Circle and Trilithons

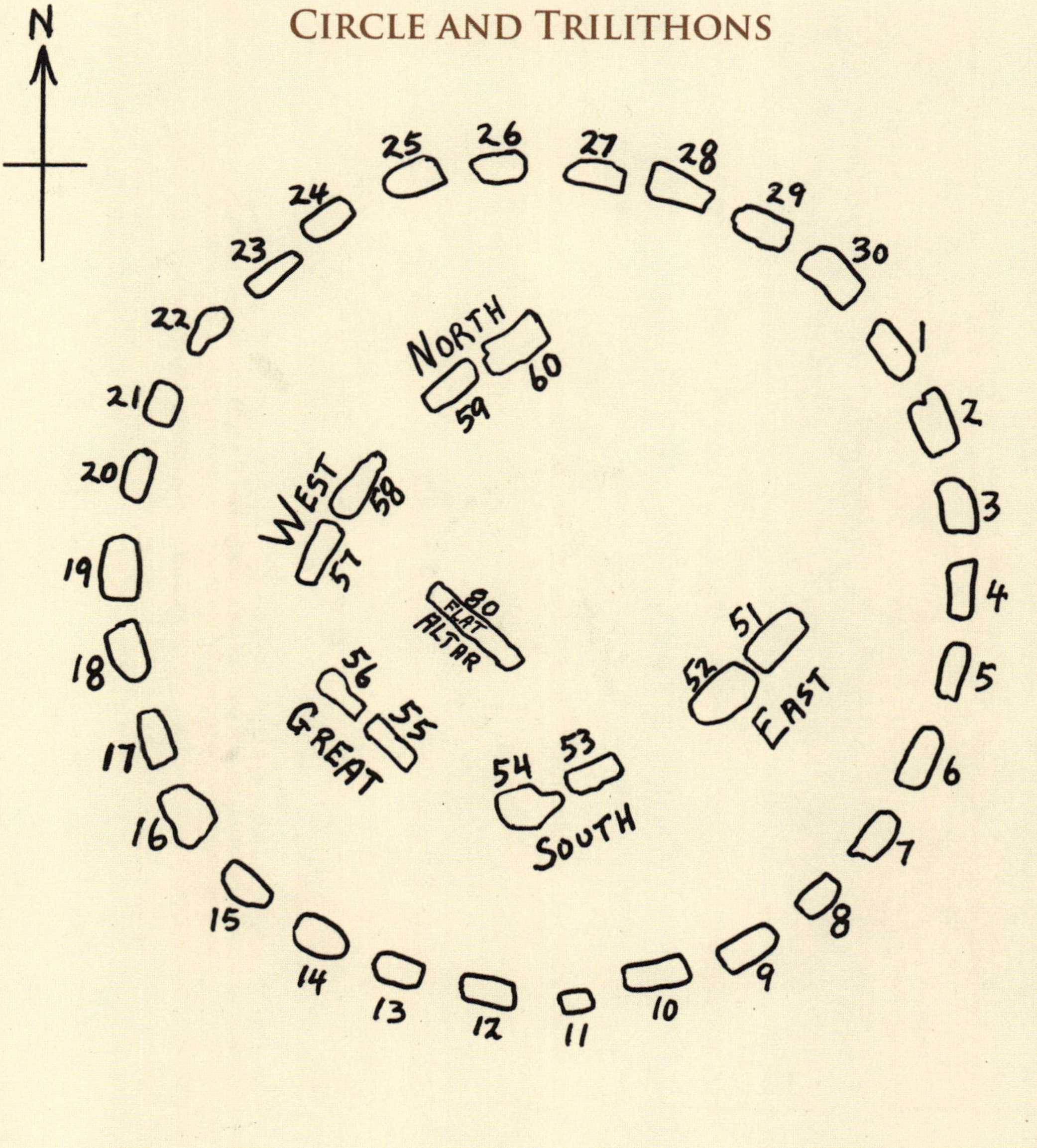

Canada's Stonehenge

Astounding Archaeological Discoveries
in Canada, England, and Wales

The Sun rose at a time and place that
changed our history.

*Rocks that speak without sound
and know without words.*

Canada's Stonehenge

Astounding Archaeological Discoveries in Canada, England, and Wales

Gordon R. Freeman

Copyright © 2009 Gordon R. Freeman
Cover and interior photographs © Gordon R. Freeman

All rights reserved. No part of this publication may be reproduced, stored in a retrieval system, or transmitted in any form or by any means, electronic, mechanical, recording, or otherwise, without the prior written permission of the author, except in the case of a reviewer, who may quote brief passages in a review to print in a magazine or newspaper, or broadcast on radio or television. In the case of photocopying or other reprographic copying, users must obtain a licence from Access Copyright.

Cover and interior design by dpict visual communications
Printed in Canada by Friesens

2009/1

LIBRARY AND ARCHIVES CANADA CATALOGUING IN PUBLICATION

Freeman, Gordon R. (1930–)
    Canada's Stonehenge : astounding archaeological discoveries in Canada, England, and Wales / Gordon Freeman.

Includes bibliographical references and index.
ISBN 978-0-9784526-1-2 (bound)

    1. Indians of North America–Alberta–Antiquities.
2. Indian calendar–Alberta. 3. Indians of North America–Alberta–Religion. 4. Stonehenge (England). 5. Preseli Region (Wales)–Antiquities. I. Title.

E98.C14F74 2008   971.23'01   C2008-902223-8

Ordering information: www.kingsleypublishing.ca

To my Beaut

READERS

Those who don't enjoy numbers and calculations may skip them and enjoy the story. Those who like numbers will get a brighter glow of the genius that has existed on the prairies these last 5000 years.

Contents

Acknowledgements	viii
A Note on the Photographs	xii
Prologue	xiii

Part One: *Ómahk*

1. Temples and Time	1
2. Setting the Stage	11
3. *Ómahkiyáahkóhtóohp*, or OldBigArrangement	23

Part Two: Stonehenge and Preseli Mountain, Wales

4. Stonehenge and Preseli Mountain	79
5. Stonehenge's Solar and Lunar Calendars	155

Part Three: History of the Christian Calendar

6. *Ómahk* Reveals a Strange Fact	185

Epilogue	225
Appendices	245
Selected Bibliography	260
List of Figures	271
Glossary	279
Index	284
About the Author	293

Front and Back Endpapers: Stonehenge maps showing the old and new (lunar calendar) numbers of Stones and Holes.

Acknowledgements

Many people during the last three decades have made this work possible. By far the greatest assistant was my wife Phyl, who comes on all field trips and listens to my chatter year-round. In the field she can't hear yelping coyotes unless they are nearby, but she can hear a bellowing bull a long way off. We passed dark winter evenings in a camper playing cribbage at temperatures between -5° and -15° C, with a single candle providing light and heat. To keep our clothing and sleeping bags dry of perspiration, each night and morning we had to get naked to get into and out of pajamas. Fortunately the skin surface is numb at winter temperatures, so it wasn't too painful. What a woman. I love you.

We thank Nancy and Junior (Fred Jr.) Bertschy for their help and warm hospitality through many years of seasons, for frequent use of a bag-phone, an occasional 4-wheel-drive vehicle, bed, dinner, and lots else.

Some of the old-timers who helped us in the large site near Majorville have passed on: Neil McKinnon, Arnold Armstrong, and Artie Nelson. Neil was manager of the cattle ranch that leased the Alberta-Government-owned 100 square kilometres of grazing land that contained the Sundial, and built a fence around 7 hectares of the main hill top when uninformed and careless people began to visit the site. Arnold owned an adjacent ranch, and in our first few years he occasionally watched us through a hunter's telescope. He didn't know what we were doing, but suspected no good and wanted to nail my hide to a fencepost. One day his son Grant dropped in from the sky to visit us. I showed him a little of what we'd found and told him of our difficulty getting official protection for the 10 square kilometres around the Sundial. After that he and his father were our strong allies. They had for years opposed people who wanted to disturb the site. Grant took me flying on several occasions to show me ancient cultural features in the larger area, or to take aerial photographs of the site and damage done by oil and gas corporations, or to drop me off to make measurements when snow blocked travel across the land, and pick me up again. Artie Nelson leased the Sundial land after Neil retired, and his son Blair carried it on until he sold the grazing lease to Lomond Grazing Corp. in December 2007. Now Lou Bertschy, one of Nancy and Junior's sons, is our contact for permissions.

Blair Nelson and Lou Bertschy obstructed petroleum corporation activity in culturally sensitive areas. They also phoned me when new activity began in the Temple zone. Each time, I went to speak with the petroleum field workers. This greatly reduced the damage done by gas well drilling and pipeline operations in the zone. I thank them and many ranchers for permission to go on their land.

We thank Shirley Armstrong, Arnold's wife, for her gracious hospitality that continues his support after his passing.

The late Jim MacGregor and Dick Forbis offered early information and encouragement.

The late Norman Lee took me in his 4-wheel-drive camper on the first three winter ventures to the site. He showed me how to live on the prairie in a camper in winter.

Since 1991 George Ball has kindly lent us *El Escarabajo Oro*, his 4-wheel-drive, 1-tonne camper-truck, for trips to the Sun Temple zone.

I contracted Geographic Air Survey of Edmonton to photograph 17 square kilometres of the Sun Temple zone in fine detail when dry grass had blown away from the stones, just before the year and a half drought ended in June 2002. The 1:3000 scale photographs are superb, and can be magnified up to 20x without loss of quality.

Colorfast Corp., Edmonton, did beautiful work with my colour photos until it closed in 2005. Now London Drugs on 149 St. in Edmonton continues the work with great skill.

I thank members of English Heritage for assistance during our visits to Stonehenge: especially the Security Officers and Maria Bush. *Maria!* We are grateful to Norman March, Bill and Jackie Hummel, and Derek and Bridget Dominey for their warm hospitality, and to Norman for use of his car. I'm sorry that this book took so long to get out Bill, and that you won't be able to comment on it. We saw a lot of life during the last fifty-six years.

Thanks to Fergus Kelly of Dublin for Celtic grammar, and to Piergiorgio Fuochi of Bologna for information about the *Meridiana* in San Petronio Basilica.

At the University of Alberta, the Chemistry Department kindly continues to provide me with space to do frontier work on complex systems. All recent members of the Science Faculty are immersed in studies of complex systems. The mushrooming subject Kinetics of Nonhomogeneous Processes (*KNP*, also called Sciences of Complexity, and now Interdisciplinary Studies) now includes ancient history and prehistory. It should spore in the Centennial Centre for

Interdisciplinary Sciences, to open in 2011 to become the Flagship of our Science Faculty. During demolition of the old Physics Building to make room for the CCIS, my abutting underground office was uninhabitable. John Vederas kindly let me use a bench in one of his research labs for eighteen months. His graduate students and Research Associates were so helpful that it was like the time when I had my own research group and the Radiation Research Centre. The RRC was a harbinger of Centres of Interdisciplinary Science, which are now becoming widespread.

I am grateful to Doug Hube for calculations and comments on astronomy through the years. Mary Mahoney-Robson graciously commented on several drafts of the book.

This book was partly written on Kedey Island in Fitzroy Harbour, Ontario. A great place to work on books, surrounded by Mother Nature's theatre. With good friends in addition to those mentioned below, Faye and Lornie Stewart, and Tom and Pat Wilson.

I thank Joseph Bellmeyer, Jack Lougheed, Mary Smellie, Ruth Thompson, Margaret Back, the late Keith Laidler, Vanja Draganić, Norman Hallendy, George Ball, Arlene Figley, Hubert Hofmann, Leah and Daniele Busi, Steven Cobb, granddaughter ∀shley Verhappen, our son Mark, and my brother John, who read all or part of drafts. Joseph is a vigorous, widely experienced ninety-seven year old—a rare gentleman of the old school. On one occasion I commented on his graciousness and he replied, pointing upwards, "My parents are up there watching, and they say '*We taught you better than that, boy!*'" Jack is a Man of the Cloth who has a way with words. Vanja has been a fellow-chemist-author for fifty years. Norman worked for forty years in the Canadian Arctic, and published an exceptional book about *Inuksuit* and Inuit.

My former colleague Jean-Pol Dodelet read an early manuscript and told me which bones needed meat where I had thought marrow was enough.

Emmanuel Anati, Catherine Dodelet, Eve Gardner, Alice Kehoe, Hugh Dempsey, Brian Reeves, and Evan Hadingham kindly read late versions of the entire manuscript and made constructive comments. Thanks Hugh for the *Napi* story and the end of the boiling.

Pinball posts during my adaptive random walk from technical to trade styles of writing were Cynthia Read, Faith Hamlin, Angela von der Lippe, John Brockman, Farideh Koohi-Kamali, Stephen Power, Colin Ridler, Bill Hamilton, Jodie Rhodes, Karl Yambert, Fred Appel,

Michael Luski, John King, and Charlene Dobmeier. The book is better for all the pings.

Charlene Dobmeier of Kingsley Publishing astutely and energetically guided the final transformations and indexing of the manuscript, and the production of the book. Thank you Alex Fraser-Harrison for your editing. Dean Pickup of dpict communications did beautiful work preparing the ABL photoscans for printing, and designing the book.

* * * *

I thank Peter Cole for permission to quote his poem *Burial Practices*. My book crosses cultures but is written in only one of the languages, so it has problems with words and their underlying ideas. I ask forgiveness of people of the Blackfoot (especially *Siksika*), Cree, *Dëne Sułiné*, and *Nakoda* (especially Pheasant Rump) Nations for some of the words used and actions described in this book to communicate with people of European background. I walked where the Grandfathers walked, and gradually absorbed some understanding. We struggle continually to minimize the desecration of sacred places by people of European heritage who have lost the concept of a sacred space. Our work is for the sake of future generations. Alex Janvier's art, wide-ranging conversations, and friendship taught me something. And thank you Peter McArthur.

I am grateful to many, especially to *Ítsiptsinamáahka* and members of his family.

Mitakuye oyasin
We are all related

A Note on the Photographs

The photographs in this book were taken with two Nikon F3 cameras with Nikkor Zoom lenses (focal lengths 35 – 105 mm, and 80 – 200 mm), on sturdy Manfrotto model 055 tripods with model 141 heads. I also made a series of detailed sketches of the Sun relative to the horizon as the Sun was rising, from naked-eye observations. The acuity of my best photographs of the Sun in the landscape is about three- to ten-fold poorer than that of my eyes. The acuity of my eyes now is less than it was fifty years ago, when I was a young man. Trained Sunwatchers in ancient times no doubt had the ability to make observations that were more accurate than those I recorded.

For most of the photos, fine detail in the distant landscape and on the horizon is more important than that in the foreground.

PROLOGUE

Two Blackfoot men hunting mule deer in the gullies along the Bow River noticed me on the isolated Sacred Hill one March afternoon. They drove their Bronco II across the prairie to check me out. Looking up from studying and photographing rocks on the hilltop, I saw the vehicle coming and walked down the hill to greet whoever it was. The place is difficult to reach at the best of times, but especially during pre-spring, so we were curious about each other's presence in this remote location west of Brooks and east of a single building called Majorville, in Alberta.

I waved and called "Hello" as they approached, but the two men were wary of me—almost as if they saw me as an intruder. We identified ourselves. I said that I was from Edmonton, and had been studying the place for several years. The younger man appeared to be in his late twenties, and the other was his uncle. They were a grandson and son of a great Holy Man who had died not long ago.

They asked what I was doing. After a spell of chat, during which they acknowledged nothing about the sacredness of the place, we went up the hill so that I could show them some of the intricate patterns I'd found that had been made of rocks.

At first sight, from a distance, the Sacred Hill seems little different from others in the area. But on its top there is a large pile of rocks—a cairn—in the middle of a big ring of stones, high above the deeply gouged valley of the Bow River to the east. The nearly circular stone ring measures thirty large paces across, three times the diameter of the cairn itself. Twenty-eight lines of stones connect the ring to the cairn.

I showed the men the large, geometrically arranged geoglyphs that represent the Sun, Moon, and Morning Star, and I explained how some of the other rock patterns work as an amazingly accurate calendar. As we went from pattern to pattern, the uncle became more and more spooked. He paced around nervously, not coming close to me.

The young man said, somewhat admiringly, "You have to be smart to figure that out."

I said, "No, you just have to tune in."

He made it clear that I was trespassing in an extremely sacred construction and told me things intended to frighten me away. Not direct threats—but he indicated things I'd done that were forbidden to all but the highest Holy Men and Women. We talked quietly and respectfully about the forbidden things, and the likely consequences.

As I spoke with the nephew I noticed his uncle go discreetly to where I knew there was a small ring of stones, and ritually make an offering of a cigarette. Holding it in his right hand, he presented the tobacco to the Western Sky, then poked a hole in the ground inside the small circle of stones and put the cigarette into it. He came back to listen to the discussion, slightly calmer.

As we walked around, I noticed that both men carefully avoided stepping on any stone, sparing even the pebbles.

After some time, the young man said to me, "You have to talk to Grama."

The uncle yelled, "No! Dad said never tell!"

His nephew shouted, "But we're gonna die! Someone has to write it down!"

The uncle looked anguished, and didn't reply.

The young man explained that his Grama is a Sun Woman, implying that she might tell me some of the tradition of this sacred place. He asked for the field notebook and pen I was carrying. I opened the notebook to the blank back page, and he printed a message: "GRAMA I --- & --- SAID IT WAS OKAY TO TALK TO G. F." (Their names are removed because of the delicacy of the situation.) He told me how to find her home, and reminded me to give her a personal gift when I got there. (It is customary to take a gift whenever visiting an Indian Elder, and I assumed that a Sun Woman, the highest Holy Woman, warranted a more significant gift.)

The nephew said that if she agreed to speak to me, I had to stay until she indicated that the meeting was over. He said it might last one minute, or all night.

It was already 5 P.M. Grama's place was an hour-and-a-half drive away, and it was a further six-hour drive from her place to Edmonton.

I said, "I have to be lecturing at the University of Alberta at 8:30 tomorrow morning, so I can't visit her this evening."

He said, "Then you'll have to arrange it through my father."

* * * *

In August 1980, my wife Phyl and I first followed a trail across 18 kilometres of rolling, treeless ranchland in southern Alberta to visit the complex circle of stones east of Majorville. As we crested knolls along the way, we could see a small bump on a hilltop in the eastern horizon, like a nipple on a supine breast. It turned out to be our destination.

The bump was the large cairn in the rayed ring of stones. The twenty-eight lines of stones—the Rays—connecting the ring to the cairn could represent an aureole around the nipple, or around the Sun. A nipple and the Sun are both sources of sustenance, and both attractors of attention.

One of my hobbies is Stone Age archaeology, an interest inherited from my father. Jim MacGregor, a retired electrical engineer and a prolific amateur Plains historian, had told me about this puzzling stone structure. He called it a "medicine wheel" and had sketched me a map to show the way to it.

When Phyl and I finally got to the remote site, we also found many other geometric patterns of rocks on the hill, making the place much more complex than the "medicine wheel" suggested by Jim's description. When I later asked archaeologists about them, they said all rocks outside the medicine wheel remain just as the melting glacier had left them ten thousand years ago (Figure P-1). Nature makes an infinite number of beautiful patterns, but these rock constructions and groupings across hectares of land seemed to be as contrived as the medicine wheel itself. You just have to zoom out to see them.

Figure P-1 Two patterns of rocks that archaeologists said are "just as the melting glacier left them ten thousand years ago."

Local ranchers have called the rayed ring and rock pile "the Sundial" for the last hundred years. Archaeologists apply the term "medicine wheel" to many somewhat similar constructions across the prairies because they look like enormous, spoked wheels, and "medicine" implies a mystical use of them by Indians. "Medicine wheel" is a loose classification of geoglyphs, patterns of cobblestones composed of a ring, lines, and a cairn, or any two of these three types of components.

The Blackfoot (*Siksika*) people who live 40 kilometres away do not talk about this place publicly. After a few years I came to know that the structure is sacred to them, and devastating experiences during the last two hundred years have taught them profound distrust of Whites. They wisely do not share what is most sacred to them with Whites.

The geometric patterns in this fascinating structure have to be read like a book. On the southwest side of the ringed cairn on the hilltop is a crescent of seven large rocks, with a larger single rock midway between the ring and crescent. The cairn, crescent, and rock are connected in such a way that, after a few years, I concluded that they are effigies of the Sun, Moon, and Morning Star—a Holy Trinity in Plains Indian religion.

Phyl and I were standing at the centrepiece of an ancient Temple.

The Sun and Moon are still worshipped directly or through symbols in many religions, including Hinduism, Judaism, Buddhism, Christianity, and Islam. Temples of the Sun and Moon were created in many places around the world, but some locations have special properties that have caused temples there to evolve during thousands of years. The site near Majorville appears to be one of these locations.

Back in 1980, the extensive rock patterns we saw on the high banks of the Bow River were a mystery, but we thought we had discovered something exciting and felt that the patterns might be readable. We became fascinated by the place. Over the next twenty-eight years we lived there for a total of seven months, eventually sampling the place during all four seasons.

Some of the discoveries we made in southern Alberta seemed relevant to controversies that we later heard about the ancient construction in England called Stonehenge. We ultimately spent thirteen weeks making observations at Stonehenge between 1989 and 2006, during which time we discovered striking similarities between the surface geometry of Stonehenge and that of the stone patterns near Majorville, Alberta. These similiaries have far-reaching implications for North American and European history.

History is something that is spoken or written; not all history is preserved on paper. Learning to read ancient patterns of stones on the ground slowly pushes back the boundaries of written history.

* * * *

We have much to learn from sacred places and the people who hold them sacred. Science alone cannot solve all the problems we face in society. There is more than one way of knowing. How does the mind work? People's perceptions are influenced by their cultural philosophy.

Whiteman's philosophy and behaviour have been greatly influenced by *Genesis 1: 27-28*, especially the words that I have highlighted in bold: "*So **God created man in his own image;** male and female he created them. And God blessed them, and said to them, 'Be fruitful and multiply, and **fill the earth and subdue it;** and **have dominion over** the fish of the sea and over the birds of the air and over **every living thing that moves upon the earth.**'*"

Has this been taken too far?

* * * *

We used to put our dead up in trees
Until the White people started robbing them
So we dug holes and covered them with earth
Now the anthropologists come and dig them out
Measure them, and take pictures

We burn our dead ones now
And keep them in a jar
And keep that jar hidden
So nobody will steal the ashes
Or the jar

— Peter Cole, 1992

Part One

Ómahk

CHAPTER ONE

TEMPLES AND TIME

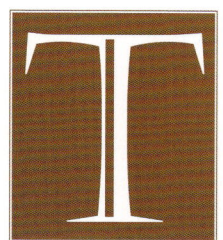ime is the fleeting dimension that can be measured only in its passing. Time is marked in most cultures by an annual series of religious observances and festivals. Units of time are provided by the Sun and Moon, and our ancestors encoded these units in temples.

As a matter of survival, animals have for hundreds of millions of years reacted to the changes of seasons, but when did mankind begin to record the days in the seasons as we do now? How did Stone Age people many thousands of years ago record time? Where is the oldest, still operational calendar ever discovered? How old is it? The answers are surprising.

Calendars are counting devices, counting days, Moon cycles (*moonths* or months), seasons, Sun cycles (years), and multiples of all these. Season counts depend on the latitude of the place; as a result, a season count in the tropics is different from that in a temperate or polar place.

Much has been written over the last forty years regarding the exquisite Mayan tropical calendar in Central America. The Mayan calendar included cycles of the Sun, Moon, and Venus. It had a 260-day sacred almanac, a 365-day secular calendar, a 584-day Venus cycle, and a 52-year (18,980-day) Calendar Round, which meshes 73 x 260-day sacred cycles with 52 x 365-day secular years. The unusual 260-day cycle is made of 13 rounds of 20 named-days, named for various animals, plants, and objects such as a flint knife and a storm cloud. These divisions are far from random: 20 is the number of fingers and toes we have, while 13 is a prime number that is considered to be mystical by several cultures.

Each day, the Sun rises in the east, reaches its highest point above the horizon at noon, and sets in the west. On the Tropic of Cancer, an imaginary ring around the Earth that denotes the northmost passage of the Sun directly overhead (latitude 23°.4 N), the Sun passes vertically overhead at noon each June 21. After June 21, the latitude of the vertically overhead Sun drifts southward, and reaches the Tropic of Capricorn at 23°.4 S on December 21 or 22 (depending on the year within the leap year cycle), then moves northward again, reaching the Tropic of Cancer on the next June 21, then back southward for the next cycle of 365.24 days.

Vincent Malmström, in his 1997 book *Cycles of the Sun, Mysteries of the Moon*, traced the 260-day sacred Mayan cycle to an earlier tropical culture at 14°.8 N latitude. At that latitude, 260 days corresponds to the time from when the Sun passes vertically overhead on the way south on August 13, to when it returns there on the way back northward on April 30. Ingenious detective work led Malmström to conclude that the 260-day sacred almanac originated on the Pacific coastal plain in Izapa, Mexico, at a date earlier than the Maya Classic Period, and that Day 1 in the almanac was August 13, 1359 B.C. During the next two millennia, this calendar and associated sacred geometries diffused northerly, westerly, and easterly from Izapa and was adopted by subsequent civilizations.

By contrast, a Mayan Long-Count calendar of 360-day years extrapolates to a beginning in 3114 B.C.

Knowledge of these calendars has been inferred from written records carved into stone and written in books of treated bark paper. The oldest calendar stela (a glyphed stone post) that has been found dates to 32 B.C., and the four surviving books are Mayan and only six to eight centuries old.

In the North Temperate Zone, crude solar calendars have been suggested to exist in two "medicine wheels"—one in Saskatchewan and the other in Wyoming.

Archeologists have designated more than one hundred medicine wheels. Their great variety indicates that different styles were used for different purposes, so medicine wheels will be renamed when more is discovered about them. I have begun the renaming.

During the 1970s, John Eddy, an astronomer from Colorado, along with two archaeologists, Tom and Alice Kehoe of Saskatchewan, studied a number of geoglyphs and concluded that two of the medicine wheels have features that point to the Summer Solstice Sun rise. The older of these two is the Moose Mountains Medicine Wheel (49°76 N, 102°70 W) on a hill east of Weyburn, Saskatchewan, estimated at two to three thousand years old. On the flat plain of southeastern Saskatchewan, a ridge of hills that reaches 200 metres above the plain seems like mountains, but it's actually a terminal moraine from glacier meltback. The second medicine wheel oriented toward the Summer Solstice Sun rise has a spectacular setting on a real mountain, 1800 metres above the plain, on Medicine Mountain in the Big Horns of Wyoming. The Big Horn Medicine Wheel (44°83 N, 107°92 W) is relatively new, only a few centuries old.

Eddy proposed that the Moose Mountains and Big Horn Medicine Wheels also have lines between pairs of small cairns or small stone rings that pointed to the heliacal rise of three stars during the period that each device was built. A heliacal rise means that the star rises just a short while before the Sun and is visible for only a few minutes until sunlight overpowers light from the star. The stars at each site were Aldebaran, which rose heliacally within a day or two of the Summer Solstice; Rigel, which rose heliacally 28 days later; and Sirius, which rose heliacally 28 days after that. The Kehoes later reported that Rigel did not fit the Moose Mountains pattern, but the Sun, Aldebaran, Sirius, Capella, and Formalhaut did.

These Solstice calendars are crude by comparison with the exquisitely complex tropical calendar developed by the Mayans and their forebears in Central America, but they indicate that ancestors of Great Plains Indians developed an astronomical calendar similar to the one we use today, containing time units of 28 days (4 weeks), and one solar year.

Eddy's conclusion that the two medicine wheels have pointers to stars and the Summer Solstice was vigorously contested, but only by people who have never made an accurate astronomical or solar measurement at one. Why the criticism? Well, fashions change with the generations, because each generation seems to want to distinguish itself from its parents. During the period around 1900 and again during the

1960s, people studying ancient sites in Europe and Egypt discovered "stone alignments" to the Sun and certain stars. The generations between 1914 and 1955 were occupied with two world wars and their aftermaths, so interest in ancient astronomical alignments was eclipsed. During the late 1970s "alignments" fell out of style among archaeologists and archaeoastronomers, perhaps partly because, in the 1960s, astronomer Gerald Hawkins overworked the concept of solar and lunar alignments in Stonehenge, as I will discuss later.

Eddy's critics took directional data reported for several dozens of noncalendrical "medicine wheels" and combined them with data for the two at Moose Mountains and Big Horn, then did orientational analysis of the geoglyph hodgepodge, and concluded that none possesses a calendrical alignment. The analysis lacked discernment.

The two critics most quoted by archaeologists and archaeoastronomers during the late 1980s and early 90s were said to be astronomers, but when I came across their articles in the late 1990s, they didn't seem to me to have that background.

I sought the critics out myself, found one in Canada and the other in the United States, and enjoyed pleasant chats with them. Both were surprised that archaeologists classified them as astronomers. Steven Haack is a wood-turner who has never seen a medicine wheel, but through great interest read a lot about them in his local library. David Vogt is an education consultant who had visited several medicine wheels, none in Alberta, and did not attempt exact measurements at any site. He obtained "alignment directions" from published reports of many medicine wheels.

To see a significant alignment you have to estimate what sort of alignment might be significant, and look at details in the entire landscape. Apparently many city-reared people have difficulty seeing and relating to fine details in a landscape. People who grow up in rural areas experience the sky and the landscape as physical and emotional presences. Christopher Tilley's *A Phenomenology of Landscape*, evidently written for city-raised anthropologists, demonstrates what is self-evident to country-raised people—that the landscape is part of the artifact.

It is ironic that one of the medicine wheels that Eddy concluded has no calendrical feature—the one near Majorville, Alberta—is part of the history-altering subject of this book (Figure 1-1). He just didn't look at it the right way. The remarkable implications of the new discoveries near Majorville reach right across the Atlantic, and across Europe, into European history and prehistory.

Figure 1-1 Aerial view of the Majorville Medicine Wheel. The ring diameter is about 28 metres, and the central cairn contains about 50 tonnes of rocks. To the lower left, a single 1-tonne rock and a 7-rock crescent have a pincerlike relationship with the cairn. Geographic coordinates 50°.585 N, 112°.411 W.

These discoveries show that genius existed on the North American Plains five thousand years ago, and probably much earlier than that.

England is home to the most renowned megalithic monument in Europe, Stonehenge (Figure 1-2). The most recent estimate of age is that the large stone circle was constructed in about 2300 B.C. (Mike Pitts; Rosamund Cleal and coauthors). Archaeologist Richard Atkinson had earlier estimated 2000 B.C.

Stonehenge includes a Circle of large Sarsen Stones and a Horseshoe U of other huge Sarsen Stones inside the Circle (see maps inside the front cover). Each Sarsen Stone in the structure was assigned a number long ago, to assist discussion of details. Sarsen is extremely hard sandstone, in which the sand grains fused together during millions of years soaking in the sea. The open end of the Horseshoe faces northeast, and northeasterly outside the Circle is another huge Sarsen commonly called the Heel Stone. A line drawn along the axis of the Horseshoe extends a little to the left of the Heel Stone. The structure of Stonehenge is almost symmetrical about this line. Almost, but not quite, as we'll see.

It has long been known that a line from the centre of the Horseshoe, or of the Circle, to the Heel Stone (Figure 1-3) points a bit to the right of where the Sun rises on the Summer Solstice. The nearness of this line to Solstice Sun rise has led a few people during the last two centuries to suggest that Stonehenge was constructed partly as a stage on which to celebrate the Summer Solstice. William Stukeley in 1740 noted that Stonehenge's principal axis pointed to the whereabouts of the Sun rises when the days are longest. In 1771, John Smith suggested that Stonehenge contains a lunisolar calendar and a zodiac.

In 1901, Norman Lockyer noted that a line from the centre of the Great Trilithon along the axis of the Trilithon Horseshoe would pass near the centre of the gap between Circle Sarsens numbered 30 and 1 (maps inside the front cover), extend to the left of the Heel Stone, and continue along the centre of the Avenue, an ancient *via sacra* (sacred path) marked by an earthen bank on each side. He suggested that this was the line along which the first flash of the Sun was seen in the morning of the Summer Solstice in the era when Stonehenge was built. Lockyer measured the azimuth of the line and the altitude of the horizon.

On the mornings of June 21 to 25, 1901, Lockyer's colleague Howard Payn tried to record the Sun's first flash from the centre of the gap between Stones 30 and 1. The only clear morning was on the 25th, when he found the first flash to be $0°.93$ to the right of the azimuth Lockyer had selected for the Avenue line. From this displacement and the calculated rate of drift of the direction of Solstice Sun rise during millennia, Lockyer estimated that Stonehenge and the Avenue were built in 1680 B.C.

✳✳✳✳

Figure 1-2 Stonehenge has remained a mystery for a thousand years. Geographic coordinates 51°.178 N, 1°.825 W. A clue to one purpose of Stonehenge has been found 7000 kilometres west of it in *Ómahk*, in Alberta, which contains the equivalent of the Rosetta Stone for Stone Age calendars.

Figure 1-3 Looking northeasterly across the centre of the Sarsen Circle to the Heel Stone far outside the Circle.

The words sunrise and sunset refer to the general events that happen every day. To accurately define the lengths of day and night, the term Sun rise refers to the first flash of the top edge of the Sun as it appears on a clear horizon. Its position can be determined exactly, reproducible at Solstices from year to year within one-twentieth of a degree, by naked eye observation on clear mornings. Also, the term Sun set refers to the *last* flash of the top edge of the Sun as it disappears below the horizon on a clear evening. It is well known by all experienced Skywatchers that exact directions of Sun rises and Sun sets, and the exact lengths of the days and nights, can be determined only in this way.

Lockyer came closest of all investigators before my own work in 1999 to finding the correct Summer Solstice Sun rise line at Stonehenge. He wrote, "Observations [of the Sun rise] were doubtless made within the sanctuary." I wonder if he recognized the difference between a Sunwatcher (a scientist) and a Priest.

Evan Hadingham, in Chapter 6 of his 1975 book *Circles and*

Standing Stones, gave an excellent summary of the history of proposals for Stonehenge's calendrics up to 1975. Lockyer's suggested Summer Solstice Sun rise line from the centre of the Great Trilithon to along the centre of the Avenue seemed to conflict with Atkinson's proposal in 1956 that the Avenue was constructed about two centuries before the Stone Circle, but the conflict noted by Hadingham disappeared in 1995, with the reversed order of construction suggested by Cleal and coauthors in their book *Stonehenge in its Landscape*.

Alexander Thom, during the 1960s, made detailed measurements in many megalithic sites in Britain, including Stonehenge. He set an exacting style that remains unsurpassed in this type of work.

In 1965, Gerald Hawkins published *Stonehenge Decoded* about calendrics and possible predictions of eclipses of the Sun and Moon. He used a computer to analyze a map of Stonehenge, by inputting the position coordinates of the various stones and holes, along with the seasonal directions of the rise and set of the Sun and Moon. It was a valuable exercise at that time, but he allowed too much tolerance in the observation directions, so the lines he selected are not the ones later obtained by direct observation of the Sun on-site. His major contribution was to suggest a credible method of using components of Stonehenge to predict the times of future eclipses. A Full Moon rises in approximately the opposite direction of the Sun set, and the other way around. However, the Full Moon rise and set directions wobble around the Sun set and rise directions in an 18.61-year cycle, caused by precession of the Moon's orbit about the Earth. If one records cycles only in whole-year periods, three Moon-wobble periods would correspond closely to two of 19 years and one of 18 years, making a total of 56 years for the triple cycle. There are 56 equally spaced "Aubrey Holes" around the circumference of the Stonehenge terrain just inside the Bank. Hawkins suggested the 56 holes were year counters for the triple cycle of the Full Moon's wobble, and were used to help predict the times of eclipses.

Astronomer Fred Hoyle later used the Aubrey Holes in an alternative eclipse-prediction method. The 56 Aubrey Holes indeed appear to be associated with cycles of the Moon.

During the last quarter century, Stonehenge calendrics suffered the same popular disfavour as did medicine wheel calendrics, apparently based upon a change of fashion, because no new measurements of the Sun were provided to counter the detailed data of Lockyer and Payn. Some of the criticisms were made in light spirit. Christopher Chippindale's 1994 book has the amusing title *Stonehenge Complete, revised edition*, then in 2004, a third edition came out entitled, *Stonehenge Complete, 3rd edition*, and still no prefix on *Complete*. Chippindale distorted some of Lockyer's data up to 18-fold, then called it meaningless.

Learning requires an open mind.

He not busy being born
Is busy dying.

    Bob Dylan, "It's Alright, Ma (I'm Only Bleeding)"

CHAPTER TWO

SETTING THE STAGE

On the prairies during the 1930s, dry winds blew away patches of tilled soil, leaving stones resting on the clay hardpan. Sometimes an arrowhead or something else manmade lay among the stones.

These were my childhood years. My father was a Canadian Pacific Railway station agent and moved from station to higher-paying station as the opportunity arose. He also had a great interest in artifacts that turned up on the wind-blown prairie of east-central Saskatchewan. During 1935 to 1939 my family spent occasional summer Sunday afternoons searching for spearheads and other stone artifacts in fields near Lanigan (a town between Saskatoon and Yorkton), and Dad gave my two brothers and me a nickel for each artifact we found. In those days a jawbreaker or licorice pipe only cost a copper (1¢), so we were well rewarded.

From Lanigan we moved to the hamlet of Sonningdale, and then to Broadacres. On a spring day when I was eleven, my older brother John and I rode our bikes 13 kilometres along trails from Broadacres to Tramping Lake, a long, narrow lake that slashes deeply through the Saskatchewan prairie. Just before the trail turned to angle down the steep bank, we noticed a circle of stones in the short, dry grass.

We went to look at it and saw other circles nearby, each about three large paces across. In one we saw a flat, white bone flush with the ground. We scratched around its edge, found it continued downward, and carefully dug it out with sharp-edged pebbles.

It was a human skull!

We cleaned it off and took it home. With all Dad's arrowheads and stone tools, what would he think of an ancient Indian skull?

He was angry—we had violated a grave! "Graveyards are not all surrounded by fences," he said. He got us into the car and drove back to rebury the skull. (There was always a shovel in the trunk of a prairie car, to use when stuck in mud or snow.)

John and I felt ashamed but didn't really understand why an ancient grave on the prairie should not be touched. Where are the Indians now? Who visits the graves anymore?

As Dad enlarged the hole we'd dug, to bury the skull deeper, he turned up neck vertebrae, which then had to be buried deeper as well. As he dug, ribs turned up. The grave had been barely beneath the surface. By the time he finished deepening the grave, I'd counted about 180 bones; there are 206 bones in an average adult human skeleton. (A new baby has about 300.)

Before putting them in the grave, I put the lower jaw on a rock, fitted the upper part of the skull to it, put a crocus in each eye socket and my cap on the head, and took its picture with my parents' Brownie box camera.

As I recall the event more than sixty years later—kids out of curiosity and ignorance digging up human bones in a remote place, bones of a race that had been vanquished a century earlier by members of the kids' race—it represents a tragic part of human nature. If a physically stronger individual attacks a weaker individual, it's considered a criminal act. If a militarily stronger nation attacks a weaker nation, it's considered a legitimate conquest. Eleven- and thirteen-year-olds of European heritage are still not being told what really happened to the Indians in North America during the nineteenth century. What would happen if they were?

Then came World War II, and in his spare time my father travelled the countryside selling Victory Bonds to farmers to help the war effort. I went with him. The persuasive argument was that if the Germans conquered Canada, our lives would become much worse. He knew what happened to the indigenous inhabitants the last time Europeans conquered this continent.

Some of the Saskatchewan villages we migrated to were near Indian Reserves. Indians were materially poor, but they didn't want to live like us. During the summer they preferred to live in tents, not spending long in one place, trapping and snaring some of their food. Most village people had little respect for them. In my late teens, I became aware of the disfiguring concept of prejudice.

* * * *

In books such as this there is always discussion about what to call the people who have lived here for millennia, now that Canada contains many people from India.

Out of respect I am using the word of a prairie Indian Elder who told me, "You people came here and called us Indians, and those animals buffalo. Now you want to change the names. I don't want to change the names."

Sacred Rings of Stones

The grave John and I found was within one of a cluster of rings of cobblestones on the west bank of Tramping Lake. I don't know whether all the rings were grave markers, or whether they were the remains of a village that had been abandoned after a death in one lodge. Sometimes the body was sealed in its lodge, and the rest of the village was moved away, leaving the tipi rings for a later return.

Tramping Lake is a salt lake in a long, deep, north–south trench that was gouged into the clay by glacier meltwater nine to ten thousand years ago. I know now that salt lakes (which animals frequent for the salt), the north–south axis, and the Sun rise and set directions east and west have special meaning to many Indians.

A transportable dwelling, a tipi, was made of several poles tied together at the top and spread out on the ground, making a cone. This frame was covered with sewn buffalo hides, and the bottom edge of the cover was anchored with pegs or stones. The stones were gathered locally, so when a tipi was moved the stones were left behind, more or less as the ring that had anchored the cover.

Thousands of tipi rings still exist on unplowed land. Hundreds of thousands were destroyed by agriculture during the last century, as farmers gathered the stones into piles so they wouldn't damage machinery.

A small fraction of the stone rings are much larger and more intricate than tipi rings. They probably had a ceremonial purpose. The Majorville Medicine Wheel is one such example.

Why a circular shape for a ceremonial place? A circle is easier to make than a square; one needs only an anchor stake, a rope, and a scratching peg. A circle has visual elegance that an imperfect square lacks. A circle has no beginning and no end. Circles are used in spiritual and philosophical metaphors around the world.

North American Plains Indians give philosophical meaning to the circular shapes of their lodges and drums. Circles relate to the horizon of creation, and to the annual cycle of apparent life and death, in which life anticipates death and death anticipates rebirth. Circles and cycles are associated with spirituality, with rhythm and balance within individual lives as parts of ongoing nature.

The Majorville Medicine Wheel is the most intricate stone ring that remains on the North American Plains. It is also the most ancient, estimated at 5000 years. The 2000-year-old Moose Mountains Sacred Ring in southeastern Saskatchewan is egg-shaped and different in style from the ring near Majorville. The approximately 300-year-old Big Horn Sacred Ring has stylistic similarities to both the Majorville and Moose Mountains Rings. There were probably other Sacred Rings of intermediate ages that have been destroyed, or have not yet been discovered.

More than one hundred intricate rings of stones on prairie hills have been designated "medicine wheels" for lack of a better name. I call them Sacred Rings to shift the emphasis toward Indian concepts, and "wheel" is not one of them. Several recent books state that all medicine wheels are on mountaintops, but only one is—Big Horn Sacred Ring.

* * * *

In early June 2003, I got permission from a Big Horn Forest Ranger in Lovell, Wyoming, to go to the Big Horn Ring, located on government parkland. Lovell is on the plain west of the Big Horn Range, 1800 metres below the Sacred Ring, which is 2930 metres above Mean Sea Level. Highway 14A, the Sky Highway, crosses the mountains to Sheridan and is closed by snow during most of the year, but it had opened the day before my visit. The road from the Sky Highway to a parking lot 2.5 kilometres from the Sacred Ring was still officially closed and potentially dangerous, but I found it passable.

The ranger had said, "Be careful walking from the parking lot to the medicine wheel, because if you slip on the snow you won't stop until you reach Cleveland."

The Big Horn Ring is on the crest of Medicine Mountain, which is edged by spectacular chimney-pot cliffs of anciently eroded limestone. Although the Sacred Ring is only about three centuries old, other features of the site indicate that the place might have been held sacred for many thousands of years. It is on the west edge of the mountain range, overlooking the plain far below to the west.

The seven so-called cairns that are part of the large Sacred Ring are not the usual piles of stones, but resemble vision quest seats, a ring or U of stones with space for your seat and legs. A few hundred metres from the summit and a little below it, on the broad shoulders of the mountain, there are a few tipi rings and several shelter-size holes down into the rock.

What luck to have the place to myself! In the snow on the walk up I had crossed fresh paw tracks—as big as the palm of my hand—of a lone wolf, which somehow gave me a fellow feeling. Maybe this was an ancient vision quest site; an isolated, difficult-to-access place where a Brave would go to fast and to seek spiritual guidance, usually from an animal spirit or the Thunder Spirit.

These ancient places have an aura about them. Storm clouds gathering above the peaks in the east added to the effect; lightning flashes and rolling thunder would have climaxed an already happy visit.

Nine hundred kilometres to the northeast, the Moose Mountains Sacred Ring is on the west edge of the Moose Mountains ridge of hills in Saskatchewan. (The local *Nakoda* insist that the *s* be added to the Whiteman's word "Mountain," and the Sacred Ring is not on the highest summit.) The location on the west edge of a highland overlooking a plain is another way in which the much younger Big Horn Sacred Ring relates to the Moose Mountains one.

My contact in the Moose Mountains was a *Nakoda* Elder. He told me the etiquette and showed me the way. I gave a gift of tobacco to the *Nakoda* Holy Man who lived at the entrance to the path to the Sacred Hilltop, and asked permission to photograph the Sacred Ring and its surroundings. The Elder took me up. At the west edge of the Ring site he presented tobacco to the Western Sky while praying, and put it on the ground, perhaps under a stone. He stayed with me for some time, no doubt to see that I was not disturbing anything, only taking compass readings along sight lines, pacing distances, and photographing from a tripod.

The egg-shaped Moose Mountains Sacred Ring has a long axis that runs northwest–southeast. The 10-metre diameter cairn in the northwest "Big-end" of the egg resembles a yolk, and the "Little-end" of the egg points southeast. An egg is an ancient symbol of fertility and rebirth, and the yolk is a symbol of the Sun; I think the Moose Mountains Sacred Ring represents a "Sun-egg," and it points approximately toward the Winter Solstice Sun rise in the southeast. (The hill could be called Sun-egg Hill; in the *Nakoda* language, *Wi-witga Baha*.)

A line of stones runs upslope from a small cairn southwest of the egg to the large yolk cairn on the summit. John Eddy suggested the line points upslope to the Summer Solstice Sun rise in the northeast, but the yolk horizon is too near for an accurate line. The line points more convincingly in the opposite direction downslope to the Winter Solstice Sun set on the distant southwest horizon. (Alice Kehoe told me that formerly a large rock on top of the original cairn gave a more precise alignment to the Summer Solstice rise, but there is no record of Sun rise along that alignment.)

I think this was a place for ceremonies to assist regeneration of the weakened Sun; to end Winter and to bring Spring.

The Beautiful Sky Moves

The brilliant Sun does not move across the clear blue sky; the sky itself moves in a daily cycle and defines the directions east and west. During the night, the moving sky is spectacularly patterned with stars, with the mottled Moon and the planets moving very slowly among them.

The Moon's shape changes from night to night, growing gradually from a thin crescent to a full disk, then shrinking slowly to a thin crescent, and finally disappearing for a couple of nights before starting a new cycle. Each night the Moon shifts its position easterly along a path among the stars, making a complete circuit around the sky in a *moonth*.

(I have coined the term *moonth* to distinguish our calendar month from the Moon-cycle period. The Moon makes a complete circuit around the sky in a *moonth*, 29 or 30 days, averaging 29.53 days.

The Gregorian calendar month is roughly a *moonth*, but its length is flexible to make twelve of them fit a solar year and a repeatable sequence of Christian festivals.)

The Sun also travels along a path among the stars, taking a year to complete a circuit around the sky. During a human lifetime, the annual path of the Sun among the stars remains constant, but it shifts slowly during a period of thousands of years. The paths of the Moon and planets through the stars are complex, each taking a different amount of time to complete a circuit.

Periodic motions of lights in the sky define amounts of time for us. From the beginning of mankind inquisitive people have probably studied the sky. On rare occasions a new light appears in the sky, then slowly fades. What was that! We call it a supernova, an exploding old star, but it must have been even more fascinating of old.

The sky is a topless source of fascination. Skywatchers are still trying to figure out how it works. For example, it is still not known whether a spiral galaxy is condensing from less dense material, or is expanding from periodic, directional explosions in its rotating, dense core (like the jets in opposite directions observed from a super-massive Black Hole). I think the latter is a model for the future, because there is almost nothing left of the time-and-space-restrictive BigBang Theory but the name. These explosions in "active galactic nuclei" throughout the universe would generate the observed low-temperature background radiation (corresponding to -270° C, or 3 kelvins, equal to 3 Centigrade degrees above the lowest possible temperature). Light from extremely distant sources would disappear by attrition. You have to visualize the not-nothing that vacuum is, and why the speed of light is constant in it. Matter and energy would be recycled on a time scale of quadrillions of years.

Patterned groups of bright stars, called constellations (together-stars), have been imagined to represent beings or things that exist on Earth. As in Heaven, so below. The periodic changes of constellations in the sky were in ancient times committed to memory as stories about doings of the constellation beings. Myths are stories based on real events.

Trying to figure out how the sky works, then and now, occupies a curious few. It has the same motivation as a man watching the swing of a full skirt on a walking woman, and figuring out what makes it do that. You have to consider the style and the properties of the cloth of the skirt, and the motions and structure of the body beneath it. Muscles, fat, and bones—especially the motions of the *glutei maximi* during the oscillating steps. Some bums even gyrate. Finding an answer doesn't decrease the attraction, because a more detailed question always follows. Major advances in science are made this way. Later, other people do something useful with the new knowledge.

From the discovered dates of the annual arrival and departure of the changing constellations in the sky and their correlation with the weather, people ritualized the periods for hunting and gathering of particular foods, the periods for preparing shelter and clothing, and for making the tools to do these things. Other people designed skirts that swing or do not swing, to match the moods of suitably structured wearers.

Genius existed tens of thousands of years ago, as it does today. Magnificent, lifelike paintings of animals on smoothed walls deep in caves have been dated back thirty thousand years near Chauvet-Pont-d'Arc, France, and back sixteen thousand years in southern France and northern Spain. How and why was this great art put in the farthest depths of the caves? There must have been a powerful motivation, which might simply have been the personal drive of exceptionally skillful individuals, guided by a belief system.

And then there are those who created the time machines that are the subject of this book. Genius on the prairies existed five thousand years ago.

* * * *

The Sun appears to us to move across the sky from east to west. Its position tells the time of day. For observers in the Northern Hemisphere where this story takes place, stars in the southern half of the sky appear to move from east to west, while those in the northern half circle the North Pole Star counterclockwise. Their positions tell the time of night.

During the last thirty years, archaeologists and archaeoastronomers have enjoyed a controversy over whether Stonehenge and certain medicine wheels contain an alignment to the Summer Solstice Sun rise. The controversy was only possible because none of the participants had ever made an exact observation of a Sun rise. An alignment of sighting gaps or stones, like back and front sights on a rifle, has to point to the Sun rise position on the horizon. The nay-sayers suggested that the rise position on the horizon is uncertain, because it might correspond to the place where the Sun's full orb is sitting on the horizon, or perhaps to where the half orb is above the horizon, or maybe to the point of the first flash of the top edge of the Sun on the horizon. At the latitude of Stonehenge and the medicine wheel near Majorville, the horizon positions of the first flash and full orb differ by about one degree, but the full orb position is difficult to determine accurately because the amount of refraction of light decreases with increasing height above the horizon, which gives the Sun's disc an oval shape. Some of the yay-sayers suggested that the rise position is that of half orb, which is even less certain than the full orb position.

Anyone who makes rise and set observations from the same spot over several years, as Skywatchers had to do in ancient times and still do, finds that the positions of the first and last flashes are the most reproducible, most nearly the same on the same date year after year. My main contribution to archaeoastronomy in the North Temperate Zone has been to rediscover the ancient technique of observation, which has provided the first dependable rise and set data during recent centuries along alignments marked by fixed back and front sights.

From day to day during a year, the positions of Sun rise and set move along the horizon, from north to south during summer and autumn, and south to north during winter and spring. At the northern extreme, the position of rise appears to remain the same for a few days, then reverses direction and begins to drift southward. The "Sun stands still" at that time, which is what the Anglo-Latin word "Solstice" means. (Sol means Sun.) The northern Sun-standstill is the Summer Solstice, which centres on June 21. A sufficiently accurate instrument can pick exactly June 21, when the drifting Sun rise position stops and turns around. The southern Sun-standstill is the Winter Solstice, on December 21 or 22, depending on the year within the leap year cycle. The Sun's place on the horizon and its direction of drift tell the time of year. The positions of the constellations visible shortly after Sun set, or at any fixed time of night, also tell the time of year.

Time Machines

A set of lines between stones on the ground could be fixed pointers, with lights in the sky moving between them to indicate the time of day or the month of the year. A time machine.

The Moon changes shape every night in a *moonthly* cycle, so the shape of the Moon tells the time of *moonth*.

We usually think of a time machine as a clock, with pointers that rotate to mark the time of day or night. On a wall of the Old Town Hall in Prague, there is a six-hundred-year-old astronomical clock that has several rotating pointers indicating the time of day or night, the time of year, and the phase of the Moon. People living in cities don't normally see a broad expanse of sky and distant horizons; they are intrigued by a mechanical device that simulates sky events. Country folk are intrigued by the fact that someone could make a machine like that that works.

On the ancient North American Plains, there were no cities. Changes in the dramatic sky were observable by everyone.

The Summer Solstice Sun rise and set positions occur on the longest day of the year. The Sun's altitude at noon is the highest that it attains above the horizon during the year. The hottest period of the year follows the Summer Solstice.

The Winter Solstice Sun rise and set positions occur on the shortest day of the year, and the Sun's noon altitude is the lowest during the year. The coldest period of the year follows the Winter Solstice.

Cardinal Directions

North, south, east, and west are called the "cardinal directions." How were they picked, and why are they called "cardinal"?

First, the term itself comes from the Latin *cardo*, meaning hinge or pivot. The stars rotate each night about a north–south pivot, with the Pole Star at the north end and the south end not visible from the Northern Hemisphere. North is simply the direction along the Earth's surface to the horizon point perpendicularly below the centre of rotation, the Pole Star. South is the direction exactly opposite to north. The directions of Sun rise during each year swing from northeast to southeast and back again, as if swinging about a hinge due east. The Sun set positions during each year swing from northwest to southwest and back, about a hinge due west. North and south are the directions toward the horizon points directly below the sky pivot-ends, east and west are the hinge-points of the Sun rise and set directions.

The names of the cardinal directions refer to positions of the Sun. "East," from the Greek ἠώς, or *eos*, means "red sky in the morning," dawn, and is the direction where the Sun rises. "West," from the Greek ἕσπερος, or *hesperos*, and the Latin *vesper*, means "evening," and is the direction where the Sun sets. "North," from the Umbrian *nertu*, means "on the left," which is the location of this direction when one faces the direction of dawn to pray. North is where the Sun never arrives, and implies darkness and cold. Finally, "south," from the Goth *sunno*, means "sun," and is the direction where the Sun is highest in the sky, and the word implies light and warmth.

OBSTRUCTIVE BIAS OF "WESTERN, EASTERN" AND "OLD WORLD, NEW WORLD" CLASSIFICATIONS

People of European background commonly classify different cultures, modes of thought, science, and religion as "Western" or "Eastern" and "Old World" or "New World." These classifications are so heavily charged with European bias that they emit sparks in non-European contexts. They form an extreme barrier to understanding the diverse cultures in the world.

The philosophy of the people in North America was evidently very different from that in Europe. For Europeans, "Eastern" meant Eastern Asia (the "Far East") and "Western" included Europe and Asia Minor (the "Middle East," the cradle of "Western" culture). It would be more insightful to use an initial, broad classification according to continent: African, North American, South American, Asian, Australian, and European. American cultures then refer to those that existed before the invasion by Europeans. Five centuries of concerted attempts to destroy American cultures have so far fallen short of the mark, and the cultures are resurging in modified forms.

Percy Bullchild, a Blackfeet Indian, in his book *The Sun Came Down*, wrote, "The truest name of our Creator of all life on Mother Earth is Holy One, or Sun. God was invented by Europeans and brought into this world to make their misdoings good." The Sun is considered to be the personification of the most immense power in creation because it governs all life on Earth. The focus is different from that of larger cosmologies.

All continents long predate human occupation, so are effectively of the same age in this context. The terms "Old" and "New" Worlds stem from a European pecking order that is no longer useful. American civilizations evolved long before the European term "Old World" came into use.

The recent classifications "pre-scientific," "scientific," and "true-scientific" do not increase our understanding. The root of the word "science," after all, is the Latin *sciens*, which means knowing, understanding. There is more than one way of knowing, and understanding is a more basic thing.

■ ■ ■

CHAPTER THREE

Ómahkiyáahkóhtóohp,

OR

OLDBIGARRANGEMENT

It gives me a feeling of amazement to hold in my hand an elegant object that was made and used by someone 10,000 years ago. We can visualize a little of the lives of people 2000 years ago, through New Testament stories and histories of Mediterranean peoples. The Old Testament stories of Abraham dating back 2000 + 2000 years are difficult to visualize except through fantasy. It's fun to visualize the begats and men "knowing" women, but I can't visualize someone 900 years old, the age given to some figures of the early Bible. (Who would want a 900-year-old woman? A 900-year-old man.) The most ancient texts that have survived have survived perhaps because they contain goodly portions of violence and sex. Human nature has remained the same.

Beyond sex and violence, we can't visualize realistic human lifestyles of 2000 + 2000 + 2000 + 2000 + 2000 years ago. At that time, the Bow and North Saskatchewan Rivers were valley-gouging torrents from melting glaciers, and long-haired elephants were part of the scene.

In 1969 my father died. His collection of stone tools, projectile points, and shards of fire-baked pottery was divided among the three brothers, since our younger sister didn't want any. By then I was a professor of chemistry at the booming University of Alberta in Edmonton. An intricate variety of projectile points hung almost unnoticed on a wall in my office at home for six years. Then, in midlife, I began enquiring about their shapes and ages, and the types and origins of the stones. The points were from 300 to 10,000 years old. Ten thousand years ago good flint had been carried more than 1000 kilometres from the Knife River in North Dakota to Saskatchewan and Alberta. The flint tools were beautifully made. The people were highly mobile and had among them skilled craftsmen.

In 1980, as I mentioned earlier, Jim MacGregor suggested that Phyl and I would enjoy seeing several patterns of stones on the ground, including three medicine wheels, and four engraved boulders called "ribstones" on hilltops. A ribstone was said to be a boulder with rows of parallel grooves pecked down its sides, which seemed to resemble ribs of a buffalo.

We drove 4500 kilometres through southeastern Alberta in eight days in late August 1980, photographed the fifteen artifacts and their sites that Jim had told us about, and were guided to two others by farmers along the way. Some of the ribstones have other symbols engraved on them, including crossed circles and human/animal hybrid faces, so ribstone is a catch-all classification like medicine wheel, and will eventually be replaced by more descriptive names.

All seventeen of the sites we visited contained additional, previously unrecognized features that are integral parts of the artifacts, for example lines of stones that extend north or northwest from the central object. The mysterious medicine wheel near Majorville has many other cultural arrangements of stones in its vicinity, patterns made by man, so it is evidently part of a much larger complex.

Questions from our brief tour enticed us into a long-term study of these things, which continues still. Throughout the 1980s, when we visited the sites we lived in our 1972 blue Ford sedan (Figure 3-1). Phyl slept curled in a sleeping bag in the front seat and I in the back, since I am much taller and the back seat is larger. Food and water were in the trunk, with cameras and tripods stuffed in the foot space of the back seat. Sometimes, in a hurry to catch a Sun set in a particular line, I drove the Ford like a pony across the prairie, and reattached the back bumper with haywire when required.

Figure 3-1 *The Blue Shrine*, our home on the hills during the 1980s. Phyl has breakfast ready and is knitting as I return from photographing the dawn and the Sun rise. June 17, 1984.

As rust holes grew in the bottom of the car, scraps of sheet metal and metres of polyethylene sheet became its lining. Finally, in 1991, after Phyl's feet got wet a few times when driving through puddles, we decided the car had to go to the scrapyard.

"One hundred twenty-five dollars!?" I protested when the scrapman told me its worth. "The V8 engine still gets 20 miles per gallon, same as when it was new!" But he held firm, and Phyl thought a bit more body should go with the engine.

I have many happy memories of that sedan, which I had named *The Blue Shrine*.

When the great sitar player Ravi Shankar first performed in Edmonton in 1973, one of my East Indian graduate students was his host, and I was their taxi driver. Kamal Jha arranged the visit because I was a fan of Ravi's music, and he toured North America occasionally.

My sky-blue Ford turned out to be good luck. Ravi told me that he is a blue-fetishist. We even had to find him a hotel room with blue walls. We walked the hotel corridors together looking for a room that had light blue walls. We found one.

After the superb, emotional concert in Edmonton's large Jubilee Auditorium, we took Ravi and his accompanists to the home of another member of the East Indian community for a late-night supper. Kamal's beautiful wife Prema was my guide in handling Indian food. She was on occasion gossamered with Ravi's admiring glances, but most memorable for me was when, upon seeing my awkwardness eating mushy food with my fingers, Prema quietly told me that, "Up to the second knuckle is alright."

The renowned Alla Rakha came to accompany Shankar on the tabla, and the trunk of my car carried their precious instruments. It was after Shankar's visit that I called the car *The Blue Shrine*.

So many happy memories … you can understand why I had trouble parting company with it at the scrapyard.

A 4-wheel-drive camper would make our lives easier in the field, but I couldn't find one for rent in Edmonton. I finally located an entomologist's camper in the University of Alberta's vehicle pool. George Ball had had a roomy camper built on the back of a 1986 GMC dual-wheeled, 4-wheel-drive, 1-tonne truck. This wasn't a play-toy like a Stupid Ugly Vehicle. George used it for collecting beetles in the Mexican mountains during the summer.

I phoned him: "Hi George. It's Gord. Will you rent me your camper truck to visit an ancient site in southern Alberta for a few days? It's 500 kilometres from here."

George: "No."

Me: "Come on, George! There isn't a 4-wheel-drive camper available for rent in the city!"

George: "I'll lend it to you."

George's camper has a yellow cab and George calls it *El Escarabajo Oro* (The Golden Beetle, Figure 3-2). We didn't have to curl up in order to lie down, there was a propane stove to heat food (but it wasn't vented, so it couldn't be used to heat the cabin), and we could actually eat off a table.

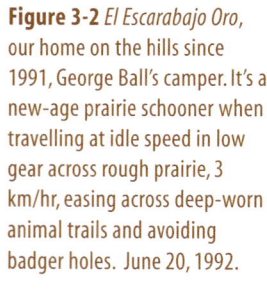

Figure 3-2 *El Escarabajo Oro*, our home on the hills since 1991, George Ball's camper. It's a new-age prairie schooner when travelling at idle speed in low gear across rough prairie, 3 km/hr, easing across deep-worn animal trails and avoiding badger holes. June 20, 1992.

The Site near Majorville, Alberta

Majorville, an Anglo-French name that hints at Big Town, consists of one small building at a crossroads far out on the prairie (Figure 3-3a). From 1908 to 1966 it was a general store and post office where local farmers bought supplies and picked up their mail. The owner lived in the back part of the building.

Lee Francis bought Majorville in 1935 and became postmaster after he came of age, twenty-one, on November 25 of that year. In 1958 Francis replaced the building with a Quonset hut on the other side of the road. He closed the store in 1966 and the post office in 1972. The building remained his bachelor home until January 2007, when, at age 92, his failing eyesight and health forced him to relocate to a seniors' home in Vulcan, Alberta. He died on March 10, 2008. Now Majorville is an empty building.

The Medicine Wheel 30 kilometres easterly of Majorville is high on a breezy hilltop overlooking the precipitous valley of the Bow River (Figure 3-4). The central cairn of head-sized rocks is surrounded by a large ring of smaller rocks, with the cairn and ring connected by 28 lines of fist-sized rocks (Figures 3-5 and 1-1).

Figure 3-3 (a) The original Majorville Store/Post Office and home as it was in about 1945. Notice the windmill generator of electric power; looking south, photo by Lee Francis. **(b)** Lee Francis at home in Majorville, age 84 years, May 19, 1999. A Quonset hut replaced the old store/post office/home in 1958.

Archaeologist James Calder and his assistants deconstructed more than half of the cairn in 1971, under the supervision of the University of Calgary's Richard Forbis. They found it to be made of eight layers of rocks separated by seven layers of dirt, containing thousands of stone, bone, and fossil artifacts. In the lower layers were dart points made by the Oxbow people about 5000 years ago. The cairn contained projectile points of styles ranging in age from 5000 to 200 or 300 years.

The artifacts were taken and added to the archaeology collection at the University of Calgary, and the rocks were heaved back into the pile. But larger rocks were returned to the upper layer in token reconstruction of the cairn.

When Phyl and I visited the site in 1980, we also found smaller rings, crescents, and cairns of stones on the same hill and on the surrounding prairie. Through the years, we found that cultural arrangements of stones extend over about 30 square kilometres of rolling prairie, equal to about 35 by 35 city blocks, cut through by the Bow River Valley.

When the glacier melted back from this area about 11,000 years ago, it left many thousands of stones and rocks on the prairie surface. However, in the zone within about 2 kilometres of the medicine wheel there are few rocks that appear to be in random positions. The thousands of random rocks have been gathered and placed in cairns, rings, crescents, and other patterns that now remain.

Figure 3-4 Looking southeast from the Majorville Medicine Wheel to a bend in the Bow River, 160 metres below and 4 kilometres away.

Figure 3-5 The Majorville Medicine Wheel. Looking north.

Aerial photographs of the site that I commissioned are useful for my study, but show too much information for most purposes. The patterns of stones were created by people on foot, and are to be viewed from ground level, where what you see is limited by the heights and hollows of the local topography. An aerial photograph shows too many rocks for an inexperienced observer, because you see the patterns down in the hollows as well as those on the heights. Different patterns have different purposes, and are not to be seen all at once. So don't read too much into the few aerial photos in this book.

There is a large crescent of rocks on the southwest side of the medicine wheel, which makes a pincerlike pattern with the central cairn and a large intermediary rock (Figures 3-6 and 1-1). The crescent seems to represent the Moon, so the medicine wheel probably represents the radiating Sun, with the central cairn as the Sun; the large rock between the Moon and Sun in Figure 3-6 probably represents the Morning Star. These are symbols of an ancient Holy Trinity; a God, Goddess, and their Son, still sacred to many Plains Indians today. The effigies seem to be the centrepiece of a widespread, lacelike, 5000-year-old Temple.

For this reason, I now call the Majorville Medicine Wheel the Sun Cairn Ring near Majorville.

The crescent Moon cupping the Morning Star was also engraved into an ancient Sacred Rock on *Kekip* Hill, 26 kilometres north of

Figure 3-6 Moon, Morning Star, and Sun effigies at the centre of a 5000-year-old Temple near Majorville. Looking northeast. The Moon crescent is 3 metres wide, the diameter of the Morning Star rock between the Sun and Moon is 1 metre, and the Sun Cairn diameter is 9 metres. This creates a ratio of 1 : 3 : 9. There is a *geometric pattern*: a straight line from the left end of the Moon through the Morning Star leads to the right edge of the Sun, and a straight line from the right end of the Moon through the Morning Star leads to the left edge of the Sun (see Figure 1-1).

the Temple. The quartzite Sacred Rock was completely covered with glyphs, even on the bottom. In times of crisis it was sometimes used as an altar for sacrifice, including blood sacrifice to the Morning Star. It was stolen off *Kekip* Hill in 1882 by Jean l'Heureux, a linguist and amateur anthropologist who had lived many years with Indians. It was presented to the visiting Governor General Marquis of Lorne during his tour of the North-West Territories. L'Heureux did, however, leave a record of what he had learned about the Sacred Rock, which he said had the Blackfoot name "*Kekip Sousouators*." He translated the name as "Flint-knife Scalp-place," which alludes to blood sacrifice. From material in the twentieth-century Blackfoot dictionaries of Uhlenbeck & Van Guik and Franz & Russell, *Kekip* seems to refer to a cutting instrument, though that precise word is not listed (*ikahk*, sever, cut). L'Heureux's translation "Flint knife" is consistent with that. *Sousouators* seems to refer to the taking of a scalp (*saáó'takssin*) during a war or a raid (*soo*), and perhaps in a suitable circumstance it was put into the Morning Star on the Sacred Rock.

The Sacred Rock suffered forced migration with the Governor General to Ottawa, then to the Museum of Man when it was constructed there, then to the Archaeological Survey of Canada collection in Bells Corners, and finally to the Canadian Museum of Civilization in Gatineau, Quebec. This rock and site are described in detail in the report *Sacred Rocks of Alberta* (2000), in my files at the University of Alberta Archives.

The waning crescent Moon cupping the Morning Star is a design used throughout the world. It is used as a symbol of Islam and is included in the design of many national flags.

* * * *

Particular directions seemed to mean something in the arrangements on the site near Majorville. Phyl and I had always found water within 3 kilometres easterly of the glyphed sacred rocks on hilltops in Alberta, and the Bow River is 2 kilometres east of the Sun Cairn Ring.

In 1980, a barbed-wire fence separating two large areas of pastureland ran through the easterly side of the Sun Cairn Ring. Farm fences on the prairie normally run north–south or east–west, and I guessed this one to be north–south. At about 60 metres from the Ring and approximately at right angles to each other, there are three constructions of rocks. If the fence were north–south, the rock sets would be southwest, northwest, and northeast from the Ring.

Although archaeologists called the complex Ring a medicine wheel, ranchers had for eighty years been calling it the Sundial, and initially it looked to me like a sunburst. So I thought the three outlying sets of rocks might have ceremonially designated the directions of the Sun sets at the Winter and Summer Solstices, and the rise at the Summer Solstice. When I later offered the suggestion to several archaeologists in Edmonton, they said Indians merely followed the migrating buffalo and weren't interested in solstices. I wondered about that.

Phyl and I returned to the site with a compass in August 1982. We found the fence to run northeast–southwest, parallel to the wide, deep valley a kilometre to the east. I had guessed wrongly. The three outlying constructions are west, north, and east from the Ring, and there is an outlying square, flat rock marking south about 60 metres from the Ring centre. The cardinal directions are marked! The solstitial Sun rise and set directions would have been much easier to determine than were the cardinal directions, so I thought that the solstitial directions were probably marked as well.

The Sun rise direction drifts northerly from day to day during the winter and spring, from late December to mid June. Observed from the same spot, the rise-point drifts northerly along the horizon. As the season approaches and passes through the Summer Solstice, the daily drift of the Sun rise point slows, stops, and reverses. When observed daily from the same place, the point of Sun rise at the Summer Solstice remains almost constant for about seven days, during which the position shifts by only one-tenth of the Sun's diameter. The direction would be easy to mark accurately with an alignment between two widely separated stones, by nudging the movable back sight to the right each morning until the direction became constant for several days.

During the summer and autumn, the Sun rise point drifts southerly. The direction of Winter Solstice Sun rise observed from a particular spot would also be easy to mark accurately. Solstice Sun set directions could be marked by the same method.

The Hunt for Summer Solstice Markers

Phyl and I returned to Sun Cairn Ring Hill in June 1983 to see if we could record the Summer Solstice Sun rise and set along stone alignments. I had calculated that the rise viewed from the hilltop should occur at about 50° east of due north, and the set should be at about 50° west of north. Using a compass, I looked across the Sun Cairn in the rise and set directions, but found no clear front sight to make an alignment in either direction. I used the compass to examine other patterns of rocks on the hill, and found a possible Sun rise line between two prominent rocks about 60 metres east and southeast of the Sun Cairn.

I found no possible alignment for the Sun set. That evening the sky was overcast, so I got no record.

The next morning was clear. In twilight, I set the camera on the tripod to look northeast across the Sun Cairn, in case we later found a suitable front sight for the Sun rise from that position. As the sky

Figure 3-7 Summer Solstice Sun rise (SSR) alignment on the southeast slope of Sun Cairn Ring Hill. **(a)** The two prominent rocks are on the left side of the photo; SSR positions during the last 5000 years are marked, beginning with that in (b) for zero kiloanni Before Present (0 ka B.P.). **(b)** The rising Sun 43 seconds after the first flash on June 19, 1988, two days before the Solstice Sun rise; the first flash position is marked, and is a negligible 0°.02 to the right of the SSR. **(c)** The camera for (a) and (b) was above the rock at the bottom of this photo, 14 metres from the nearer prominent rock and 59 metres from the farther one. The dashed line is the present SSR line.

lightened, it first became intensely coloured with the dawn, then the colours faded as Sun rise approached. When the tip of the Sun flashed on the horizon, I photographed it to locate it in the landscape, then ran with the camera about 60 metres southeast to find where the Sun appeared relative to the alignment of the two prominent rocks. By the time I got there, the top of the Sun had moved slightly to the right of the alignment, and by the time I took the picture along that line, the Sun had just cleared the horizon and its top was about two Sun diameters to the right of the alignment. The angle of the path of the rising Sun is about 30° above horizontal, so the first flash would have appeared in the line. The two rocks apparently formed a Summer Solstice rise observation line, but it would have to be confirmed another time.

The visit was for only one night, because we were continuing on to glyphed Sacred Rock sites elsewhere. We would return another year.

Nearly half of all my attempts to photograph a Sun rise or set in the site near Majorville have been foiled by clouds. We also recorded rises and sets from other locations, so it was June 1988 when I got a clear photograph of Sun rise along the line of these two prominent rocks (Figure 3-7). The first flash was to the right of the farther prominent rock, a one-tonne white limestone, but a deeply embedded smaller rock was beneath the rise position (Figures 3-7a & b). Although the naked eye can easily see the sharp edge of the rising Sun as well as the landscape, Figure b has to be printed darker to show the Sun's edge. Fine detail on the horizon is more important than that in the foreground.

The Solstice rise and set directions shift slightly during thousands of years, due to a slow change of the tilt of the Earth's spinning axis relative to the axis of the Earth's orbit around the Sun. During the last five thousand years, the tilt has decreased by $0°.6$ and the Summer Solstice rise and set directions have become $1°.1$ less northerly. The rise positions along this line are marked for each thousand years (a term used to express this length of time is "kiloanni," or ka) back to 5 ka B.P. in Figure 3-7a. (B.P. stands for "Before Present," as in before the present year; it should not be confused with B.C., "Before Christ," or B.C.E., "Before Common Era," which are years before year one in the Christian calendar.) It appears that the original rise line was between the two prominent rocks, but when the rise shifted to the right of the white limestone, a smaller rock was placed as the new front sight. The distance between the two prominent rocks is too small for an accurate Solstice marker line. Humps and notches in the distant cliffs of the river valley could have served as accurate markers.

The back sight rock is much smaller than the front sight white limestone and could presumably have been moved easily, yet as the Sun rise direction drifted during the 5000 years, a smaller front sight rock was placed unaesthetically beside the limestone rather than move the back sight. Perhaps the Sunwatcher wanted a more precise, smaller front sight, or maybe the position of the back sight rock was fixed in an additional pattern that did not change with time. In any case, the small shift of the front sight meant that the Skywatchers made precise observations, so we looked elsewhere in the Temple zone for a longer Sun rise line.

An Accurate Summer Solstice Sun Rise (SSR) Observation Line

It's a long time between Sun rise and Sun set, so Phyl and I spent most of each day exploring the large site. We looked for cairns, rings and lines of stones, large rocks, and other patterns.

Three hills of equal height in a northeast to southwest string are the highest hills in the area (Figure 3-8). On the summit of each is a cairn, the largest being the Sun Cairn on the northeast hill, and the smallest being on the southwest hill. The Summer Solstice Sun rises in the northeast, so I photographed the rise from the cairn on the southwest hill.

The first flash on June 21, 1987, was slightly to the right of a rock on the distant west shoulder of Sun Cairn Ring Hill (Figure 3-9a). The rock is easily seen with naked eyes, but is barely visible in the photo, so Phyl stood behind it for photo 3-9b.

Figure 3-8 The core of the enormous Temple zone near Majorville is comprised of cairns on the tops of three hills of equal height, 919 metres above Mean Sea Level. Each of the three hills touches the distant horizon in this southwest view from near the principal Sun Cairn on Sun Cairn Ring Hill. The middle hill is 1.3 kilometres away, the southwest hill 1.8 kilometres.

Figure 3-9 SSR from the cairn on the southwest hill.
(a) First flash of the Sun on June 21, 1987; the position was corrected for a slight mirage. **(b)** Phyl standing behind the middle foresight rock of (c). **(c)** Looking northeast to Phyl standing behind the rock of (b) and one to the left; there is another to the right. The SSR would have occurred at these foresights in the periods marked. **(d)** Looking northeast across the cairn on the summit of the southwest hill in 1996, the positions of SSR are marked in thousand-year steps back to 5 ka B.P. In 5 ka B.P., the foresight was the bottom of the V made by the intersection of two hillsides. **(e)** Looking southeasterly at a series of rocks, with the Global Positioning System (GPS) instrument beside Phyl's position in (b). **(f)** Looking southwesterly at the GPS instrument as in (e), and Phyl at the edge of a ring of rocks; the arrow marks the back sight cairn of (b) and (d).

The horizon-marker rocks shown in Figure 3-9c could have marked the SSR in the era from about 1200 years ago to 400 years ago.

I have found over the years that foresights for some of the marked Sun rises and sets are the bottom of a V made by intersecting profiles of rocks or hills. In Figure 3-9a there is a V made by intersecting hillsides to the left of the first flash. The SSR had been above the bottom of this V 5000 years ago. When the SSR drifted sufficiently to the right of the bottom of the V, apparently a rock was placed as a foresight, and another rock was placed every four centuries or so. Locations of the SSR are marked in thousand-year steps back to 5 ka B.P. in Figure 3-9d, a photo taken after the fence had been removed by the new lease holders of the land.

The last stone marker was placed about 400 years ago. The next adjustment would have been made at about the present time, but the European invasion had destroyed much of the Indian culture by about two centuries ago.

The discovery that the hillside V corresponded to the SSR foresight 5000 years ago was a happy surprise. It came while analyzing the pictures several years after the SSR had been photographed. My life is at times a chain of surprises, mostly pleasant. For this SSR line, the first surprise came shortly after the first flash appeared, when I noticed the tick on the horizon a bit to the left of where the first flash had been. I felt that the tick would be a rock. I walked the kilometre-and-a-half to check, and it was. A later surprise was when I saw another rock, 3 metres southeast of the first, closer to the first flash position. There are additional rocks to the northwest (Figures 3-9e and f), which were a puzzle until I noticed the 5 ka B.P. V-sight. The rocks marking positions southeasterly of the V-sight could be sequential foresights as the SSR direction became less northerly with time.

The back sight is a cairn on the narrow summit of the southwest-most of the three equal-height hills, so its position has been fixed for 5000 years. As the SSR direction shifted, the foresight was corrected each half-millennium or so. This amazing calendar had been kept accurate almost continuously for 5000 years. The calendar was evidently disrupted only when Europeans invaded the territory a few centuries ago.

Ómahkiyáahkóhtóohp

A Blackfoot Elder told me that a name for the large patterns of rocks near Majorville is *Ómahkiyáahkóhtóohp*, a Blackfoot word meaning "Old, Big Arrangement," which I join together in the Blackfoot manner to "OldBigArrangement." If you want to try saying the word, the *h*'s are aspirated, and the accented vowels are emphasized.

I apply the name to the widespread set of patterns distributed over about 30 square kilometres of hilly prairie (diameter about 6 kilometres), approximately centred on Sun Cairn Ring Hill.

Ómahkiyáahkóhtóohp is probably not what Blackfoot call the place among themselves, but is what the Elder was willing to make public. For ease of pronunciation, the word is shortened to *Ómahk*, which means "big, old." So each time the full word appears in this book, you may pronounce only the *Ómahk*.

Summer Solstice Sun Set

Fifty metres north of the Sun Cairn Ring there is a complex arrangement of rocks that I call the North House, for lack of a better name. The rock patterns that were constructed at the four cardinal directions from the Sun Cairn Ring are decreasingly complex in clockwise order from the West House to the North, East, and South Houses. The West House is a finely engineered construction, and the South House is a single, square, flat rock. I wonder what the sequence of complexities signifies. Their distances from the Sun Cairn Ring perimeter decrease in the same order, from 70 metres west to 40 metres south.

On the Summer Solstice in 1990, I photographed the setting Sun across the top of the North House. The last flash occurred directly above a cairn on the summit of a knoll one kilometre away (Figure 3-10a). The last flash was a pinpoint of light on the horizon about 15 seconds after this photo was taken, and its position is marked. Phyl is standing behind the foresight cairn in Figure 3-10b.

The North House back sight is a cluster of rocks (Figure 3-10c). Looking back from the foresight cairn, one sees the North House back sight as a small V on the horizon (Figure 3-10d). The tripod for the Sun set photography is faintly seen in the middle of the V.

40 CANADA'S STONEHENGE

Figure 3-10 Summer Solstice Sun set (SSS) from the North House. June 21, 1990. **(a)** Last flash of the Sun. **(b)** Zoom of (c); Phyl is standing behind the foresight cairn 930 metres away. **(c)** Looking across the North House in the SSS direction. **(d)** Looking back across the foresight cairn to the North House, visible as a tiny v with the tripod in it.

The Solstice last-flash position along this line in June 2000 differed by only one-fifteenth of the Sun-diameter; one-thirtieth of a degree.

My searches and discoveries within this ancient Temple are like examining an exquisite Fabergé egg, but on a scale of kilometres!

In the present era, the Solstice Sun set line is accurate within one-twentieth of a degree, $0°.05$, which means that it was probably adjusted within the last two or three centuries, during the eighteenth century. The first European to penetrate these southern Alberta prairies was David Thompson, who made mapping and trading expeditions there during 1799 to 1811. This is striking evidence of loss of Indian culture after the invasion by Europeans.

* * * *

Ómahkiyáahkóhtóohp Temple has an aura. I always feel contented there, occasionally enthralled. But when writing about it, I am sometimes weighed down by thoughts of the Europeans who invaded the territory and nearly destroyed the civilization that built the lace-like patterns and the astonishing calendar. Human nature is so complex that what is considered vicious depends on point of view. Genocide kills more than people. It kills a civilization that took thousands of years to grow. Genocide seems to have gone on since the migrations of peoples began. Read the Old Testament.

From time to time, I also think of the colonists who came to North America during the seventeenth to twentieth centuries to "pioneer in the empty land." Although most were migrating away from oppression, I wonder if they knew that *pioneer* meant *peon* or *foot soldier*. My ancestors migrated from Blackfriars (now the area of Blackfriars' Bridge and St. Paul's Cathedral in London) to Massachusetts Bay in 1630. They remained on the east coast of New England and then in Nova Scotia for three centuries. They were part of the beachhead of English colonization, part of the struggle between Englishmen and Frenchmen to dominate "the New World," using Indians as pawns. *Pawn* also means *foot soldier*, and as chessplayers know, they are relatively disposable.

Pioneers and pawns are disposable people, and even pioneer scientists enjoy the survival challenge that is sometimes rewarded with the "high" of amazement at the occasional discovery we make.

* * * *

Dick Forbis visited us on Sun Cairn Ring Hill one day in the late 1980s. As I mentioned earlier, his graduate student Jim Calder had excavated half the "Majorville Cairn," as the Sun Cairn was called in 1971. Dick didn't know that the structure and site were still held deeply sacred by Indians, but after the excavation he had wondered about the nature of the place.

He said that one time he had driven there with his son, and they stayed the night in the car to see whether spirits would visit them. "I fell asleep, and nothing happened."

I took his picture in the nearly-always-present wind beside the big pile of stones, and later sent him a copy.

He wrote back, "It's a pity you can't see the wind."

I replied: "You can see the wind. Look at the grass stalks."

* * * *

Siksika Reserve was an area north of the Bow River to which the Siksika tribe was restricted after 1877, when Treaty 7 was forced upon the southern tribes on the Western Canadian plains. The present Siksika First Nation is much smaller than, and shifted from, the original allotment, but even in 1877 the neighbouring sacred *Kekip* Hill and *Ómahk* Sun Temple zone were confiscated by the Canadian government.

Maps of this area of the North-West Territories published from 1882 to the early 1900s labeled a highland zone of about 500 square kilometres "The Rocky Buttes," bordered on the north and east by the winding Bow River. The mapmakers marked three prominent hills near the east edge of the zone. *Ómahkiyáahkóhtóohp* is the east-central 30 square kilometres of The Rocky Buttes, including the three prominent hills. The name "The Rocky Buttes" might have been given because most of the hills in the eastern part of the highland have cairns on them. The name was dropped a few years after the Province of Alberta was founded in 1905, and the tendency of Whites has been to think that there is nothing special about the zone.

Farther north, 250 kilometres north-by-east from *Ómahk*, in 1866 the venerated Flying Stone, a large, iron meteorite, had been taken from its sacred Wolf Ears Hill on the orders of Reverend John McDougall, to assist conversion of Indians to Christianity. Nonetheless, Indians continued to leave offerings at the Flying Stone's place on the summit of the Sacred Hill until the late 1930s. The Flying Stone is now in the Aboriginal Culture display of the

Alberta Provincial Museum and is described in my report: *Sacred Rocks of Alberta*. (Strangely enough, after years of my asking successive personnel and Directors of the Museum to move the sacred meteorite from the Minerals display to the Aboriginal Culture display, it was finally moved because the new Director, Phil Stepney, had a Freeman grandmother, Hazel (Freeman) Landals, with Freeman ancestors in 18th century Nova Scotia and 17th century New England, as I do.)

Winter Solstice Sun Rise

When *The Blue Shrine* was our mobile home, it could not get to the site in snowy conditions, so our visits were limited to summer and autumn. One of our neighbours, Norman Lee, was a retired member of the Royal Canadian Mounted Police. Norm was an enthusiastic outdoorsman and hunter both summer and winter, who trained trophy-winning black Labrador retrievers. He had a half-tonne 4-wheel-drive truck with a canopy on the back, into which he had built a sleeping platform, storage drawers, cupboards, and a propane furnace. In March 1988 he offered to take me to the site. One of his black Labs lived in the tiny quarters with us. The dog scoured the site with its nose and slept on Norm's feet. As a teenager, I had worked with dogs trained to herd cattle, but the behaviour of this sport dog had an air of trained precision. It seemed to match Norm's high-powered rifle with telescopic sight.

Norman got us into the site and out again without trouble. The following December the snow wasn't deep, so he thought he could pull his trailer there. He was seventy-one, which seemed old to me then, and I was admiringly grateful for a chance to record the Winter Solstice Sun. I was fifty-eight at the time. When I was about twenty, anyone more than ten years older than me seemed old. It seems strange that the perceived age gap between me and the beginning of "old" has stayed at ten years during the last fifty-eight years.

We got across the prairie to the site by avoiding snow patches as much as possible. Snow fell a couple of days later (Figure 3-11), but I didn't give it a thought, and Norman didn't mention it. One day I asked him how he passed the time.

He said, "My job is to keep you as comfortable as possible." Good God, I had no idea. I'd thought it was just another adventure for him. No wonder he was successful at anything he tackled. That attitude toward others is a philosophy of life.

Figure 3-11 Winter at the site, December 1988. **(a)** Norman Lee's truck and camper on December 19 after a blow. **(b)** Looking northeast at the Rayed Sun Cairn on December 20.

The morning before the Solstice there was a thin layer of cloud on the horizon viewed from the hilltop, but there was a possible upward-sloping Sun rise observation line from the West House V Rocks to a rock at the clear horizon above the cloud layer (Figure 3-12a). The Sun rise direction in the morning before the Solstice would be less than one-hundreth of a degree from the Solstice rise direction. When the first flash appeared, the horizon rock disappeared into the Sun (Figure 3-12b). What luck! The Sunwatchers had even avoided a layer of cloud near the cold ground by having an upward-sloping observation line to catch a first flash on a horizon above the cloud layer!

Later that day, more snow fell. The weather and sky conditions remained poor, so about an hour before Sun set time we decided that we had better leave. By the time we packed, hooked up the trailer, and headed out, the light was dimming. But it was no longer snowing. Norm drove through small drifts by ramming them in 4-wheel-drive. A few kilometres from the hill, an attempted ram ramped the truck up onto the snowbank, lifting the wheels off the ground. With the deteriorating driving conditions, Norm had abandoned the usual caution to "get into trouble in 2WD and get out of it in 4WD."

Unperturbed, Norman got out a shovel and dug snow away from the truck. The trailer was still in shallow snow, so he could back up after returning the truck wheels to the ground. When I took over the shovel, Norman used a piece of board to scrape snow from beneath the truck.

By the time the wheels were on the ground and the trailer backed up, twilight had gone. But the white ground kept the dark from being pitch. I walked around to find a path through manageable snow. When I found one, Norm followed me in the truck. When we got to snow of unthreatening depth, I rode until the depth became doubtful. Then I walked back and forth, sometimes knee-deep in snow, to find a way—like a landlubber lead-swinger, only looking for shallow instead of deep.

After an hour or two we wound up at a fence, and went northerly along it to where I knew there was a gate. Soon after the gate we reached a power line that was our guide to the trail that led to the road.

From that point, it was seven more hours to home.

The next visit during winter season was in George Ball's *El Escarabajo Oro*. The Mexican *Golden Beetle* would get some variety in outlook and challenge.

Figure 3-12 Winter Solstice Sun rise viewed from the West House V Rocks. The camera is 5 metres northwest of the grey granite that forms the left arm of the V. December 20, 1988. **(a)** 08^{h}48^m. **(b)** 08^{h}55^m.

Winter Solstice Sun Set

Nancy and Junior Bertschy (Figure 3-13) live next to a gravel road, and are the closest inhabitants to Sun Cairn Ring Hill—19 kilometres away by our usual route. They give us permission to cross their land. We stop to visit each time on the way in, and again after we come out. We always let them know the date we expect to come out of the area, and if we are two days late, they'll come to look for us.

Fortunately, we have never been two days late, but on a couple of occasions they've come to check on us anyway. When we come out Nancy usually offers us cake or pie, or a meal if that's the time we arrive.

Junior used to ask laughingly, "Are you any smarter than when you went in?" I always replied, "I know more." Nowadays my age shows *outside*, but not *inside*, so he asks things like, "What have you two kids been up to this time?" He gets a great chuckle after we've come out from a few winter days in the unheated camper.

Their hospitality extends to a bed during the occasional quick trip by car from Edmonton, and a 4-wheel-drive vehicle for the prairie. *El Escarabajo Oro* is a lumbering machine not suited for a quick trip to check something out, such as a gas well surveyed to be drilled in the site, and that might have to be moved or stopped.

In December 1993, Phyl and I drove the last 10 kilometres to the site through fog, with visibility occasionally down to a few metres. It was the only thick fog I've seen on the prairie in winter, and it was white, not yellow smog like an old-time London pea-souper. There were no banks of snow to trap us when I steered by guesswork, driving very slowly in 2-wheel-drive.

Heavy hoar frost crystallized on the grass and fence (Figure 3-14a). If you dress warmly and think warmly, it's not the cold, it's the *humidity* (Figure 3-14b).

The reverse of the Summer Solstice Sun rise (SSR) line in Figure 3-7a is a possible upward-sloping Winter Solstice Sun set

Figure 3-13 Nancy and Junior (Fred Jr.) Bertschy and son Fred (III), December 17, 1992. Sons Lou and Steve and daughter Tammy were elsewhere. After a night of extreme cold and wind, we had left Sun Cairn Ring Hill a couple of days earlier than expected. In the ice-hazed morning, the sky threatened a storm and Phyl thought we were finished. The camper's cold engine had to be cranked a while before it started, resting the cold dual batteries to recover between crankings. Nancy had been worried about us, and was very glad when we arrived.

(WSS) observation line (Figure 3-15a). The grey granite horizon marker is the back sight of the SSR line, and might be the foresight of a WSS line. The rock projects seductively above the horizon in the WSS direction. Haze had prevented clear photographs of the Sun along this line in December 1992, so I was trying again in 1993.

Figure 3-14 (a) Hoarfrost on the barbed-wire fence at the base of Sun Cairn Ring Hill. December 17, 1993. **(b)** Priestess in an ancient Winter Solstice Sun rise observer's chair. December 18, 1993, sky overcast.

Figure 3-15 Winter Solstice Sun set alignment from the East House to an upslope horizon marker. The tripod on the horizon is for a different, horizontal WSS line, across the visible horizon marker and to a marker below the distant horizon. **(a)** The observation line is too hazy, 16^h29^m December 16, 1992. **(b)** to **(f)** December 19, 1993, camera 55 metres from the horizon marker and as low to the ground as possible; look carefully at the Sun entering the rock on the horizon: **(b)** 16^h04^m; **(c)** $16^h06^m00^s$; **(d)** $16^h06^m10^s$; **(e)** $16^h06^m30^s$; **(f)** a clear view of the line, 16^h32^m.

Figure 3-16 Winter Solstice Sun set observation line of 5000 years ago. The line is from a sculpted red granite, along the southeast edge of the large white limestone, to a domed grey granite on the horizon, which is the receiver of the Sun. Granite to granite is 50 metres. October 4, 2004.

On the afternoon of December 19, 1993, I put the tripod 12 metres northeast of the SSR foresight—the flat rock on the left side of the East House white limestone—and set the camera as low as possible to still see the horizon marker straight ahead. The Sun descended toward the horizon rock and finally touched it (Figure 3-15b). Gradually, the Sun disappeared into the rock! Figures 3-15b to e show the movie, with the rock finally glowing from the engorged Sun.

Five thousand years ago, the WSS direction was $1°1$ farther south, to the left. The back sight of this line was to the right, a sculpted red granite 4 metres northeast of the east corner of the white limestone, pointing to the grey granite dome on the horizon (Figure 3-16).

The WSS observed from the East House and the WSR observed from the West House (Figures 3-12 and 3-15) are lines that have both back and front sights on Sun Cairn Ring Hill. At Sun rise the *foresight rock* disappears into the Sun, and at Sun set the *Sun* disappears into the foresight rock. What does that symbolize? As the Sun continues to rise after the rock-absorbing first flash, the rock gradually becomes visible again, and the Sun moves away from it. Does that symbolize the Sun coming out of the rock? The Sun enters the underground through a rock and leaves it through a rock? Does the Sun spend the night in rock? Is rock sacred? I had thought that cairns and large rocks were just permanent markers of Sun rise and set observation lines, but these rock foresights might have a greater significance.

Stone, *Inyan* in the *Lakota* language, is sacred to *Lakota* and the related *Nakoda* and *Dakota* people. People in many tribes refer to their own tribe as The People, sometimes The Real People or The Original People. Tribe names that are familiar to Whites were assigned by outsiders and are often pejorative, such as Blackfoot (also Blackfeet, perhaps because of black moccasins) or Little-rattlesnake (Ojibwa word *Natowessiw*, shortened by the French to Sioux, referring to the *Lakota* and their relatives). The word *Lakota* refers to several bands of people and means allies, or friends.

One summer day a *Nakoda* Elder in Saskatchewan took me to a sacred pattern of stones. After putting an offering of tobacco under a particular stone and praying, facing west, he suggested that I do the same, and walked down from the hilltop. When I had done so, he came back. He was violating tradition by showing me these things so that I could communicate something for the sake of future generations.

During conversation, I asked him how the *Nakoda* refer to themselves. He gently touched the side of a stone in the effigy with the toe of his boot.

"*Inyan!*" I said. Stone.

There followed a silence. I remembered that a branch of *Nakoda* living in the foothills of the Rocky Mountains is called Stoney.

Stones. On the March day that the two *Siksika* men saw me on Sun Cairn Ring Hill and came to investigate, the atmosphere became highly charged as I quietly showed them some of my discoveries. As we walked around they avoided stepping on any stone, even the pebbles.

In 1971 Whites had ripped apart and robbed half of the Sun Cairn!

Equinox

I had found Summer and Winter Solstice Sun rise and set observation lines between cairns and rocks that mark the first- or last-flash directions, with tiny errors of less than one-fifth of a Sun-diameter. Along a particular alignment, the Solstitial Sun rise or set from year to year occurs at the same place on the horizon within less than one-tenth of a degree. The enormous *Ómahkiyáahkóhtóohp* complex contains several observation lines for each of the season dates. Some lines are several kilometres long, others less than 100 metres; some are horizontal to a distant horizon, and others slope a few degrees upward to a near horizon to avoid a thin layer of cloud on the distant horizon. It seems that during the last 5000 years, more than one society built its own lines for the same season-pivot dates. The Sun-standstills, at the northerly and southerly extremes of rise and set directions, are the most obvious characteristics of the Sun's annual cycle along the horizon.

These markings were quite easy to find. I then looked for alignments that mark the Equinox Sun rise and set directions. After initial failures, I increased the chance of finding them by loosening the error restriction to one Sun diameter, half a degree.

I found none.

Fortunately, most of the observations were not on the appointed day. The site is 18 kilometres away from a road. Sometimes weather and ground conditions prevented us from reaching the site on a particular date (Figures 3-17 and 3-18). Sometimes the Sun rise or set was hidden behind clouds. Over a period of years, we photographed Sun rises and sets from a few days before an Equinox to a few days after it. We found alignments of stones that marked the rises and sets three days before the Equinox in March, and three days after the Equinox in September. Puzzling.

In March 1991 there were several days of clear skies, allowing a series of Sun sets and rises to be photographed as they moved across stone alignments.

Figure 3-17 In March 1991 the ground was wet and the gumbo was greasy. Our 4-wheel-drive camper-truck had trouble with the hills. Horses had less trouble. At 1 P.M. on March 17, two cowboys came looking for six two-year-old horses. Ranch horses sometimes run wild for their second year, after branding, weaning, and growing large enough not to be prey to coyotes. At two years of age they are caught and trained for riding. That morning I'd lit a candle in the camper before getting dressed to photograph the Sun rise. The young horses saw the light in the window and came galloping to investigate. After a couple of minutes of looking and sniffing, their curiosities satisfied, they went galloping off again. I told Locky McKinnon (white hat) and Ryan Brown (cap) where to look.

Sun Sets

A sight line that points to one last flash in March and to another in September goes from the Sun Cairn to three small cairns that make a V on top of a knoll nearly a kilometre to the west (Figures 3-19 and 3-20).

Figure 3-18 On June 21, 1990, I walked the prairie looking for cairns and rings of stones. At about 5 P.M. six yearling horses spotted me and came galloping over half a kilometre to check me out. I stood smiling in welcome as they approached. They galloped full speed right up to me, stopped abruptly and huddled round. A couple of them sniffed my bare arms and approved. I talked quietly to them for a minute, then slowly opened the camera and raised it to take their picture. After another minute, they galloped away as suddenly as they'd come. These are the horses that the cowboys came looking for the following March.

Figure 3-19 A sight line that marks only one Sun set in March and one in September is from the top of the Sun Cairn to a V of small cairns on a knoll a kilometre away (arrow). The present top of the Sun Cairn is not at the centre of the photo, partly because the south half of the Cairn was disassembled and robbed in 1971, and the Cairn was not properly reassembled.

Figure 3-20 Zoom of the Sun set line of Figure 3-19.

Figure 3-21 Setting Sun on March 16, 1991, viewed from the Sun effigy as in Figure 3-19.

A multiple exposure of the setting Sun on March 16 is in Figure 3-21. The last flash of the Sun was south (left) of the foresight on the knoll (Figure 3-22).

The last flash on March 17 was directly above the foresight on the knoll (Figure 3-23).

On March 18, the set point was to the north of the foresight. Figure 3-24 shows the positions of the last flash each day from the 16th to the so-called Equinox on the 20th. The Sun observation line picked the set on the 17th, three days before the Equinox.

Figure 3-22 Last flash of the Sun on March 16, 1991, viewed from the Sun effigy as in Figure 3-20. The last flash occurred to the left of the front sight (arrows).

Figure 3-23 About 13 seconds before the last flash on March 17, 1991, viewed from the Sun effigy. The last flash was directly above the front sight.

Figure 3-24 About 15 seconds before the last flash on March 18, 1991, viewed from the Sun effigy. The last flash was to the right of the front sight. The positions of the last flash on the 16th to the 20th are marked. The Equinox Sunset on the 20th was far to the right of the front sight.

Sun Rises

A sight line that points to one first flash in March and to another in September has a rifle-like V back sight made of 1-tonne rocks (Figure 3-25). In fact, these heavy rocks were finely adjusted, wedged, and shimmed so that when viewed from different directions they also make V back sights for the rises and sets of the Sun at both the Winter and Summer Solstices. That's why I call them the *V Rocks*. They are a pivot for six calendrical Sun observation lines that mark the annual swing of rise and set directions. The V Rocks are a rock-pivot, a *stonehinge*. (More about this term later.)

The foresight for one first flash in March and one in September is a pair of deeply embedded smaller rocks that make a V, 79 metres to the east, near the Sun Cairn Ring. To observe the Sun rise, one stands on the slope below the V Rocks, and visually nests the foresight V in the bottom of the back V (Figures 3-25 and 3-26). The line extends to touch the north rim of the Sun Cairn Ring.

On March 17, 1991, the first flash of the rising Sun appeared south of the bottom of the nested V sights, on a sort of chair (Figures 3-27 and 3-28).

58 CANADA'S STONEHENGE

Figure 3-25 An observation line that marks only one Sun rise in March and one in September has a back V sight made of several 1-tonne rocks, and a front sight V of two smaller rocks embedded deeply in the ground 79 metres to the east. The tips of the front sight can be seen nested in the bottom of the back sight. The Sun Cairn is on the right, and its Ring extends to this sight line.

Figure 3-26 Zoom of the view in Figure 3-25. A camera was placed on the left rock of the front sight to increase its visibility.

Figure 3-27 First flash of the rising Sun on March 17, 1991.

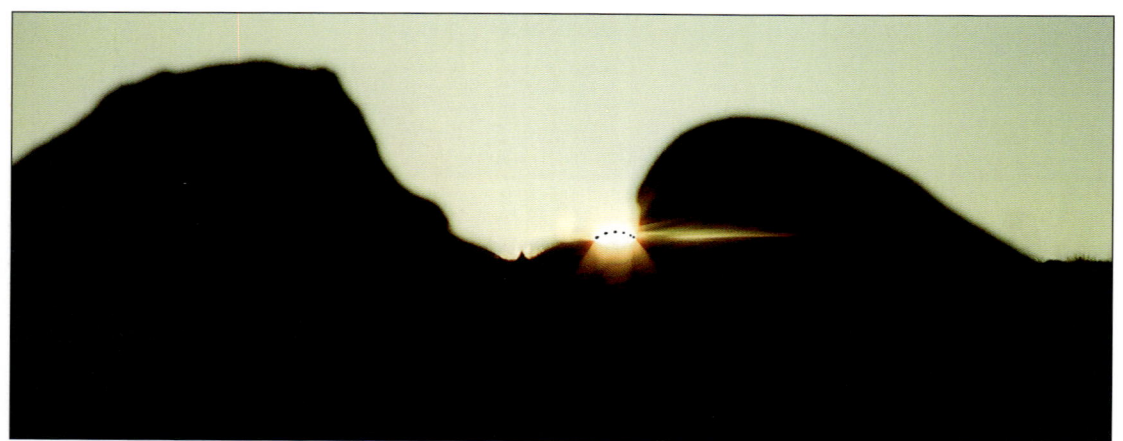

Figure 3-28 March 17, 1991, about 50 seconds after the first flash.

Figure 3-29 March 18, 1991, about 10 seconds after the first flash in the bottom of the nested Vs, shown in the frontispiece.

On March 18, the first flash was in the bottom of the nested Vs (Figure 3-29, see also the Frontispiece).

On March 19, the first flash occurred on the north arm of the V sight. The Sun in Figure 3-30 is a bit indistinct due to haze but was sharply visible to the naked eye. The edge of the Sun is more distinct in the photo negative than in the print, and was much sharper to the naked eye than in the negative.

On March 20, thirteen hours before the Equinox, the first flash was farther up the north arm of the V sight (Figure 3-31). The Equinox occurred at 20^h02^m Mountain Standard Time on the 20th, so the Sun rise closest to the Equinox was on the 21st, still farther up the north arm of the V.

Figure 3-30 March 19, 1991, about 12 seconds after the first flash, north of the bottom of the Vs.

Figure 3-31 March 20, 1991, first flash. The Equinox occurred 13 hours later. The Sun rise closest to the Equinox was on the 21st, farther up the north arm of the V.

The rise picked by the bottom of the nested V sights was on March 18, three days before the Equinox Sun rise.

The night selected by these observation lines was March 17 to 18, 1991. In the autumn of 1991, these lines picked the night of September 25 to 26, three days after the Equinox, which was at 05^h48^m MST on September 23.

There are other sight lines within the widespread *Ómahkiyáahkóhtóohp* that also select these dates of Sun rise and set.

Maps of the Calendrical Sun Sight lines

For the sake of people who like maps, Figure 3-32 is a contour map of the Temple core, which contains the three high hills of equal altitude. Casual readers might want to skip the details, which are given for those who wish to check the work. Each of the three hills holds a Cairn: the main Sun Cairn is on the northeast hill, Sun Cairn Ring Hill, and is labeled 11' (the numbers are GPS data-list numbers, in the order in which they were measured); the Secondary Sun Cairn is labeled 36; the southwest-most of the three is labeled 44, in the lower left corner, which I call Solstice Cairn for lack of a better name. The Summer Solstice Sun rise (SSR) observation line in Figure 3-9 transposes to Figure 3-32 as Cairn 44 to Cairn and Rocks 23 on the west shoulder of Sun Cairn Ring Hill. The Summer Solstice Sun set line (SSS) of Figure 3-10 is shown as North House Cairn 14 on Sun Cairn Ring Hill to Cairn 24 on the knoll in the top centre of Figure 3-32. The Equalday/night Sun set line (ESS) in Figure 3-23 is represented by 11' to 28' at the map centre.

The shorter observation lines are drawn on an aerial photo of Sun Cairn Ring Hilltop, Figure 3-33. The first SSR line found, Figure 3-7, passes across Horizon Marker Rock 52 to East House Rock 15 on the right side of Figure 3-33. The reverse of this line is the WSS shown in Figure 3-15. The Winter Solstice Sun rise (WSR) observation line of Figure 3-12 is on Figure 3-33 as V Rocks North Grey Granite 93" to Horizon Marker Rock 110'. The Equalday/night Sun rise line (ESR) of Figure 3-29 is from the bottom of the West House V Rocks V 93' to the Horizon Marker Rocks 108 and 108' on Figure 3-33.

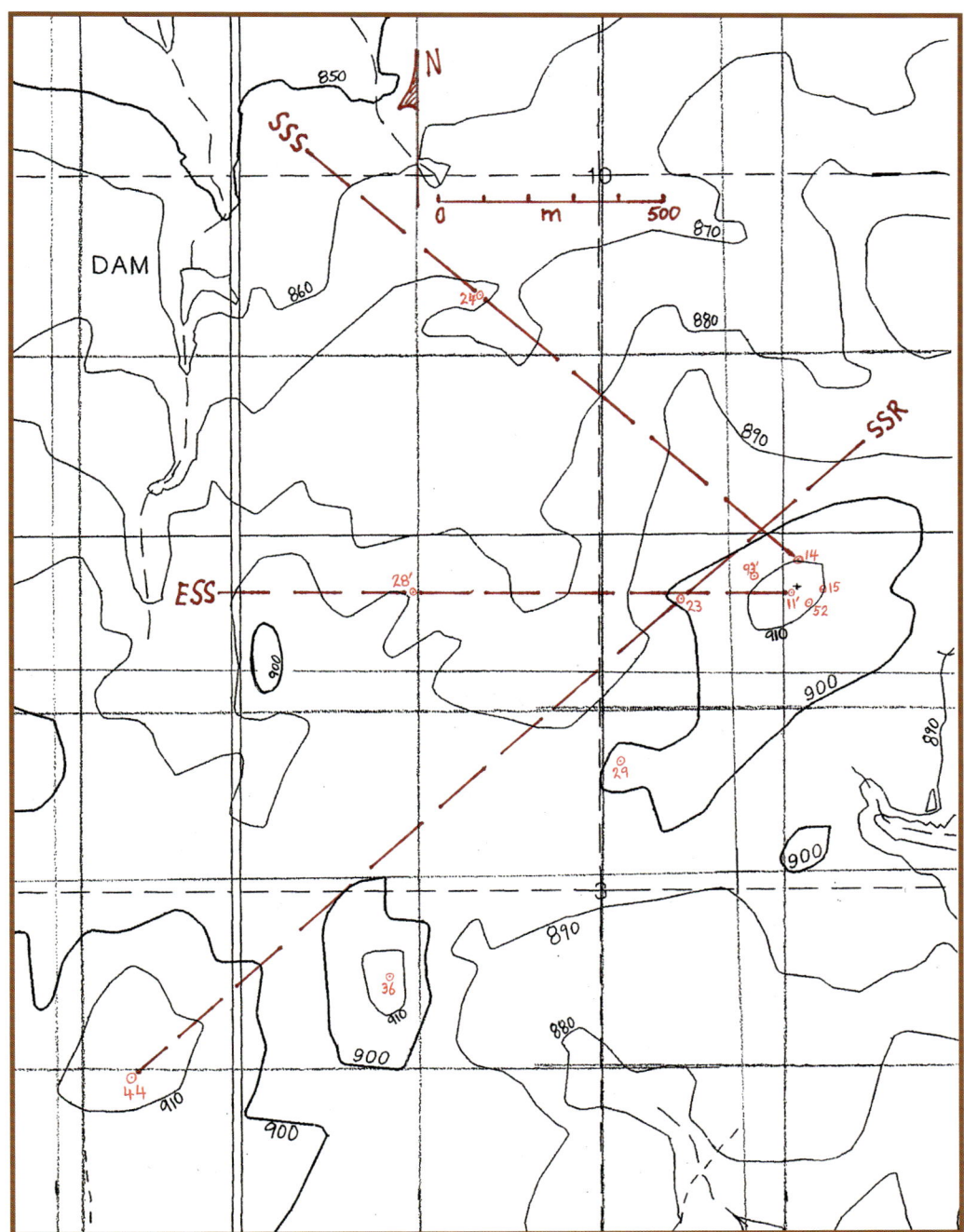

Figure 3-32 Calendrical Sun sight lines on a contour map that contains the three highest hills in *Ômahk* Temple core. The vertical contour interval is 10 metres. The red numbers are GPS data-list numbers that label the location of relevant cairns or large rocks. The summits of the three hills hold cairns GPS-11' (Sun Cairn Ring, right centre), GPS-36 (Secondary Sun Cairn, lower left centre), and GPS-44 (Solstice Cairn, lower left corner). SSR = Summer Solstice Sun rise (observation altitude to distant horizon = -0°3), SSS = Summer Solstice Sun set (altitude = 0°0), ESS = Equalday/night Sun set (altitude = +0°1). The map is from the National Topographic System Series, part of Alberta Map NTS 82 I/9 SW (1997). © Department of Natural Resources Canada. All rights reserved.

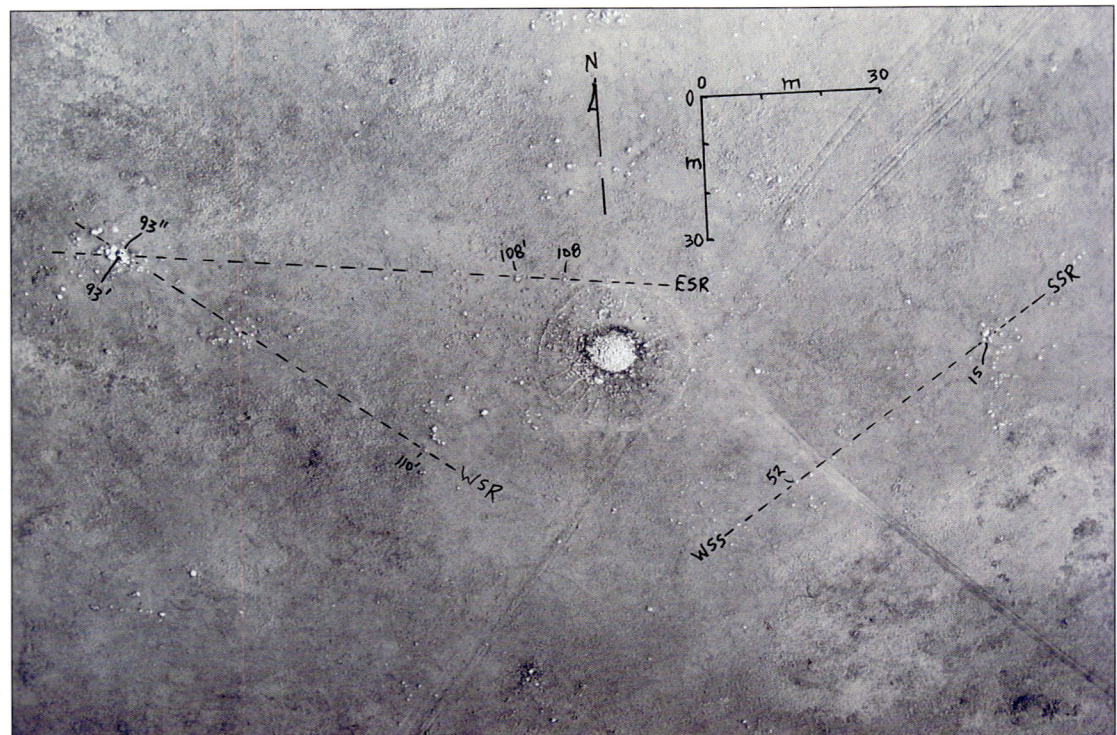

Figure 3-33 Calendrical Sun observation lines drawn on an aerial photograph of Sun Cairn Ring Hilltop. The numbers are GPS data-list numbers of the relevant Cairns and Rocks. 93' represents the bottom of the V in the West House V Rocks. SSR = Summer Solstice Sun rise line Horizon Marker Rock 52 to East House Rock 15 (observation altitude to the distant horizon = -0°.3), and the reverse 15 to 52 is a Winter Solstice Sun set (WSS) line (altitude = +1°.3). ESR = Equalday/night Sun rise line 93' to Horizon Marker Rocks 108 and 108' (altitude = +5°.2). WSR = Winter Solstice Sun rise line V Rocks North Grey Granite 93" to Horizon Marker Rock 110' (altitude = +3°.1). Notice the crescent Moon to the upper right of Rock 110'.

WHAT HAPPENED TO EQUINOX?

When convinced that the Sun rises and Sun sets selected by the observation lines were three days before the Equinox in March and three days after it in September, I looked for an explanation in the library.

The annual *Astronomical Almanac* and its *Supplement* produced by the United States Naval Observatory had what I was looking for. As experienced Skywatchers have always known, the only practical way to determine the exact positions and times of the Sun rise and set is to take them as those of the first and last flashes of the top of the rising and setting Sun. Extensive Tables in the *Almanac* list the times of the first and last flashes on a horizon horizontally in front of the observer, zero-degree observational altitude, at different latitudes and longitudes.

The *Almanac* shows that at the latitude and longitude of Ómahkiyáahkóhtóohp, 51° N and 112° W, the night of March 17 to 18, 1991, was less than half a minute from exactly twelve hours long, the Equalnight. The other Equalnight in 1991, September 25 to 26, was also less than half a minute from exactly twelve hours long.

However, the time of an *Equinox* is selected "theoretically" as the time when the centre of the Sun is directly above the Equator, and the "theoretical" Sun rise is when the *centre* of the Sun is *physically* horizontal from the observer. "Theory" treats the Sun as if it were a tiny dot, instead of its actual broad disk. The radius of the Sun is one-quarter of a degree, and the near-horizontal light of the first flash from the Sun's tip is bent downward more than one-half of a degree as it penetrates the Earth's atmosphere, so the first flash of sunlight appears when the centre of the Sun is more than three-quarters of a degree below the horizon. So the observed rise time is a few minutes before the "theoretical" Sun rise.

Similarly, the last flash occurs a few minutes after the "theoretical" Sun set. At the latitude of *Ómahkiyáahkóhtóohp*, five minutes are added to each end of the day and taken from each end of the night. The so-called Equinox days are 12.2 hours long and the nights are 11.8 hours. So the 12.0-hour-day/12.0-hour-night, or the Equalday/night, occurs two to three days, an average of 2.8 days, before the Equinox as the days lengthen in March, and two to three days after the Equinox as the days shorten in September.

The Equal*days* at Ómahkiyáahkóhtóohp are all within two minutes of exactly twelve hours long, and occur on March 17 and September 25 every year. The Equal*nights* in 1990 and 1991, and in the last two years of each leap year cycle, were March 17 to 18 and September 25 to 26. In the first two years of a leap year cycle, for example 1988 and 1989 or 2004 and 2005, the Equalnights were March 16 to 17 and September 24 to 25. The Equalnight dates oscillate back and forth across the Equalday date at this longitude, spending two years on each side during each leap year cycle.

The 5000-year-old calendar in *Ómahkiyáahkóhtóohp* is extremely accurate.

Equalday/night occurs when the Sun rises due east and sets due west in a flat landscape. Appendix A.7 shows how to make an accurate east–west line by using only the rotating stars and Sun as direction finders. The method is much more accurate than a magnetic compass. At an Equalday/night, the Sun rise viewed from the west end of the east–west line occurs above the east end of the line, and the Sun set viewed from the east end occurs above the west end of the same line, with an accuracy of half the diameter of the Sun.

During the months of March and September, the positions of Sun rise and set move along the horizon by one-and-one-third Sun diameters per day, so the same-line marker of both rise and set works only one day each March and one day each September. The dates are determined exactly. Once the dates are known from observations in a flat landscape, separate lines to the first and last flashes of the Sun on those dates can be marked anywhere.

March 17 is a familiar date, St. Patrick's Day. The ancient Irish people evidently celebrated the Spring Equalday. The modern Irish still celebrate it with a pagan festival, Christianized to the extent of naming it after their patron saint. However, the modern Irish did not welcome the information that March 17 is the Spring Equalday, and has been the Equalday for thousands of years. Perhaps it gives too formal a recognition to the pagan roots of the St. Patrick celebrations. Leprechauns and other fairies are now considered simply folklore. We consider other people's religions to be superstition.

The Old Irish, *Gaeilge* name for Equalday is *là leathach*, day in halves, or half daylight. The term has fallen into disuse. Modern Irish people speak of *eacaineacht*, an Irishization of the English word equinox, and the date is March 20, not March 17.

Unfolding Equalday/night, Equinox, and SZM (pronounced zem)

New discoveries uncover new problems when explanations are elusive. What happened to Equinox?

"Equinox" is Anglo-Latin for "Equalnight." The *Oxford English Dictionary* and *Merriam-Webster Dictionary* state that an equinox is either of two times per year, March 20 or 21 and September 22 or 23, when the day and night are equal in length *all over the Earth*, owing to the Sun's crossing the Equator. The ancient time machine in *Ómahkiyáahkóhtóohp* demonstrated that at 51° north latitude, the dates of equal-length day and night are March 17 to 18 and September 25 to 26. The modern *Astronomical Almanac* agrees with the 5000-year-old time machine, and shows that there is *no* place on Earth where the day and night are of equal length on March 20 or 21 or September 22 or 23.

Why are the dictionaries wrong? How did the correct information get lost, or discarded?

Large dictionaries in at least eleven European languages give definitions equivalent to those in the *Oxford English* and *Merriam-Webster* dictionaries. The error is a European phenomenon.

If the Earth's spinning axis were parallel to the axis of the Earth's orbit around the Sun, the Sun would rise nearly due east year-round, and set nearly due west. However, the spinning axis tilts 23°.4 away from the axis of the orbit, which causes the direction of Sun rise to swing back and forth between northeasterly and southeasterly during each year, and Sun set between northwesterly and southwesterly. The extremes away from due east and west are at the Solstices, when the North Pole tilts directly toward or away from the Sun.

Five thousand years ago, the tilt was a little greater, 24°.0, which, at the latitude of *Ómahkiyáahkóhtóohp*, made the directions of the Solstice Sun rises and sets 1°.1 farther from due east and west than they are today. The directions of rise and set at an Equalday/night are always due east and west in a flat landscape. The tilt is broadside to the Sun at an Equalday/night, so the change of tilt doesn't affect them.

In an accurate solar calendar, the *dates* of the Solstices and Equalday/nights would not change during ten thousand years. So the errors in European dictionaries need explaining.

The Sun is highest above the horizon, at its zenith, at noon Suntime each day. The Sun's zenith is highest at the Summer Solstice and lowest at the Winter Solstice. Halfway between the zenith extremes is what I call the Sun Zenith Midaltitude, abbreviated SZM, which is pronounced *zem*. SZM is difficult to determine accurately by naked eye and is not marked in the *Ómahkiyáahkóhtóohp* calendar. The SZM dates are March 20 or 21 and September 22 or 23, depending on the year within the leap year cycle. That's when the Sun crosses the Equator.

How SZM came to be called Equinox, and why dictionaries contain the word "equinox" and not "equalnight" or "equalday" is a fascinating story that unfolds in Chapter 6. Dictionaries in all European languages, and in American and Chinese, need to be revised.

The exact number of days in a year can be counted from one March Equalday/night to the next or from one September Equalday/night to the next. Equalday/nights are the key to an exact solar calendar.

The calendar in *Ómahkiyáahkóhtóohp* is slightly more accurate than the Gregorian calendar we use. Each year has 365 days for three years; then 366 days are needed in the fourth year to allow the Sun set and rise to cross the Equalnight lines and enter the next cycle. Further corrections of one day are needed occasionally to keep the calendar synchronized with the solar cycle.

One way of synchronizing the calendar with the Sun is the Gregorian way: every 100th year is not a leap year and has 365 days, except that every 400th year is a leap year and has 366 days. A further correction needs to be added to the Gregorian series, for each 3200th year to have 365 days. The Gregorian calendar has existed for only 425 years, so it will do for us. But the calendar in *Ómahkiyáahkóhtóohp* has existed for 5000 years, and its Equalnight lines are still accurate. Equalnight lines for direct observation of the Sun do not need corrections. Only our bookkeeping schemes need correction.

Sky on the Ground

Solar and lunar calendars

The 5000-year-old solar calendar in *Ómahkiyáahkóhtóohp* is by far the oldest accurate calendar that has been demonstrated by on-site observations to still work. The device must have been refined through many generations by people who were gifted with great curiosity. The calendar would have been useful to the regulators of society, but the great accuracy might have appealed only to the nerds of the time; nerds are everywhere and forever. Weather and seasons change along the Sun cycle, but without great precision.

There is also a lunar calendar in *Ómahkiyáahkóhtóohp*. The Moon changes shape every night during its *moonthly* cycle, beginning as a right-hand thin crescent, growing to a full disk, shrinking to a left-hand thin crescent, then disappearing for two or three nights, and reappearing for another cycle of 29 or 30 nights. The Moon's nightly change of shape and its easily discernable phases of No (New) Moon, straight edge (First and Last Quarter Moons), and circular (Full Moon), make it a convenient counter of nights, weeks (quarter *moonths*), and *moonths* (months).

The maximum number of nights that the Moon is visible during one of its cycles is 28. (The thinnest crescents of the New and Old Moon are not commonly seen, because these crescents at their thickest part are only about one-fourteenth of the Moon-diameter, and the sky is twilight.) Twenty-eight lines of stones join the Sun Cairn to the surrounding Ring (Figure 3-34). Perhaps the lines relate to the maximum number of visible Moon shapes. Four of the lines are in the cardinal directions, which divide the ring into quadrants. There are 7 lines in each northern quadrant and 5 in each southern quadrant. I wonder what the unequal numbers of lines in the northern and southern quadrants signify. The numbers 4, 5, and 7 were all held sacred in many ancient societies. They still are by many people: 4 cardinal directions, each is now addressed even during some Christian ceremonies; 5 Islamic prayer times each day; the Jewish-Christian-Islamic God rested on the 7th day, after 6 days of Creation; Lucky 7.

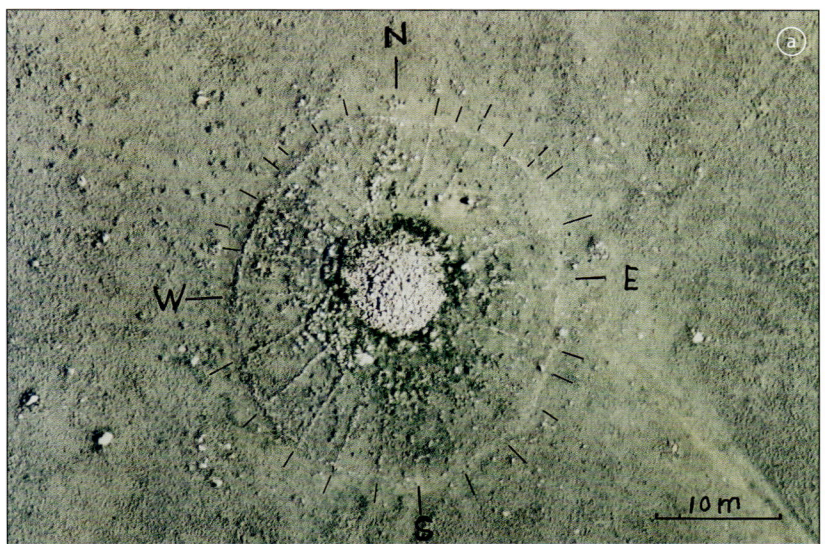

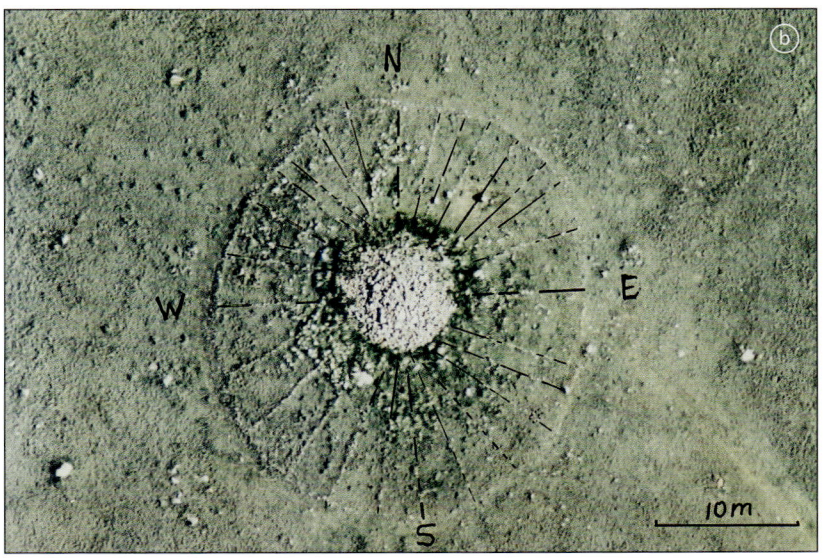

Figure 3-34 Sun Cairn Ring on a hilltop in Ómahkiyáahkóhtóohp. **(a)** 28 Rays of stones join the Cairn to the Ring; ticks outside the Ring indicate their locations; Rays in the cardinal directions are labeled (distortion in the photo is caused by the non-flat ground and the off-centre aerial camera). **(b)** The Rays are highlighted; there are 7 in each northern quadrant, and 5 in each southern quadrant.

Some of the stone lines between the Cairn and the Ring have been damaged by visitors during the last half-century and are not easily seen, so line locations are marked in Figure 3-34b. The lines are most visible in twilight, when walking around the outside perimeter of the Ring looking obliquely inward.

The number 28 is widely associated with the Moon. For example, there are 28 Mansions in some lunar zodiacs. The Moon is sacred in Islam, and there is an effigy of the waning crescent Moon on the peak of every mosque. There are 28 letters in the Arabic alphabet, which was developed for writing the Koran (*Al Q'ran*, The Recitation) during the seventh and eighth centuries A.D. This is compared with 26 letters in the earlier Latin alphabet, 24 in the classical Greek, and 22 in the much earlier Hebrew alphabet.

As an aside, through the years I have asked many Muslims, including a few *Imams* (Leaders), what the Moon on top of the mosque signifies, and why the Moon is always the waning crescent. The answers have always been, "I don't know," or an evasive, "I'll try to find out for you." The information might be restricted to Islamic Leaders.

The Full Moon is directly across the sky from the Sun, so the Full Moon rises opposite where the Sun sets, and sets opposite where the Sun rises. Therefore, the Full Moon near the Summer Solstice rises near where the Winter Solstice Sun rises, and sets near where the Winter Solstice Sun sets, when viewed from the same place. Near the Winter Solstice, the Full Moon rises and sets near where the Summer Solstice Sun rises and sets.

There are about twelve-and-a third Moon phase-cycles in the annual Sun cycle. The extra fraction of a Moon cycle from year to year makes the date of a "Solstitial Full Moon" jump around within fourteen days on either side of a Solstice. This causes the Solstitial Full Moon rise and set directions to dance irregularly about the other-Solstice Sun rise and set directions by up to two Sun-diameters, one degree, on either side. In addition, the axis of the Moon's orbit around the Earth is inclined by five degrees to the axis of the Earth's orbit around the Sun, and the Moon-orbit-axis precesses in a cycle that takes nearly nineteen years. This causes the Solstitial Full Moon rise and set directions to oscillate to nearly twenty Sun-diameters on either side of the Sun rise and set directions in a lunar-standstill 18.6-year cycle. The name is sometimes rounded off to lunar-standstill nineteen-year cycle.

The lunar-standstill 18.6-year cycle is marked in *Ómahkiyáah-kóhtóohp*. The southern extreme of the Summer Solstice Full

Moon rise, viewed from the Sun Cairn, occurs at the bend in the river shown in Figure 3-4. The northern extreme of the Winter Solstice Full Moon rise occurs at another big bend in the river to the northeast. Is it a coincidence that big bends in the river occur at the northerly and southerly extremes of the Full Moon rise viewed from the Sun Cairn? Or was that one of the reasons for building the Sun Cairn at that place?

The Moon's orbit around the Earth oscillates back and forth across the Earth's orbit around the Sun. Occasionally the Sun, Earth, and Moon happen to be exactly in line, which causes either the Sun or Full Moon to be eclipsed! The Sun gets eclipsed when the Moon is exactly between the Sun and Earth, and the Full Moon gets eclipsed when the Earth is exactly between the Sun and Moon. I wonder what the Oxbow Skywatchers thought about eclipses 5000 years ago.

Constellation effigies

About three kilometres south of the Sun Cairn, on sides of certain knolls in a zone that stretches about three kilometres east-to-west, there are rock patterns that appear to represent constellations. One pattern looks like the brightest part of Orion, while another looks like Draco or Gemini. Clusters of five to seven rocks at several places seem to represent The Pleiades. The Pleiades, a cluster of young stars, is a dust-like apparition to the upper-right of Orion that has captured imaginations in many cultures.

"As in Heaven, so on Earth" is a concept in many religions, including that of the *Lakota* and their relatives. Was the Bow River in the Temple Zone the Earthly representative of the Milky Way? The path of souls?

Christians also have this concept, as the Lord's Prayer includes the line, "Thy will be done on Earth, as it is in Heaven."

The constellations in the night sky change in a cycle similar to the Sun's. The weather, Sun, and constellations serve as season and year counters.

People about 2300 years ago constructed ground-patterns that seem to represent constellations in the vicinity of the Black Hills in the north-central United States, on a much larger scale than those in *Ómahkiyáahkóhtóohp*. They used the seasonal shifts of the constellations to guide their annual migration cycle between summer and winter camps among the patterns on the ground. This information has come to me from Ronald Goodman through his book, *Lakota Sky Knowledge*. Their celestial Sacred Hoop is a winter constellation that includes the intriguing Pleiades and the bright stars Capella, Castor, Pollux, Procyon, Sirius, and Rigel. Objects on the Earth are taken to mirror objects in the Sky and are still used ceremonially.

On the prairie in Alberta and Saskatchewan there are several cobble outlines of a man. For example, there is one near Dorothy and another near Steveville in Alberta, and two near Cabri Lake in Saskatchewan. I think they represent Orion—but that's not a sword hanging between his legs, and the stones on either side of its top are not a hilt guard. He's a mighty fertility symbol. One Blackfoot interpretation is that he is *Napi*, Creator and Trickster. *Napi* has a very long penis that frequently would reach between the legs of a young woman, even if she were swimming in the middle of a lake and he were standing on shore.

The Cerne Abbas Giant, whose outline is cut through the turf down to the chalk in England, has an erect penis in near-normal proportion, but he brandishes a large club. He might represent the constellation Hercules, but I hope the club wasn't intended for a lady who had caught his attention.

Enormous effigies of constellations, much larger than those described above, were made by Mexicans, Egyptians, Cambodians, and others around the world. The ones in Alberta might be among the oldest, perhaps 5000 years.

Ómahkiyáahkóhtóohp remains nearly intact because it is in a remote place. Whitemen did not recognize it as something worthy of destruction while they were trying to destroy the ancient Indian culture during the nineteenth and twentieth centuries.

There are natural gas deposits beneath *Ómahkiyáahkóhtóohp*. In recent years, gas wells have been drilled closer and closer to the central three hills that hold the core of the Temple. Several artifacts have been damaged. The high officials I've encountered in petroleum companies are money-grubbers who don't seem to care that they cause damage to irreplaceable prehistoric documents—and the ancient stone patterns *are* documents that we are learning to read. Alberta Government Officials who are charged with protecting such places are inadequate to the task.

But country folk who live off the land respect it, and respect others who have lived off the land. Fortunately, most of the petroleum and gas company field workers seem to be country folk. They have sometimes allowed me to move projected gas-well sites, and shift proposed access roads and pipeline right-of-ways to less destructive places, and even to erase a proposed well from the plan—all to minimize damage to this extremely important place.

When you learn to read prehistoric artifacts, they become historic. *Ómahkiyáahkóhtóohp* is a unique 5000-year-old document.

Ranchers who lease or own parts of the large site support its preservation. They recognize it as an invaluable record of people who lived off that land long ago.

The era of concerted attempts to destroy Indian cultures is nearing its end, and study of *Ómahkiyáahkóhtóohp* will continue for generations.

In 1971 only 16 hectares of *Ómahkiyáahkóhtóohp* was protected by designation as an archaeological site, and it didn't even enclose the entire "medicine wheel." After several years of my persistent requests during the 1980s, Alberta Government archaeologists increased the designated area to 65 hectares, including the entire Sun Cairn Ring Hill. I keep agitating to increase the designated area, and it is slowly happening.

Where Did They Live?

Tipi rings in the immediate area of the Sun Cairn Ring are too few to have accommodated the many people who probably constructed and used the enormous Temple. However, a few kilometres north of the Temple, on the north side of the winding Bow River, there are many hundreds of tipi rings 3 to 8 metres in diameter. These are the remains of habitation lodges. The people lived *north* of the sacred ground. The Sun Temple was to their *south*, like the zenith Sun.

Modern "Medicine Wheels"

The name "medicine wheel" that was applied to certain rings or radiating lines of stones has outlived its usefulness. Some of the radiating rings are Blackfoot death lodge memorials to honoured men. Some are venerated sacred rings, the significance of which I have not yet learned. At least two are complex, coded Sun effigies, and two or three others might be as well. When enough is learned about individual structures, they will be given appropriate descriptive names.

Lakotas and people of several other North American Indian nations now use objects called "medicine wheels" in a medical/spiritual/mental health sense. The symbol is a circle with a cross in it, representing the Circle of Life and Spiritual Balance. The message is that one should try to maintain one's self near the middle of the Circle, avoiding extremes. There are variations in details of the colours, construction, and interpretation of the cross and circle from one group to the next, but the symbol always represents "the Balanced Way."

In the Voodoo religion the cross represents the "crossroads," the intersection of the horizontal mortal plane by the vertical spiritual plane. The right angle between these planes is sacred. Voodoo is a Dahomey, African *Fon* word meaning Spirit.

The circled-cross is also a common, ancient petroglyph, sometimes representing the Earth and its Four Directions, and at other times perhaps a star.

Heaven on Earth

Star patterns on a clear night, the faintly glowing Milky Way passing through them, display the creativity and power of Nature. A partly cloudy sky before Sun rise or after Sun set can be flooded with rich reds, oranges, yellows, greens, blues, and mauves. In some cultures, the dawn sky represents the Goddess of Dawn in a colourful gown. Is there also a Goddess or God of Dusk?

It's a small mental leap from awareness of the power of Nature to the concept of God. God is usually placed beyond reach above the stars. Fascination with the sky can lead to reverence of the place from which it is studied, often a high hill, then the place is dedicated to God. Such is the sacred Sun Cairn Ring Hill in *Ómahkiyáahkóhtóohp*.

Phyl and I have lived in the isolated *Ómahkiyáahkóhtóohp* for a total of seven months, in all seasons. Being there with Phyl is like Heaven on Earth for me, but conditions are sometimes a little uncomfortable for her. When a 130-kilometre-per-hour wind rocks the camper at night, she crawls down from the sleeping platform above the truck cab and lies on the bench by the table. One December, our sleeping bags preserved us through a -20°C night and brought us cautiously into the day.

In the summer, Phyl is nervous of the occasional territorial bull and inquisitive coyote, but the delicate flowers, flitting birds, soaring golden eagles, and staring antelope are beautiful. Coyotes sing to each other, especially at sundown and sun-up. Sometimes during the day a coyote watches me, and periodically yelps, barks, and sings. I yelp, bark, and sing in reply. There is a language of yelps, barks, and songs.

One June afternoon, Phyl and I were a third of the way down the steep, 90-metre-high east bank of the river, recording details of an ancient standing marble that is an Equalday/night back sight. After a while, we heard loud yelps and barks from the bank top about 30 metres north of us.

I looked up and saw a large coyote seated on his haunches, calling to the west. Answers dimmed by distance came from several coyotes two or three kilometres west.

When Phyl saw him, she cringed and moved away from the animal to try to hide, but there was no sheltered place on the steep bank. Her motion caught the coyote's attention and he stared at us. Then he came a few metres down the bank to try to figure out what kind of strange creatures we were in a place like that.

A moment later, he decided not to risk our being unfriendly and went up the bank and away.

Phyl's fright had grown while the animal was studying us. She decided to go back to the truck two kilometres to the southwest. She climbed back to the top of the bank, saw no coyote, and headed out.

After a few minutes, I heard her screaming in terror. I rushed up the bank and ran in the direction of the screams. No Phyl or coyote visible—just shrill sound.

Then Phyl crested a rise hurrying toward me. She cried, "He was coming toward me smiling and wagging his tail!"

I laughed and called back, "Your screams terrified the poor animal! Coming toward you smiling and wagging his tail? He just wanted to shake your paw and smell your genitals! He's gone now!"

On rare occasions when a bull and cows are nearby, the bull knows I'm not going to challenge him for his harem, so he ignores me. When a bull is first put with a couple of dozen cows on the range in the spring, after a quickie or two he usually courts each lady with gentle persistence. He patiently follows her as she grazes, sometimes licking her sides with great massaging sweeps of his giant tongue, then patiently follows her again.

When she arrives at the mood she stops grazing; at this signal he becomes two-legged, hugs, plugs, and injects her in about five seconds, then returns to four-leggedness and exhales forcefully a few times, then stands on two legs again and repeats the primal process, then maybe another round until he is sated and his breathing returns to normal. A big investment of time for a climax that's over so quick. Sound familiar? Then on to the next lady, for about forty ladies during the summer. I don't know on how many days the same cow stands still for a return session. A happy man repeats his courting and mating with the same lady for as long as they both live.

If I crouch down for a while to examine something on the ground or to make notes, cows that are not at the moment the object of the bull's attention gather closely around to watch what I'm doing. They back off a bit when I stand up, since I am taller than they.

At the end of summer, bulls are tired and lethargic, in need of a winter's recovery. The primal hip-dance doesn't put a spring in their step, as it does for us who don't do it as a job. Playful heifers, young girl cows, see mating as a game and sometimes try to pluglessly mount each other.

Antelope loping past stop at a safe distance to watch me, whether I'm walking or stationary. Mule deer try to hide in gullies. Pincushion cactus berries are sweet and juicy in September. Large, ripe puffballs have brown honeycomb patterns on their off-white skins. Small

mushrooms grow on old cow dung. Moss grows on the buried side of translucent quartz embedded in the turf. Life really wants to happen, and it does.

And then there are the stones that thousands of years ago were moved by man to make specific patterns, the reason for our being there. In writing that, it occurred to me that I identify with the pattern-maker.

In Figure 3-35, the Sun Cairn Ring Hill is on the horizon, *El Escarabajo Oro* is off to the right, and the river is behind us and down 90 metres. Phyl keeps us alive, walks the plain, and finds cultural features. We have looked down from this cliff top onto the back of a flying golden eagle.

Figure 3-35 The main beauty in my life since 1950, Phyl. Sun Cairn Ring Hill is on the western horizon three kilometres away. The Bow River is ninety metres below. Golden eagles sometimes nest in the steep, clay bank. September 27, 1996.

PART TWO

STONEHENGE AND PRESELI MOUNTAIN, WALES

CHAPTER FOUR

STONEHENGE AND PRESELI MOUNTAIN

ngland's Stonehenge has been the subject of study and of folklore for at least nine hundred years. In the twelfth century, the Norman poet Maistre Wace mentioned Stonehenge in one of his epic poems:

Stanhengues ont nom en englois,
Pières pandues en françois.

Stonehenges are the name in english,
Hung stones in french.
    Le Roman de Brut, lines 8385-6, Maistre Wace, A.D. 1155

Fascination with this circle of giant stones continues to this day. It is located about 120 kilometres west-by-south of London.

The wonder of Stonehenge is in the elegance of the capped circle of enormous shaped and smoothed stones, and its enclosed mysterious construction of five even larger capped stone pairs arranged in a U, the whole surrounded by a ditch and bank.

The hung stones, or stonehenges, are presumably the capstones, the lintels, on the uprights in the megalithic building (Figure 4-1). The name "Hung Stones" rings with wonder at how the 20-tonne stones were lifted 5 metres in the air and placed atop the 50-tonne posts, at a time so long ago that no folk memory of it remained by the time Wace wrote *Le Roman de Brut* in the twelfth century. The feat was ascribed to giants or magicians. It was known even nine centuries ago that the huge stones were not of local origin and had been transported over long distances to the Stonehenge site. Geoffrey of Monmouth, in about A.D. 1130, wrote that the wizard Merlin had magically, or by superior engineering, transported the entire sacred structure from Ireland, where it had been called The Round-Dance of Giants; like a Romanian hora danced by thirty giants, each with his arms on his neighbours' shoulders (Figure 4-2).

* * * *

Figure 4-1 The South Trilithon (Three-stone-thing) within Stonehenge Circle. The 20-tonne lintel is 5 metres above ground, atop the 50-tonne uprights. Looking south, April 11, 1989.

Figure 4-2 Stonehenge Circle, with missing stones sketched in. The 8-tonne lintels are 4 metres above the ground, atop the 30-tonne uprights. A round-dance of giants? Looking west, September 25, 2002.

The origin of the name Stonehenge seems to be lost in prehistory. My work, combined with information in the *Oxford English Dictionary* and the writings of Geoffrey of Monmouth before A.D. 1138, brings a possible meaning to the name different from the "hung stones" given by Maistre Wace in 1155.

Geoffrey of Monmouth wrote that the name of the structure was *Stanheng* in Saxon and *Stanhenge* in English. Before A.D. 1000, *stan* in both Old Saxon and Old English meant "stone," while *heng* in Old Saxon and *henge* in Old English meant "hinge," that on which something turns, a pivot. *Stonehinge*, or *Rock Pivot*. This interpretation jumped out at me while I was reading Monmouth's *Historia Regum Britannie*, because I had been using the name Rock Pivot for two decades in descriptions of the calendar in *Ómahkiyáahkóhtóohp*.

The 5000-year-old time machine in *Ómahkiyáahkóhtóohp* contains several Rock Pivots about which the seasonal Sun rise and set directions turn back and forth to the same marked positions year after year, making a calendar. The intricate structure of Stonehenge contains similar calendrical Rock Pivots, Stonehinges, about which the seasonal Sun directions swing annually to marked positions, shown later.

The name *Stonehenge* might reveal more about uses of the structure than has been realized during the last nine hundred years. The great engineering skill of the ancient people was matched by their knowledge of the motions of the Sun, Moon, and stars through the sky.

* * * *

The first construction of stones at this site about 4400 years ago was made of about eighty "Bluestones"—bluish-grey, hard, coarse basalts weighing about 4 tonnes each. The Bluestones had been laboriously transported from their source on Preseli Mountain in southwestern Wales, about 240 kilometres west-northwest from Stonehenge. Monmouth had the right direction of the Temple's origin. The particular Bluestones and the Stonehenge site must have had exceptional properties for these heavy rocks to be transported over such an enormous distance.

It was H.H. Thomas in 1923 who, by comparison of rock characteristics, identified Stonehenge's source as large mounds of bluestones, called *carns*, in a three-square-kilometre zone on the east end of Preseli Mountain. Particular *carns* within that zone were selected in 1974 by Richard Atkinson, by Timothy Darvill and Geoffrey Wainwright in 2005, and by Olwen Williams-Thorpe and coworkers in 2006, after analysis of the rocks. In September to October 2006, I visited Preseli Mountain and several of the *carns* from which the Stonehenge blocks were purportedly "quarried." From my observations and measurements, I concluded that these particular *carns* are part of a large sacred area, a Temple, which might have been raided by invaders from the east. Monmouth's story again. A preliminary description is given at the end of this chapter.

* * * *

The first construction of Bluestones at the future Stonehenge site was later dismantled and replaced by the present Trilithons and Circle, made of about 73 Sarsens. The Sarsens weigh from about 8 to 70 tonnes each. They were hauled about 30 kilometres from their source near Marlborough in the north.

The particular site of Stonehenge had special significance to the people long before construction in stone was begun. A large circular terrain 100 metres across had been set apart there about six centuries earlier, by digging a deep ditch around it and throwing the dirt and chalk up to make a bank around the edge of the terrain (see the Ditch and Bank in the map inside the front cover). There was probably a construction of wood within the terrain before it was replaced by a succession of stone structures.

Four thousand years ago, the transport and shaping of the heavy, hard rocks, and erection of the spectacular building were great feats of engineering.

So, what does all this have to do with *Ómahkiyáahkóhtóohp*? How did *Ómahk* lead to Stonehenge, and ultimately to Preseli Mountain in Wales, 7000 kilometres away?

While studying *Ómahkiyáahkóhtóohp*, I learned of a flurry of controversy over the existence of a calendar in Stonehenge. Technical arguments commonly feed on fashion, conjecture, and inadequate data. Stonehenge is about half a millennium younger than *Ómahkiyáahkóhtóohp*, but they are still of the same general era.

The Stonehenge calendar controversy was based on crude observations, English Heritage maps of Stonehenge, Ordnance Survey maps of the countryside, astronomical calculations, and preconceptions. Arguments against a calendar were strengthened by poor arithmetic and presumed inabilities of people in England 4000 years ago.

One Professor expressed doubt that anyone at that time could record numbers up to more than 180 and halve a large number. Howard Payn's accurate observation of the Sun rise on June 25, 1901 (reported by Norman Lockyer) was discounted by the contrary folk. Christopher Chippindale called Lockyer's selection of a known geographic azimuth, differing from his measured Sun rise direction by 0°.03, bizarre, and said it made the Solstice Sun rise alignment meaningless! Chippindale misrepresented Lockyer's data by using unmentioned scale distortions up to eighteenfold in maps in the 1994 edition of his *Stonehenge Complete*. But no other accurate observations of Sun rises or sets were published.

So, I expanded my study across the Atlantic Ocean. Accurate observations leave little wiggle room. The flippant argument could be settled by compelling facts.

A Hunch

The speculation about a calendar in Stonehenge seemed wild by comparison with the accuracy of the 5000-year-old solar calendar I had found in *Ómahkiyáahkóhtóohp*. If ancient Skywatchers in southern England marked the directions of season-pivot-date Sun rises and sets as accurately as did Skywatchers in southern Alberta, alignment errors in Stonehenge assumed by writers during the last half-century were at least twenty times too big. Most of the calendrical lines of cairns and rocks in *Ómahk* are about a kilometre long. I wondered if there is a similarly long observation line for a Sun rise or set at Stonehenge.

In winter 1988-89, I applied to English Heritage for permission to enter Stonehenge Circle in April of 1989. During a trip to England for a chemical-physics conference that month, I wanted to scan the Stonehenge landscape for a Solstitial Sun rise or set marker about a kilometre away from the Circle. The long application form and subsequent letters, telexes, and phone calls did not produce the permission before I left Edmonton. After my arrival in England, I made two more phone calls to English Heritage at Stonehenge from Bowness-on-Windermere, and permission finally arrived by telex on the last day of the conference. Protective security had been wrapped tightly around Stonehenge since my wife and I wandered freely

Figure 4-3 Looking from between Stonehenge Circle Sarsen 1 and Bluestone 31 to Bell Barrow 15, which is 950 metres southwest (arrow). Numbers assigned by English Heritage to the Sarsen Stones and Bluestones are shown in the Map inside the front cover. The left side of the mound might have been the front sight for the Winter Solstice Sun set. The horizon was treeless 4000 years ago, and the Solstice setting Sun might have appeared to enter the mound. Great Trilithon Sarsen 56 remains standing.

through it in 1956. Back in 1956, while a student at Oxford, I'd heard about the peculiar structure called Stonehenge and was curious to see it. We parked a friend's car beside the road and crawled under the fence, not seeing a gate—we were the only people there!

In 1989, I was granted one hour on April 11, beginning half an hour after the site had closed to tourists at 6 P.M. Bill Hummel, the same friend who had loaned me his car in 1956, drove me there from Steventon, Oxfordshire. Different car.

During the afternoon I wandered around the gargantuan Circle at Avebury in the drizzle, wearing Bill's rain cape while he read a book in the car. By the time we reached Stonehenge for the appointed entry at 6:30 P.M., the Sun had come out and I took the photos in Figures 1-3 and 4-1.

Within a few minutes I'd spotted the mound about 1 kilometre southwest of the monumental Circle (Figure 4-3). A line from the Circle's centre to the Heel Stone in the northeast was known to be inaccurate for the Summer Solstice Sun rise, but the mound to the southwest viewed *through* the Circle from the far side near the Heel Stone seemed a possible line for the Winter Solstice Sun set. This mound is identified as Bell Barrow 15 in maps issued by English Heritage.

Several people have speculated about possible Winter Solstice set lines but not this one, and no attempt to *observe* a Winter Solstice Sun rise or set at Stonehenge has ever been published.

Winter Solstice

On a photograph similar to Figure 4-3, I drew the guessed path of the Winter Solstice Sun setting into the left side of the Bell Barrow. I sent it to an English Heritage Inspector of Ancient Monuments, who agreed to try to photograph the Sun along that line the following December. Clouds spoiled the attempts in 1989 and 1990, and the inspector could spare no more time for it. Foggy sights such as Figure 4-4 are beautiful but are not useful to Sunwatchers. Fog is a cloud on the ground, which occasionally drifts across the landscape at inconvenient times.

Norman March, a dynamic Oxford University Professor who lived in Englefield Green west of London, had often invited Phyl and me to visit and stay awhile. In August 1995 I reached the age of sixty-five—the time when professors in Alberta are severed from their students. Withdrawing from lectures and students was like withdrawing from an addiction. I realized then that lectures are like a performance on stage, and performers never want to quit. We thrive on the feedback from the audience. But after compulsory retirement from teaching, for the first time in thirty-seven years I was free in December, so Phyl and I visited Norman for three weeks to watch for a break in the clouds during a Sun rise or set at Stonehenge.

Figure 4-4 View in the Winter Solstice Sun set direction from the Heel Stone on an unlucky day, December 5, 1997.

Nights were long during December, but they weren't entirely for sleeping. We got up at 5:20 A.M. to quietly have breakfast and leave without waking our host. Milk is delicious in England; the milk-fat content of 5% makes it velvety. Into a mug of milk I stirred two heaping teaspoonfuls of dark Nescafé (*By Appointment to the Queen* printed on the label) and two heaping teaspoonfuls of sugar, then heated it in a microwave oven. This is a strong version of Norman March's recipe. *Smoooth*.

Then I drove through the dark maze of streets, roads, strangely marked roundabouts, and Motorways toward Stonehenge. Several times we found ourselves at the town of Bagshot, with no idea how we got there and no recollection of how we got back on a road toward Stonehenge the last time! Trial and error always got us to Stonehenge before 7:30 A.M., to check in and set up the tripod and camera in a selected place before showtime a few minutes after eight.

The Sun rises were all overcast during the 1995 visits. But the setting Sun kindly made a showing.

Sun set

There is a chain-link fence between the A344 highway and the Heel Stone, shown in the upper-right corner of the Map inside the front cover. On the afternoons of December 5 and 8, the Sun descended in partly clear skies. I didn't have permission to enter the Circle those days, so I photographed the setting Sun from outside the fence, behind the southeast and northwest edges of the Heel Stone. When the Sun sank behind the Circle, I moved along the fence a metre or so, such that the Sun appeared in a gap between the stones from time to time. The line of descent approached the southeast side of the distant Bell Barrow 15. The line guessed in 1989 was roughly correct, but for an accurate record a clear sky was needed on an afternoon when I had access to the Circle.

December 11 was the lucky day. Clouds can appear quickly, so I recorded the Sun as it descended the last few degrees to the horizon. The camera was placed slightly within the Circle between Sarsen 1 and Bluestone 31 to obtain a broad enough view, as for Figure 4-3. This allowed extrapolation of the Sun's path across a band of cloud if necessary, and behind the trees to the unobstructed horizon of 4000 years ago. The set point on the 11th also had to be shifted to the left by accurately calculated amounts to the location on the Solstice ten days hence, and to the Solstice position of 4000 years ago.

The sky became hazy, but the Sun remained sharply visible as it descended into the trees on the low ridge that holds Bell Barrow 15 (Figures 4-5 and 4-6). Photo-prints are much less sensitive to contrast than are eyes, so the photos had to be printed dark enough to see the edge of the Sun, but that blacked out the Barrow. The treetops serve as a scale to measure the Sun and Barrow positions to reconstruct the event on a clear photo (Figure 4-7). In the absence of trees, the Sun would have been seen entering the left, southeast side of the Barrow. The last flash of the Sun would have been at the top of the Bell Barrow.

Figure 4-5 Setting Sun at $15^h52^m30^s$ on December 11, 1995, viewed from behind the northwest edge of Bluestone 31. The treetops provide a measuring scale to transfer the Sun position onto a photograph in which Bell Barrow 15 is visible (Figure 4-7).

Figure 4-6 Setting Sun visible through the trees at $15^h54^m50^s$ on December 11, 1995. The last flash was hidden by the trees.

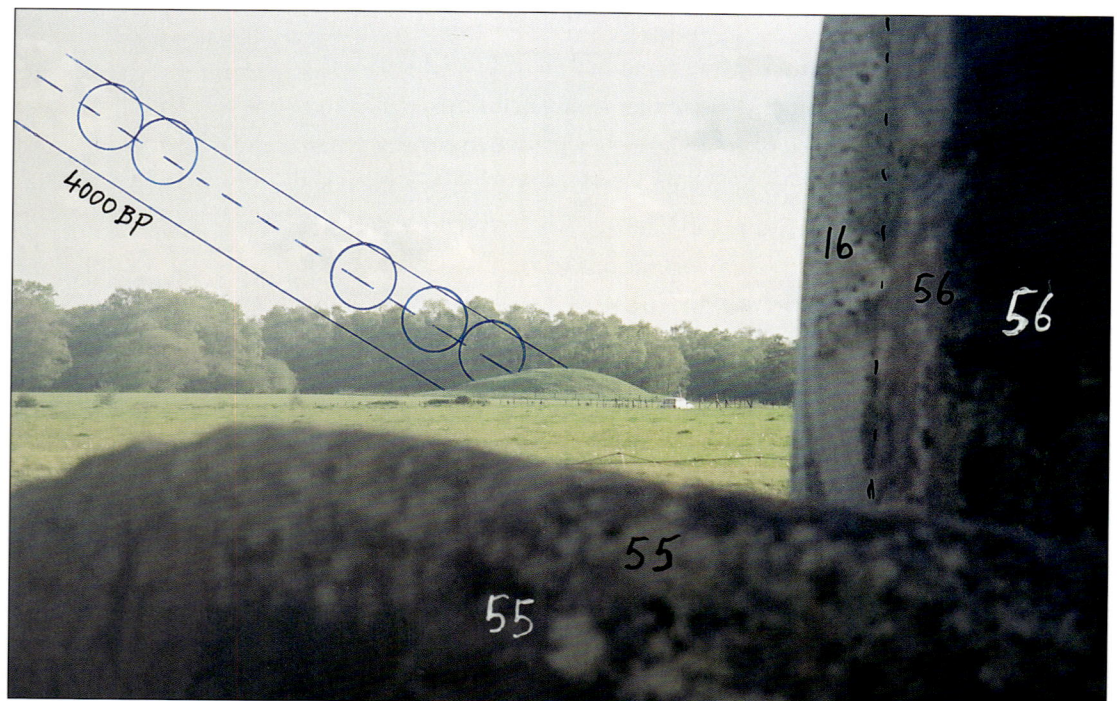

Figure 4-7 Reconstruction of the path of the setting Sun on December 11, 1995, from images in a series of photographs at $15^h41^m00^s$ to 54^m50^s. This view shows the entire Bell Barrow 15. The path of the upper limb of the Sun extrapolated to give the last flash at the top of the Barrow. The path on the Solstice, December 21, 1995, is 0°61 to the left (dashed line to the side of the Barrow). The path on the Solstice 4000 years ago was another 0°92 to the left, with the last flash in the southeast groin of the Bell Barrow.

The Solstice occurred on December 21. The setting Sun would have been 0°61 left of the path on the 11th (Appendix A.6 and Figure 4-7). The path on the Solstice 4000 years ago was a further 0°92 left, about the width of your little finger nail held as far in front of you as your arm will reach (Appendix A.5). During the period in which Stonehenge was built, the Sun along this line disappeared into the angle where the dome meets the flare of the Bell. The Winter Solstice Sun entered the southeast groin of the burial mound.

This ancient Winter Solstice Sun set observation line extended back to the Heel Stone. Four thousand years ago, someone standing at the centre of the Heel Stone could look between Sarsens 1 and 30, across the Circle centre, through the narrow gap between the Great Trilithon Sarsens 55 and 56, out of the Circle between Sarsens 15 and 16, to see the Winter Solstice Sun disappearing into the groin of the distant Bell Barrow 15 (Figure 4-8). The fallen Trilithon Sarsen 55 now blocks the view of the Barrow for someone standing at the Heel Stone, so a ladder helps (Figure 4-9).

The width of the gap between Sarsens 1 and 56 at the level of the horizon in Figure 4-8 is three-quarters of the Sun-diameter. If the space between the erect Great Trilithon Sarsens 55 and 56 were half a metre at the viewing level, the angular width of the gap seen from

Figure 4-8 View along the Winter Solstice Sun set sight line of 4000 years ago, from the front of the Heel Stone. The edge of the flat "Slaughter Stone" 95 is in the centre foreground, in a hole, and was at one time covered with dirt. It might have been been shifted from its original location during the last millennium or two. The horizon is behind the fallen Sarsen 55 of the Great Trilithon. September 25, 2002.

Figure 4-9 Looking back along the Winter Solstice Sun set sight line to the Heel Stone, from beyond Stonehenge Ditch. Derek Dominey is on a ladder to see over Sarsen 55 to the southeast groin of Bell Barrow 15. April 1, 1997.

STONEHENGE AND PRESELI MOUNTAIN

the Heel Stone would have been half a Sun-diameter. The last flash would have been visible in the Trilithon gap for about eleven days.

In late autumn, one could begin to watch the Sun set approach its Winter Solstice position. During the month preceding the Winter Solstice, one could stand inside the Circle at the Great Trilithon gap and watch the southward progress of the Sun set between Circle Sarsens 15 and 16. Eighteen days before the Solstice, the Sun tip slid down the right, northwest side of the Bell Barrow (Figure 4-7). On following evenings, the last flash moved slowly left across the dome, finally reaching the angle between the dome and the flare on the southeast side. After a few days of repeated entry into this angle, this groin, the last flash slowly reversed its path and moved back across the dome. About thirty-seven days after the Sun tip had slid down the northwest side of the dome, it slid down it again. The actual date of the Solstice was halfway between the two slide events.

The line guessed in 1989 was correct. Experience at *Ómahkiyáhkóhtóohp*, an older Temple at the same latitude in Alberta, was transferrable across a continent and an ocean to Stonehenge.

For some reason, driving home *from* Stonehenge after dark was easier than driving *to* Stonehenge before light. But one time I did misunderstand signs, wandered off the M3 Motorway and had an interesting passage through dark villages while trying to find the Motorway again, actually channelling beneath it once. Providence finally spit us back onto the M3 and all I had to do was guess which way was toward home.

Bell Barrow 15

To get to Bell Barrow 15 from Stonehenge, one has to cross Trunk Road A303. During daylight the A303 is usually full of speeding cars and trucks. The trick is to find an interval between projectiles that is greater than the time needed to run across the road, carrying tripod and camera. I think some drivers catch their breath when a pedestrian hurries across, while others cheer the runner into the scrummage. Something like a rugby game.

The tripod was set on the southeast groin of Bell Barrow 15 (Figure 4-10), and from it the reverse of the Winter Solstice Sun set line was photographed (Figure 4-11). The Heel Stone is seen in the gap between the tall Trilithon Sarsen 56 and Circle Sarsen 1.

Figure 4-10 Reverse view of the Winter Solstice Sun set sight line. The tripod is in position for Figure 4-11, on the southeast groin of Bell Barrow 15 between its dome and flare. April 1, 1997.

Figure 4-11 Zoom of the reverse view of the Winter Solstice set line. The middle of the Heel Stone is visible beyond the gap between the central Trilithon Sarsen and the Circle Sarsen to its right.

STONEHENGE AND PRESELI MOUNTAIN

Richard Colt Hoare excavated Bell Barrow 15 two hundred years ago. The concave top on the left side, where the dashed line touches the Barrow in Figure 4-7, might indicate that he dug into the southeast side. He found a primary interment of an adult male on an elm plank (buried as the mound was built). There was also a grooved dagger in a wooden case, and a small dagger, a richly ornamented drinking cup, and antlers. Traces of three wooden poles extended from the primary interment to the top of the Barrow, which make the Barrow unique in the area. Some Barrows contained wooden mortuary houses, but not with poles extending to the Barrow surface. The poles might have been Sun markers, and considered to be transmitters to the crypt.

I found no convincing evidence about whether the Heel Stone was erected, and Bell Barrow 15 constructed, before the Sarsen Trilithons and Circle, or afterward. Was the initial Winter Solstice Sun set observation line from the Heel Stone to the left groin of Barrow 15? Or was 15 built and the Heel Stone erected to refine the line through the Circle?

The Slaughter Stone 95, whether it was always horizontal or originally erect, must have been in a position that did not block the Winter Solstice Sun set sight line. (Stone 95 received its exotic name from someone who thought it looked like a sacrificial altar, with basins for blood; Christians tend to think of sacrifices in other religions as slaughter, so he called it a Slaughter Stone. Stone 95 was probably not an altar at all, but was more likely a standing-stone, later knocked down and buried by members of a new religion.)

Sun (Heel) Stone

The 70-tonne Heel Stone seems elaborate to simply mark the observer's position for the Winter Solstice Sun set (Figure 4-12). It probably had a more complex purpose or was part of an earlier design. In profile from the southwest it looks like a turtle's head. The turtle is an ancient symbol for water in many countries, and represents female nature. Water is basic to generating and sustaining life, which nurturing females do.

The Heel Stone is at the Stonehenge end of the 2.8-kilometre Avenue that leads to a river, called Avon, the Celtic word for river.

Sun rise

I calculated that the Winter Solstice Sun rise sight line through Stonehenge 4000 years ago pointed to 129°, making an acute angle of 79° with the set line (Appendix A.5). There is no distant horizon marker near 129° from the Circle, so a narrow observation line had to be constricted by the stone structure itself.

I walked along the northwest arc of the Bank, using a compass to find a 129° sight line that passed all the way through the Sarsen Circle, but narrow enough to fix the Winter Solstice Sun rise direction. An exciting, almost hidden possibility was a narrow gap that passed into the Circle between Sarsens 21 and 22 and through a large notch that had been hammered into the gap between the West Trilithon Sarsens 58 and 57! The sight line continued above the entire length of the flat Altar Stone 80, and out of the Circle between Sarsens 8 and 9. The notch in the Trilithon is mainly in Sarsen 58 and has hammer marks all over its surface.

On December 12, 1997, I aimed the camera along the Altar Stone from its northwest end, to see a broad span of the southeasterly horizon. Under a beautifully clear sky the exhilarating first flash of the Sun appeared (Figure 4-13)! I then moved the camera to outside the West Trilithon to see the Sun through the narrower gap, then outside the Sarsen Circle to the Bank to see the Sun in the ancient, narrow Winter Solstice Sun rise line (Figures 4-14 and 4-15). *Wow!* In all the speculation during the last four centuries, nobody had guessed the line!

The first flash on the Solstice, December 21, would be 0°.50 to the right of that on December 12. Four thousand years ago, it would have been a further 0°.92 to the right (Figure 4-13).

Figure 4-12 Heel (Sun) Stone seen from the southwest. Turtle head? It is 5 metres high, 2 metres wide and thick, and weighs about 65 tonnes. April 11, 1989.

STONEHENGE AND PRESELI MOUNTAIN

Figure 4-13 First flash of the rising Sun on December 12, 1997, viewed from the tripod shown in Figure 4-15, at 08ʰ04ᵐ15ˢ. On the Solstice, December 21, 1997, the rise point was 0°.50 to the right. The Solstice rise 4000 years ago was a further 0°.92 to the right, southerly.

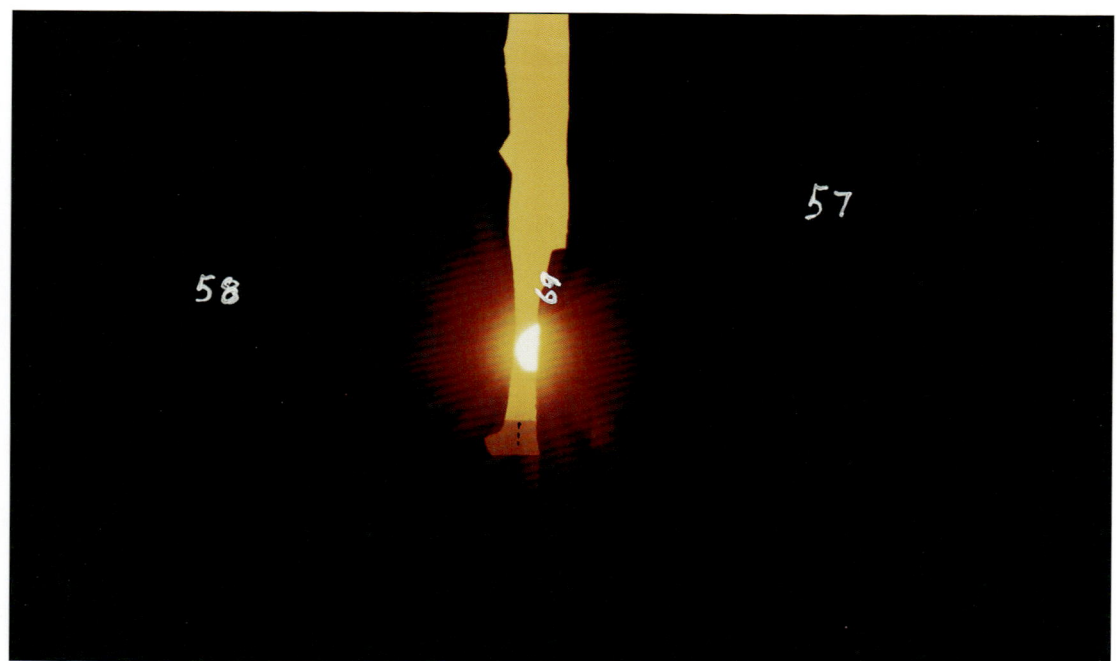

Figure 4-14 Zoom of the Sun in the Winter Solstice Sun rise sight line of 4000 years ago, seen from the Bank near Aubrey Hole 40 (Figure 4-17), December 13, 1997, 08ʰ13ᵐ00ˢ, eight minutes after Sun rise. The position of the Winter Solstice first flash on the horizon 4000 years ago is marked.

Figure 4-15 The Winter Solstice Sun rise sight line of 4000 years ago, looking southeasterly from near Aubrey Hole 40. The empty tripod can be seen at the northwest end of the Altar Stone, from where Figure 4-13 was taken. Note the large notch that was hammered into the side of Sarsen 58, to the left of the tripod. December 12, 1997, 08^h23^m.

The rising Sun moves southerly from left to right each day, so it passes above the ancient Winter Solstice rise point a few minutes after the Solstice rise now (Figure 4-14). In this photo, the position of the first flash on the Winter Solstice 4000 years ago is marked on the horizon in the narrow gap of the West Trilithon. The gap is actually confined between Trilithon Sarsen 58 and Bluestone 69 on the far side of it. The first flash appeared in this gap about four days before the Solstice and remained there a total of about nine days.

If the camera for Figure 4-14 had been a handwidth lower, the

STONEHENGE AND PRESELI MOUNTAIN

Figure 4-16 Reverse of the Winter Solstice Sun rise sight line, seen from the east edge of South Trilithon Sarsen 53. The observation line passes along the Altar Stone 80, through the gap between Bluestone 69 and West Trilithon Sarsen 58, to Phyl near Aubrey Hole 40. The tripod is in the position used for Figure 4-13. December 12, 1997, 08^{h}34^m.

horizon would have appeared at the level of the notch in Sarsen 58. The first flash 4000 years ago would have appeared in the left side of the notch about seven days before the Solstice and would have remained in the notch for about fifteen days.

I also captured the first flash on December 13, 1997. It gave the same Solstice rise positions as those shown in Figure 4-13, within one-twentieth of a Sun-diameter.

A reverse view of the Winter Solstice rise sight line from the east edge of South Trilithon Sarsen 53 shows the broken end of the Altar Stone 80 (Figure 4-16). The Altar Stone is still in its original position, though broken and pressed into the ground by the falling Great Trilithon Sarsens 55 and 156. During the last half-century, many people have suggested that the Altar Stone was originally vertical, although no appropriate seat-hole has been found for it in the chalk beneath the sod. However, there is a posthole in the chalk near each end of the Altar Stone. The posts probably supported an altar in an earlier wood version of the Temple.

This sight line 4000 years ago had the Winter Solstice Sun rise entering the Circle by intimately brushing Circle Sarsen 8, perhaps through a notch (Figure 4-17). A notch would have weakened the Stone and made it easier for vandals to break off pieces and cart them away. Maybe that's why only a fragment of Sarsen 8 remains.

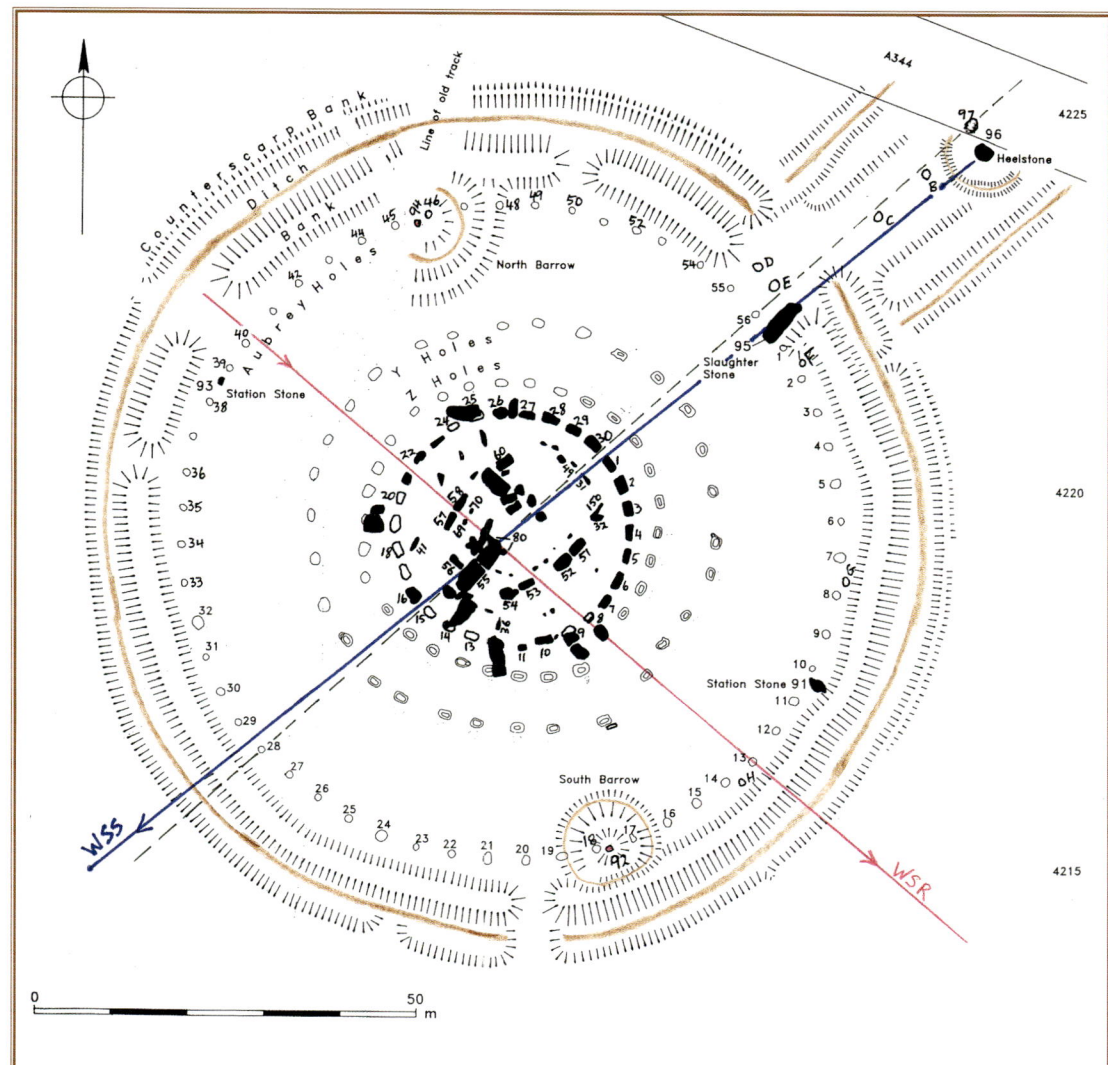

Figure 4-17 Winter Solstice Sun rise (WSR, red) and set (WSS, blue) observation lines through Stonehenge 4000 years ago. The lines cross in the middle of the Altar Stone 80. The base map is a modified composite of several in R. M. J. Cleal and coworkers (1995), and G. S. Hawkins (1965), all produced by English Heritage, Ancient Monuments Branch. © English Heritage. Estimated positions of the missing Circle Sarsens have been added. Black spots are stones that remain, some no longer upright; open spots represent missing stones. The various ditches are coloured brown. The diameter of the Sarsen Circle is one-third that of the terrain inside the Bank, the same as the ratio of the diameter of the Sun Cairn in *Ómahkiyáhkóhtóohp* to that of the ring around it.

STONEHENGE AND PRESELI MOUNTAIN 97

Winter Solstice at Stonehenge

The Winter Solstice Sun set observation line was built for drama. It begins at a massive rock that from the Circle looks like a turtle's head, passes through the Circle along the axis of the Trilithon Horseshoe, through the narrow gap in the tallest of the five Trilithons, called the Great Trilithon, and ends at the groin of a burial mound on the horizon.

Does this observation line symbolize a life story? It begins at a female symbol, birth from water, passes through the centre of a complex structure, and ends where the Sun enters a death symbol. Does the entry of the low and weak Sun into the groin of the mound anticipate regeneration? Does the mound also represent a pregnant belly? A double symbol of death and rebirth?

The entry of the Winter Solstice Sun into a mound on the horizon is somewhat analogous to its entry into a horizon-marker rock in *Ómahkiyáahkóhtóohp* (Figure 3-15).

The Winter Solstice Sun rise observation line is almost hidden, perhaps known only to the Skywatchers, Priests and Priestesses. It passes through the southwest segment of the Sarsen building, along the Altar in the inner sanctum between the Trilithons (Figure 4-17).

The Winter Solstice Sun set and rise observation lines cross significantly in the middle of the Altar.

Summer Solstice

The line from the centre of the Sarsen Circle to the distant Heel Stone is roughly in the direction of the Summer Solstice Sun rise. This seeming agreement has held people in thrall. The view from the Altar provides a dramatic stage for the rising Sun in June (Figure 1-3). Four thousand years ago, the Summer Solstice Sun rose three Sun-diameters to the left of the Heel Stone, and passed well above it eight minutes later. About sixteen days before the Solstice, the Sun rose behind the tip of the Heel Stone. The rise point drifted to the left from day to day until the Solstice, and returned to the Heel Stone sixteen days after it. The Solstice itself was slung in the hammock of the month between the Heel Stone events.

The Winter Solstice observation lines through Stonehenge Circle, especially the beautifully hidden Sun rise line along the length of the Altar Stone, led me to suspect that there would be an entire solar calendar equivalent to the one in *Ómahkiyáahkóhtóohp*. That would require accurate Summer Solstice observation lines that cross the entire Circle.

We returned in June 1999 to check lines that I had tentatively selected in 1995.

By 1999, Norman March had retired as Professor of Theoretical Chemistry at Oxford University and moved to become a guest Professor of Theoretical Physics in *Rijks Universitair Centrum Antwerpen* in Belgium, so we couldn't continue to stay at his home in Englefield Green during our further visits to Stonehenge. Professors in Oxford have to retire at age sixty-seven, which is two more years than we in Alberta get. But neither of us has a mind to quit.

In any case, summer nights are short, so we had to stay nearer Stonehenge to be on site for both sets and rises of the Sun. For June 1999, Bill Hummel's wife Jackie booked us into Solstice Bed & Breakfast in Amesbury, 3 kilometres from the site. Solstice B&B used to be a farmhouse, but Amesbury grew to engulf it. We made Solstice B&B our Stonehenge base from then on.

We have enjoyed several B&Bs on working farms in Britain and Ireland. The farmhouses were quite different from those on the prairies where I had worked as a farmhand.

Each June night we went to bed at about 11 P.M., and I got up again at 3:20 A.M. The early mornings were steeped in heavy dew. The drenching dew helps to keep the countryside green, but wets the feet and trousers of visitors not properly dressed!

The larger Temple outside the Sarsen Circle

I assumed that an accurate Summer Solstice Sun rise observation line would cross the entire Sarsen structure, so the observer's station would be southwest of the Circle. The line would not involve the Heel Stone, and there is no mound to the northeast that could have served as a distant front sight. Something in the Sarsen structure had to serve as foresight from a place southwest of the huge Ditch around the structure (see the map inside the front cover). I walked southwesterly from the Ditch, looking for a possible, clearly distinguishable, Summer Solstice Sun rise observation point.

An accurate sight line for the rise or set of the Sun needs a front sight that appears less than one-half Sun-diameter wide, about the thickness of a dollar coin or a Euro held at arm's length. A large front sight must be viewed from a long distance. The 4000-year-old Summer Solstice rise line might somehow have involved the Great Trilithon, Stones 55 and 56 in Figure 4-17. If so, the observation place would have to be far from the Trilithon, in the southwesterly direction, about 229° (Appendix A.5).

Sun rise

Southwesterly 350 metres from the Great Trilithon there is a "Disk Barrow" that has two tumps and a surrounding oval ditch. This so-called Oval Twin Disk Barrow 10 (OTDB 10) has diameters 36 metres northeast and 30 metres northwest. The Disk Barrow is about a thousand years older than the Trilithons and has been nearly levelled by plowing. Its ditch is easily seen, but the two tumps are indistinct. Richard Colt Hoare excavated the tumps two hundred years ago and found a primary cremation burial in one, but did not record which one. A cremation burial means burnt bones. A burial is called primary if it was placed there as the mound or tump was built, and secondary if it was dug into the side of an existing mound.

During our visits in June 1999, many mornings were misty. I put the camera on the southwest side of OTDB 10 each morning, in case the Sun peeked through an opening in the cloud. Occasionally the sky was clear at 4 A.M., and I'd watch a fog bank move in from the north or east, hiding first the horizon, then the brightening sky, and sometimes Stonehenge itself, while Bell Barrow 15 to the southwest remained uselessly visible. One morning in dense fog and twilight, I walked nearly blind through the grey fluid from Stonehenge Ditch toward OTDB 10, counting paces to know when to expect the Barrow ditch. The stinging nettles in the ditch let me know when I'd found it. As I waited for the Sun to rise, the fluctuating fog stripteased me with visibility ranging between about three and forty metres. The grey slowly lightened with the dawn, and thinned after sun-up.

For forty-six years my research has been to measure and visualize what goes on inside complex systems. The fascinating subject has an unfriendly name, Kinetics of Nonhomogeneous Processes, shortened to KNP. The mental framework of KNP makes everything interesting. If the Sun disk didn't show up, other changes caught my attention, the clouds or mist, or awakened jackdaws flying around the stones.

My mantras are, "Fluctuations is where it's at!" and, "Everything is KNP!"

The first few mornings at OTDB 10, I put the camera 12 metres southwest of it and aimed across the centre of the oval to the centre of Stonehenge. Bright spots that appeared in the clouds from time to time after Sun rise indicated that I was too far to the southeast, so I looked inside the ring for a tump northwest of centre, which might have been the Summer Solstice rise observation station. I found no obvious tump below the long hay and stinging nettles, but there was a hint of a north and a south tump. I selected the north tump as the tripod base.

On the morning of June 12, the dew was so heavy that walking to OTDB 10 through the hay field was like walking through knee-deep water. I wiped condensation off the camera lens before each shot (Figure 1-2). Back at the car after Sun rise time, I emptied water out of my shoes, took off my trousers, and wrung them out.

The upper limb of the rising Sun became sharply visible through the haze above a band of cloud on June 17, 1999, though Figure 4-18 records it less clearly. The time-sequenced positions of the top of the Sun in Figure 4-19 were put onto a copy of Figure 4-18, and the path of the rising Sun was extrapolated back to the level of the ancient treeless horizon to find the first-flash position (Figure 4-20). This path was moved 0°.09 left, northerly, to obtain the path on the 21st (Appendix A.6), and another 0°.94 left to find the Summer Solstice first-flash position 4000 years ago (Appendix A.5). The rise point would have been just above the Circle lintels in the gap of the Great Trilithon.

Figure 4-18 The Sun peeks above the cloud, 0°.65 above ground level at the formerly treeless horizon. Viewed from the north tump in OTDB 10. June 17, 1999, 05^{h}01^{m}40^s.

Figure 4-19 Three exposures of the rising Sun on June 17, 1999, from the same position as Figure 4-18. The edge of the Sun and the landscape could be seen clearly with naked eyes, but photos must be printed very dark to show the edge of the Sun through the haze. The level of the treeless horizon above the Circle lintels is shown by a line. The position of the top of the Sun disk in Figure 4-18 was marked on this photo, and the curve of the rising top was extrapolated back to the horizon.

Figure 4-20 Summer Solstice Sun rise viewed from the north tump in OTDB 10. The line for June 17 was shifted 0°.09 left for the Solstice on June 21 (dashed line), and another 0°.94 left for the Solstice 4000 years ago (Appendices A.5 and A.6).

Seen from OTDB 10, the part of the Great Trilithon gap that protruded above the Circle lintel would have looked like a tall, narrow window high above the ground (Figure 4-21). The gap above the Circle would have been about two metres high and less than one metre wide. The angular width of the window seen from OTDB 10 was about one-quarter the width of the Sun. The window width was double the maximum variation of the observed Solstice rise position from year to year due to different atmospheric conditions.

Photographs of a similarly hazy rising Sun on June 13, 1999, shifted $0°.36$ to the Solstice, gave the same Solstice rise position within a twenty-fifth of the Sun's width.

The Sun rise would have remained in this window for at least nine days bracketing the Summer Solstice. That was enough time for at least one thrilling appearance of the first flash in the Trilithon window, even if the weather were as bad as now. The Solstice might have been celebrated during the entire stand-still period of five, possibly seven days.

The Trilithon window *above* the Sarsen Circle made a spectacular display of the Summer Solstice Sun rise. I had expected to find an accurate Summer Solstice rise line, but the art and engineering that shaped and erected rocks that weighed up to 60 tonnes each, to put a magnificent, massive slit-window 5 metres in the air to frame the Sun rise, was amazing.

Figure 4-21 Looking northeast from the north tump in Oval Twin Disk Barrow 10, 350 metres southwest of the Great Trilithon (Sarsens 55, 56, 156), September 25, 2002. Four thousand years ago, light from the Summer Solstice Sun rise passed from the treeless horizon (dotted line) just above the Circle lintels, through the Great Trilithon window.

Four thousand years ago, 12 days before the Solstice, the northward-drifting rise point observed from OTDB 10 would have emerged from the left side of the SouthTrilithon (Sarsen 54), and 25 days later the southward-drifting rise point would have returned there. The rise point would have reached the right edge of the Great Trilithon about 8 days before the Solstice, and returned there 17 days later.

OTDB 10 is the same age as Stonehenge Ditch and Bank, which was created nearly a thousand years before the Sarsen building. OTDB 10 might originally have been the observation place for the Summer Solstice Sun rise above a post in the centre of the domain enclosed by the circular Bank. There seems to have been a Stone a bit northerly of the present Heel Stone (seat hole 97 in Figure 4-17), which might have been a later front sight for the Solstice rise. By the time the Trilithons and Sarsen Circle were built, the Solstice line had moved one-third of the Sun diameter to the right. A new, elegant Summer Solstice Sun rise front sight was included in the Sarsen structure (Figure 4-21). Sarsen 97 was either removed or moved to the present Heel Stone position for a different purpose. The Summer Sun rise viewing position remained the same, within a metre.

The original Summer Solstice Sun rise alignment from the north tump of OTDB 10 to a post in the centre of the circular domain would have dated to about 5 ka B.P., nearly contemporary with the earliest dated calendar lines in *Ómahkiyáahkóhtóohp*.

Views along the Summer Solstice Sun rise sight line

Is there anything of note along the three-kilometre Summer Solstice Sun rise line from OTDB 10 to the southeast shoulder of Larkhill?

The Oval Twin Disk Barrow is no longer visible from a distance, especially when covered in long hay. But the complete oval ditch is unmistakable when you walk into and around it.

The interior of the Sarsen Circle can be seen on approaching the ruins of the Circle from OTDB 10, because most of the Sarsens of its southwest section have been destroyed. In Figure 4-22, I sketched the approximate positions of the missing Sarsens to show the relative sizes of the Circle and the Trilithon Horseshoe. There was probably a gap in the lintels of the Circle between Sarsens 10 and 12 (no lintel 111 or 112), for reasons given in Chapter 5.

The Summer Solstice Sun rise line within the Circle passed above the centre of the Altar (Stone 80), as did the Winter Solstice Sun set line in the opposite direction (Figure 4-17).

A ceremonial marker of the Summer Solstice rise and Winter Solstice set 5000 years ago might have been the line between Aubrey Holes 28 and 56 in Figure 4-17. It was too crude to have been used for an accurate calendar. The line as it exists now is shown in Figure 4-23, with Phyl standing above Hole 56. The Summer Solstice rise line of 4000 years ago passed to the right of Phyl, to the treeless horizon below the arrow. The line passed to the left of Heel Stone 96 and above the ceremonial Avenue in the field beyond the Heel Stone. A portion of the Avenue's left ditch is visible as the shadow beyond the fence in Figure 4-24, to the left of the Heel Stone.

Figure 4-22 Sarsen Circle seen from 20 metres southwest of the Ditch, along an extension of a line between Aubrey Holes 28 and 56 (Figure 4-17). The positions of the missing Sarsens in the Circle and Great Trilithon are sketched. Note the gap in the lintel Circle between lintels 110 and 113. December 13, 1997. Jackdaws start flying around shortly after Sun rise.

Figure 4-23 View from Stonehenge Bank 5 metres southwest of Aubrey Hole 28, to Phyl standing over Aubrey Hole 56, December 13, 1997. The arrow points to the Summer Solstice rise point 4000 years ago, viewed from the north tump in OTDB 10.

Figure 4-24 View along the northeast segment of the Summer Solstice Sun rise sight line, from midgap between Circle Sarsens 30 and 1. Phyl is halfway between Aubrey Hole 56 and the edge of Slaughter Stone 95, December 13, 1997. The shadow of the Avenue's northwest ditch is visible to the left of the Heel Stone, beyond the fence. The Summer Solstice rise point 4000 years ago, seen from OTDB 10, is marked by the arrow.

Figure 4-25 Possible remains of the tiny Peter's Mound on Larkhill, reported by Alexander, Archibald, and Alexander S. Thom in 1974. Ordnance Coordinates (14334 43967). It is now a rabbit warren or something similar. September 24, 2001.

The northeast horizon of the Summer Solstice Sun rise line is on Larkhill. Trees on this part of the hill now block the view back to Stonehenge. About 20 metres south of the 4 ka B.P. line's horizon-point is a tiny mound, called Peter's Mound by Alexander Thom and his sons Archibald and Alexander in 1974. It is too small to have been a major horizon marker and is riddled with small animal burrows, perhaps rabbits (Figure 4-25). The surrounding area contains no burrows that Phyl and I could see. Thicker soil in the tiny mound makes it easier to dig.

We walked in the reverse of the Solstice rise direction, skirting trees and a housing development below the sight line. A sign along one of the housing streets read:

DANGER

BEWARE OF CHILDREN

At the north edge of the enigmatic Cursus, a 2.8-kilometre long east-west "runway" (Latin *cursus*) that passes 900 metres north of Stonehenge Circle, the Circle came into view (Figure 4-26). We could see the border ditches of the Avenue leading to the Sarsen Circle 1.5 kilometres to the southwest. The narrow gap in the Great Trilithon above the Circle was on the left side of the remaining tall Sarsen. The Summer Solstice Sun rise observation point in OTDB 10 was 1.9 kilometres away, below the Circle lintel viewed from this spot.

The ancient observation line for the Summer Solstice Sun rise could be restored by removing a swath of trees between the Cursus and the northeast horizon.

Figure 4-26 View from the north edge of the Cursus, back along the Summer Solstice Sun rise sight line. The central shrub is at the south edge of the Cursus. Shadows of the ditches that border the Avenue are visible above the outer edges of the shrub. OTDB 10 is 350 metres beyond the remaining tall Sarsen, on its left side. The camera here is at the elevation of OTDB 10, and 27 metres below the Solstice rise point on the horizon. Bell Barrow 15 is 900 metres beyond the Sarsen Circle, on the right. September 24, 2001.

Sun set

The Summer Solstice Sun set observation line through the Sarsen Circle should pass through the same gap as the Winter Solstice rise line, in the reverse direction along the Altar Stone (Figure 4-17). People have wondered why the Altar Stone is not at right angles to the axis of the Trilithon Horseshoe, or to the line from the centre of the Sarsen Circle to the Heel Stone. A symmetrical arrangement would seem to favour a right angle, 90°, between the Altar Stone long-axis and the Horseshoe axis, whereas the actual angle is about 82°. The reason for this angle is that the Horseshoe axis and Altar long-axis nearly paralleled the Summer Solstice rise and set observation lines 4000 years ago, and the acute angle between them was 82°.

I recorded the setting Sun along the Altar Stone line, but within a broad view of the northwest horizon to allow extrapolation of the last flash position to other dates. I put the camera near the northwest end of the Altar Stone, and aimed through the notch that had been hammered into the gap of the West Trilithon. The setting Sun was visible through haze on June 12, 1999 (Figure 4-27). The treetops on the horizon provide a scale for measurement and comparison. The position of the Sun's top edge in Figure 4-27 was marked on a photo of the Sun just before it disappeared behind the trees (Figure 4-28). Then the descent path was extrapolated to the level of the ancient treeless horizon. This set point of June 12 was then shifted 0°.46 northerly, to the right,

Figure 4-27 Setting Sun on June 12, 1999, viewed from the northwest end of the Altar Stone, through the notch in West Trilithon Sarsen 58. 21^{h}10^m.

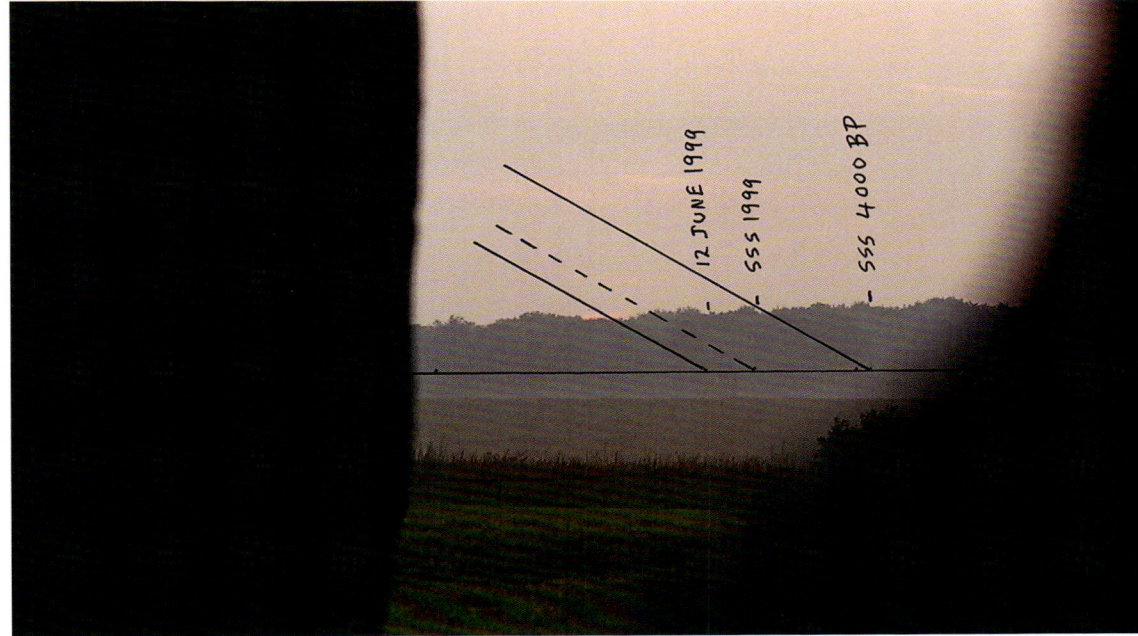

Figure 4-28 Top of the Sun at the treetops on June 12, 1999, 21ʰ14ᵐ. The position of the top of the Sun in Figure 4-27 was marked on this photo, and the line was extrapolated to the level of the treeless horizon 20 metres below the present treetops. The set position was shifted 0°.46 to the right for the Solstice on June 21, and another 0°.94 to the right for the Solstice 4000 years ago.

to the Solstice set position on June 21 (Appendix A.6), and another 0°.94 northerly to the Solstice position of 4000 years ago (Appendix A.5).

A similarly hazy setting Sun was recorded on June 15, 1999. The extrapolated Solstice set positions were one-thirteenth Sun-diameter to the right of those in Figure 4-28. Even with hazy Suns, the Solstice set positions extrapolated from two different days were the same within 0°.04.

I feel a direct mental connection with the people who designed and built the place thousands of years ago each time I see the Sun's first or last flash along an anciently marked line. In fact, any time I now happen to see the first or last flash of the Sun on the horizon, I feel pleasure a bit like the flutter I get any time I unexpectedly see Phyl these last fifty-eight years.

The position of the last flash of the Summer Solstice Sun 4000 years ago is visible from the southeast Bank of Stonehenge Ditch (Figure 4-29). The treeless horizon would have appeared at the level of the notch in Sarsen 58. The angular width of the notch in this view is 0°.23, and of the narrower gap above it is 0°.08, one-seventh of the Sun-diameter. From the southeast Bank, the last flash would have been visible in the notch for about two weeks bracketing the Solstice, and by raising the eyes a bit higher, visible in the narrower gap for about a week.

Was anything visible on the horizon at the Summer Solstice set point

Figure 4-29 Summer Solstice Sun set sight line of 4000 years ago, seen from the southeast Bank of Stonehenge Ditch, June 12, 1999. The treeless horizon in this view would be at the level of the notch in Sarsen 58.

seen through the gap in the West Trilithon in 4 ka B.P.? The Sun set point was in the Lesser Cursus, two kilometres to the northwest. The set point was actually at an "Oval Enclosure" within the east end of the Lesser Cursus, a 13x15-metre oval space now detectable only by its shallow ditch in the bedrock chalk. It is marked on the map in Figure 4-52.

There might have been a wooden structure at the Oval Enclosure, visible from Stonehenge. A trace of the Enclosure ditch was discovered in a magnetometer survey (scanning the surface with a delicate magnetic instrument) by A. Bartlett and Clark in 1993 and published by A. David and A. Payne in 1997. The Lesser Cursus, and possibly the Oval Enclosure, are about 5000 years old. They have been leveled by plowing or other means, and are now only detectable by geophysical methods or aerial photography.

* * * *

During September of 2001 and 2002 I walked the low crest that holds the Lesser Cursus, but saw no trace of Cursus or Enclosure. The place is now a hay field.

Stonehenge cannot now be seen from the Lesser Cursus, due to trees in the intervening Fargo Plantation. The name "Plantation" means that the area has been re-treed. The view back along the Summer Solstice set

line from the east edge of the trees shows no trace of a Barrow that could have served as a front sight (Figure 4-30).

Preservation of what remains of the Temple around Stonehenge has been given high priority by English Heritage, so trees will probably be removed from several places to restore the treeless horizons of 4000 years ago.

The Summer Solstice Sun rise observation point was an Oval Barrow, and the Summer Solstice set horizon point was an Oval "Enclosure." What did an oval signify?

Figure 4-30 View back along the Summer Solstice Sun set sight line from the trees at Fargo Plantation. Looking 130° to Stonehenge, 1.4 km away. June 15, 1999.

Summer Solstice Calendrical Lines and the Design of Stonehenge

The Summer Solstice *rise* sight line began far outside the Sarsen Circle and crossed the Circle centre. This line from Oval Twin Disk Barrow 10 seems to have been in use before the Sarsen structure was built, and was probably used as the axis in the design of the Trilithon Horseshoe (Figure 4-31). The front sight of the earliest Summer Solstice rise line from OTDB 10 might have been a pole at the centre of the Aubrey Circle.

The Summer Solstice *set* sight line went along the top of the flat

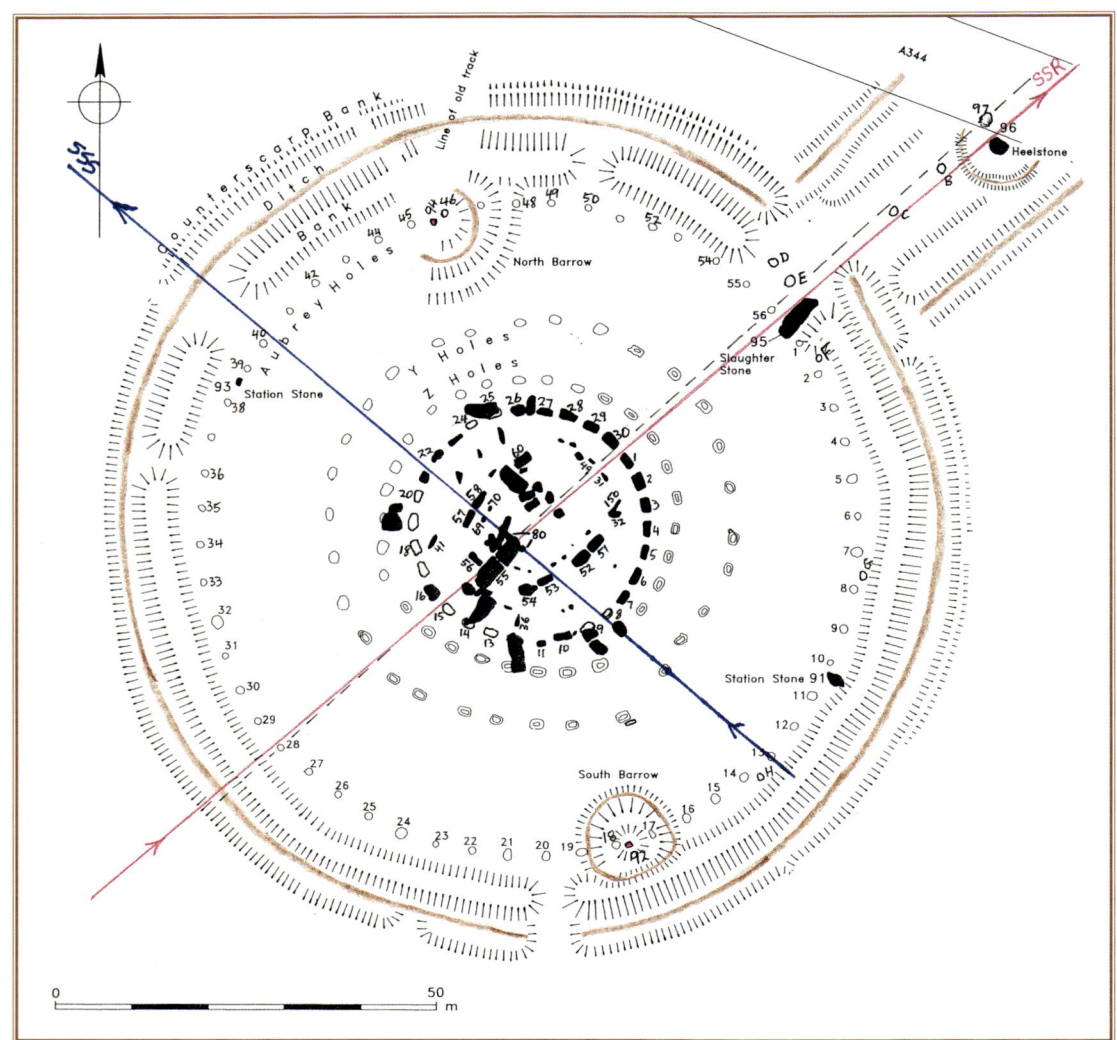

Figure 4-31 Summer Solstice Sun rise observation line (SSR, red) across Stonehenge 4000 years ago, and set observation line (SSS, blue) through the Circle. The lines cross above the Altar Stone, number 80. The base map is the same as that in Figure 4-17. © English Hertiage. The various ditches are coloured brown.

Altar Stone 80, so the set line was one of the determining factors of the location and orientation of the Altar within the Sarsen Circle (front endpapers and Figure 4-31). The line brushed the northeast edge of the South Trilithon and went through the gap in the West Trilithon, so it must also have been used in designing the Trilithon pattern.

The Winter Solstice Sun set and rise sight lines through the Circle are only slightly offset from the reverse of the Summer rise and set lines (Figures 4-17 and 4-31), so they all contributed to the design of the Sarsen building.

Sun rise and set sight lines at the Solstices were used in determining the orientation and placement of the huge Sarsens and the Altar when Stonehenge was designed. Stonehenge was indeed a Temple to the Sun, although it was also much more than that.

The Avenue and Solstice Sun Sight Lines

The most spectacularly engineered feature of the Solstice Sun sight lines was the upper window in the Great Trilithon, which framed the Summer Solstice Sun rise viewed from the north tump in OTDB 10. The Summer rise line northeast of the Sarsen structure was directly above the Avenue, but the Avenue was not visible from the observation point in OTDB 10. Was it significant that the Avenue was directly below this sector of the Sun rise line?

The main use of the Avenue might have been for ritual approach to Stonehenge while the Winter Solstice Sun was setting. I walked the Avenue to check its structure.

Beginning at the Circle, the Avenue extends about 600 metres in a straight line northeasterly down a slight slope into Stonehenge Bottom (Figure 4-52), where it bends and goes easterly up onto King Barrows Ridge, and finally goes southerly down to the Avon, a total length of 2.8 kilometres. I stood at the Avenue bend in Stonehenge Bottom and looked up the straight portion toward Stonehenge. No trace of Stonehenge was visible, even though I stand 1.85 metres tall. I walked southwest up the Avenue from the bend, and Stonehenge rose gradually from the horizon. At about 20 metres from the bend, the lintels of the Trilithons came into view. At 40 metres, I could see the Circle lintels (Figure 4-32). At about 55 metres from the bend, the Circle uprights were nearly completely visible (Figure 4-33).

Figure 4-32 Looking along the Avenue from about 40 metres southwest of the bend. Camera height: 1.6 metres. The Sarsen Circle lintels are visible. September 20, 2001.

Figure 4-33 Looking along the Avenue from about 55 metres southwest of the bend. Camera height: 1.6 metres. The top of the Sun Stone (Heel Stone) is indistinct below the top of the Circle lintel.

Figure 4-34 Looking along the Avenue from about 270 metres southwest of the bend, not quite halfway to the Circle. Camera height: 1.6 metres. The Sun Stone (arrow) projects above the Circle lintels but is still below the tops of the Trilithons. Different parts of the Sarsen structure come into view as one proceeds southwest up the straight part of the Avenue from the bend.

The first 70 metres of Avenue southwest of the bend have a slightly steeper slope than the remaining portion to the Circle.

One cannot see the Sun Stone (Heel Stone) until its top projects above the Circle lintels (Figure 4-34). At about halfway from the bend to the Circle, the top of the Sun Stone reaches the height of the top of the Trilithons, and the Sun Stone becomes more prominent as one continues along the Avenue (Figure 4-35).

As one walks up the Avenue from Stonehenge Bottom, first the tops of the Trilithons emerge from the horizon, then the Sarsen Circle, then the Sun Stone. It seems intentional that Stonehenge is not visible from the bend, and that there is this sequence of emergences from the horizon as one proceeds up the Avenue. Earth might have been moved in Stonehenge Bottom to increase the slope of the first 70 metres southwest of the bend, to completely hide Stonehenge from view at the bottom and create the emergence effect.

It would be interesting to photograph the Winter Solstice Sun set from the Avenue 60 or 70 metres southwest of the bend. Would the setting Sun 4000 years ago have appeared to enter the Sarsen Circle

114 CANADA'S STONEHENGE

Figure 4-35 View from mid Avenue, about 25 metres from the Sun Stone.

between Sarsens 8 and 9? At that time, light from the rising Winter Solstice Sun entered the Circle between Sarsens 8 and 9 to pass along the Altar, viewed from the northwest Bank of the circular domain. Gap 8-9 might also have been the gate for the setting Winter Solstice Sun to enter the Circle viewed from the Avenue.

In *Ómahkiyáahkóhtóohp* there is a sight line, sloping slightly upward to the southwest, which exactly marks both the Summer Solstice Sun rise (Figure 3-7a) and Winter Solstice set (Figure 3-15a), viewed from opposite ends. The effect is spectacular to those who realize how much people had to know 5000 years ago to create it. For the same sight line to serve both the Summer Sun rise and Winter Sun set, the slope must be slightly higher in the set direction than in the reverse, rise direction, to balance the offsetting effects of light refraction by the atmosphere and the radius of the Sun. At Stonehenge, the upward slope of a Winter Solstice set observation line from the Avenue to the Sarsen structure would be slightly greater than the slope of the Summer Solstice rise line from OTDB 10 to the horizon on Larkhill. To those in the know, having the Winter Solstice set and the Summer Solstice rise follow the same exact line in opposite directions is a turn-on.

There is also philosophical appeal in having the two most significant seasonal solar events share exactly the same observation line in opposite directions. The Sun set at the Winter Solstice signifies the end of the weakening of the Sun, when it passes through its crisis and gradually strengthens again. The Sun rise at the Summer Solstice signifies the end of the strengthening of the Sun, followed by its gradual weakening again. It symbolizes the universal life cycle of birth, strengthening, weakening, death, and rebirth. The philosophical crisis is the passage from death to rebirth. The designers of *Ómahkiyáahkóhtóohp* on the North American Plains had the wit and ability to make such a line 5000 years ago. It seems likely that the designers of Stonehenge Temple in their turn did too.

We experience many personal strong-weak-strong cycles during our lives. The dearly departed Ann Landers advised, "When life hands you a lemon, make lemonade." The seasonal Sun cycle has been an important personal metaphor for millennia.

Equinox and Equalday/night

Strange as it may seem, during a century of speculation about a possible calendar in Stonehenge, nothing was published about an attempt to observe an Equinox Sun rise or set there. Come to think of it, I haven't come across an attempt to observe a Sun rise or set along any marked line other than the Summer Solstice rise over the Heel Stone seen from the Circle centre, with the exception of Payn and Lockyer's perceptive work in June 1901. Speculation is so much fun, and so easy to do, that nobody after 1901 took the trouble to make accurate observations.

The observation lines for the Winter Solstice Sun set and Summer Solstice Sun rise were majestic, constructed with the most massive rocks in the Stonehenge building. By contrast, the Winter rise and Summer set observations shared the same, almost hidden gap through the Circle, passing along the top of the Altar Stone and through a large notch that had been hammered into the gap of the West Trilithon. Now, what about the March and September Equinoxes? Or the Equalnights that were rediscovered in *Ómahkiyáahkóhtóohp*? Accurate horizon astronomy can pick out the Equalday/nights, not the Equinoxes. Were the Stonehenge builders concerned with that?

During the winter of 2000–2001 I sent Bill Hummel a letter asking about the expected clarity of skies during March and September in southern England. He replied that the average number of clear days in March is four, and in September is five, so we should come in September.

During a single visit to England, there is little likelihood of having sky clear enough to see both the last and first flashes of the Sun that begin and end the same night. Clouds were not the only hindrance at Stonehenge. In 2001 I had competition from a tour company to gain special access to the Circle in the evenings.

However, the positions of Sun rise and set move smoothly along the horizons from day to day. In September, the positions move south by one-and-a-third Sun-diameters, two-thirds of a degree, each day. This rate remains steady for nearly six weeks straddling the Equinox and Equalnight (Appendix A.6). So, if a set and rise can be recorded within a few days of those nights, the sought positions on the horizon can be accurately determined by extrapolation (Appendix A.1).

Figure 4-36 Looking southeast at a large notch hammered into the southwest side of West Trilithon Sarsen 58, probably using sarsen mauls, to widen the angle of view through the gap. December 5, 1997.

The notch in the southwest edge of West Trilithon Sarsen 58 (Figure 4-36) was part of the Summer Solstice Sun set and Winter Solstice Sun rise observation lines. An even bigger notch had been hammered into the south corner of this Sarsen to make a hole due east–west through the Trilithon (Figure 4-37). An east–west sight channel extends through the entire Circle, but is only one-third of a degree wide (Figure 4-38). It is much narrower than the two-thirds of a degree that the Sun rise and set points move along the horizon each day. I first made observations through a wider gap on the north side of Sarsen 58, to locate the rise and set points on the horizon and extrapolate them to the Equinox and Equalnight positions.

Figure 4-37 Looking east through the notch in Sarsen 58, greatly enlarged in the south side by hammering away part of the south corner. There is also a notch in Sarsen 3 on the far side of the Circle, and the side above the notch has been hollowed somewhat. September 24, 2001.

During our vigil in September 2001, the Sun set was completely clear only on the 20th, and the Sun rise only on the 28th. There was a thin band of cloud on the horizon below the Sun at set on the 24th, and at rise on the 27th. I extrapolated the four set and rise positions to points on the treeless horizon where the set and rise would bracket the Equinox and the Equalnight. The Sun set observation line for the Equalnight seemed to be the one across the Circle and through the notch. The Sun rise observation line for the Equalnight seemed to be a narrow version of the one I'd been using, the gap between the north edge of West Trilithon Sarsen 58 and the south edge of Sarsen 2 on the far side of the Circle, and on out to the north edge of a mound on the horizon a kilometre away, called New King Bowl Barrow 28. The set and rise of the Equinox were far away from any alignments we found.

We returned in September 2002 to check the lines.

I tried to book special access into Stonehenge during all the early mornings and late evenings of September 24 to 27, 2002. All the early mornings were granted, but a tour company had booked the late evenings of the 25th and 26th. For one such evening in 2001, I had persuaded a Stonehenge Official to let me into the site before the tour group arrived and to leave after the group, because my work kept me apart from the tour and didn't interfere with it. But this time there was a different Official, a firm regulation had come down from above, and the *no* was adamant.

What luck! Everything is KNP!

Flowing energy that meets an obstruction gets redirected, and sometimes produces something unexpected! Have you watched the shifting ripple pattern in water flowing around a rock that juts sharply into the edge of a stream? Watch it carefully for a few minutes, the big eddies and the little eddies, and maybe you'll get an inkling about the nonhomogeneous processes that are everywhere in nature, including in ourselves.

Six mounds are prominent among the trees on the horizon east of Stonehenge, on a low, north–south ridge a kilometre away (Figure 4-39). They are called New King Barrows 27 to 32, and the horizon was treeless when Stonehenge was built. This is known because woodland pollens are different from grassland pollens. Archaeological pollen samples indicate that 4000 years ago the area had been cleared of trees and was used for grazing.

Figure 4-38 Looking west along a possible Sun set line to mark the beginning of the Equinox or Equalnight, from two metres inside the Circle from the gap between Sarsens 2 and 3. The large notch in Sarsen 58 makes a triangular opening to the horizon. September 24, 2001.

STONEHENGE AND PRESELI MOUNTAIN   119

Figure 4-39 New King Barrows Ridge seen from inside the Sarsen Circle, looking east between Sarsens 2 and 3, September 27, 2001. Barrows numbered 27 to 30 are Bowl Barrows (shaped like a simple bowl upside down, surrounded by a ditch), in a south–north line 1.2 kilometres east. Numbers 31 and 32 are Bell Barrows (shaped like a bell with dome and flare, surrounded by a ditch). The line of 30 to 32 veers somewhat to the east.

Do the Barrows tie in with the design of Stonehenge? The north edge of one of them, number 28, seemed to be the position of the first flash of the rising Sun that ended the 12.0-hour night, viewed through the Sarsen Circle. The next Barrow north, number 29, seemed a possible place from which to see the last flash of the setting Sun directly above the Circle to begin the 12.0-hour night. The difference of direction from Stonehenge to the two Barrows was about the needed two degrees. I went to examine the Barrows. They were unkempt and little visited, but the vista of Stonehenge seemed to invite observations of the Equalnight Sun set from there. A bit like the feeling I had five years earlier about Oval Twin Disk Barrow 10, when I found it in the hayfield and decided to record the Summer Solstice Sun rise from that place.

Sun Sets Viewed from New King Bowl Barrow 29

On September 23, 25, and 26, 2002, I photographed the Sun sets from the top of New King Bowl Barrow (NKBB) 29, about 40 metres north of the edge of NKBB 28. The west horizon was clear all three evenings! It gave me a rush each time. The last flash on the 23rd and 25th occurred behind trees, and the positions were obtained by extrapolation to the tree bases 20 metres below their tops (Figure 4-40). The dot of the last flash recorded on the 26th was only one-hundredth of a degree wide, which is not uncommon to see during vigils under clear sky, but is not often captured on film in my work (Figure 4-41). The sets on the 25th and 26th were both directly above the Sarsen Circle!

Figure 4-40 Sun set on September 25, 2002, viewed from the top of New King Bowl Barrow 29, 18h57m27s, and the last flash was 28 seconds later. The last flash on the 26th was seen at the place marked (Figure 4-41), and that on the 23rd was extrapolated to the base of the 20-metre-high trees.

Figure 4-41 Last flash on September 26, 2002, 18h55m37s, seen from the same place as Figure 4-40. Sun set locations are marked for dates from that nearest the Equinox, September 22nd in 2002, to the 27th. During a leap year cycle, the September Equalnight set position regresses one-sixth of a degree north in each of the three 365-day years, then the 366-day year brings the Equalnight set back to the original location. The set positions are marked for September 25 and 26 throughout a leap year cycle, in the years marked. EN represents locations of Sun sets that begin the Equalnight every year, and end the Equalday in the first two years of each leap year cycle; ED marks the locations of Sun sets that end the Equalday in the last two years of each leap year cycle.

The last flashes on the 24th and 27th were outside the edges of the Sarsen Circle (Figure 4-41), so the Sun set swept across the Circle on the 25th and 26th. The Equinox was at 04^{h}57^m Universal Time (UT) on the 23rd, and the closest Sun set to it was on the 22nd at 18^{h}07^m UT. The set point would have been far north of the Circle. The Equinox was not a marked date in this part of the Stonehenge calendar. The *Astronomical Almanac* produced by the U.S. Naval Observatory shows that, at the latitude and longitude of Stonehenge, the night of September 25 to 26, 2002, was 12.0 hours long. The day of September 26 was also 12.0 hours long, whereas the day of September 23 was 12.2 hours long. The *Almanac* showed that at Stonehenge, the length of the night that began on the 25th was equal to the length of the day that ended on the 26th, within two minutes. The Equalday/night was from the last flash of the Sun on the 25th to the last flash on the 26th, both of which occurred directly above the Sarsen Circle when viewed from the top of NKBB 29.

As in *Ómahkiyáahkóhtóohp*, the Equalday/nights are marked in the Stonehenge calendar, and Equinoxes are not.

The Sun set and rise directions for an Equalday/night do not shift during 5000 or 10,000 years, while those for a Solstice do. Accurate Equalnight Sun set and rise observation lines that were built 4000 or 5000 years ago are still accurate now (Appendix A.5).

LEAP YEAR CYCLE AND THE DESIGN OF STONEHENGE!

The solar year is nearly a quarter day longer than the 365-day year, so 365 days after the present Equalnight, the new Equalnight Sun set and rise positions fall a bit short of the present ones. Every fourth year, an extra day is needed for the Sun to reach Equalnight set and rise positions. In *every* year, the Equalday and night are each within two minutes of exactly twelve hours long. To maintain this balance, every fourth year has 366 days, with occasional exceptions to give an average year of 365.2422 days.

The horizon Sun set points on September 25 are shown for a leap year cycle in Figure 4-41. Each September, there is only one night and one day that is each within two minutes of being exactly twelve hours long. The 12.0-hour *night* in the autumn at Stonehenge is September 25 to 26 every year. For the first two years in a leap year cycle, the 12.0-hour *day* is September 25, and for the last two years in the cycle, it is the 26th. The situation is similar in March, with the Equalnight always the 17th to 18th. The Spring and Autumn Equalnights at Stonehenge have constant dates, and the Equalday dates flip-flop back and forth across them during the leap year cycles. Half the twenty-four-hour Equalday/nights in a leap year cycle begin and end at a Sun rise, and half begin and end at a Sun set.

At the longitude of *Ómahkiyáahkóhtóohp*, one-third of the way around the world from Stonehenge, the Equalday dates are constant at March 17 and September 25, and the Equalnights flip-flop across them during the leap year cycles.

The Sun set locations on September 26 in the last two years of the cycle at Stonehenge are part of the Equalday/night zone on the western horizon. Any Sun set that occurs within $0°.4$ of the average position (central line in Figure 4-41) participates in an Equalday/night.

While marking the Sun set positions for a leap year cycle on Figure 4-41 and the clearer Figure 4-42, I was astonished to see that the most southerly set position is directly above the south edge of the most southerly Trilithon Sarsen, and the most northerly set position is above the north edge of the most northerly Trilithon Sarsen! And the average Equalday/night Sun set position is above the centre of the Sarsen Circle! Most discoveries grow slowly, and just produce a warm feeling in the discoverer. This was one of the rare, sudden discoveries that jump off the paper while making a measurement, and reverberate in the mind for several days!

Figure 4-42 The extreme positions of the Equalday/night Sun sets in Figure 4-41 are marked relative to the Sarsens on this brighter photo, 18^h12^m on September 26, 2002. The set locations during a leap year cycle move back and forth between the most southerly Trilithon Sarsen (54) and most northerly (60); the middle of this range is at the centre of the Sarsen Circle. The long lines mark the outside edges and centre of the Circle; the dashed lines mark the Equalday/night Sun set extreme positions and the north and south extremes of the Trilithon structure (the top of the most northerly Trilithon Sarsen 60 is barely visible above the lintel of Circle Sarsen 1; the lintel of this North Trilithon would have been clearly visible, but has fallen); dotted lines mark the gaps in the North and South Trilithons.

The variation of Equalday/night Sun set positions during a leap year cycle, viewed from the top of NKBB 29, determined the size of the Trilithon Horseshoe pattern! Furthermore, the north–south distance between the gaps in the North and South Trilithons is 16 metres, one-half the 32-metre outside diameter of the Sarsen Circle! The gaps in the North and South Trilithons are not in an exact north–south line, but the size of the Sarsen Circle is evidently related to the Trilithon pattern by this factor of two.

Before the Sarsen Circle was built, a pole at the centre of the Aubrey Circle could have served as the front sight for the Equalday/night Sun set seen from the top of NKBB 29. The centres of the Aubrey and Sarsen Circles are 0.5 metre apart north–south, making an angle of only $0°.02$ from the 1200-metre distance of NKBB 29, one twenty-fifth of the Sun-diameter. If Bowl Barrow 29 was built after the Aubrey Circle and its surrounding Bank and Ditch were made, the Barrow must have been positioned as an observation place to see the average Equalday/night Sun set above the centre of the terrain within the Bank.

The Trilithon Horseshoe had to be built before the Sarsen Circle because the huge Trilithons are enclosed by the Circle. We now have clues to the choice of their sizes.

Barrow 29 was the observation place for Equalday/night Sun sets over the middle of the Aubrey Circle and the surrounding 5000-year-old Bank and Ditch. The diameter of the terrain within the Bank is three times that of the Sarsen Circle. The above clue to the choice of size of the Sarsen Circle might lead to a clue to how the diameters of the roughly one-thousand-year-older Bank and Ditch were chosen. The factor three seems significant. Three seems everywhere to be a sacred number. Within the initial Temple, was there a wooden structure of the same diameter as the later stone structure? And were dimensions within the wooden structure related to the leap year span of the Equalnight Sun set positions viewed from NKBB 29?

Equalday/night Sun Set Sight Line Through the Sarsen Circle

Now, back to the view through the Circle itself.

The only clear Sun set when I had access to the Circle in 2002 was on September 24. I placed the camera inside the Circle in the suspected Equalnight set line aimed through the notch in West Trilithon

Sarsen 58, to capture the set in a broad enough sweep of horizon to allow extrapolation to positions on other dates. The hawthorn bush on the horizon was a calibration marker (Figure 4-43). The last flash positions on the 22nd to the 27th are 0°̣20 north of those determined for the same dates in 2001, which agree well enough with the 0°̣17 calculated for the leap year cycle shown in Figure 4-44.

In 2006, the last flash recorded along this line on September 25 was at the place marked for September 25, 2002 in Figure 4-44, as expected, with an uncertainty of 0°̣05.

The narrow observation line through the entire Circle appears as a slender triangular hole at about chest height (Figure 4-45). The line is confined by the north edge of Circle Sarsen 3 and passes through the deepest part of the notch in West Trilithon Sarsen 58. The north edge of Sarsen 3 above the notch was pared away to reach the required viewing angle across the Circle (Figure 4-46).

The east–west gap through the Circle seen from the east Bank appears as a narrow slit at the horizon (Figure 4-47). The position of the last flash crosses this line twice per year during its annual north–south swing cycle.

Figure 4-43 Last flash of the Sun on September 24, 2002, seen from the suspected Equalday/night Sun set line across the Sarsen Circle. The camera was 0.5 metre east of the north edge of Bluestone 70. A hawthorn bush 340 metres away on the left horizon serves as a calibration marker. The set positions on the 22nd to 27th are marked.

Figure 4-44 Leap year cycle of shifts in the Equalday/night Sun set position. The dates are September 25 and 26 in the years marked. The average set position is marked with a longer line. The Equalday/night has ended when the Sun set position has crossed the narrowest slit observable from the east Bank (Figure 4-47). The camera was one metre east of the north edge of Bluestone 70.

Figure 4-45 The Equalday/night Sun set observation line is through the slender triangle that contains the horizon, framed by Circle Sarsen on the left and the notch in West Trilithon Sarsen 58 on the right. The set following the Equalday/night has crossed this line from the right each September and from the left each March. The camera was fou paces east of Circle Sarsen 3, September 24, 2002.

Figure 4-46 Looking east at Circle Sarsen 3. The north (left) edge of the Sarsen above the notch was pared away to attain the Equalnight Sun set sightline from the east Bank, through the Circle and the notch in West Trilithon Sarsen 58.

Figure 4-47 Equalday/night Sun set observation line viewed from the east Bank, September 24, 2002. The last flash on the western horizon has crossed this narrow slit from right to left on September 26 each year, and from left to right on March 18.

Equalday/night Sun Rise Sight Line Through the Circle

Figure 4-48 Rising Sun on September 25, 2002, viewed between Sarsens 2 and 3 in the suspected Equalnight Sun rise sight line. The camera was placed to record enough horizon to allow extrapolations to rise positions on other dates. The position of the top of the Sun was extrapolated back to the horizon, and to rise points on the 23rd to 27th. The mound from which the Sun rose on the 26th is New King Bowl Barrow 28. The rise positions during a leap year cycle are shown. The dates are September 25 and 26 in the years noted. The average position is marked with a longer line.

The leap year cycle would also appear in the first flash positions on the east horizon. How was it marked?

On September 25, 2002, I placed the camera within the Circle, peering out between Sarsens 2 and 3. The Sun rose one Sun-diameter north of the base of New King Bowl Barrow 28 (Figure 4-48). On September 26, the Sun would have emerged from the north slope of Barrow 28 as marked on the photo, but the sky was overcast. The slightly raised horizon on the Barrow increases the shift between the 25th and 26th, and broadens the span of the critical Equalday/night rise positions a little. This same device was used in *Ómahkiyáahkóhtóohp*, where the Sun "seat" in the south arm of the V Rocks increased the span between the Sun rise positions on the critical two mornings (Figures 3-27 and 3-29).

128 CANADA'S STONEHENGE

Comparison with observations in 2001 showed that the rise position extrapolated to a particular date was accurate to within one-eighth of a Sun-diameter. The shift of an Equalnight rise position from one 365-day year to the next is three times that much and easily detectable.

The average Equalday/night Sun rise position during a leap year cycle is at the north edge of NKBB 28.

The Sun rise that occurred closest to the Equinox was on the 23rd. It would have appeared far to the left, not visible along this line from the west side of the Circle (Figure 4-49).

* * * *

The Equalday/night rise line, marked ER in Figure 4-50, cuts off the 12 northernmost Sarsens of the Circle, and isolates the North Trilithon from the other 4. It cuts across the Sarsen Circle one-third of the north–south diameter from the *north* end; there's the factor 3 again. These details seem to have been a significant part of the design.

Figure 4-49 Sun rise sight line for September 25, 2002, viewed from about 40 metres west of the Ditch. To record the average rise line for a leap year cycle, the camera would have to be 0.5 metre to the left, which would make the gap between West Trilithon Sarsen 58 and Circle Sarsen 2 slightly wider than seen here. The position of the first flash has crossed this line from left to right on September 26 each year, and from right to left on March 18.

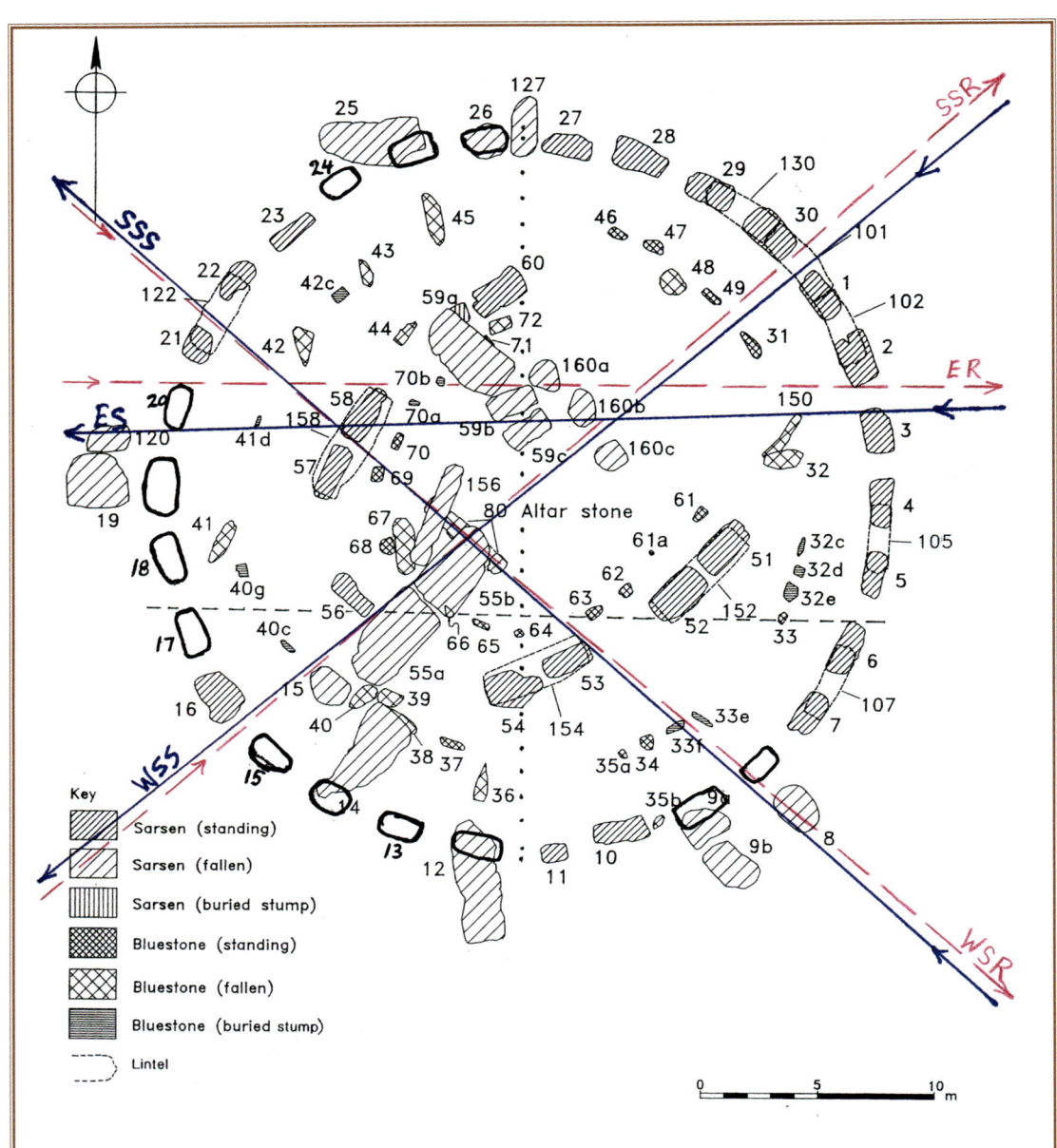

Figure 4-50 Map of the 4000-year-old solar calendar observation lines across the Sarsen Circle. The close-hatched areas show locations of the bases of standing stones. Loose-hatched areas represent fallen stones and fragments. Observation lines that pass through close-hatched areas go through notches or past narrow parts of the stones. Figure 14 of *Stonehenge and Its Landscape* (1995) by R. M. J. Cleal and coworkers, © English Heritage, was modified to sketch the approximate positions of the 30 Circle Sarsens. The Altar Stone, number 80, is broken in two pieces. SSR, SSS = Summer Solstice Rise, Set; ER, ES = Equalday/night Rise, Set; WSR, WSS = Winter Solstice Rise, Set. The ES and ER lines are the same now as 4000 years ago. The SSR, SSS, WSR, and WSS lines are 0°93 farther away from due east and due west than are the present ones. The short-dash east–west line cuts the Circle north–south diameter (dotted line) one-third of the diameter from the south end, and is coupled with the ER line (see text).

An analogous east–west line across the Circle one-third of the north–south diameter from its *south* end cuts off the 12 southernmost Sarsens of the Circle. This line intersects the Great Trilithon at its gap, between Sarsens 55 and 56, and leaves a *central* 3 Sarsens each on the *east* and *west* sides of the Circle (Figure 4-50). A lot of symbolism seems to be encoded in the design.

People who like numbers will have fun with the 3 and 3 x 4 = 12, and with the structures that each particular segment of the Circle contains. People who have trouble with arithmetic will think that this analysis would go too far. I don't know how far the ancient architects took number crunching. Much of this simply accompanies the elegance of the design. But I suspect that numerology began more than 5000 years ago.

Maps of Season-Pivot-Date Sun Sight Lines across Stonehenge and Its Landscape

The 6 observation lines for the Sun rises and sets on the 4 season-pivot dates involved 4 gaps through the Sarsen structure.

The subtly positioned observation lines for the spiritually charged Summer Solstice *set* and Winter Solstice *rise* shared the same path along the Altar and through the West Trilithon gap.

The spectacularly positioned observation lines for the emotionally charged Summer Solstice *rise* and Winter Solstice *set*, viewed from far outside the Circle, shared the gap in the Great Trilithon, but at different heights above ground. The Summer rise line passed *above* the Circle lintels, while the Winter set line passed near the ground *between* the Circle uprights. This could be vertical symbolism of strength and weakness. The Summer rise occurs in a massive stone frame above the stone Circle, while the Winter set occurs along the ground.

The Equalnight *rise* and *set* observation lines shared the gap between Circle Sarsens 2 and 3, but they *straddled* the notched West Trilithon Sarsen 58 and Sarsen 20 on the west side of the Circle.

The six season-pivot Sun observation lines are extrapolated across the Bank and Ditch in Figure 4-51. The "Heel Stone" 96 in the northeast corner of the map was the observation place for the Winter Solstice Sun set. The Summer Solstice Sun rise was observed from

OTDB 10, far off the southwest side of the map. I think the other four rises and sets were viewed from the Bank, to give the viewer a bit more height. This was especially important for the Equalnight set. At present, there is no Bank at the viewing place for the Winter Solstice rise, although there might have been 4000 years ago.

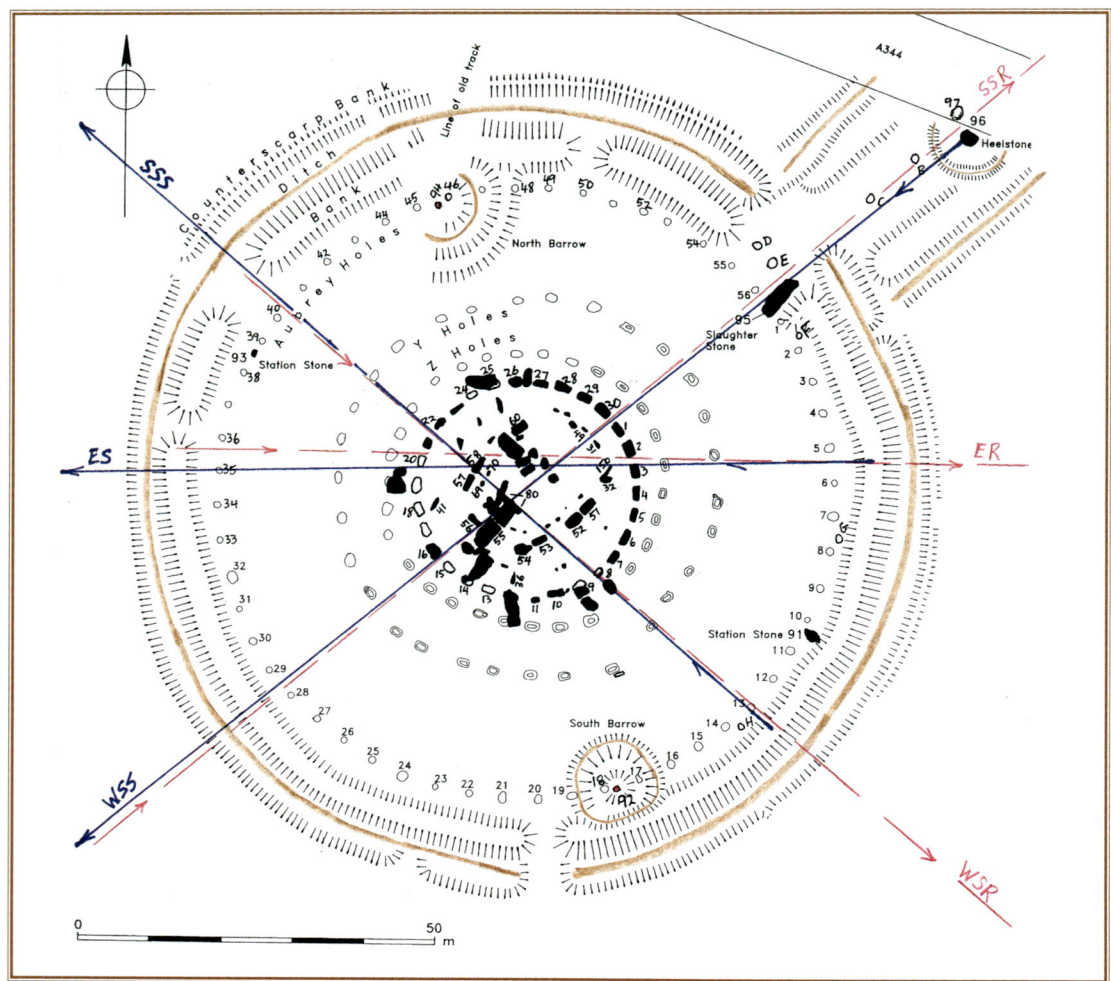

Figure 4-51 Map of the 4000-year-old observation lines for the solar calendar, extrapolated across Stonehenge Ditch and Bank. The base map is the same as that in Figure 4-17, © English Hertiage. The Sun observation lines are labeled as in Figure 4-50. Ditches are marked brown.

The most spectacular observation lines were the opposing pair of the Summer Solstice rise and Winter Solstice set, which seems to imply public ceremonies at those times. The other two pairs were almost hidden. The Summer set and Winter rise pair along the length of the Altar seems to have had great spiritual significance. The largest dissimilarity was in the Equalday/night set and rise pair, which holds Sarsens 58 and 20 in a pincer (Figure 4-50), and might have symbolized the clamping of the exact dates of the Spring and Autumn Equalnights. Sarsen 58 is the *north-Rock* in the West Trilithon. In *Ómahkiyáahkóhtóohp*, a pair of Equalday/night set

He was a very perceptive man. Stukeley excavated it and found a flint layer, below which were scattered broken and burned bones "seeming to be of oxen, dogs &c." No excavation has been reported for any of the other New King Barrows, and nobody seems to know why they are called *New King* Barrows. A windstorm in 1987 uprooted some of the large beech trees on the Barrows, and the resulting root-holes exposed their crudely layered structure.

Colt Hoare excavated Bell Barrow 11 in about 1815, and found a primary cremation and bone tweezers beneath a large inverted urn. *Primary*

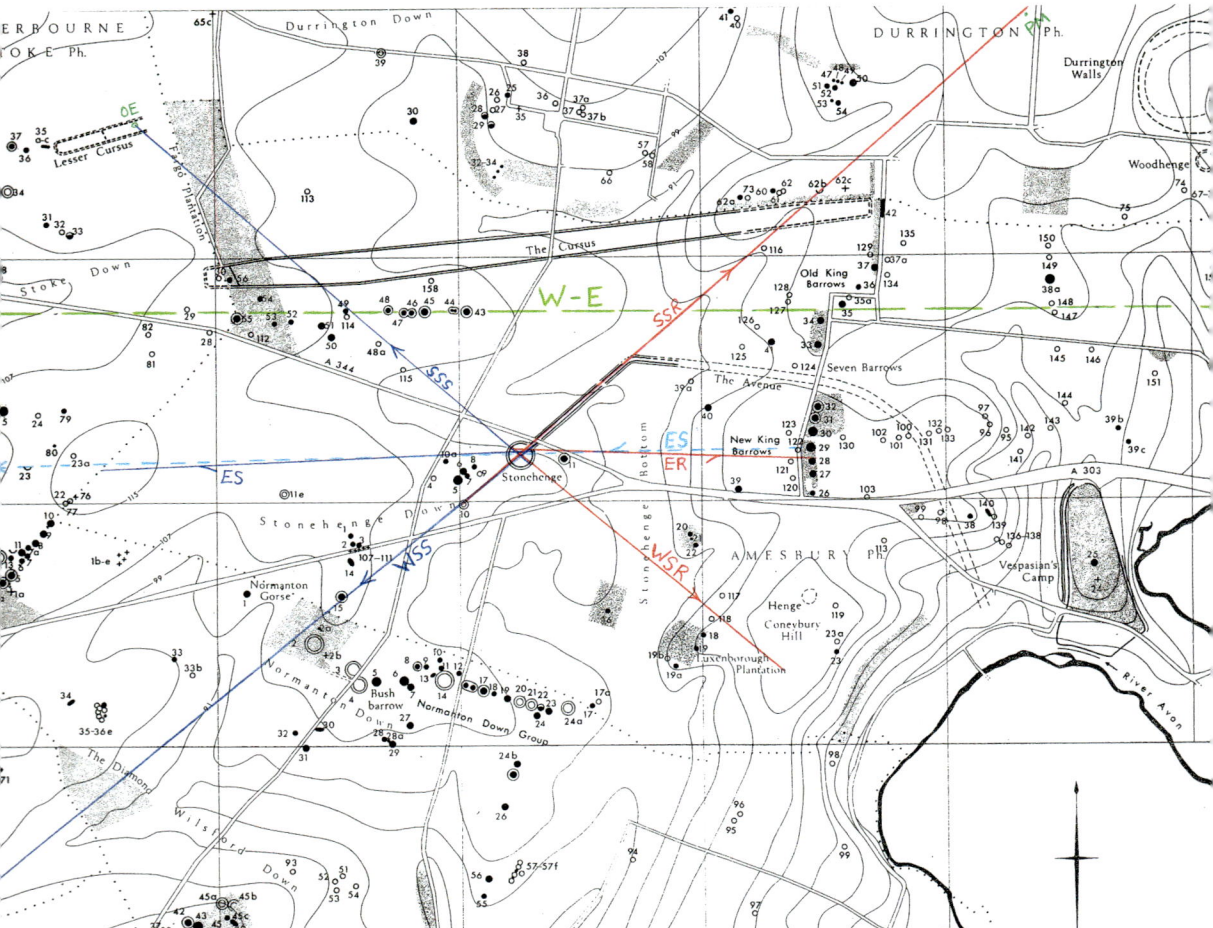

Figure 4-52 Map of the 4000-year-old solar calendar observation lines through Stonehenge, extended to the distant horizons. The observation lines are labeled as in Figure 4-50. The light-blue short-dash line is for Equalnight Sun set seen from New King Bowl Barrow 29. The green long-dash line through the tops of the Cursus Barrows 43 to 49 is exactly west from the top of Beacon Hill 8 kilometres to the east. A horizontal, exactly east–west line goes from Beacon Hill to a crest south of Chitterne, 20 kilometres to the west. Stonehenge is 120 kilometres west-by-south of London and 11 kilometres north of Salisbury. "Barrow Distribution Map 2," in the back pocket of Royal Commission on Historical Monuments (1979), *Stonehenge and Its Environs*, was modified to include Peter's Mound (PM in the northeast corner) and the small Oval Enclosure (OE) in the Lesser Cursus. The contour interval = 7.6 metres. Reproduced by permission of Ordnance Survey on behalf of HMSO.© Crown copyright 2008. All rights reserved. Ordnance Survey Licence number 100048180.

means that the burned bones, tweezers, and urn were placed in the mound as it was built. Bell Barrow 11 might have been built after the Equalnight rise line from the Circle to NKBB 28 had been established.

The four New King Bowl Barrows 27 to 30 are in a north–south line. The number four and the cardinal directions are considered sacred in some religions. These Barrows viewed from between Circle Sarsens 2 and 3 could have served as markers of Sun rise positions for ten days on either side of an Equalnight (Figure 4-39). That would have given a three-week period to obtain a clear Sun rise to check the calendar each spring and autumn, in case there was poor seeing weather.

The annual dates of the Equalday/nights are easily determined in a flat landscape. How to do it is shown in Appendix A.7. After being determined in a flat landscape, these dates could be marked anywhere. They were included in the design and construction of Stonehenge, where the land is not flat.

Plans are afoot to restore the landscape around Stonehenge as nearly as possible to its condition of 4000 years ago. It would cost about one hundred million British pounds ($200,000,000), so English Heritage well appreciates that the local landscape is an integral part of the Temple. The east horizon is now partly shrouded in beautiful, century-old beeches with huge gnarls. They would have to be removed to restore the calendric clear horizon of 4000 years ago. This idea naturally upsets present-day environmentalists. Removal of the beautiful trees is not the only environmental concern. Each evening that we were on New King Barrows Ridge, a young woman came by with a bat-voice detector. She walked along the ridge to record the flight paths of bats. Restoration of the ancient Stonehenge landscape might disturb the present flight pattern of local bats. The restoration seems worth the sacrifices.

BARROWS AND SUN SIGHT LINES

The Equalnight set and rise lines involved *north* edges of Barrows.

The front sight of the Winter Solstice set line is the *left* groin of Bell Barrow 15. The front sight of the Equalnight rise line is the *left* edge of Bowl Barrow 28 (Figure 4-52). The Winter Solstice rise line is restricted by a narrow gap through the Stonehenge structure and has no external Barrow as a front sight. In the reverse direction, extension of the Winter rise line crosses the *left* edge of Cursus Bowl

Barrow 49. This could have been used as a sight line from the northeast edge of Aubrey Hole 13 (*left* edge seen from the Circle, Figure 4-51) for the construction of that part of the Sarsen Circle and Trilithons. All these positions are the left edge of something when viewed from the Sarsen Circle. Did left signify something?

Cardinal Directions

Within *Ómahkiyáahkóhtóohp*, the cardinal directions are marked by lines of cairns across the prairie. In some instances, the directional accuracy of the north–south and east–west lines is an astonishing one-tenth of a degree, one-thousandth part of a right angle. The cairns are separated by distances from about 100 metres to a string of them along 4 kilometres. I measured the directions and distances between the cairns with the aid of a supersensitive Trimble Global Positioning System, by computer deconvolution of the collected data from simultaneously collected Base Station data. The accuracy of some of the cardinal direction lines was such a surprise that I figured out how to make them without using a compass or clock. One only needs the annual cycle of the nearly stationary North Star and the March or September rises and sets of the Sun over flat land (Appendix A.7).

The cardinal directions are held sacred in many cultures. On the Canadian prairies, Indians address the four cardinal directions in prayers. In Christian churches, the altar is supposed to be at the east end, so the congregation will look to the Priest in the direction of Sun rise, which represents Resurrection. If for some reason, such as convenience, the altar is not in the east end of the church, the altar is *taken to be the Liturgical East*. If a church will fake the symbol of Resurrection, it will fake other things as well.

At Stonehenge, my mirrored compass and the known direction of magnetic north gave directions accurate to one degree.

The north–south diameter of the Sarsen Circle is from mid gap between Sarsens 26 and 27 to mid gap between Sarsens 11 and 12 (Figure 4-53). The east–west diameter is from mid Sarsen 4 to mid Sarsen 19 (now missing). When these diameters are extended through the Aubrey Circle, one finds that the Aubrey and Sarsen Circles have the same north–south axis, and that the Sarsen east–west axis is 0.5 metre north of the Aubrey east–west axis.

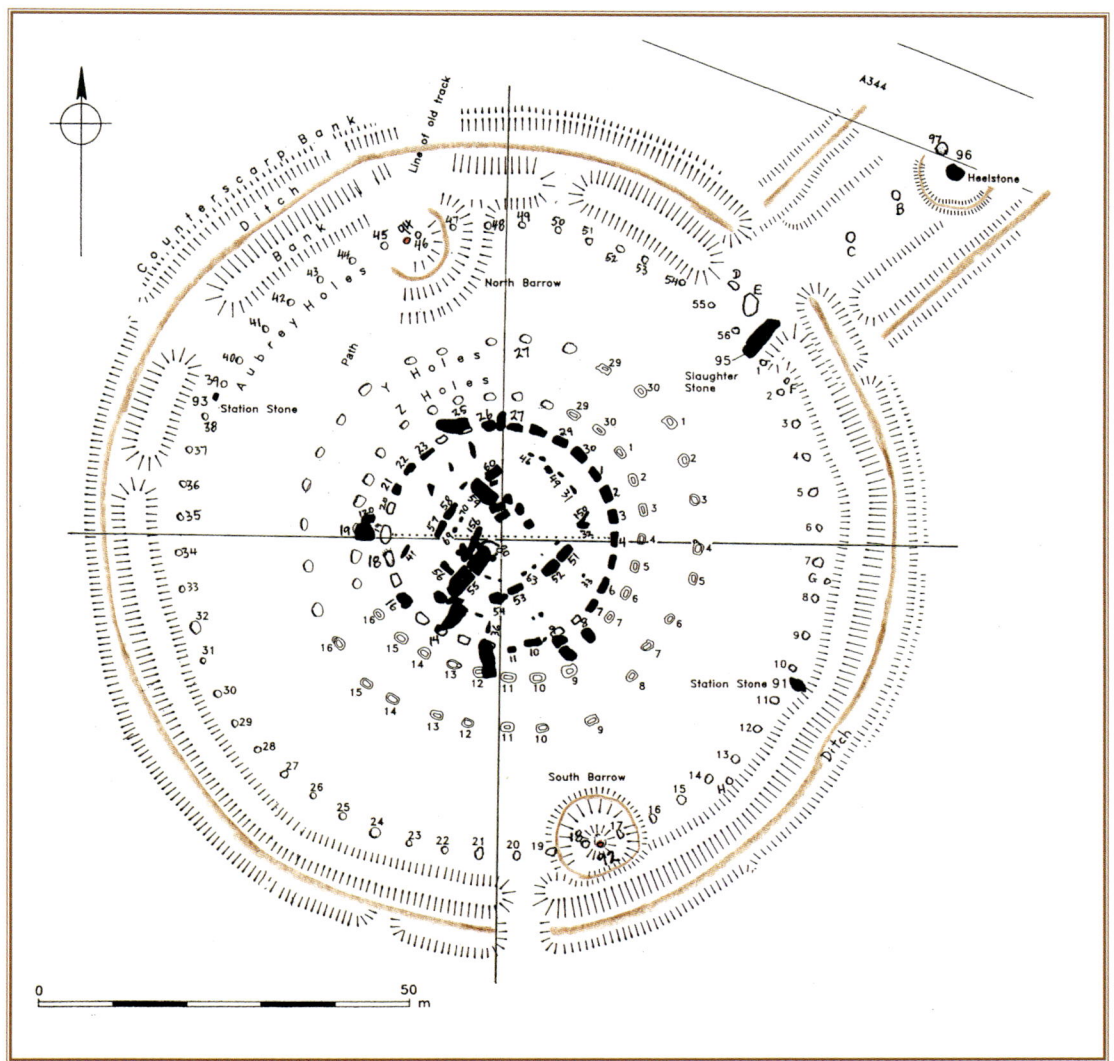

Figure 4-53 Map of Stonehenge showing north–south and east–west diameters of the Aubrey and Sarsen Circles. The Aubrey Circle is a ring of 56 enigmatic holes around the perimeter of the area confined by the circular Bank and Ditch. This earthwork predates the stone structure by nearly one thousand years. The Sarsen Circle is the dark spots numbered 1 clockwise to 30, with missing rocks represented by open spots. The five Trilithons are the dark spots 51 to 60. The Bluestone Circle, from which most of the stones have been removed, is dark spots 31 clockwise to 49. The map is a modified composite of several produced by English Heritage. The base map is the same as that in Figure 4-17, © English Heritage. Brown indicates a ditch.

The cardinal axes divide the Aubrey Circle symmetrically into 4 quadrants, each containing 14 Aubrey Holes. The number and placement of Aubrey Holes are not yet clearly understood. For example, why do the axes pass through the centres of gaps between Holes, rather than across Holes or posts that they might have held? Did the number 14 have special significance? The 56 Aubrey Holes are twice the number 28 of Sarsen Circle lintels, and twice the 28 Rays in the

Sun Cairn Ring of *Ómahkiyáahkóhtóohp*. But in the Sun Cairn Ring, one Ray lies in each of the four cardinal directions. Furthermore, the 7, 7, 5, 5 distribution of Rays in the quadrants of the Sun Cairn Ring (Figure 3-32) is more complex than the uniform 14 Holes in each Aubrey quadrant.

The cardinal axes do not divide the Sarsen structure into symmetrical quadrants, but part of the structure is understood. For example, the Sarsen Circle is a night-counter for the Moon cycle, described in the next chapter.

One cannot see all the way through the Sarsen Circle along either cardinal axis. From the north Bank, one can see *into* the centre of the Circle along the south axis, but the view south *out of* the Circle is blocked by South Trilithon Sarsen 54 (Figure 4-54). However, the top of Sarsen 54 was carved away so the Trilithon gap just below the lintel reached the north–south axis.

From the south Bank, one can see along the north axis only one-fifth the way across the Circle to South Trilithon Sarsen 54 (Figure 4-55). Circle Sarsen 12 has fallen, but when upright it was the same height as Sarsen 10. There was probably no lintel between Sarsens 10 and 12; Sarsen 11 is too short to support lintel ends, and there is a reason to have no lintel between Sarsens 10 and 12. The absence of a south lintel on the Circle allowed clear passage of light from the zenith Sun through the triangular gap in the South Trilithon to cast a pointer of light along the south–north axis within the inner sanctum of the Circle, as described in the next chapter.

Figure 4-54 Looking south (180°) along the north–south axis of the Sarsen Circle from the north Bank. The top left side of Sarsen 54 in the South Trilithon had been hammered away to make a triangular gap that reaches due south, marked by the line above it in the photo.

and rise observation lines also holds the *north-Rock* of the West House V Rocks in a pincer.

The so-called "North Barrow" and "South Barrow" within the Bank in Map 4-51 are not due north–south of each other, had different structures, and are enigmas. A line from Stonehole 92 in the South Barrow to Stonehole 94 in the North Barrow has the direction 342°, and passes through the centre of the Circle and the centres of Sarsens 10 and 25. This seems to select the two Sarsens for some reason. Special functions of these Sarsens are mentioned in the next chapter.

The observation lines are extended across the landscape in Figure 4-52. All the Barrows are numbered in this map.

The Summer Solstice rise line begins at OTDB 10 southwest of the Sarsen structure, crosses above the Circle centre, follows the Avenue to its bend, and terminates a bit north of the tiny Peter's Mound on the northeast horizon. The summer set line begins at Stonehenge southeast Bank, crosses the Circle above the Altar, brushes the northwest edge of Barrow 49 on Cursus Ridge, and terminates at the Oval Enclosure in the Lesser Cursus.

The Winter set line begins at the Heel Stone northeast of the Circle, crosses the Circle centre, crosses the northwest arc of OTDB 10 and the southeast groin of Bell Barrow 15, and might extend to a slightly higher horizon four kilometres southwest. The Winter rise line begins at the northwest Bank, crosses the Circle above the Altar and ends on Coneybury (Rabbit-warren) Hill. We found no end-marker on Coneybury Hill, but a geomagnetic survey of the area might show something. Curiously, Peter's Mound is also a rabbit warren.

The horizon of the Equalday/night set observation line through the Circle is the summit of a gentle knoll about two kilometres west of the Circle. The line brushes the *north* edge of the small, elongated Barrow 10a, which has been nearly obliterated by cultivation. Colt Hoare excavated the Barrow sometime before 1810 and he found nothing. Was it constructed to mark the Equalnight set line before the Sarsens were erected? The Equalday/night Sun rise line through the Circle brushes the *north* edge of the ditch of Bell Barrow 11, 160 metres east of the Circle, and ends at the *north* edge of New King Bowl Barrow 28 a further 1000 metres east. What was the significance of all these *north* edges in the Equalday/night observation lines?

William Stukeley determined in 1723 that the fifth Kings Barrow south of the Avenue (NKBB 28) was "full east from Stonehenge."

Figure 4-55 Looking north (0°) along the south–north axis of the Sarsen Circle from between Aubrey Holes 20 and 21. Note the half-size Sarsen 11 in the south arc of the Circle, in front of South Trilithon Sarsen 53. The line above the South Trilithon marks due north. The triangular gap in the South Trilithon makes a pointer of zenith Sunlight along the ground within the inner sanctum of the Sarsen Circle, described in the next chapter.

Figure 4-56 Looking west (270°) along the east–west axis of the Sarsen Circle from the Bank. The axis passes through the middle of Sarsen 4, marked by the line.

STONEHENGE AND PRESELI MOUNTAIN

Figure 4-57 Looking east (90°) along the west–east axis of the Sarsen Circle from west of the Ditch. The axis passed through the middle of Sarsen 19, now fallen and partly destroyed, and past the south edge of the West Trilithon, marked by the line. The knob on top of Great Trilithon Sarsen 56 is a tenon that fitted into a mortise in the lintel, now fallen with Sarsen 55, the mate of 56.

Views into the Circle along the east–west axis were completely blocked, by Sarsen 4 from the east (Figure 4-56), and Sarsen 19 from the west (Figure 4-57). The cardinal axes of the Sarsen Circle were apparently important to the structure inside the Circle, not to views into the Circle from the outside. Perhaps the blocked east–west axis shielded the secret of the Equalnight set and rise observation lines and removed them from religious ritual. Then Priests could claim special knowledge of the occasion, as happened later in the Christian religion. The complexity of the leap year cycle could be left to the Skywatchers, and not disrupt a smooth annual sequence of religious rituals.

From the centre of the Circle, one could see outside only to the north. The habitations near Ómahkiyáahkóhtóohp were several kilometres north of the Temple. Are these two north-characteristics related? Three kilometres north of Stonehenge is the local highland, now Larkhill Military Base. Four kilometres north–northwest of Stonehenge is a Neolithic camp called Robin Hood's Ball, a causewayed enclosure on the crest of a low ridge.

The Trilithons are not arranged symmetrically within the Sarsen Circle quadrants. There are *five* Trilithons, which form a "Horseshoe." The numbers three (*tri*) and five must have had special meaning for these people 4000 years ago, as they did for the *Ómahkiyáahkóhtóohp* people 5000 years ago, and still have for many people today.

The Trilithon Horseshoe opens to the northeast, and the northeast quadrant of the Sarsen Circle contains no Trilithon. The northwest quadrant contains the complete North and West Trilithons, represented by Sarsens 59–60 and 57–58 in Figure 4-53. By comparison, north and west are the most massively marked directions on Sun Cairn Ring Hill in *Ómahkiyáahkóhtóohp*. The southwest quadrant of Stonehenge contains the tallest Trilithon, sometimes called the Great Trilithon, Sarsens 55–56, and half of the southernmost Sarsen 54 in the South Trilithon. By comparison, south is the least massively marked direction in *Ómahk*. The southeast quadrant of Stonehenge contains the other three-quarters of the South Trilithon and the entire East Trilithon.

Each Trilithon except the East one participates in the solar calendar. The East Trilithon provides symmetry to the structure, but might have had other purposes. The combined solar-lunar calendar described in the next chapter offers a clue.

Parts of Stonehenge were destroyed during the last 3000 years. The main destruction was in the southwest quadrant, which is in the Winter Solstice Sun set direction. Were the destroyers concerned mainly with the ritual significance of these stones? The crucial calendar stones remain, so maybe the calendar continued in use.

An enormous amount of energy and ingenuity was spent on the construction of Stonehenge and the associated Barrows. It must have been built during a period of relative peace, possibly due to the military superiority of the builder society. Societies that have only minor wars for several generations become cerebral. Spirituality and art are honoured, while physical aggression is suppressed. We call such societies advanced civilizations. Little-used militaries become weak. Sooner or later a less evolved, more warlike society comes along and destroys the advanced civilization. Greece–Egypt, Rome–Greece, Gaul (Germanic Peoples)–Rome, and so on through Mongolia, Spain, Britain, and who's next? Unique elements of the advanced civilization, such as libraries and temples, are destroyed or plundered. We call the warlike societies barbarian.

The main barbarians in the Western Hemisphere during the last 500 years were Spaniards and Englishmen in the Americas, who destroyed libraries, temples, and civilizations here.

Stonehenge Bluestones and the King Arthur Legend

About 4400 years ago, an enormous amount of energy was expended to drag more than 300 tonnes of Bluestones more than 300 kilometres over a winding route of land and water from Preseli Mountain in southwest Wales, to install them within the Ditch-and-Bank-enclosed Temple on the Salisbury Plain. What made the Bluestones so special? Our twenty-eight years of experience at ancient sites in Alberta might provide clues. We have found that in millennia-old sites, the landscape is part of the artifact, and the same is true of Stonehenge. What about Preseli Mountain in Wales?

In October 2006, Phyl and I visited southwestern Wales to assess the overall landscape from which the heavy Bluestones were taken.

We drove across the highest pass on Preseli Mountain, hoping to find a B&B on the mountain. No luck. We wound up at the Harries' farm B&B near Eglwyswrw, six kilometres north of the east end of Preseli Mountain. As the source of the Stonehenge Bluestones, Atkinson favoured an enormous heap of bluestones near the east end of the mountain, Carn Meini.

Pat Harries and Maggie St. George Sproule, a geologist/archaeologist who lives in Crymych two kilometres east of the east end of the mountain, told me how to get to Carn Meini.

From a parking spot at the edge of a narrow road, I walked along a farm lane and crossed a stile, then walked west-southwest two kilometres up the gentle slope through sheep pasture and bracken to a 30-metre-high mound of bluestones that I thought was Carn Meini. It was noon Daylight Time and the Sun was high, so the Sun was in the direction south-by-east. I climbed the mound and saw two more enormous mounds of huge rocks at 200-metre intervals to the southwest! I had a flash of the three hills of equal height in the core of *Ómahkiyáahkóhtóohp,* at intervals of one kilometre northeast to southwest. Things are bigger in Canada. I recognized the nature of the landscape, and didn't know whether Carn Meini was the name of one of the mounds, or of the set of three. I could see other mounds on distant hills; local summits on the broad mountain. I had to study the whole mountain to put them in context.

Mynydd Preseli, Preseli Mountain in north Pembrokeshire, covers an area about ten kilometres east–west by four kilometres north–south. It wasn't spectacular as mountains go, more like a very large hill with rock outcrops. It has several peaks; the highest is *Foel Cwmcerwyn*, Vatvalley Hill, 536 metres above Mean Sea Level in the western half of the Preseli bulge. Vatvalley is like half a 150-metre-high vat on the east side of the summit, which broadens into a valley.

The source of the Stonehenge Bluestones was one or more of the huge Cairns, *Carnau*, on the eastern half of Preseli Mountain at about 365 metres above Mean Sea Level.

Each of the Preseli peaks holds ancient structures that have been named. Some of the names printed on Ordnance Survey maps have been altered during the last century, so I have updated published names to those on the 2006 map, except for two cairn name errors on the 2006 map. Names that were broken into two words in the English fashion on the map are rejoined in the Welsh fashion, since that is the language used for them.

H. H. Thomas (1923) and R. J. C. Atkinson (1979) reported that the main varieties of bluestone in the Stonehenge monoliths occur naturally only in a 1 square mile area (3 square kilometres) at the eastern end of Prescelly (Preseli) Mountain, between the summits of Carn Meini and Foel Trigarn. These names correspond to those on the 1909 OS map of North Pembrokeshire, sheet 210. According to the 2006 OS map OL35, the name of the mountain is properly spelled *Preseli*. The name Carn Meini, which means "Stone Cairn," was confused with that of a village one kilometre to the south, given as Carnmeini on the 1909 map, but in 2006 corrected to *Caermeini*, which means *Stone-rampart*, possibly in reference to the string of *Carnau* on the crest one kilometre north. The village has three portions strung out along one kilometre east–west, *Caermeini Uchaf, Caermeini Ganol,* and *Caermeini Isaf*, which mean Stone-rampart Highest, Middle, and Lowest, referring to the steepness of the road.

Carn Meini on the 1909 map is labeled *Carnmenyn*, Butter-cairn, on the 2006 map.

Carn Gyfrwy on the 1909 map is labeled Sheepfold on the 2006 map, but it is actually a 30-metre-high cairn that looks like a saddle from the southwest and northeast (Figure 4-58), so it must be *Carngyfrwy*, which means Saddle-cairn. This is the mound I had climbed, thinking it was Carn Meini. The supposed sheepfold might be the remains of a 20-metre-diameter ring of stones with a corridored north entrance, below the east side of the Cairn (Figure 4-59).

Figure 4-58 *Carngyfrwy* near the east end of Preseli Mountain, seen from 300 metres east-northeast. It looks like a saddle, and its name means Saddle-cairn.

Figure 4-59 Looking east from the east-top of *Carngyfrwy* to the remains of a 20-metre-diameter ring of stones 30 metres below, with a corridored north entrance. Is this the "sheepfold" labeled on OS map OL35?

The three Cairns at about 200-metre intervals northeast–southwest on this hilltop are *Carngyfrwy* in the northeast, *Carnmenyn* in the southwest, and one in the middle that I call *Carnganol*, Middle-cairn (Figure 4-60). *Carganol* is incorrectly labeled Carn Gyfrwy on the 2006 map. This multicairn hill should have a distinctive name, and I call it *Foelteml*, Temple-hill, for reasons that follow.

Foel Trigarn on the 1909 map means "Three-cairn Hill," presumably in reference to the three smaller, closely spaced cairns on its summit. However, on the 2006 map the site is called *Foeldrygarn*, which means *Hinge-cairn-hill*. The Welsh word *dry* means "hinge, revolve, reverse." *Drych*, a mirror, reverses the direction of light and reverses the image of something reflected in it. Hinge-cairn casts our thoughts back to the solar Stone-hinges in Stonehenge and the Pivot-Rocks of *Ómahkiyáahkóhtóohp*.

144   CANADA'S STONEHENGE

Figure 4-60 Looking 234° from mid-top of *Carngyfrwy* to the gap in *Carnganol*, Middle-cairn, at about 200 metres, and the northwest end of *Carnmenyn*, Butter-cairn, at 400 metres. I call this multicairn hill *Foelteml*, Temple-hill.

I learned these things only after visiting sites on *Mynydd Preseli* and noticing surprising similarities with alignments of hills and cairns in *Ómahkiyáahkóhtóohp*.

The central three hills of *Ómahk* each reach 919 metres above Mean Sea Level, in an approximate northeast–southwest line 1.8 kilometres long. The three large cairns of nearly equal height on *Foelteml* make a northeast–southwest line 400 metres long. It seemed to be a small-scale version of the Temple Hills in *Ómahkiyáahkóhtóohp*.

I walked from the top of *Carngyfrwy* to the gap in *Carnganol*, and to the northwest portion of *Carnmenyn*. Looking back along the line of Cairns from the bottom of the V in the northwest part of *Carnmenyn* (Figure 4-61), I saw *Foeldrygarn* 1.8 kilometres away in line with the northwest edges of the three Cairns, with an azimuth of about 50°, approximately the azimuth of Summer Solstice Sun rise, and in the opposite direction, of Winter Solstice Sun set! The altitudes of the summits of *Foeldrygarn* and *Carnmenyn* above Mean Sea Level are nearly the same, 363 metres and 365 metres, respectively—a remarkable similarity with the central portion of *Ómahkiyáahkóhtóohp*. Someone should record the seasonal Sun rises and sets from *Foeldrygarn* and *Carnmenyn*. They are at 51°.96 north latitude, 4°.70 west longitude, only 87 kilometres farther north than Stonehenge. The rise and set azimuths of the Sun and Full Moon would be similar to those at Stonehenge and *Ómahkiyáahkóhtóohp*.

STONEHENGE AND PRESELI MOUNTAIN   145

Figure 4-61 (a) Looking northeast from below the V-sight in the northwest end of *Carnmenyn*. The northwest ends of *Carnganol* and *Carngyfrwy* are in line with the summit of *Foeldrygarn* 1.8 kilometres away, at azimuth 50°. **(b)** Looking from up on the V-sight in *Carnmenyn* along the line in (a). The dots outline the cairns, which are indistinct in the photo.

On the northeast side of *Carnmenyn*, there is an impressive, 20-metre-long, chapel-like Sanctuary oriented north–south, bounded by huge rock end-panels (Figure 4-62). On the southwest side of *Carnmenyn*, there is a 15-metre-long Sanctuary oriented east–west, bounded by less opulent rock end-panels (Figure 4-63). The cardinal direction pairs are honoured by separate Sanctuaries, with the bulk of *Carnmenyn* between them. The axis of the East–West Sanctuary extends 1.4 kilometres due west to *Carnbica* (Pointed-cairn) on the ridge crest across a small valley.

Figure 4-62 A 20-metre-long North–South Sanctuary below the northeast side of the V-sight in *Carnmenyn*. **(a)** Looking south from the north end rock panel to the south panel, 7 metres high. **(b)** Looking north from the south end rock panel to the north panel, 3 metres high.

STONEHENGE AND PRESELI MOUNTAIN 147

Figure 4-63 A 15-metre long East–West Sanctuary below the southwest side of the V-sight in *Carnmenyn*. **(a)** Looking east from the west end rock panel to the east panel, 3 metres high. **(b)** Looking west from the east end rock panel to the west panel, 2.5 metres high. *Carnbica* (Pointed-cairn) is on the crest 1.4 kilometres away at azimuth 271°. *Beddarthur* (Arthur's grave, a stone ring between marks | |) is just below *Carnbica*, 1.2 kilometres from the camera.

An oval of standing-stones, 1.2 kilometres due west of the East–West Sanctuary in the line to *Carnbica*, is called *Beddarthur* (Arthur's grave!). Arthur, the legendary sixth century A.D. Welsh War Leader, is referred to in English as King Arthur. Arthur is said to have won many battles against the invading Anglo-Saxons in the era around A.D. 500. He is the most renowned character in British folklore. So, why is he said to have been buried in this thousands-of-years older site, in a ring of stones 1.2 kilometres due west, across a small valley, from the East–West Sanctuary in *Carnmenyn*?

The legendary Arthur's grave has also been claimed for two other places sacred to Celtic people: Stonehenge and Glastonbury Abbey. Stonehenge is 1.2 kilometres due west, across a small valley, from New King Bowl Barrows 28 and 29; the same direction and distance as for *Beddarthur* and *Carnmenyn*, and also with a small valley between them! Were NKBB 28 and 29 sacred for an earlier reason? Are they equivalent to the East–West and North–South Sanctuaries of *Carnmenyn*? NKBB 28 and 29 are in a north–south line, and are due east of Stonehenge. Do these coincidences relate to the transport of Bluestones from Preseli Mountain to the

Temple on the Salisbury Plain 4400 years ago?

Glastonbury Abbey was built 1.2 kilometres due west of the peak of Glastonbury Tor, a pregnant-belly-shaped hill that has been held sacred for many thousands of years. The Welsh feminine word *tor* means belly. This purported grave of Arthur is the same direction and distance from an ancient sacred mound as in the other two stories! Was there an ancient sacred ring of stones at the place where the Abbey was built? A Sun Temple? What does the recurring distance of 1.2 kilometres represent? There is no valley between the *Tor* and Abbey, because the *Tor* projects 130 metres above the surrounding lowland. The origin of Glastonbury Abbey is lost in the mists of time but is believed to have existed in the sixth century, the legendary time of King Arthur.

There are many Arthurian legends, and several of them claim that Stonehenge Circle in England was moved there from Ireland (where it was called The Round Dance of Giants) at the orders of Arthur's uncle Ambrosius Aurelius. The huge stones of the Round Dance were said to possess magical properties. Ambrosius sent his younger brother Uther Pendragon, with twelve thousand men and the magician Merlin, to Ireland to seize the Round Dance monument and transport it to the Salisbury Plain. Which they did. Uther later fathered Arthur on someone else's beauteous wife. Some legends claim that Ambrosius and Uther were buried in Stonehenge. Others claim that Arthur and his successor Constantine III were also buried there. Warriors all.

Were stories of Arthur transported from southwest Wales to southwest England along with the Bluestones? A Neolithic trade route between southern England and Ireland ran along Preseli Ridge. A large temple and hero's grave on the mountain would be known to the traders. Were the stories Christianized by Celts 3000 years later at Glastonbury, after Celtic Britons had heroically battled the invading Anglo-Saxons? Is the 1500-year-old English Arthurian legend an embellished 4500-year-old pre-Celtic myth?

The relationship between Preseli Mountain, Stonehenge, Glastonbury, and Arthurian myths now opens a new cycle of investigation of that whole area. *Foelteml* on Preseli Mountain is an extremely sacred place, in the same category as Stonehenge, Glastonbury, and *Ómahkiyáahkóhtóohp*. The Bluestones on *Foelteml* were so sacred 4400 years ago that eighty of them, up to four tonnes each, were moved to the Salisbury Plain. Exceptional battle-axes were made from the very hard dolerite, which is coarse basalt. That might be a clue to the sacredness of the Bluestones to warriors. Neolithic

Battle-Ax cultures, some say Cults, are well documented in Europe. Maybe War Leader Arthur was a Demigod to a warring people.

What is the probability that the northwest ends of the three Cairns on *Foelteml*, separated by 400 metres, would accidentally line up exactly with the three smaller cairns on *Foeldrygarn* 1800 metres away? It is negligible. Many multi-tonne bluestones were moved northwestward in *Carnganol* and *Carngyfrwy* to make the line straight, and were moved in *Carnmenyn* to make the terminal V-sight in its northwest section. I think that *Foelteml*, *Foeldrygarn*, and also features on the ridge 1.5 kilometres west of them that holds *Beddarthur*, *Carnbica*, *Carnbreseb* (Crib-cairn), and *Carnalw* (Meetingplace-cairn?), contain a solar calendar, and possibly a lunar calendar.

On the 2006 Ordnance Survey map OL35, near the summit 400 metres south of *Carnbica* is marked *Carnsiân*, Jane's Cairn. Jane's identity seems to have been lost. Somebody's daughter or girlfriend in the nineteenth century?

The cairns on *Foeldrygarn* have depressions in them, as does the Secondary Sun Cairn in *Ómahkiyáahkóhtóohp*. I have seen depressions in a few other cairns in sacred sites in Alberta, too tidy to have resulted from plundering the cairns, and too small to have been vision-quest seats. I don't know what the depressions represent, but they might represent similar things in Wales and Alberta. Offerings and prayer objects are left in them sometimes, and culturally inconsiderate people collect them. It's like stealing from the collection plate in a church.

Richard Atkinson, Cyril Fox, and others quoted by Atkinson felt Preseli Mountain was an ancient sacred place, perhaps one of the chief religious centres of Britain. I support the idea that a sacred enclosure or construction of Bluestones existed there, and that it was dismantled and moved to Stonehenge 4400 years ago. I think it was on *Foelteml*. Was it in what now appears to be the remains of a ring of stones that has a corridored entrance in its north side (Figure 4-59)? Was it a sacred building confiscated by invaders from the east? An Arthurian myth says that a sacred ring of giant stones in Ireland was captured by an English army led by Arthur's father, and that the superhuman task of transporting the stones to England was performed by the magician Merlin. The myth has the directions right. This seems to have been a theft similar to the much later incident in A.D. 1801–1803, when Lord Elgin plundered the Parthenon in Athens and shipped marble statues and friezes to London.

The Skywatcher and the Priest

Skywatchers in ancient times were what we now call scientists. No doubt some of them tried to figure out how the moving sky works. The Sun follows the same narrow path through the constellations from year to year, and the time for a complete circuit defines the solar year, 365.24 days on average. The exact fraction wouldn't have to be known, because the length of the year would occasionally be increased by one day above the usual 365 when needed for the Sun rise and set to reach the Equalday/night observation lines.

The most important Sun observation lines for the Skywatchers' time machine were probably those that marked the Sun rises and sets of the Equalday and night.

The Moon follows a path similar to the Sun's through the constellations, but the Moon wobbles back and forth across the Sun's path. The Moon makes a circuit through its phases from Full Moon to Full Moon in a *moonth*, 29.53 days on average. However, a complete circuit of the Moon through the constellations takes only 27.32 days because the constellations are moving slowly in the opposite direction. As with the Sun, the fractions don't have to be known exactly, because a whole day would be added when needed to complete the cycle.

The Moon's path wobbles back and forth across the Sun's path once each 230.2 *moonths* on average, a whole *moonth* being added to the 230 every five or six cycles. The builders of Ómahkiyáahkóhtóohp and Stonehenge knew the Moon-wobble cycle (see Chapter 5).

Five of the stars wander disturbingly forward and back along the Sun's path through the constellations, not across it, periodically moving into and out of the Sun. Each of these stars was called a wanderer by Greeks, πλάνης, *plánes*, planet, with cycle periods ranging from eighty-eight days for Mercury to twenty-nine years for Saturn.

Shooting stars are luminous projectiles that sometimes hum, and occasionally boom into the Earth. Comets are ghostly. All these things have cycles, more or less.

Such things are measured initially simply because someone wonders about them, not because the information is needed for something practical.

There have always been a few nitpickers driven by curiosity. We don't have names from early millennia, but a few examples from recorded history are K'ung Fu-tse (Confucious, 551–479 B.C.), Erastothenes (about 276–196 B.C.), Al-Khwarizimi (died in A.D. 849, from whose name we get "algorism" and "algorithm"), Ibn Sina (Avicenna, died in 1037), Umar Khayyam (Omar Khayyam, about 1044–1123), Roger Bacon (about 1220–1292), Leonardo da Vinci (1452–1519), Tycho Brahe (1546–1601), Isaac Newton (1643–1727), and Albert Einstein (1879–1955).

Priests and Priestesses probably ministered to people and performed the annual rituals, as they do today. The most important Sun sight lines for the ritual Temple were probably those for the Winter Solstice Sun set and the Summer Solstice Sun rise, which demonstrated the annual cycle of the Sun's weakness, then strength, then weakness again, as summer follows winter and winter follows summer. It's a metaphor for the lives of people and of nations. Sun sight lines that mark these extreme season-pivot dates were constructed to provide dramatic events.

The weak Sun during the Winter Solstice period, viewed from a large Sun (Heel) Stone, entered a large burial mound at the end of each day. At the end of the Solstice period, the Sun began to strengthen, and after about two weeks moved away from the mound. During the Sun's departure period the mound might have been regarded as a pregnant belly.

The strong Sun during the Summer Solstice period, viewed from a small burial tump, rose each day in a heavy stone window that was high above the ground. After the Solstice period the Sun began to weaken, and moved away from the elevated heavy stone window.

Weakness anticipates strength, and strength anticipates weakness.

STONEHENGE THEN AND NOW

Stonehenge appears to have been a Temple to the Sun and Moon. During the last 3000 years many of the original stones have been removed, possibly broken up for building stones by zealots of new religions. Fortunately, the stones crucial to the working of the calendar remain.

Most of the remaining stones have been straightened or re-erected during the last century. However, there are seat holes in the solid chalk bedrock beneath each erect stone. These seats, and the fact that the erect stones stand plumb-vertical and their tenons fit into the mortises of the lintel stones, put the present positions within a few centimetres of those 4000 years ago. The uncertainty of the original positions is slight compared to the 30-metre diameter of the Sarsen Circle. The accuracy of the calendar lines is not affected.

■ ■ ■

Chapter Five

Stonehenge's Solar and Lunar Calendars

here was a large turnover in custodian and security personnel between 1995 and 2006, but all those we interacted with had a great interest in Stonehenge. Their minds were more open and absorptive than those of professional archaeologists, some of whom surprisingly professed to "know all we want to know about Stonehenge." In partial defence of the local archaeologists, they perpetually have to deal with a lunatic fringe of Stonehenge enthusiasts; they grow tired and withdraw into their shells. My success would have been less dramatic if some Custodians and Security Officers had not helped me sail close to the wind. I am grateful.

The greatest physical danger of working in the large Stonehenge site is that one might step in sheep dung. Sheep is the next most pungent dung after human. I walked all the season-pivot Sun rise and set lines across the landscape, and examined many mounds and ditches. Of the quarter million steps I took in the area during the years, I think only two were bad ones. My early years as a farm labourer stood me in good stead.

* * * *

The solar calendar encoded in the Sarsen building at Stonehenge is 4000, possibly 4300 years old. The extra 300 years would not affect the Equalday/night observation lines and would shift the Solstice observation lines by only one-ninth of the Sun-diameter more northerly in summer and southerly in winter.

The Sarsen building also encodes a lunar calendar, involving the circle of 29 large and one small upright Sarsens, and 28 lintels. There was a gap in the south arc of the lintel circle. Strategically placed gaps in the Sarsen building are crucial in the calendars, like pauses between words in poetry.

The dates that characterize the Sun and Moon cycles are their direction-pivot dates. The directions of rise and set of the Sun or Moon on these dates were included in Stonehenge as gaps that allow someone on one side of the building to see a narrow piece of horizon in that direction on the far side of the building. A particular pivot date was when the Sun or Moon rise or set was within, or traversed, the appropriate gap.

The accurate calendar in *Ómahkiyáahkóhtóohp* was constructed in the middle of the Mesoindian Period of the North American Plains (8 to 2 ka B.P.), and early in Canadian archaeologist James Wright's Period III (6 to 3 ka B.P.). The Stonehenge Sarsen building and its encoded calendars were built nearly a millennium later, at the end of the Neolithic Age of Europe. The calendars are Stone Age devices.

Encoding of symbols in a complex stone structure was carried to perfection 4000 years after construction of *Ómahkiyáahkóhtóohp*, in Chartres Cathedral southwest of Paris. One small example of the rich symbolism that permeates the cathedral's construction and decoration is the eleven-circuit labyrinth laid into the floor; 11—another sacred prime number. The labyrinth is divided into four quadrants (and there's the sacred 4 again), as are the Sun Cairn Ring in *Ómahkiyáahkóhtóohp* and the terrain within the Ditch and Bank at Stonehenge. At the centre of the labyrinth is a seven-circle rosette (and there's the sacred 7), which is variously used as a symbol of enlightenment, the Sun, a womb (rebirth), the Flower of Life, and other uplifting ideas. In *Ómahkiyáahkóhtóohp* I interpret a rosette of stones as The Pleiades, a misty, multifoetal constellation in the sky.

The driving force for the expenditure of so much labour on a Temple must have been an intense, hierarchical religion that was supported by a large populace.

* * * *

The Sun is necessary for life. In northern lands heat and light from the Sun become perilously fragile each winter. Most religions in the North Temperate Zone entwine the Sun's annual cycle of strength and weakness into an annual cycle of symbolic rituals. A Solstice lasts about a week, whereas an Equalday/night lasts only twenty-four hours. In some theologies, the brief period of the Spring Equalnight after a cold winter symbolizes the act of fertilization; sexual coupling. Some Spring Fertility Ceremonies included sexual intercourse between Priests and Priestesses, or between domesticated food-animals, and sometimes between exotic pairs. In some societies, the sensuous populace participated. Nine months later, the longer Winter Solstice period is in some theologies a symbol for the slower process of birth. It is actually a symbol of the connection between death and rebirth in the cycle of life and death.

The Spring event is predominantly male-driven—seed planting—and the Winter event is predominantly female—death and birth. Women create life. They also usually oversee our entry into life, and our departure from it.

The Moon is less obviously connected to life/death conditions. The lunar calendar is connected only indirectly to ceremonies in most major religions, with the exception of Islam.

The Islamic lunar year (the Hijri calendar, counting the time since the Hijra, Mohammed's flight from Mecca to Medina in A.D. 622) is about 11 days shorter than a solar year, so each successive Hijri year begins about 11 days earlier in the solar calendar. There are 103 Hijri years in each solar century. The Hijri calendar revolves through the solar cycle once each 33 solar years and does not reflect solar seasons. The Hijri calendar was devised in Saudi Arabia, where the desert climate does not produce the extreme solar seasons experienced farther north. A symbol of Islam is a waning crescent Moon. Why it is a *waning* crescent is a closely guarded secret. Could it be because the thinnest waning crescent is seen shortly before Sun rise?

In the Moon's *moonthly* cycle the New Moon appears as a thin-line crescent, low in the western sky shortly after Sun set, near where the Sun had been, and it sets soon thereafter. Each succeeding night the crescent gets thicker and more visible; it has shifted southerly (left) among the stars and sets about fifty minutes later. On about the 7th night the Moon appears as a half-circle, called the First Quarter, and near the time of Sun set it is in the south, only halfway across the sky. The Quarter Moon grows to gibbous, and after about another 7 nights is a complete circle, the Full Moon, rising in the east near the time of Sun set. The Full Moon sets in the west near the time of Sun rise. The circular face of the Moon then begins to decay on the side that was initially round. After about 7 nights it appears as the other half of the circle, the Last Quarter, and is in the southern sky near the time of Sun rise. The Quarter Moon decays to a crescent and gets thinner and thinner for about 7 nights until it disappears into the rising Sun. After two or three nights with no visible Moon, it appears again on the other side of the Sun as a thin-line New Moon to begin a new cycle.

The Moon's shape is different on every night that it is visible during its cycle, and is used to distinguish each night in the lunar month, the *moonth*.

SOLAR CALENDAR: STONEHINGES AND A WHITE BULL'S HEAD

Solar cycles and hinges of stones

When the Sun rises and sets farthest north, its height above the horizon at noon is the highest of the year, and daylight lasts longest. When the Sun rises and sets farthest south, at noon it is lowest, and daylight is shortest.

Sun altitudes are difficult to measure accurately, because there isn't a scale fixed in the sky to compare them with. But directions of Sun rise and set observed from a given place are easily determined as points on the horizon. If there are no natural structures as reference points at the season-pivot locations, rocks are placed to make artificial structures on or directly below the horizon.

In Stonehenge, the Summer and Winter Solstices and the March and September Equalday/nights are marked by Sun rise and set observation gaps through the Sarsen building. Some of the Sun sight lines for these season-pivot dates share the same stone, which provides an elegant physical link between the seasons. The shared stone, such as Sarsen 58 in the West Trilithon, acts as a hinge about which the Sun rise or set swing back and forth in an annual cycle.

West Trilithon, a Stonehinge and a White Bull

Sarsen 58 in the West Trilithon is a solar Stonehinge. It hinges four sight lines for season-pivot dates (Figure 4-50). The large notch hammered into the south corner of the Sarsen is part of three sight lines: Winter Solstice Sun rise, Equalday/night Sun set, and Summer Solstice Sun set. The fourth line is for the Equalday/night Sun rise, which brushes the north edge of the Sarsen.

The West Trilithon also contains the image of a White Bull's head in the space below the lintel (Figure 5-1). The Bull's horns are visible also from the east and west axes outside the Circle and from positions along the Winter Solstice rise and Summer Solstice set observation lines. The horned Bull is an ancient international symbol of the fertilizing male, often associated with the Sun.

In Hindu mythology, Nandi is the White Bull mount of Śiva, the god of destruction and restoration, analogous to the death and rebirth cycle. White Bulls were also popular in Greek mythology. Zeus in the form of a White Bull seduced the mortal princess Europa and sired Minos. Minos became king of Crete and married Pasiphae, daughter of the Sun-God Helios to whom White Bulls were sacred. Passionate Pasiphae lusted for a beautiful White Bull, which mounted her and sired the Minotaur.

Figure 5-1 Head of a White Bull outlined by the space below the lintel of the West Trilithon, between Stones 158, 57, 58, and 122. The Bull would have been visible from southeast of Stonehenge Ditch, below the lintel between Circle Sarsens 7 and 8. September 27, 2002.

A White Buffalo, although a heifer, was sacred to Plains Indians, for whom buffalo were the main source of sustenance.

Sex not only sells stuff now, it causes stories to be passed along for a *looong* time.

When Stonehenge was built, the land around it was used for grazing. Many cattle bones were found in Stonehenge Ditch, and cattle bones carbon dated to 2300 B.C. were found in the Avenue ditches.

In the era of Stonehenge Ditch 5000 years ago, the Sun in the month of the Spring Equalday/night was in the Bull constellation, later called *Ταῦρος* in Greek and *Taurus* in Latin. The Full Moon, on the opposite side of the sky to the Sun, was in the Bull constellation in the month of the Autumn Equalday/night. Perhaps the ancient Britons also identified that constellation as a Bull, and venerated a White Bull. It would be interesting to know what they called the other Equalday/night constellation, across the sky from the Bull. Its symbol was probably symmetrical to produce equal sides (equal day and night), as does the Bull's head. About 2400 years later, Babylonians picked the symmetrical Ram's head and the symmetrical Equal-arm Balance to represent the Equalday/night constellations that surrounded the Sun and Full Moon at that time. Babylonians called the constellation opposite the Bull a Scorpion; its symbol has a hooked tail which lacks symmetry, so would not have represented a period of Equalday/night in the era of the Bull.

The West Trilithon has a counterpart in the 5000-year-old calendar in *Ómahkiyáahkóhtóohp*. The West House V Rocks on Sun Cairn Ring Hill (Figure 3-25) are a solar Rock Pivot, a Stonehenge, which participates in Sun rise and set lines on all six season-pivot dates. Five of the sight lines pass through the bottoms of V's in the centre-top of the rock structure, but the Equalnight *set* line brushes the *north* edge of the West House structure. By comparison, the Equalnight *rise* line at Stonehenge brushes the *north* edge of the West Trilithon.

Buffalo Bulls were venerated animals on the plains. A Buffalo Bull skull, painted symbolically red on one side and black on the other, has been venerated in the annual Sun Dance of prairie people for centuries, perhaps millennia. In *Ómahkiyáahkóhtóohp,* red represents the direction south and black represents north.

I have seen a Bull skull altar used with great emotion in a female *Hounsi* ritual during a Voodoo Ceremony in Haiti. The Bull altar was on the west side in an *Hounfort* (Temple) in Port-au-Prince.

I was the only White invited to an eight-hour night Ceremony, during which five babies were blessed. It's a long story.

The complete set of six season-pivot Sun sight lines in the Stonehenge calendar involves two rock pivots, each serving four sight lines: West Trilithon Sarsen 58 and Altar Stone 80.

The Altar, a Stonehinge

The Altar, Bluestone 80, about 4.5 metres long and weighing about 6 tonnes, was broken and pressed into the ground when two of the Great Trilithon Sarsens fell on it, but it remains in its original orientation. The Winter Solstice Sun rise and Summer Solstice Sun set observation lines lie along its length.

The Winter Solstice set and Summer Solstice rise lines cross the Winter rise and Summer set lines at the middle of the Altar. The middle of the Altar is a Stonehinge.

The acute angle between the Summer Solstice Sun rise and set lines 4000 years ago was 82°, and that between the Winter Solstice rise and set lines was 79°. This explains why the Altar Stone is oriented about 80° to the axis from the Circle-centre to the Sun Stone, rather than a symmetrical 90°. This lack of symmetry led people who didn't know about the Sun sight lines to suggest that the Altar Stone had originally been standing on end and got knocked over, although excavations have failed to locate an appropriate seat hole in the bedrock chalk for a standing Altar Stone.

South Trilithon and the Small Sarsen in the south arc of the Circle; more Stonehinges

The oldest part of the Stonehenge complex is the 100-metre diameter terrain surrounded by the Bank and external Ditch. There are two causeway entrances to the terrain, a broad one through the northeast arc of the Ditch and Bank, and a narrow one through the south arc. The Heel Stone and Avenue were later oriented toward and connected to the northeast causeway, which was apparently associated with ceremonies at the Winter and Summer Solstices. The south causeway might have been the normal entrance to the terrain. It was directionally connected to the daily zenith of the Sun.

Nearly a thousand years after construction of the Ditch and Bank, the Sarsen structure was built. The cardinal directions and the directions of the season-pivot Sun rises and sets were marked more thoroughly in it. Looking north along the south causeway, one sees the Circle Sarsen that is much smaller than all the others (number 11 in Figure 5-2). Directly behind the small Sarsen is the gap in the South Trilithon. There was no lintel on the small Sarsen. The 28 lintels on the Sarsen Circle left an opening in the south arc between Sarsens 10 and 12. Each clear day, rays from the zenith Sun enter the Trilithon Horseshoe area through the gap in the South Trilithon, not blocked by a Circle lintel. A rod of light projects northward from the South Trilithon into the central area of the Circle and ends at the shadow of the Trilithon lintel.

The camera for Figure 5-2 was pointed slightly west of true north. The true north–south diameter of the Sarsen Circle extends southward to the clockwise edge of the south causeway (Figure 4-53), just as the Solstice Sun sight lines pass the clockwise edge of the northeast causeway (Figure 4-51). What does this mean?

* * * *

How far does the daily noontime rod of light on the ground reach from the South Trilithon, and does it mark anything? The bottom of the South Trilithon lintel is 5.2 metres above the ground. During the Summer Solstice period the Sun is highest, and the rod of light from the Trilithon gap reaches the base of Bluestone 64, just north of the Trilithon (Figure 5-3). Through the late morning and early afternoon, the tip of the light rod moves along a curve from near Bluestone 65, bent toward Trilithon Sarsen 53.

Figure 5-2 In the foreground is the south causeway entrance to the circular terrain within the Ditch and Bank. The small Sarsen 11 marks the south entrance to the Sarsen Circle. There was no lintel to Sarsen 11, so the Circle of 28 lintels was open from Sarsen 10 to 12. The gap in the South Trilithon, between Sarsens 53 and 54, is directly beyond small Sarsen 11. The camera is pointed 355° to the small Sarsen. September 25, 2002.

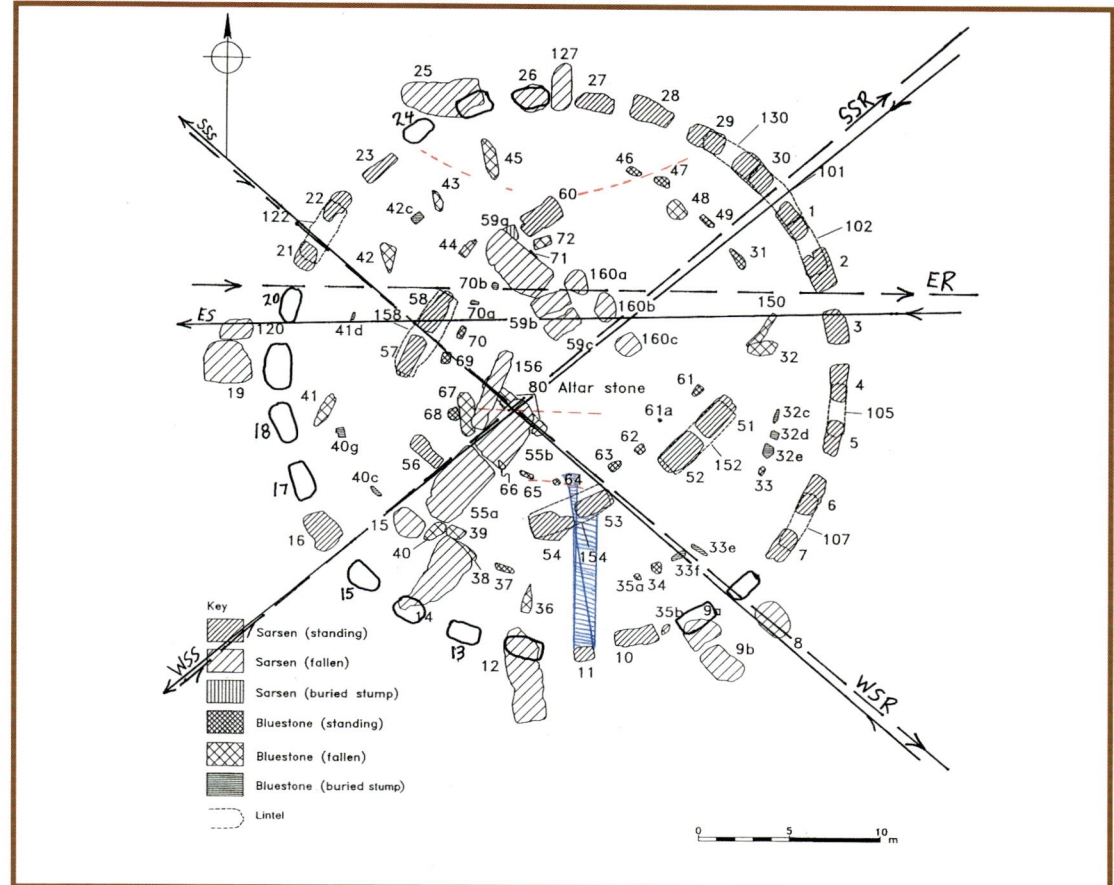

Figure 5-3 On this map, red - - - represents lines traced on the ground by the tip of a rod of light made by Sun rays passing through the gap in the South Trilithon. Summer Solstice: curve from Bluestone 65 through 64. Equalday: straight line from near Bluestone 68, crossing the Altar Stone at the intersection of the Summer and Winter Solstice Sun rise and set lines. Winter Solstice: curve from Circle Sarsen 24 to 29, by way of Bluestone 45, North Trilithon Sarsen 60, and Bluestone 46. The blue shaded patch at the bottom is the shadow of Sarsen 11 from the zenith Sun during the Winter Solstice period, reaching to near Bluestone 64 through the South Trilithon gap. The base map and symbols are the same as those in Figure 4-50, © English Heritage.

On the Equalday, the tip of the rod of light moves along a straight west–east line, from about the north edge of Bluestone 68 toward the north edge of Bluestone 61a. At about 11 A.M., the tip of the light rod passes across the centre of the Altar Stone, where it intersects the crossings of the Winter and Summer Solstice Sun rise and set lines! The Altar centre is a Stonehinge for all the season-pivot dates! The Altar would be a focus of ritual celebrations.

At the Altar's centre, the intersection of the two Altar-long Solstice observation lines and the Equalday light-rod passage present an interesting sequence: Winter Solstice Sun rise, Equalday Sun zenith, and Summer Solstice Sun set. Winter rise, mid zenith, and Summer set.

STONEHENGE'S SOLAR AND LUNAR CALENDARS 163

The sequence seems to look to the future, as does the Plains Indians' uplifting philosophy that winter is a harbinger of spring.

Back to the rod of light projecting northerly from the South Trilithon gap.

The light rod from the South Trilithon is longest during the Winter Solstice period, when the Sun zenith is lowest. The longest rod of light occurs during the shortest days. A symbol of hope? Religion enters our subconscious being mainly through symbols. At noon, the rod of light reaches the north side of the North Trilithon, Sarsen 60 (Figure 5-3). The tip of the rod would have entered the Circle floor near the base of Sarsen 24, moved eastward to illuminate the lower front of the North Trilithon, penetrating the gap toward Bluestone 45, and departed the north-most Trilithon Sarsen about noon. The line traced on the ground by the tip of the light rod bends away from the South Trilithon.

The end of the light rod each day traces a curve that bends toward the South Trilithon from early April to early September, and bends away from the Trilithon from early October to early March. For about a week on either side of an Equalday, the line is sufficiently close to straight that neither the exact Equalday nor Equinox can be selected by the straightness of the line.

The lintel of the South Trilithon is a Stonehinge for zenith sunlight. The seasonal change of length of the light rod on the floor of the chamber could serve ceremonial purposes but is not precise enough for a calendar.

The rod of zenith sunlight is mainly confined to the area enclosed by the Trilithons, which could be the most sacred inner room of the Temple, the Holy of Holies. The length of the light rod correlates with the length of night, which is an artistic contrast of light and dark.

The shadow of the short Sarsen 11 also marks the time of year in a symbolic fashion. The Sarsen is 2.7 metres high. During the Winter Solstice period, the shadow of the short Sarsen near noon each day penetrates the gap in the South Trilithon and reaches just past Bluestone 64 (Figure 5-3). During the Summer Solstice, the rod of light from the South Trilithon penetrates to Bluestone 64, and during the Winter Solstice the shadow of the short Entrance Sarsen penetrates to that stone. The rod of light in summer and rod of shadow in winter match the light and dark seasons of the year.

The interplay of light and shadow dramatizes works of art. It is also an important component of the ancient sculptings of sacred quartzites on prairie hilltops.

Season Intervals

The Solstices and Equalnights do not divide the year into equal quarters. The period from Spring Equalnight to Summer Solstice is 96 days, from Summer Solstice to Autumn Equalnight is also 96 days, but from Autumn Equalnight to Winter Solstice is 87 days, and from Winter Solstice to Spring Equalnight is 86 or 87 days, depending on the year within the leap year cycle. So the Big-end of the egg-shaped year has the Summer Solstice at its middle, and the Winter Solstice is at the middle of the Little-end. This seems like the Moose Mountains Sun-egg, with the year egg-shaped in time, not space.

The lighter part of the year, when daylight is longer than the night, lasts 191 nights. The Summer Solstice is in its centre and is called Midsummer in some old languages. Why was June 21 called Mid*summer*? It was because our word summer comes from the Sanskrit *sama*, which means half a year, and it came to mean the warmer half. The darker part of the year when night is longer than daylight lasts 172 or 173 nights. The Winter Solstice is at its centre, also called Midwinter because our word winter comes from the Indo-European root *wed-*, which means wet. In the Middle East and Europe, the darker part of the year is wetter than is the lighter part.

The Landscape and the Calendar, Sun Observation Lines for Season-Pivot Dates

Was the Winter Solstice Sun observed from the Avenue to set into the Sarsen Circle?

The map in Figure 4-52 includes labels of all the Barrows in the vicinity of Stonehenge. The map in Figure 5-4 contains more detailed ground elevation contour lines at a smaller interval, and shows the steeper slope of the Avenue near its bend northeast of the Circle. It would be interesting to record the Winter Solstice Sun set from a little below the 90-metre contour in the Avenue, to find out if the Sun appeared to set into the left, southeast side of the Sarsen Circle 4000 years ago. Such a line would provide another similarity with the design of *Ómahkiyáahkóhtóohp*.

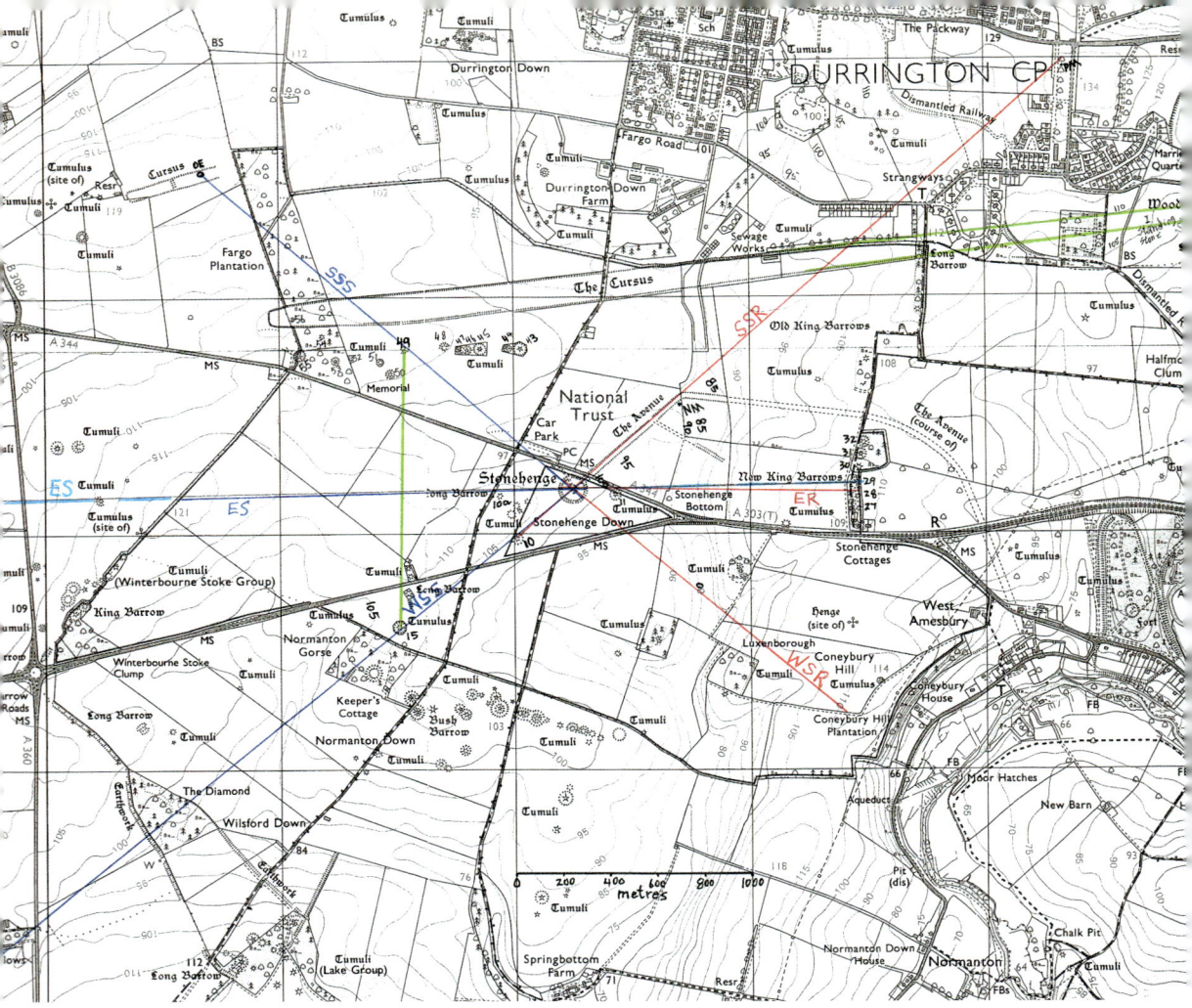

Figure 5-4 Seasonal Sun observation lines on a map with 5-metre contour intervals. Red = rise, blue = set, green lines mark relationships between features. A portion of Ordnance Survey Pathfinder 1221 (1988) was enlarged and features were added: PM is Peter's Mound near the Summer Sun rise northeast horizon; NM is Newall's Mound near the Avenue bend; OE is an Oval Enclosure ditch near the east end of the Lesser Cursus. Some of the Barrows are labeled with their Amesbury Goddard number. Reproduced by permission of Ordnance Survey on behalf of HMSO. © Crown copyright 2008. All rights reserved. Ordnance Survey Licence number 100048180.

Rise and set horizons seen from the Sarsen Circle

The Sun rise and set horizons seen from the Sarsen Circle have different characteristics. The rise horizons are across the lowland of Stonehenge Bottom, and are the first ridge beyond it. In the set directions the distant horizons are each $0°.1$ to $0°.2$ above a nearer ridge. I wonder if this difference served a purpose?

The soil is thin above bedrock chalk, so change of surface level by erosion or buildup of soil could not have been more than a few centimetres, and would not have changed the sight line altitudes appreciably.

Summer and Winter Solstice Sun set Barrow symmetry in the site plan

The Summer Solstice Sun set observation line crossed the northeast edge of Bowl Barrow 49 near the Cursus, while the Winter Solstice Sun set into the southeast groin of Bell Barrow 15. There is a remarkable symmetry in the positions of Barrows 49 and 15 relative to the Sarsen

Circle (Figure 5-4). The two Barrows are each about 920 metres away and about 40° north or south of due west from the Circle centre.

There is a low ridge between Barrows 49 and 15, so one Barrow might not have been visible from the other. Yet Barrow 49 is nearly due north from 15, only 1°, 1180 metres away.

Bowl Barrow 49 has been nearly destroyed by plowing or digging. Was Barrow 49 destroyed at the same time as the Oval Enclosure at the Summer set horizon?

The Equalday/night rise and set observation lines through the Circle touch Barrows

The Equalnight sight lines differ from the Summer and Winter Solstice sight lines with respect to Barrows. The Solstice Sun set sight lines cross Barrows, but the rise lines do not. However, the Equalnight Sun rise sight line touches the north edge of two Barrows, and the set line passes the north edge of a much smaller one. Do these similarities and differences mean something?

The Cursus is cut symmetrically by the Summer Solstice rise and set lines

I was surprised to find that the Summer Solstice Sun rise and set sight lines cross opposite ends of the Cursus symmetrically (Figure 5-4). The Cursus is straight and 2.8 kilometres long, the same length as the bent Avenue. The Cursus is outlined by ditches that run the length of the north and south edges, and has a Barrow at each end. It runs not quite due east–west, but 6° north of east. The centre of the Cursus is only 1° west of the centre of the Aubrey and Sarsen Circles, and is 850 metres north of it. The Summer Solstice Sun rise and set lines cross the south ditch 450 metres from the ends, and cross the north ditch 330 metres from the ends. The south ditch bends near where the Summer set line crosses it, and runs closer to west. The north ditch bends where the Summer rise line crosses it, and runs closer to east. These near-symmetries are a puzzle.

It appears that the Cursus and Avenue were created at about the same time, as suggested by Atkinson, but later than his Bluestone-double-circle Phase II that preceded the Sarsen structure by several centuries. The correlations of the Cursus and Avenue with the Solstice Sun observation lines through the Sarsen Circle suggest that the Cursus and Avenue are contemporary with or later than the Sarsen structure.

The Sarsen building was made strong by the mortise and tenon technique used for construction in wood. The calendrical gaps through the massive stone building are very accurate. I wonder whether a full-scale model in wood preceded the stone structure. After accurate dimensions were obtained by adjusting the wooden structure, it would have been dismantled and replaced by the accurately shaped and placed Sarsens.

Woodhenge and the Cursus

Three kilometres east-northeast of Stonehenge was an ancient construction, traces of which were noticed in an aerial photograph of the area in the 1920s. The place is called Woodhenge.

The remains of Woodhenge are six concentric, slightly oval rings of post stumps, at the centre of which is the grave of a sacrificed child with split skull. The rings are surrounded by a 60-metre diameter ditch and 80-metre diameter bank. The south straight ditch of the Cursus projects eastward to the south edge of Woodhenge bank, 1350 metres from the east end of the Cursus (Figure 5-4). The Cursus north straight ditch projects eastward to the north edge of the largest oval of posts.

A slight ridge hides Woodhenge and the Cursus from each other, so why was Woodhenge placed on an eastward extrapolation of the Cursus? A large rock, 1.8 metres long by 1.5 metres wide, called the Durrington Stone, lies 950 metres east of the Cursus in the Woodhenge line. If it were standing on end 4000 years ago, it would have been visible from the Long Barrow at the east end of the Cursus and would have marked the line to Woodhenge. Woodhenge is on the east edge of the local highland, which then drops 25 metres to the Avon. Woodhenge might have been associated with observation of Sun rise year-round. Did the child-sacrifice have something to do with that?

I mention in passing that Avon, pronounced the same way in Welsh but spelled *afon*, means river. Saying River Avon in southwest Britain is like saying River Fleuve in Canada. Or spout bec on our milk cartons.

Lunar Calendars

Most northern peoples schedule religious ceremonies on a lunisolar calendar. Weather and lifestyle are governed by the solar cycle, but the daily shape-change of the Moon makes the lunar cycle the most convenient to count the days.

Four exact phases of the Moon are easily identifiable, the First Quarter (straight edge on left side), Full (perfect circle), Last Quarter (straight edge on right side), and No Moon (called New Moon in modern almanacs, but not visible because the Moon is too near to the bright Sun). There are usually two No Moon nights, so the date of this phase is the least well defined observationally. An observer's New Moon is the first-visible thin-line crescent after the No Moon nights, and it is rarely seen by anyone other than a loonie, a nitpicker.

The most popular exact phase to record is the Full Moon, because the circle is elegant in its perfection. The period from one Full Moon to the next Full Moon is sometimes 29 and sometimes 30 nights. The numbers do not alternate regularly from cycle to cycle; there might be two or three 29s in a row, then one or two 30s, then one 29, then two or three 30s, and so on. The Moon has rocking movements of several kinds, called librations, which slightly affect the phase we see at a given time. The three-year sequence in 1998 through 2000 was: 30, 29, 29, 30, 29, 29, 30, 29, 30, 29, 30, 30, 29, 30, 30, 29, 30, 29, 29, 30, 29, 29, 30, 30, 29, 30, 30, 30, 29, 30, 29, 29, 29, 30, 29, 30. Eighteen 30s and eighteen 29s, with an average of 29.5 nights per Moon cycle.

The Circle of Stonehenge contains 29 large Sarsens and one small one. The Circle refers to the Moon cycle and is a lunar calendar. For the long term counting of nights by a device, no serious error is introduced by assuming a regular alternation of 29 and 30 nights per cycle.

Sarsen Circle Moon counter

Symmetry was important in the design of the Sarsen Circle. The north–south diameter of the Circle passes between the small Sarsen and its neighbour to the west, traditionally numbered 11 and 12 (Figure 4-53). The small Sarsen 11 represented the 30th night in every second Moon cycle, and symmetry suggests that Sarsen 12 represented the 29th night in every cycle. This means that night numbering proceeded counterclockwise, mimicking the change of position of the Moon at successive dusks (Figure 5-5).

Circle and Trilithons

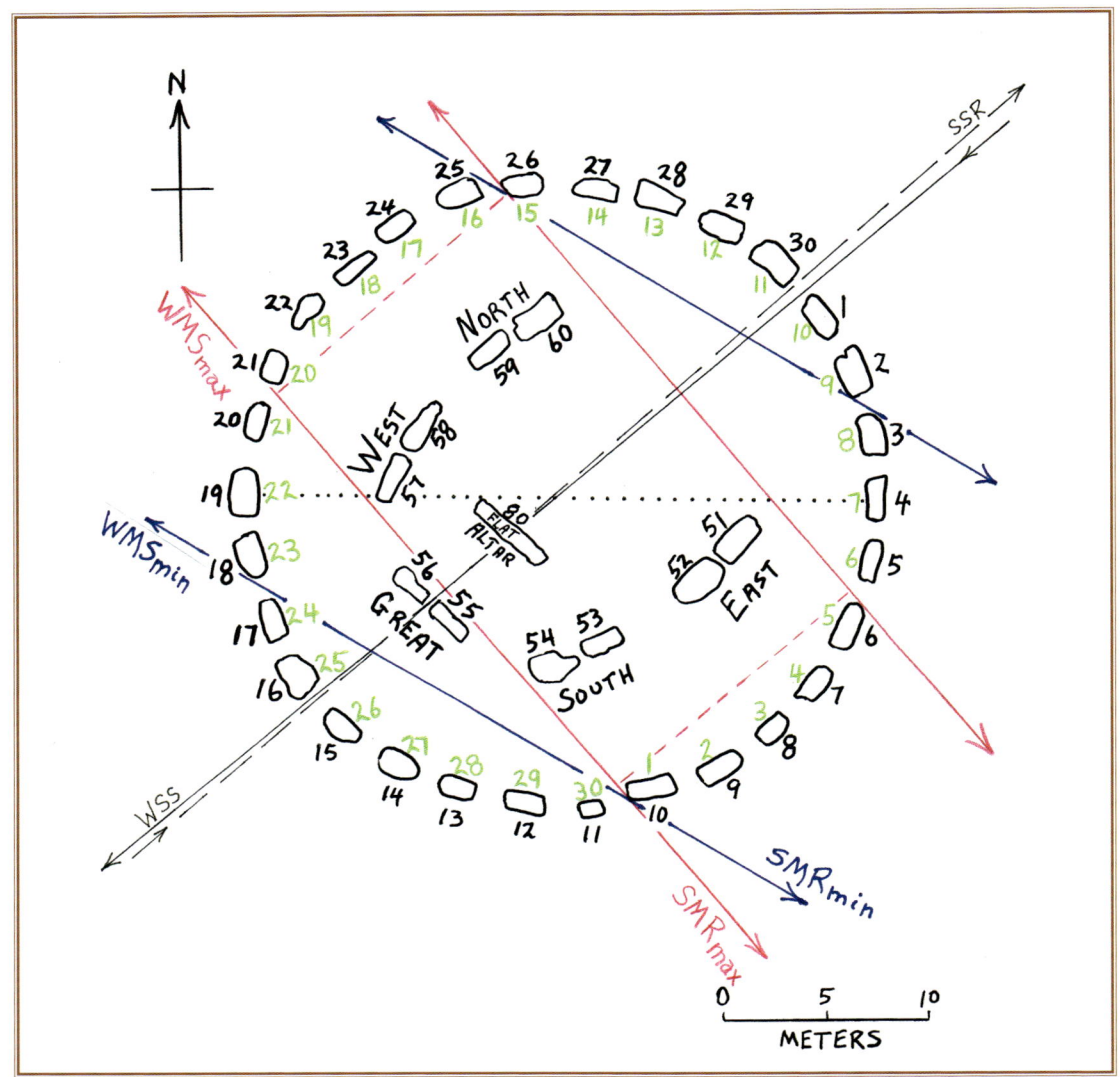

Figure 5-5 Lunar calendar in the Sarsen Circle. The sequential night counters are the new, counterclockwise Sarsen green numbers printed inside the Circle. New number 1 in the lower right represents the first-visible thin-crescent New Moon after the No Moon nights. New number 29 represents a No Moon night every month, and small Sarsen 30 represents a No Moon night every second month. The red lines WMS_{max} - SMR_{max} that run Sarsen new 20 to new 1 and new 16 to new 5 mark the directions of the northerly maximum of the Winter Solstice Full Moon set, WMS_{max}, and the southerly maximum of the Summer Solstice Full Moon rise, SMR_{max}, in the lunar-standstill 18.6-year cycle. The rectangle formed within the Circle by the Moon-max lines encloses the West, North, East, and South Trilithons. The lines for Summer Solstice Sun rise, SSR, and Winter Solstice Sunset, WSS, are nearly at right angles to the maximum Moon directions. Two observation lines for the least northerly Winter Moon set and least southerly Summer Moon rise, WMS_{min} – SMR_{min}, are shown in blue. Summer Solstice Full Moon rise directions swing about a hinge at Sarsen new 15 to sweep across the three east-most Sarsens new 6 to 8. Winter Solstice Full Moon set directions swing about a hinge at Sarsen new 1 to sweep across the three west-most Sarsens new 21 to 23. The dotted line is the Sarsen Circle east–west diameter.

The counter-stone for the New Moon's first-visible crescent was the Sarsen traditionally numbered 10. Proceeding counterclockwise, the Full Moon occurred at Sarsen 27, at the north end of the north–south diameter of the Circle. I have renumbered the Circle Sarsens in Figure 5-5 to show the night-counting sequence. The night of the first-visible crescent is represented by Sarsen new 1; Full Moon night by Sarsen new 14; the night of the last-visible crescent is usually at Sarsen new 27 or 28; the No-Moon nights are represented sometimes by new 28, always by new 29, and every second cycle by the small Sarsen new 30.

There were 28 lintels on the Sarsen Circle, as there are 28 Rays in the Sun Cairn Ring in *Ómahkiyáahkóhtóohp*. Did they represent the maximum number of visible Moons per cycle? In both Temples the solar and lunar calendars are entwined.

Viewed from the small Sarsen new 30, the east half of the Circle has the shape of the New Moon crescent, and it counts the waxing-Moon nights. The west half of the Circle has the shape of the Old Moon crescent, and it counts the waning-Moon nights. The crescent shapes may be remembered easily as D, Dew = New, and C, Cold = Old.

There is a narrow northwest–southeast gap through the Sarsen Circle, which separates the Great Trilithon on the southwest side of it from the other four Trilithons on the northeast side (Figure 5-6). The gap passes the southwest sides of Sarsens old 21 and 10 (new 20 and 1, Figure 5-5). This gap is nearly perpendicular to the Trilithon Horseshoe axis and to the Circle-centre to Sun Stone line, and is therefore approximately perpendicular to the Summer Solstice Sun rise and Winter Solstice Sun set observation lines. The gap is a sight line that marks the direction of the most southerly Summer Solstice Full Moon rise, SMR_{max}, and in the opposite direction (Figure 5-7), the most northerly Winter Solstice Full Moon set, WMS_{max}. The Full Moon rise and set directions reach these extremes once each 18.6 years, in the lunar-standstill 18.6-year cycle. The ancient Skywatchers might also have known of the *lunar-phase 19-year cycle*, which has a period of 19.0 years, now commonly called the Metonic cycle after a Greek who lived only 2500 years ago.

Figure 5-6 Observation line in 4000 B.P. through the Sarsen Circle and Trilithons for the most southerly rise of the Summer Solstice Full Moon in the lunar-standstill 18.6-year cycle, SMR_{max}, viewed from the northwest Bank. In the opposite direction (Figure 5-7), this line marks the most northerly set of the Winter Solstice Full Moon, WMS_{max}. The numbers on the Stones are the traditional ones for readers' convenience. September 27, 2002.

The lunar-standstill 18.6-year cycle gap cuts significantly between Sarsens new 30 and 1, which mark the end of one lunar cycle (*moonth*) and the beginning of the next.

The axis of the Moon's orbit around the Earth precesses due to attraction toward the Sun, with a period of 18.6 years. The precession causes the Solstitial Full Moon rise and set directions to swing back and forth about 10° on either side of the Solstitial Sun rise and set directions. The angles are presently about 8° north and 11° south of the Sun directions at both Solstices. So every 18.6 years the Full Moon nearest the Winter Solstice sets in the northwest nearly perpendicular to the Winter Solstice Sun set, and rises nearly perpendicular to the Sun rise. Near the preceding or following Summer Solstice, the Full Moon rises nearly perpendicular to the Sun rise, and they set nearly perpendicular to each other.

The Sun and Moon at Stonehenge were celebrated as a couple in their Summer Solstice rises and Winter Solstice sets. That emphasizes the Summer rise and Winter set—probably as a philosophical metaphor of rise and fall in life.

The right angle, 90°, was considered special in ancient times, presumably because it is the angle between the sacred cardinal directions and between vertical and horizontal. The accurate cardinal directions can be determined by using only the cycles of the stars and Sun, as described in Appendix A.7. The vertical direction is easily determined with a plumb line and was needed to make the tall standing stones in the Trilithons and Circle stable.

At Stonehenge 4000 years ago, the angle between the Winter Solstitial Sun and Full Moon sets, and between the rises, reached 88° once each 18.6 years, and at an adjacent Summer Solstice the Sun-Moon angle grew to 92°. The average of the Summer and Winter maximum angles between the Sun and Moon directions was 90°.

There was a second narrow gap across the Sarsen Circle in the WMS_{max}–SMR_{max} direction. It passes the northeast sides of Sarsens new 16 and 5 (Figure 5-5). The two Moon-maximum lines made a rectangle within the Circle that enclosed the West, North, East, and South Trilithons, and grazed the inner surface of the Great Trilithon. The East Trilithon was not associated with any of the Sun observation lines that I found, but it is part of the symmetrical set of four Trilithons enclosed by the Moon-maximum lines of the 18.6-year cycle. The Moon-maximum lines and the Trilithons might have defined the space of the most sacred inner room, the *sanctum sanctorum*.

The artistry of this building is amazing.

Figure 5-7 Observation line in 4000 B.P. for the most northerly set of the Winter Solstice Full Moon, WMS_{max}, in the lunar-standstill 18.6-year cycle, viewed from the southeast-by-south Bank.

The two observation lines for the Moon maximum directions of Summer-rise and Winter-set divide the Circle Sarsens into three groups of ten, the central ten being two groups of five. The southwest group includes Sarsens new 21 to 30, which are nine normal Sarsens plus the small one. Might these represent the 9.3 years of the half lunar-cycle, the time between the maximum and minimum angles of the Solstitial Full Moon rises and sets away from the corresponding Sun directions? These angles are also the maximum and minimum away from due east and west.

The small Sarsen might have represented the fractional time unit in any cycle that included it. If so, are the minimum Sun-Moon angles also marked by gaps?

Lunar-standstill 18.6-year cycle hinges, and Circle symmetry

Yes, the Sarsen building did include two narrow observation lines for the minimum Sun-Moon angle, labeled WMS_{min}–SMR_{min} in Figure 5-5. One was between the southwest sides of Sarsens new 1 and 23, and the other was between the northeast sides of Sarsens new 16 and 3. The gaps new 30-1 and 15-16 were Moon-cycle hinges, and the max–min angle from each hinge swept out *three* Sarsens of the Circle. The centre Sarsen in each set of three was new 7 or 22 (old 4 or 19), the centres of which were the east–west diameter of the Sarsen Circle!

The solar and lunar calendars in Stonehenge are full of surprises!

Gap new 20-21 is in both a WMS_{max}–SMR_{max} line and the Equalday/night Sun rise line. Gap new 8-9 is in an SMR_{min}–WMS_{min} line and in both the rise and set lines of the Equalday/night. Entwined Sun and Moon! Husband and Wife. God and Goddess.

It's amusing to think of the times since 1996 that I've been told by Stonehenge experts in England that they know all they want to know about Stonehenge, or that there is nothing else worth learning about it. The word "student" derives from the Latin *studeo*, which means to be eager. It's a lifetime thing for the good ones.

The Moon rise and set observation lines divide the 30 Circle Sarsens into groups of 3, 5, and 7. In *Ómahkiyáahkóhtóohp*, the 28 Rays in the Sun Cairn Ring are divided into groups of 1, 5, and 7 (Figure 3-32).

* * * *

Ómahkiyáahkóhtóohp (50°.6 N), Stonehenge (51°.2 N), and *Foelteml* (52°.0 N) are at similar latitudes, so the interplay of Solstitial Sun and Moon rise and set directions is similar at the three Temples. In *Ómahkiyáahkóhtóohp*, the lunar-standstill 18.6-year cycle is marked by cairn alignments and big bends in the Bow River, but the cycle has so far been only partially recorded there. Observations supported by calculations for 5000 years ago indicate that the maximum angle between Sun and Full Moon rise or set viewed from the Sun Cairn were 90° at the Summer Solstice, 88° at the Winter Solstice, with an average of 89°. *Ómahkiyáahkóhtóohp* is near the minimum latitude 50°.4 N, where the maximum angle between the Sun and Moon rise or set directions reaches 90°.

Calculations from equations in the Appendices indicate that, at *Foelteml* 5000 years ago, the angle between the Winter Solstice Sun and Full Moon rise directions, and between the set directions, increased to the sacred right angle 90°. The angle between the Summer Solstice Sun and Full Moon directions at rise or set increased to 94°. *Foelteml* is at the maximum north latitude where the cycling Solstitial Sun-Moon angle stops at 90°, so perhaps the Winter Solstice was emphasized. The right-angle WMS_{max} might be marked by the line *Carnmenyn* to *Carnbreseb*, or *Carngyfrwy* to *Carnalw*. Someone should check them during 2023 to 2025, bracketing the next period of extremes of the rise and set directions in the Moon cycle.

Moon counting with Y and Z Holes, and the cycle marked by Station Stones

There is a spiral of two rings of Holes outside the Sarsen Circle, the Y ring with 30 Holes and the Z ring with 29 (Figure 5-8). In maps of Stonehenge, the Y and Z Holes are traditionally numbered according to the old numbers of the nearest Sarsen, and some people assume that Hole Z8 is missing, implying that the project was abandoned before completion. But the two-ring spiral is complete and represents two Moon cycles.

The system of Y and Z Holes was created several centuries after the Sarsen Trilithons and Circle were constructed, perhaps about 1800 B.C. The new Holes do not seem to be more accurate than the Sarsen Circle for counting Moons. Perhaps they were easier to use, by moving a marker from one Hole to the next each night. Or perhaps some of the Sarsens had fallen and people did not know how to re-erect them. Or maybe Priestesses after a few centuries got tired of using the same old things.

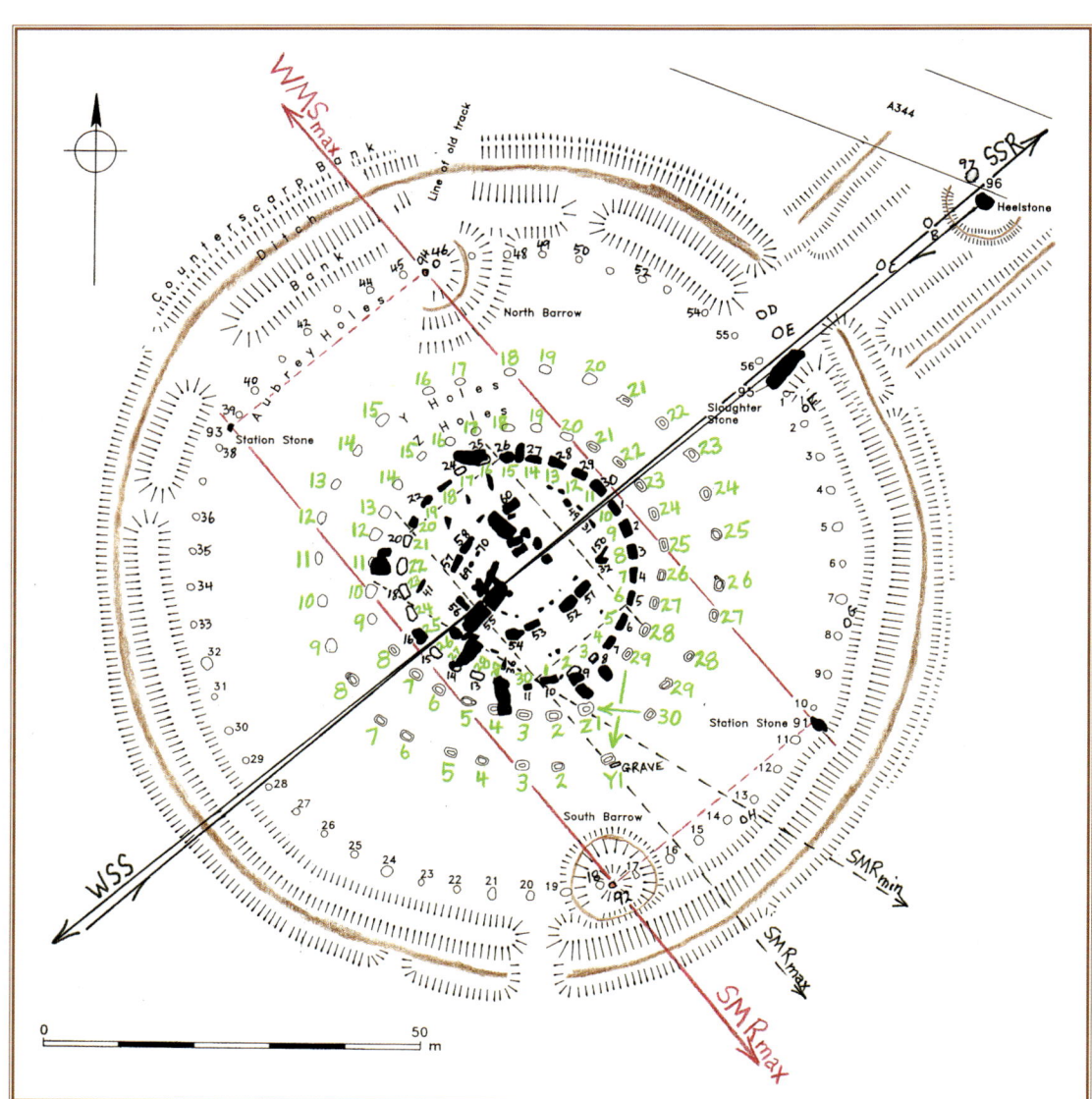

Figure 5-8 Lunar calendar outside the Sarsen Circle, Y and Z Holes. The two-ring spiral begins at the outermost Hole, marked by a grave, now numbered Y1 for the first-visible New Moon in the two-*moonth* cycle. The numbers increase clockwise. All new numbers are in green. The inner ring begins at the Hole now numbered Z1, for the first-visible New Moon in the second *moonth*. The traditional numbers of the Holes were changed to make an appropriate sequence for the lunar calendar. The Station-Stone almost-rectangle 91, 92, 93, 94 cuts through the Y-Z spiral, with long sides marking the extreme directions of the Summer Solstice Full Moon rise, SMR_{max}, and Winter Solstice Full Moon set, WMS_{max}, in the lunar-standstill 18.6-year cycle. The designers used the SMR_{max} and SMR_{min} lines through Sarsen gap new 30-1 to pick the locations of the Holes Y1 and Z1. The date was perhaps about 1800 B.C. The base map is the same as that in Figure 4-17, © English Heritage. Holes marked by a double ring have been excavated. The various ditches are coloured brown.

The traditional numbering of the Holes in earlier maps must be changed to display the lunar calendar. Only the new numbers are displayed in Figure 5-8.

The Y Hole farthest from the Sarsen Circle, old number Y9, is the beginning of the inward spiral. This Hole has a grave near its southeast edge and is the only Y or Z Hole marked by a grave. I have numbered it Y1. Other numbers increase clockwise to Y30. The cycle then passes westerly to Z1 in the inner ring, and so on to Z29, then southerly back to Y1. Z1 is the largest and deepest of the Y and Z Holes, so both Y1 and Z1 are unique.

The newly numbered Holes Y29 and Z29 are relatively small. Y29, old number Y7, was therefore thought to be unfinished. No Moon is visible on the twenty-ninth night of a cycle, which correlates with the small size of the Holes numbered 29. Also, on the thirtieth night in every second cycle, the Moon is not visible. Hole Y30 is of average size, but its distance from Y1 is nearly twice the average spacing.

How were the starting points of the two rings of Holes selected?

The SMR_{max} line through Circle gap new 30-1 extends to touch Hole Y1, which begins the two-*moonth* cycle. This observation line through the Circle was part of the original Sarsen structure, built several centuries before the Y and Z Holes were dug. The line seems to have been chosen to locate the beginning of the new lunar calendar outside the Circle. Furthermore, the SMR_{min} line though gap 30-1 extends through Hole Z1 and seems to have been chosen to locate the beginning of the second ring in the spiral.

There are four *Stations* outside the Sarsen Circle, marked by Station Stones 91 and 93 and the presumed Stone Holes 92 and 94 in the South and North "Barrows" (Figure 5-8). The Stations are intermingled with the Aubrey Holes to maximize the length of the almost-rectangle that they form. The long sides are not quite parallel to each other; the northeast side has a one-degree smaller azimuth and points to WMS_{max}, while the southwest side points to SMR_{max}. Stations 91–94 and 93–92 mark the lunar-standstill 18.6-year cycle more accurately than do the SMR_{max}–WMS_{max} sight lines through the Circle.

The Station lines are tangent to the Sarsen Circle, which suggests that the Station Stones were installed after the Sarsen Circle was built. Within the Circle, the two SMR_{max}–WMS_{max} lines are tangent to the space enclosed by the set of Trilithons, the most sacred space within the Temple, the Holy of Holies. The tangent arrangement of the Station rectangle suggests that the entire Sarsen Circle became the Holy of Holies, perhaps because emphasis on the Sun increased in the religion.

The fifty-nine Y and Z Holes and the four Stations were apparently constructed to move the lunar calendar outside the Sarsen Circle, which then could be dedicated exclusively to the Sun.

The short sides of the Station rectangle are approximately parallel to the Circle-centre to Sun Stone line, and therefore point roughly in the directions of the Summer Solstice Sun rise and Winter Solstice Sun set. But the short sides merely complete the almost-rectangle, as they do in the internal rectangle, and are not calendric Sun markers.

Sarsens new 1 and 16 in the Moon-cycle pivots of Figure 5-5 are the old numbers 10 and 25, which were previously mentioned as being selected by the diagonal line between Stations 92 and 94. Now this diagonal appears to be part of the design that integrates the Station rectangle with the Sarsen Circle. The enlarged lunar calendar rectangle continues to clasp the Sun Holy of Holies. In Plains Indian art, the Crescent Moon is sometimes depicted as the Goddess' spread thighs that are the Sun Catcher.

For easy reference to the lunar calendars in Stonehenge, the new numbers of the Circle Sarsens and of the Y and Z Holes are in green on the maps inside the back cover.

The design of the greater Stonehenge Temple contains a lot of coded information that remains to be deciphered.

Lunisolar Calendar, a Temple to the Moon and Sun, Site Selection

Why are some places holier than others? How does the human mind work?

About 5000 years ago, the gentle west slope of a broad gully at 51° north latitude was selected for the construction of a large circular Ditch and Bank, with causeway entrances at the northeast and south sides of the enclosed domain. This was the first construction phase of the site on which Stonehenge was later built. The gully is now called Stonehenge Bottom, which sounds funny to all but the English.

The enclosed domain was built on the broad west slope rather than on a crest, perhaps to obtain Sun sighting-lines to horizons that were relatively uniform in altitude and not too far away. The large amount of energy spent in developing the site during about fifteen hundred years probably had to do with its latitude. At 51° N latitude, once each nineteen years the Solstitial Suns and Full Moons rise and set in directions separated by a sacred right angle. Finding the periodic right angle in the slow wobble of the Full Moon about the Solstitial Sun rise and set directions was an early example of discovering order within chaos. Seeking order within chaos is now fashionable again in science. As I mentioned earlier, my broad research subject is Kinetics of Nonhomogeneous Processes (KNP), and we say that when you learn to read noise it is no longer noise. Heavy Metal music fans know that. No doubt people have found excitement in finding order within chaos for the last forty thousand years.

The broad causeway across the northeast Ditch and Bank into the enclosed domain seems to have been a ceremonial entrance. It was a forerunner of the northeast–southwest sight line from the Heel Stone to the Great Trilithon for observing the Winter Solstice Sun set, and of the line from the Great Trilithon gap to the Avenue centre for ceremonially viewing the Summer Solstice Sun rise from within the Circle.

The great breadth of the northeast causeway is sufficient to accomodate a line from the domain centre to the right edge of the causeway for the Summer Solstice Sun rise, and to the left edge of the causeway for the northern maximum of the Winter Solstitial Full Moon rise in its 18.6-year oscillation about the Sun directions.

The narrow causeway to the south side of the sacred domain might have been the normal entrance, from the direction of the daily zenith Sun. The south causeway was the forerunner of the small Sarsen in the centuries-later Circle, and of the rod of light that passed through the South Trilithon gap into the Inner Sanctum. The narrow south causeway suggests that the zenith Sun had ritual significance to people 5000 years ago.

* * * *

The design of the Sarsen Trilithons and Circle included refined observation lines for the Sun rise and set on the season-pivot dates, and observation lines for the Full Moon rise and set at the extremes of the lunar-standstill 18.6-year cycle. The observation lines had to be known before construction was planned. The unique Oval Twin Disk Barrow 10 southwest of the Circle must have been placed to be an observation point for the Summer Solstice Sun rise above the centre of the circular domain. Later, but before the Trilithons were constructed, the large Sarsen 97 might have been erected northeast of the Ditch to be the Summer Solstice rise foresight.

New King Bowl Barrow 29 on the east crest of Stonehenge Bottom was probably constructed as the observation point for the average Equalday/night Sun set to occur above the centre of the circular domain during each leap year cycle. My head still rings with surprise at the discovery that the oscillating sweep of Equalday/night Sun set positions seen from NKBB 29 during a leap year cycle determined the size of the Trilithon Horseshoe! The space enclosed by the five Trilithons contained the Altar, and presumably was the Holy of Holies for Sun worship.

It was no surprise that the twenty-nine large Sarsens and one small one in the Circle tracked the nightly Moon in its two-*moonth* cycle, but the Sarsens need to be renumbered. The new numbers increase in the counterclockwise direction, mimicking the night-to-night shift of Moon position among the stars. It may take a couple of generations for the renumbering to gain general acceptance (the new numbers are in Figures 5-5 and 5-8, and on the Back Endpapers). It was a surprise that the lunar-standstill 18.6-year cycle was marked by four intricate gaps through the Circle, with several symmetries in the design. The locations of the hinges for the Moon cycle (more *stanhenges*!) increase the emphasis on the Winter Solstice *sets* of the Sun and Moon and their Summer Solstice *rises*. The hinge for the Winter Full Moon set directions is at the Sarsen that counts the New Moon, Sarsen new 1. The hinge for the Summer Full Moon rise directions is halfway around the Circle.

The Winter Solstice sets of the Sun and Moon and Summer Solstice rises were emphasized in the calendar, and therefore in the religion.

The placement of the Winter-Moon-set hinge between Sarsens new 30 and 1 might indicate that the Old Year was taken to end at the last No Moon night after the Winter Solstice, and the New Year began at the next visible New Moon.

When the lunar calendar was moved outside the Sarsen Circle, the positions of the beginnings of the *moonths* in the two-*moonth* cycle, Holes new Y1 and Z1, were picked away from the hinge between Sarsens new 30 and 1 in the extreme directions of the Summer

Moon rise. The new numbers of the Holes increase in the clockwise direction, reinforcing the larger emphasis on the Sun.

The four external *Stations* 91, 92, 93, and 94 seem to have been constructed as part of the Y and Z Hole lunar calendar. The long sides of the Station rectangle are tangent to the Sarsen Circle and clasp the Circle in an intimate embrace.

The picture that emerges from all this is that the original Sarsen structure was a Temple of the female Moon, designed to be penetrated by light from the male Sun year-round and in special places on season-pivot dates. The Trilithon enclosure, the Holy of Holies, suggests a womb, a place that the male emanation must reach. Later, the religion evolved in a way that the Sun took precedence over the Moon. The Y and Z Holes and the four Stations were created to make a Moon Temple outside the Sarsen Circle, the Circle then being dedicated solely to the Sun. The female Moon Temple now clasped the male Sun Temple in the rapturous reproductive mode. The Moon was the Suncatcher.

In *Ómahkiyáahkóhtóohp*, the observation lines for the lunar 18.6-year cycle also scissor the Solstice Sun lines in sexual embrace. The Moon nests the Sun and they produce the Morning Star.

ABANDONMENT OF STONEHENGE TEMPLE AFTER 1500 B.C.

Stonehenge seems to have been abandoned as a Temple some time after 1500 B.C. By that time, the Solstice Sun rises and sets had drifted significantly out of the observation lines through the Circle, and the Full Moon nearest the Autumnal Equalnight had drifted away from the Bull constellation, into the Ram. Might these have been reasons for Skywatchers and Priests to cease using the edifice for its original purposes?

A cooling climate in the Northern Hemisphere might also have contributed to changes in religious ritual, to increase emphasis on the Sun. Quimby's summary of ancient climate changes, derived from ocean-bottom sediments, pollen, and other factors, indicates that the period about 4500 B.C. to 2000 B.C. was exceptionally warm, and that the climate cooled between 2000 B.C. and 1000 B.C. The glaciers that had been retreating advanced again (the Cochrane advance) during the latter period.

The Next Century at Stonehenge and on Preseli Mountain

There are four Bowl Barrows in a south–north line on New King Barrows Ridge one kilometre east of Stonehenge (numbers 27 to 30 in Figure 4-39). Four is a sacred number; the number of cardinal directions. The middle two Bowl Barrows participated in calendrical lines; Barrow 28 was the horizon marker for the Equalday/night Sun rise sight line through Stonehenge, and Barrow 29 was the observation point for the Equalday/night Sun set across the centre of Stonehenge. The two Barrows might have been built at the time of an earlier wood structure within the circular Ditch and Bank.

The outer Bowl Barrows 27 and 30 could have supplemented the Equalnight markers, to accommodate bad viewing conditions by extending the range of calendar calibration dates. Were there other purposes of the outer Barrows?

The pattern of Stonehenge and the surrounding Barrows includes a code. The code can only be solved a bit at a time, by exact observations and measurements on site. A new century of discovery has been opened at Stonehenge by the discovery that, when viewed from New King Bowl Barrow 29, the range of positions of the Equalday/night Sun set in a leap year cycle equals the north–south span of the Trilithon Horseshoe. The artistic interweaving of Sun and Moon observation lines in the Sarsen building leads me to suspect that the third member of the Celestial Holy Trinity, Venus, is also marked by observation lines through the Temple. They will be sought during the next cycle of investigation.

Extensive study on Preseli Mountain has begun with the discovery of probable solar and lunar calendars there, which involve the three hills *Foelteml*, *Foeldrygarn,* and the hill that holds *Carnbica*, *Beddarthur*, *Carnbegeb*, and *Carnalw*. Direct observations of the Sun during several years are needed on Preseli Mountain to illuminate the workings of the *Foelteml* calendar.

The number 3 is included in the Preseli Mountain Temple in a different way from in the other two Temples. The diameter of the Sarsen Circle is one-third that of the terrain inside the Bank, the same as the ratio of the diameter of the Sun Cairn to that of the Sun Cairn Ring. But on Preseli Mountain, the number 3 enters as the number of *Carns* on each of *Foelteml* and *Foeldrygarn*.

The three Temples and their time machines have a lot in common. It seems that the Preseli Mountain Temple predates Stonehenge and might be contemporary with *Ómahkiyáahkóhtóohp*.

Ómahkiyáahkóhtóohp is still relatively complete and about a half-millennium older than Stonehenge, so a further understanding of Stonehenge and its neighbourhood may be obtained by studying *Ómahkiyáahkóhtóohp*. The 7000-kilometre distance between the two similar Temples increases their intrigue.

■ ■ ■

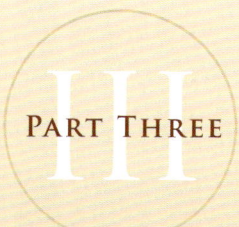

Part Three

History of the Christian Calendar

CHAPTER SIX

Ómahk REVEALS A STRANGE FACT

A calendar is a counter of cyclic changes of lights in the sky. Cycles of the Sun, Moon, planets, and stars give us days, weeks, months, years, and ever-increasing clusters of years. The lights are marvels. Their patterns, motions through the sky, and cycles seem increasingly wondrous as we learn more about them. Our minds are drawn beyond ourselves toward something much larger. In ancient times, calendars were considered sacred, as was all advanced knowledge, including prescriptions in Holy Books for living a good life. Calendrical devices, readable calendars, were constructed in sacred places. *Ómahkiyáahkóhtóohp* and Stonehenge were sacred places. They still are.

All calendars in widespread use are frameworks for annual cycles of religious festivals. There are Muslim, Christian (two of them), Jewish, Hindu, Taoist (Chinese), and other calendars. The Christian Gregorian calendar is used for civil purposes in many countries, but each religion uses its own calendar to regulate its ritual cycle.

The ritualization of time through periodic habits and ceremonies increases our sense of well-being. We habitually do certain things at regular times, so we don't have to mull over a decision every time. We have daily schedules for personal hygiene, eating, working, and sleeping. Muslims have a daily schedule for prayers. Christians like to count down the days to Christmas and to Easter. We like to see milestones along roads, and highway signs telling how far remains to go.

The activity and rest cycles of most animals and plants follow the light and dark phases of the twenty-four-hour day. A woman's menstrual cycle has approximately the same period as the Moon cycle and is named for it (from Latin *menstrualis*, monthly, the *moonthlies*). Weather and the availability of food tend to follow the annual Sun cycle. These things separately and together are sources of wonder and often lead to an idea of God, especially in times of great stress: great cold or heat, drought, flood, cyclone, infertility. The fertility of women is thought in many cultures to be influenced by the Moon Goddess.

Temples

An event that captures our imagination produces wonder if we don't know its cause. Wonderments that occur again and again reflect a mysterious higher power. Repeated wonderments acquire an aura of sacredness. Observation of repeated wonderments at a particular place transfers wonderment to the place itself. Five thousand years ago, something wondrous happened repeatedly at 51° N latitude to cause these enormous, intricate Temples to the Sun and Moon to be developed at that latitude in Western Canada, England, and probably Wales. Each Temple occupies many square kilometres of land. I wonder if there was (and is?) a related Temple near 51° N latitude in Kazakhstan, which was an ancient source of Indo-European culture. We should look for a Temple that contains an accurate calendar in the Kirgiz Steppe of northern Kazakhstan.

The word "temple" comes from the Latin *templum* and the Greek τέμενος. *Templum* did not originally refer to a building. It meant a broad, open place set apart for observation of omens, often among the stars and planets. Prophets sought omens of future events. If the omens were the rise and set points of the Sun, the predicted events were the season-pivot dates. Through millennia, probably before the Sumerian and Egyptian civilizations of 5000 years ago, prophecy grew beyond calendrics to include human events. A calendrical prophecy might be the next date of an Equalday/night, or the date of an eclipse of the Sun or Moon. A human event might be success or failure in an endeavour. Calendrics seem to have become a minor part of prophecy by 2500 years ago, when learned people thought calculations were more important than observations (an egg-head Cult of Mathematics). Prediction of human events became the main concern of Astrology, which means "Star discourse," or what the stars say. The stars were asked to predict an auspicious date to begin a battle, or to make a business deal, or to get married.

Ómahk is a Temple in the original Greek and Latin sense of τέμενος and *templum*, but is twice as old as what we commonly consider to be the ages of ancient Greece and Rome.

As temples evolved, they came to include a structure of some sort in the centre. Five thousand years ago in east-central Ireland, an enormous "Cairn and Passage Grave," now called Newgrange, was built in a temple. The "Passage Grave" contained an accurate Sun rise alignment that marked the Winter Solstice. The large, intricate building probably had a much greater purpose than being a tomb and a calendar marker. What was it?

Newgrange, *Nuaghrian*

In an oxbow of the River Boyne 40 kilometres north of Dublin, Newgrange is constructed of millions of rocks, with a few layers of turf separating layers of rocks in the pile. It is a huge, dome-shaped mound girdled by vertical stone slabs and faced on the southeast side with white quartz. About 82 metres in diameter and 11 metres high, it is two-and-a-half times the diameter and twice the height of the Stonehenge Sarsen Circle built nearly a thousand years later. A passage penetrates the mound from the quartz-faced side, a tunnel 24 metres long sloping slightly upward to the northwest (Figure 6-1).

For the first 19 metres, the passage is about 2 metres high and 0.8 metre wide, somewhat larger than needed to walk upright in it. It then widens into a 5x7-metre cruciform of three compartments, with a corbelled ceiling rising to 6 metres. The ground plan of the 5200-year-old passage resembles a Celtic Cross; so that symbol predates the Celts in Ireland by two millennia. Broad stone slabs in the passage walls and ceiling, and some of those around the exterior base of the mound, are engraved with spirals and geometric forms.

The long, narrow passage was accurately engineered. There is a horizontal slit-window in a "roof box" 2 metres above the floor of

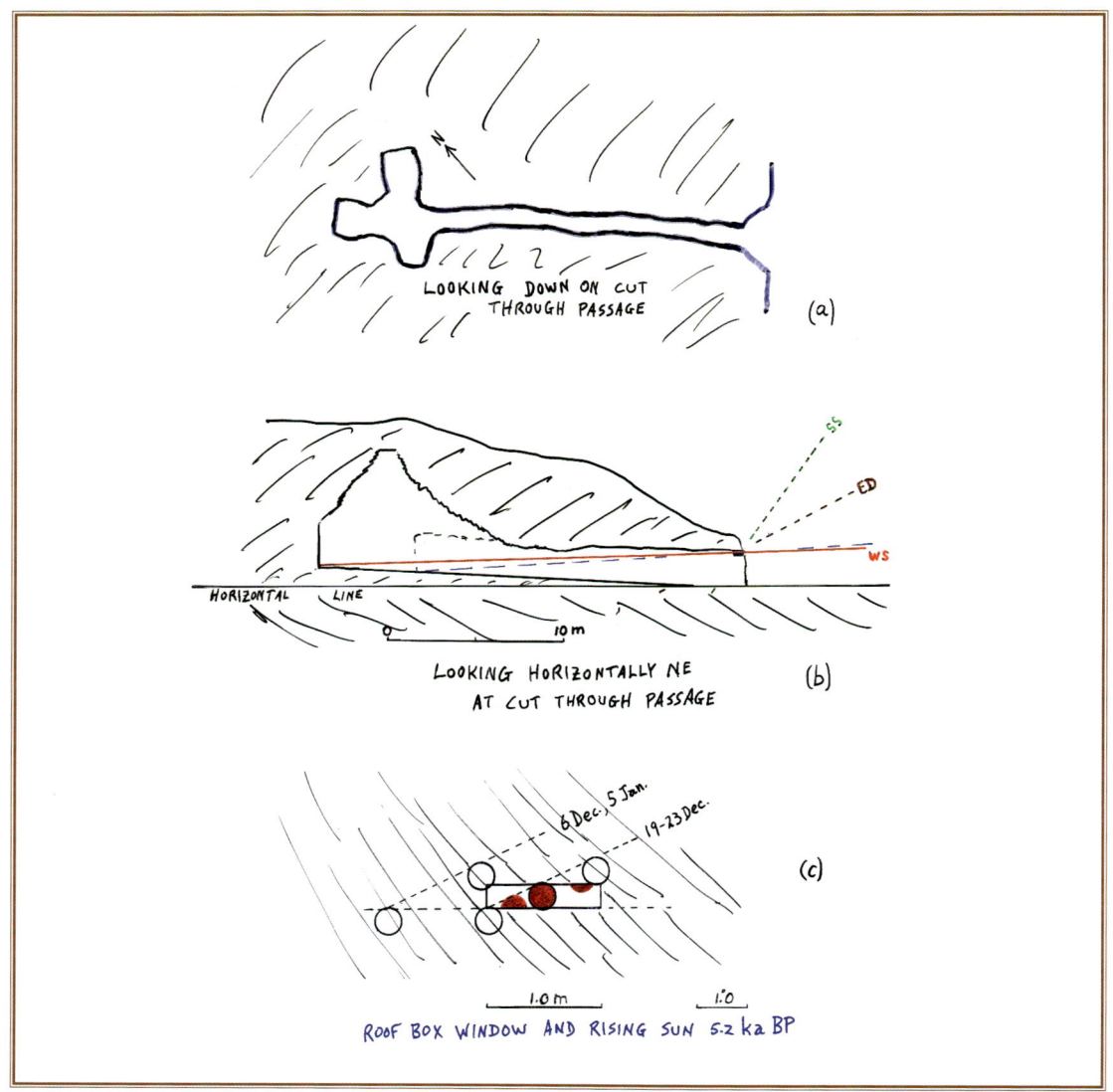

Figure 6-1 The tunnel in Newgrange, a 5200-year-old Sun Temple in east-central Ireland (53°7 N, 6°5 W). **(a)** Looking down at a horizontal cut through the passage and inner chamber. The passage is 19 metres long, the cruciform chamber is 5x7 metres, from entrance to back wall is 24 metres. Passage and chamber outlines in (a) and (b) are adapted from material of Tom P. Ray in *Nature*, 1989, volume 337, pages 343–345. **(b)** Looking horizontally northeast at a vertical cut through the passage and chamber. The floor of the passage slopes upward about 4°. The altitude of the distant southeast horizon from the back wall is 0°9. The window in the "roof box" above the entrance is an average 0.2 metre high and 1.0 metre wide. The line marked WS represents the sunbeam during five to nine days of Winter Solstice 5200 years ago, penetrating to the back wall. The dashed line represents the sunbeam entering the inner chamber about two-and-a-half weeks before the Solstice, and withdrawing from the chamber about two-and-a-half weeks after the Solstice (Sun altitude 3°0). The Sun's zenith altitude at this azimuth is also shown for the Equaldays (ED, 25°) and Summer Solstice (SS, 53°). **(c)** Roof box window sketch, as it might have been seen 5200 years ago from the floor of the end compartment. The average height of the window corresponds to 0.9 x Sun-diameter. The Sun rises along a slope 25° above horizontal. The decreasing altitude of the Sun during December reached the upper left corner of the window about two weeks before the Solstice, was mostly below the lower left corner for five to nine days of Solstice, then rose again and departed the window about two weeks after the Solstice. On about December 10 the full disk of the Sun became visible in the left side of the window. Each subsequent day the disk appeared farther to the right, reaching the middle of the window for the Solstice period, then moved back to the left. The final appearance of the full disk was on about January 1.

the entrance. When the Sun is low enough in the southeastern sky, possibly beginning in October, its light can pass through the horizontal, crevasse-like slit into the passage for a brief period each morning. As the Sun descends lower and lower from morning to morning, its light penetrates farther up the passage, and in December reaches the floor of the inner chamber, and finally the floor of the end compartment. During a visit to Newgrange in 1998, I noted that the sky could not be seen down the passage from a standing position in the inner chamber, so I put my head on the dirt floor at the base of the stone basin in the end compartment to see the tree-dotted horizon in the "roof box" above the entrance. In 2006 I returned for more precise observations. Placing my head sideways at the base of the end stone basin, closing one eye at a time, the eye that was 5 centimetres above the floor saw the tree-dotted horizon in the roof box, but the eye that was 12 centimetres above the floor saw only land and trees that were below the horizon. Unfortunately, I was not allowed to photograph the view down the passage from the compartment floor. Attempts to obtain permission from higher officials failed. However, local expert William Battersby guided me to the particular trees on the southeast ridge that I had seen through the roof box from the end compartment.

Five thousand years ago, during the week of Winter Solstice, light from the rising Sun illuminated the base of the back wall for a few minutes each morning. The entire back compartment would be illuminated by reflection from the floor. The passage was probably intentionally sloped a little upward to decrease the length of passage needed to show these effects, and thereby reduce the needed size of the roof box window and the corresponding width and height of the passage.

The end compartment was illuminated in this way for about ten minutes after Sun rise each day during the Winter Solstice period (Figure 6-1c). Near a Solstice, the Sun rise and set positions on the horizon stand still. At the latitude of Newgrange, the Sun rise remains at the same spot on the horizon for nine days, within one-fifth of the Sun-diameter, the thickness of a dime or half the thickness of a Euro held at arm's length.

The tunnel in Newgrange measures the height of the Sun above horizontal in a fixed, narrow band of southeasterly directions during December and January. It selects the minimum altitude of the year, which in the window is the horizon itself at the Winter Solstice. Newgrange focuses entirely on the Winter Solstice, ignoring the Equaldays and Summer Solstice. The rising Sun crosses in front of the passage every day of the year but is usually too high to be seen through the roof box window by someone in the passage. Light from the Sun only penetrates the roof box into the tunnel during the months that straddle the Winter Solstice.

By contrast, the more accurate calendrical lines in *Ómahkiyáahkóhtóohp* and Stonehenge record the direction of the Sun at a fixed height, the horizon, and pick out the directions of the first and last flashes on season-pivot dates. The rise and set directions swing back and forth through a wide angle between the Summer and Winter Solstices each year, and, to my amazement, the Equalday/nights are also picked out by observation lines.

The end compartment in Newgrange would have been fully illuminated during the Winter Solstice period until about 2000 years ago, but it is less illuminated now. The slowly decreasing obliquity of the ecliptic moved the Solstice position of the Sun's full orb in the roof box from the centre 5200 years ago (Figure 6-1c) toward the left side. The Solstice full orb touched the left edge of the window about 1500 years ago, and since then a decreasing part of the orb appears in the left side of the window at the Solstice. Perhaps the shift of the full orb position is why the passage was constricted by placing a stone slab against the southwest wall 15 metres from the entrance, so that now only the left, northeast, portion of the window is visible from the end chamber.

The direction of the Winter Solstice Sun's first flash now is $1°.3$ less to the south than it was 5200 years ago, so it is $0°.6$ higher above the horizon in the direction out of the passage, and its rays cannot reach the back of the inner chamber.

The southeast façade of Newgrange mound, which faces the rising Sun during the Winter Solstice season, is made of brilliant white quartz. The Old Irish word for quartz is *grianchloch*, sunstone. White quartz has had a spiritual quality for people around the world for thousands of years, perhaps because of its whiteness, translucence, and hardness. One can see white quartz in fractured pieces, and an occasional fist-size lump, in certain areas of *Ómahkiyáahkóhtóohp*. Furthermore, the anciently engraved Sacred Rocks in Alberta are quartzite, described in my 2000 report, *Sacred Rocks of Alberta*.

Classifying Newgrange as a passage grave, which simply refers to the tunnel and the chambers that contained a few human bones, is like classifying Notre Dame Cathedral in Paris as a passage grave because its crypt contains the remains of a few humans. Notre Dame was built 800 years ago, 4400 years after Newgrange, so Notre Dame's architecture is correspondingly more complex.

Newgrange is a Sun Temple. It has been suggested that the name "Newgrange" dates only to Norman times, about 900 years ago. *Grange* means "granary" in Norman. But "New" is not a Norman word, and surely the Normans didn't call the stonepile "newgranary." In English, "grange" means a farm, or farm buildings, including a granary. In view of the aggressive history of the English in Ireland and elsewhere in the world, one can imagine them establishing a new farm at this ancient site and applying their own name to it. But would they call the stonepile "newfarm?"

There is an oral tradition in the Boyne Valley area of Newgrange that tells of sunlight penetrating the edifice at a certain time of year. I think the ancient Celts knew about Newgrange, and continued to use it as a Sun Temple. The old bones might have been revered, as Christian relics are today.

The Old Irish (Celtic) language is *Gaeilge*. The *Gaeilge* word for "new" is *nua*. Nearly the same sound. A word similar in sound to "grange" is *grian*, which means sun. In *Gaeilge*, words get joined together with slight modification: *Nuaghrian*, Newsun. The place was perhaps *Teampall Nuaghrian*, Newsun's Temple.

During the two months preceding the Winter Solstice, as the Sun got lower and lower in the sky, each morning when the rising Sun passed southeast of the Temple, its rays penetrated deeper into the passage. About two-and-a-half weeks before the Solstice the rays reached the large inner chamber, then gradually approached the end compartment. During the week of Solstice the rays illuminated the end compartment, as the Sun "stood still" at its minimum altitude and strength. The Sun appeared on the horizon directly in front of the window above the entrance. Then the Sun began to increase in altitude and strength again, and the beam gradually withdrew from the end compartment. About two-and-a-half weeks after the Solstice it withdrew from the large inner chamber. So the Sun illuminated the large inner chamber for a few minutes each morning during about five weeks straddling the Solstice. During the following month the beam penetrated less and less deeply each morning, as the strengthening Sun withdrew from the passage.

The Oldsun entered the Newsun's Temple to be regenerated. The language of the builders of this ingenious Temple is not known, but one can leap forward 2000 years to the era of the Celts and imagine an Old Irish ceremonial announcement at the Winter Solstice:

Faigheann an tSeanghrian bás; beirtear an Nuaghrian
The Oldsun dies; the Newsun is born!
A more literal translation has the imagery of succession:
The Oldsun gains death; the Newsun arrives at birth!

The passage and chamber are analogous to a vagina and womb. The process that generates new life involves many intense emotions.
Nuaghrian is contemporary with *Ómahkiyáahkóhtóohp*.

About a thousand years before the Stonehenge Trilithons and Sarsen Circle were built, the ancient Irish accurately knew the motions of the Sun and had the engineering ability to construct the intricate Newgrange building. At about that time or not many centuries later, they probably recognized Equalday (which in *Gaeilge* is *lá leathach*, day in halves, or half daylight), March 17 and September 25.

* * * *

I mention in passing that the art styles of the Newgrange people about 5000 years ago, the Celts 3000 years ago, and the Vikings 1000 years ago all emphasize spirals and intersecting rings. It's the sort of pattern I see on a calm Ottawa River surface when I'm rowing the boat, as water drips off the oars at each return stroke. The three peoples went to Ireland in their separate times from someplace else. Did they originate in a common place? Does their similar art have a similar rowboat origin?

On many occasions, I've wondered what was going on in Kazakhstan in western Asia 6000 years ago. Did some people migrate westward from the area of the Aral Sea, going north of the Caspian Sea into Europe, while others went southward toward Persia and India? The Indo-European family of languages is called *Indo-* because the Sanskrit roots of many words were thought to originate in India. But Sanskrit did not originate in India. The Sanskrit language and Vedic religion, which was the precursor of Hinduism, seem to have been located in the vicinity of Kazakhstan about 6000 years ago. They migrated southward about 5000 years ago. The Vedic religion venerated the Sun and bears strong similarities with early Judaism and other early Middle Eastern religions, such as the precursor of Zoroastrianism. The southward migration was one of conquest aided by horses, which provided military strength. Were there also periodic migrations by boat westward from the Caspian Sea? The Volga River flows from near the Baltic Sea in the west, across northern Europe to the Caspian. If people migrated up the Volga and to the Baltic, then Scandinavia, Germany, and the British Isles would have been within easy reach.

* * * *

The Sun worship evident in Newsun's Temple in Ireland is well suited to northern peoples, because of the killing cold in winter. The most intense praying occurs in asking for help, rather than in giving thanks.

The Zodiac and Equalnight in Calendar Development

Many cultures around the world have zodiacs, using the same groups of stars but imagining different images in them. How did the twelve constellations of the zodiac get selected, and how do they relate to the calendar? Are the Equalnights and Solstices clearly marked in the zodiac?

Although all calendars are based on the apparent motions of the Moon, Sun, and stars, each religion sets itself apart by placing emphasis at different places in the cycles. Some calendars place the beginning of the day at Sun set (Hebrew, Muslim, Phoenician), some at midnight (Taoist, Roman, Gregorian), and some at Sun rise (Hindu, Babylonian, Egyptian). Some calendars take the year as the 365-day period from one Spring Equalnight to the next, adding a 366th day every fourth year to allow the Sun rise to reach the Equalnight observation line before beginning a new cycle. The Gregorian calendar does this, although it begins counting the days in each new year ten or eleven days after the Winter Solstice. Some calendars, such as the Hebrew, take the year as twelve Moon cycles, 354 days, adding a thirteenth *moonth* every two or three years to adjust the lunar calendar to the solar cycle of seasons. Our food and weather cycles follow the Sun cycle more closely than they do that of the Moon, so most calendars are anchored to the Sun.

But the waxing and waning Moon cycle is dramatic, and relatively rapid. Everyone seems to find the circular Full Moon beautiful. Only loonies, Moon connoisseurs, seem to be excited by seeing the thin-line crescent of the New Moon as it first appears, and of the Old Moon just before it disappears. *Ómahkiyáahkóhtóohp* and Stonehenge show that cognoscenti measured the Moon cycle accurately many thousands of years ago. There is a saying that the Moon is more important than the Sun, because the Moon gives light at night when it's needed!

If the sky is clear, one sees a Full Moon once every 29 or 30 nights. The Full Moon is seen against a background of star patterns. At each succeeding Full Moon, the star pattern that surrounded last month's Full Moon has moved nearly one-twelfth of a circle, 29°, to the west of the current Full Moon. Successive Full Moons move 29° eastward each *moonth* through the patterns of stars. After twelve Full Moons, the next one returns to about 11° short of the place of the first Full Moon among the stars, a fist's width at arm's length, to begin a new cycle. Every two or three years, a thirteenth *moonth* is needed to bring the Full Moon back near the original starting place.

One can make a chart of the stars seen near the Full Moon each Gregorian month during a year. The twelve charts combine to make a complete band of stars around the sky (Figures 6-2 and 6-3). If one marks in the sky chart the positions of all the Full Moons for the eight years 1990 to 1997, one finds that there are ninety-nine positions in the band. Five of the years contain twelve Full Moons each. If these Moon positions are numbered successively one through twelve for each year, all the ones fall in a cluster, all the twos in a cluster, and so on. The other three years each contain thirteen Full Moons. Each of the two Moon positions in December 1990 are labeled twelve, the two in September 1993 are labeled nine, and those in July 1996 are labeled seven. Both Moons occur in the appropriate month segment. Over many years, two Moons occur in every month except February, which is usually two days too short to get a second Full Moon.

The band of stars along the annual path of the Full Moon consists of twelve equal compartments, each 30° wide. The same band of stars and twelve compartments have been identified by several cultures around the world. To assist remembering the location of each compartment in the sky, the star pattern in each compartment was imagined to represent the image of a different animal, a ζῶον, *zöon*, a living being. The word zoo comes from the Greek. The twelve animals and humans in the band of stars along the Full Moon's path

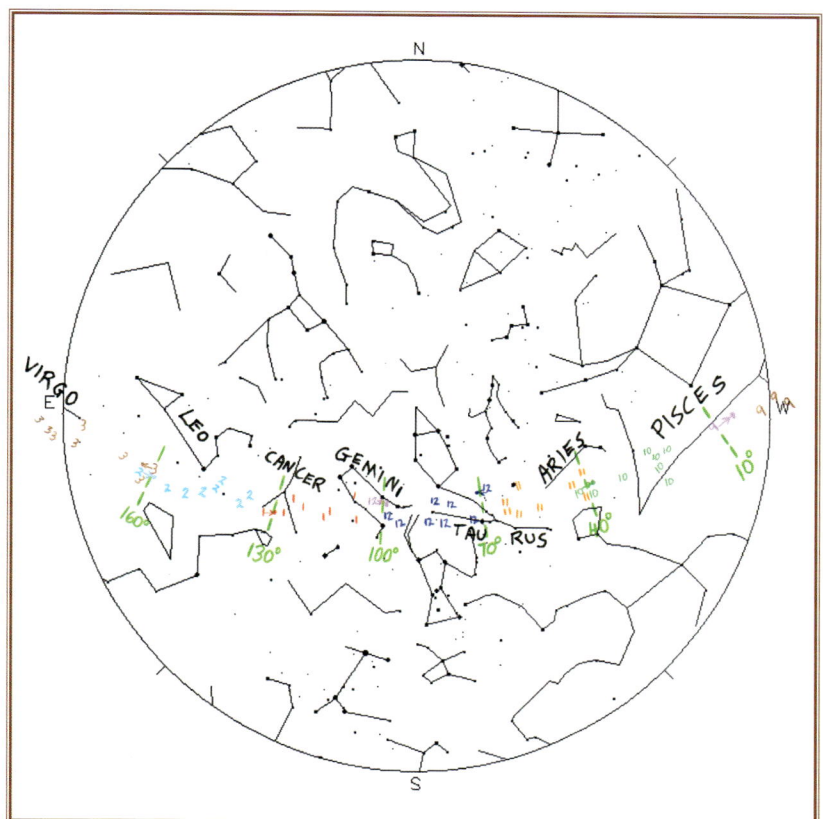

Figure 6-2 Positions of the Full Moon in September through March, 1990 through 1997, against the star patterns seen from Stonehenge. Zodiac constellations are named in the chart. Numbers designate months: 1 = January, 2 = February, ... to 12 = December. Dates and times of the Full Moon at Stonehenge were obtained from the Web site **http://aa.usno.navy.mil/data/docs/MoonPhase.html**. Sky maps containing the Full Moon were obtained from **www.fourmilab.to/yoursky**. Sometimes the Moon passed through the Full stage in daylight. For observation consistency, the sky map was generated for the midnight nearest the Full Moon time, at the beginning (0^h10^m) or end (23^h50^m) of the day on which the Moon passed through the Full phase. The vertical dashed lines border 30° segments of the circle around the sky, which best fit the Full Moon positions in each month. When the position at midnight fell a little outside the segment boundary, recalculation to find the position near dawn for a morning Full Moon, or dusk for an afternoon Full Moon, moved the position to the appropriate segment boundary (indicated by a small arrow and dot).

make up the zodiac, ζῴδια, *zódia* in Greek. The animals and humans and their seasonal comings and goings are related through stories, or myths, for teaching and for entertainment.

The particular set of living beings named in Figures 6-2 and 6-3 was selected by the Babylonians about 2500 years ago and adopted by the Greeks, then by the Romans, and on down to us. Other cultures imagined different animals or Gods, or objects, in the same twelve compartments of stars. Many cultures developed zodiacs, and myths to go with them.

One of the animals in the Babylonian zodiac was replaced by an Equal-arm Balance, to represent the lunar month in which the Spring Equalday/night occurred. The Arabic term for the Equalday/night is still *Al Istiwáa*, which means The Balance. Another Arabic term for Equalday/night is *Al Ítidal*, which also means The Balance. The Latin word for equal-arm-balance is *libra*, the name we use for the constellation.

The Babylonian New Year began with the first visible New Moon after the Spring Equalday. The following Full Moon appeared in The Balance (Libra). In the present era, the Full Moon that follows the Spring Equalday appears between Virgo and Leo, in March or April. During the last 2500 years, the seasons have moved a bit more than one constellation toward the west in the zodiac. The seasons regress through the entire zodiac every 26,000 years, due to precession of the Earth's spinning axis. Now the logic behind the name The Balance has been lost, since Libra no longer frames the Full Moon that follows the Spring Equalday/night. The constellation name *Libra* is now sometimes translated as "Scale," which is

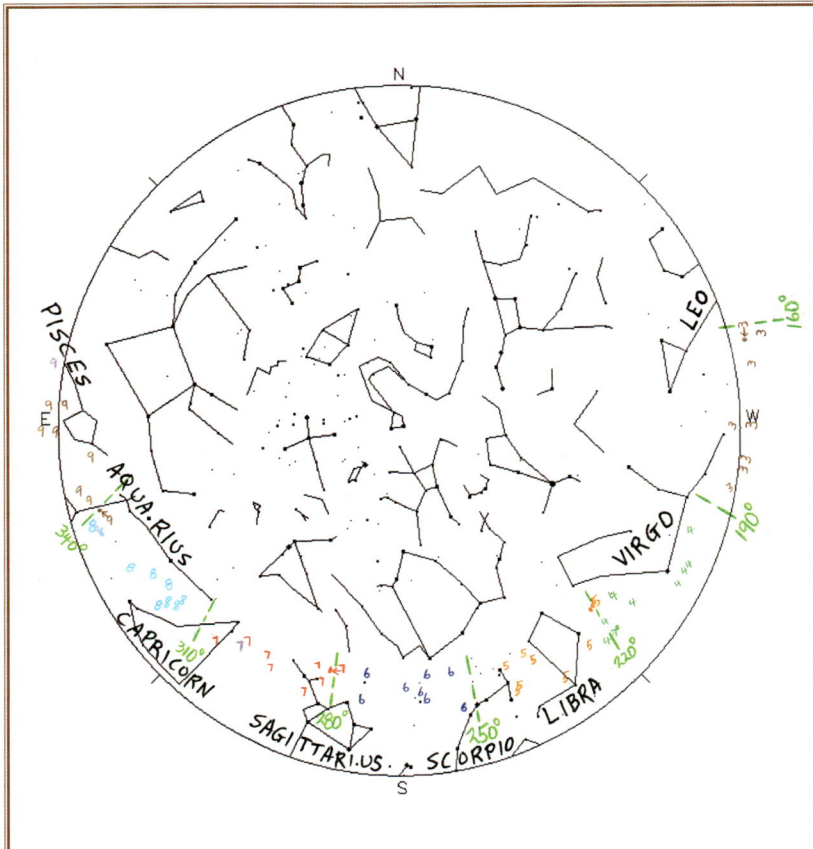

Figure 6-3 Positions of the Full Moon in March through September, 1990 through 1997, against the star patterns at Stonehenge. See the legend of Figure 6-2.

too general to be an appropriate image because "*libra*" requires "equal arms" for "balance."

When the Full Moon was in The Balance, the preceding New Moon had been near the Sun on the opposite side of the sky, in the constellation Ram, which in Latin is *Aries*. This is the reason why *Aries* is traditionally associated with the March Equalday/night in our literature, although the Sun on the Equalday now sits in the constellation Fishes, *Pisces,* approaching Water Carrier, *Aquarius,* and the nearest New Moon from year to year flits between the two constellations.

The Spring Equalday now occurs two days after the middle of March. I wonder if in a solar calendar about 2500 years ago, February was assigned 30 and 31 days in the leap year cycle, which would put the Equalday at the middle of March, and if that is the root of the astrological significance of what the Romans called the Ides of March. The Latin *iduo* means to divide, and perhaps *Idus* of March anciently referred to not only the month divided in halves, but to the day divided in halves. If the Moon happened to be Full, which is the half-point of the Moon cycle, on the March Equalnight, one had the three Ides of the day, month and Moon together! Beware the Ides of that March! It would happen each nineteenth year, in the *lunar-phase 19-year cycle*.

The double Ides of day and Moon occurred on the Equalday/night of March 17 to 18, 2003. The double Ides in March 2003 has entered history as the date the Christian United States of America invaded Islamic Iraq, on the day of the Jewish festival of Purim. The world's only remaining superpower consumes huge amounts of petroleum every day, and Iraq has lots of it. History repeats itself because human nature doesn't change.

* * * *

History procedes in spirals, rather than simply repeating itself. During the sixteenth to nineteenth centuries, Christianity was used as a Walrus' handkerchief by the Spanish and English superpowers to hide from the eyes of God the Carpenter the pillage and slaughter of people on other continents. The false front used by Americans now is Feminism/democracy. During the last fifty years English-speaking people have tried to win many *guerrillas*, a Spanish word meaning little wars, so we need a punchy English word for *guerrilla*. I suggest "**warino:** irregular war waged by small bodies acting more or less independently." The suffix "-ino" means small, as in neutrino. Like neutrinos, participants in a warino are difficult to detect, and individual impact events are irregularly spaced. The participants, *guerrilleros*, may be called "freedom fighters" or "terrorists," depending on your point of view. When warino replaces the present word "insurgency," American politicians might understand—if they wish to—what is happening now in the Middle East. I think American military strategists already know the difference, but industrial chieftains and politicians use language to obfuscate rather than to inform the public.

* * * *

The Full Moon is on the opposite side of the sky to the Sun. The Moon's orbit around the Earth wobbles a bit, so the Full Moon's path through the stars wobbles back and forth across the band shown in Figures 6-2 and 6-3. The Sun follows a much steadier path across the sky, near the centre of the Moon band. The Moon's path periodically crosses the Sun's path. If the Moon happens to cross the Sun's path when the Moon is exactly between the Sun and the Earth, the Moon blocks the Sun's light from reaching the Earth. The Sun is eclipsed. If the Earth happens to be exactly between the Sun and Moon when the Moon crosses the Sun's path through the stars, then the Sun's light cannot reach the Moon. The Full Moon is eclipsed.

Eclipses of the Sun can occur only during a No Moon period, the New Moon in almanacs. Eclipses of the Moon occur only in the Full Moon period. Eclipses can only occur when the Moon is in the Sun's path. This is why the Sun's path is called the Ecliptic, shown in Figures 6-4 and 6-5.

The Full Moon rises in the opposite direction to where the Sun sets, at about the same time. So the Full Moon near the Summer Solstice rises approximately where the Sun rises at the Winter Solstice. The Full Moon near the Winter Solstice rises approximately where the Sun rises at the Summer Solstice. The wobble of the Moon's orbit produces the north–south scatter of the points in Figures 6-2 and 6-3.

* * * *

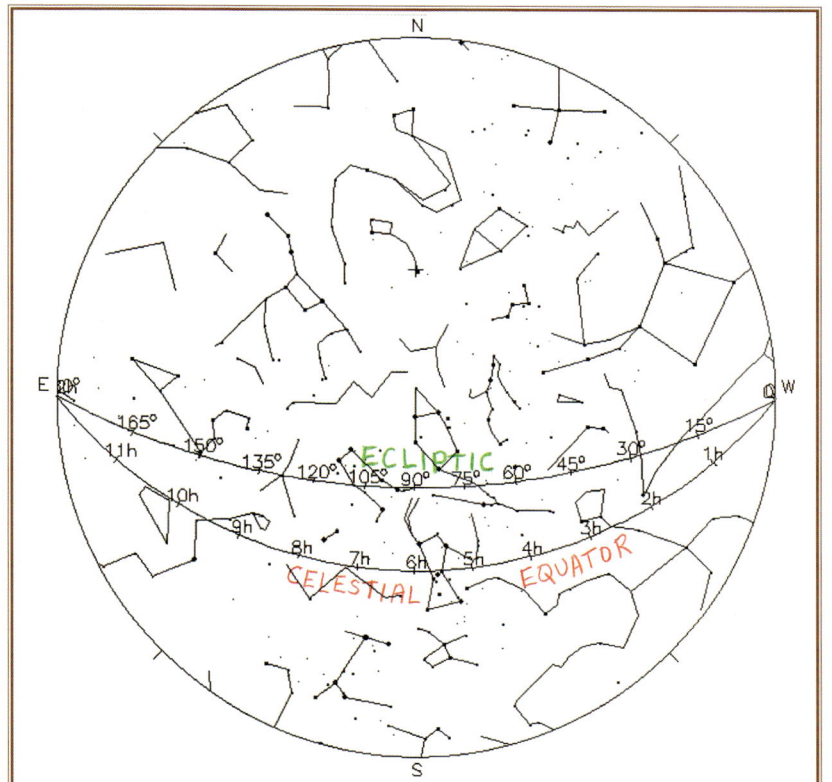

Figure 6-4 Background sky map for Figure 6-2, showing the Ecliptic and Celestial Equator. The Ecliptic is the apparent path of the Sun across the sky in its annual cycle. The Celestial Equator is the sky directly above the Earth's Equator.

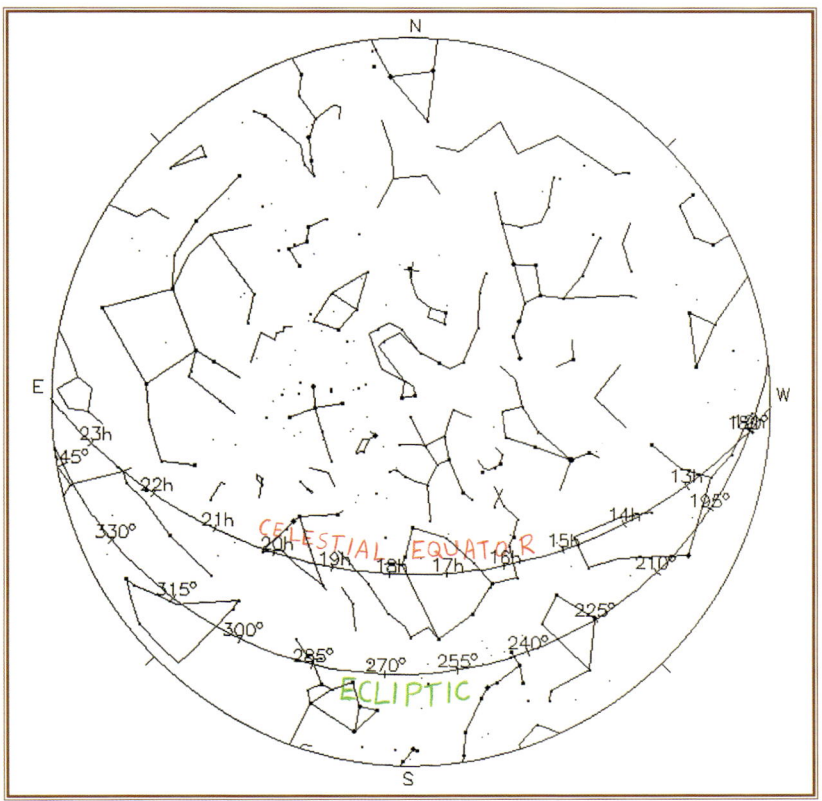

Figure 6-5 Background sky map for Figure 6-3, showing the Ecliptic and Celestial Equator. See the legend of Figure 6-4.

The Equalnights were marked in a general way in the Babylonian zodiac about 2500 years ago, by the symmetrical symbol of an Equal-arm Balance on one side of the sky and of a Ram's head on the opposite side. But the 5000-year-old solar calendar in Ómahkiyáahkóhtóohp marks the *exact* dates of the Equalnights, which is what the Anglo-Latin word Equinox originally meant. The exact dates are also marked in the somewhat younger Stonehenge. And yet the definition of Equinox is now wrong in all European languages. To investigate how that came about, we have to look briefly at the history of calendars and what events in the sky they are purported to represent.

Astronomy and Astrology

Astrology, the Greek ἀστρολογία, telling of the stars, originally meant what we now call astronomy, an account of the positions and motions of the stars. Not just the stars as we define them, but all the lights in the sky, including wandering planets, ejaculated meteors, and ghostly comets. It dealt with predictions of physical events such as the season-pivot dates, dates of eclipses, and so on. It was later extended to foretelling human events from which stars were visible and how they were moving relative to each other. The meaning "telling of the stars" changed to "what the stars say," and the word astronomy, ἀστρονομία, was used to mean physical astronomy.

Astrologers and astronomers were the ancient equivalent of present-day scientists. They looked for omens, such as the positions of Sun rise and set on the horizon to foretell the date of the next Equal-day/night or Solstice. They looked for conjunctions of particular planets with particular constellations, or with the Moon or another planet. These were thought to be associated with human fortune or misfortune.

The place where observations were made was the Temple, which was a sacred place.

The changing seasons have major effects on human lives. Present-day celebrations that are held near season-pivot dates, such as Christmas, Easter, Passover, and St. Patrick's Day, are carryovers from prehistoric times but are now given names associated with each particular religion.

The Equalnight date was exactly determinable. The counting of years was straightforward. However, the naming of years was influenced by politics, so the accumulation of an accurate long-count of years through several political regimes was difficult.

Some events in the sky generate fear or amazement. Occasionally, the Sun is eclipsed. The source of life is extinguished. At other times the Full Moon is eclipsed. The Goddess of Fertility, Mother Nature, is attacked. Times of crisis!

Eclipses occur in nearly regular cycles, and Skywatchers gradually worked out how to predict them. Perhaps it was then that prophets extended their prowess to predict events less dependable than seasons and eclipses. When they tried to predict human events from celestial and other omens, year counting and foretelling the season pivot-dates became secondary. Then calendars became a mess through lack of attention to accurate observations of the sky lights, and excessive attention to theory. Theory can be manipulated by politics. Accurate observation data cannot.

The Egyptians kept in touch with the sky. They took the solar year to be 365.25 days. Their solar calendar purportedly dates back to 4240 B.C. Several calendars have a purported year-one date of five or six thousand years ago. In the Jewish calendar, it is 3761 B.C. In the Mayan Long-Count, it is in 3114 B.C. In the Taoist calendar, year-one is 2697 B.C.

Complex mathematics developed along with writing, starting about 4000 years ago. Mathematics and writing developed in Vedic Persia and India, in Mesopotamia, and Egypt. The Greeks learned writing from the Phoenicians about 2600 years ago. The Greek Thales is often credited with learning astronomy and mathematics from the Egyptians, also about 2600 years ago, while others suggest that Greek advances in astronomy and mathematics followed the territorial conquests of the Macedonian Alexander about 2300 years ago. Alexandria became renowned for astronomy. Greeks made mathematical models to seek a physical understanding of the cosmos, separate from their mythological understanding of it.

It should be emphasized that models are only approximations of reality. Results from model calculations do not usually agree exactly with observed facts.

During the second and first centuries B.C., Rome developed into a superpower. Romans had a crude calendar. By the time Julius Caesar became chief, Rome had conquered Greece and had absorbed many of the refinements of Greek civilization. That included involvement with Egypt. While 54-year-old Julius was messing around with the 22-year-old Macedonian Queen Cleopatra of Egypt, he learned about the Egyptian solar calendar. The next year, in 45 B.C., he installed a slightly modified form of it as the Roman calendar. There were to be 365 days in each of three years, and 366 in the fourth, in a leap year cycle. We call this the Julian calendar. It took a few decades to apply it properly, so dates didn't settle down until A.D. 4. (All the dates in this brief epoch are essentially the same in the Julian and the present Gregorian calendars.)

The Julian calendar was in force as Christianity developed into an international religion, and was the framework on which the Christian festival cycle was eventually hung.

The Easter Date Problem: a.d. 190 to 2009

The date of Easter in the Gregorian calendar is officially stated as the first Sunday after the first Full Moon that occurs on or after the Spring Equinox (fixed at March 21). How did that come about?

Modern dictionaries in at least eleven European languages, and in American and Chinese, state that an Equinox is one of two times per year, March 20 or 21 and September 22 or 23, when the day and night are of equal length all over the Earth. Why bother to specify "all over the Earth?" And why do not all languages, such as Japanese, Hindi, Arabic, and Hebrew, make this specification?

The true dates of the Equalday/nights were marked in *Ómahkiyáahkóhtóohp* 5000 years ago, and in Stonehenge at least 4000 years ago. The accuracy of these ancient calendars illuminates the genius of some of the people who lived on the North American Plains and in England many thousands of years ago, and shows how much attention they paid to detail. Nitpickers are forever. At a time long before Julius Caesar, the Latin word *aequinoctium* meant exactly what it said, equalnight. The ancient-ancient Latin word *aequidiarium*, the ancient Greek *ἰσημερία*, and the ancient Irish *lá leathach* meant what they said, equalday. At some time between then and the time of compilation of European dictionaries, the information was discarded or lost. What happened? It is extraordinary that discovery of a Stone Age calendar in Canada should give insight into part of European history.

* * * *

The average length of a Julian year is slightly greater than a solar year, so Julian dates fall behind solar dates by one day every 128 years. If the length of the solar year had been accurately tabulated by the leap year cycle, the date of the Spring Equalday/night would have remained the same. However, by A.D. 1000, the Julian dates were eight days behind the solar season-pivot dates; if the Spring Equalday/night had been on March 21 to 22 in 45 B.C., in A.D. 1000 it would have slipped to March 13 to 14. It took another 582 years to legislate a refit of the calendar to the solar year. Such a long time to settle such a seemingly simple observational problem must have involved a complex political problem.

Religion in its spiritual form does not cause wars. Politics do. The rule "Do not do to others what you would not like done to you" is basic to spirituality and fosters peace. But politics are involved in any large organization, religious or not. Politics fashion the interrelatedness of the people within the organization, and the relations with other organizations. Politics sometimes require coercion. Organizational ritual involves politics.

The Easter date problem was to obtain a lunisolar formula that would give the same date for Easter everywhere on Earth.

The political background of the Easter date problem stretches back 1900 years. The writing of history is a plastic art. Even the translation of a text from its original language into another is a plastic art. That's why Muslims say that The Koran (*Al qur'An*, The Recitation) can only be read in Arabic. All translations of the Koran are only interpretations of it.

After understanding the Easter date problem, I retranslated some of the related Latin writings, especially about Eusebius, Bishop of Caesaria, to see the extent to which earlier translations had been shaped by the politics of the translator. Politics affect which writings are made public, or are suppressed or destroyed. Some of my own writings experienced that problem during the 1990s! Historic examples include the destruction of Mayan books by Spaniards during the sixteenth century, and the suppressive influence of the Inquisition on writings of Nicolaus Copernicus during 1513 to 1543, and of Galileo Galilei during 1615 to 1642.

In the early centuries of Christianity, the date of Easter was directly connected to that of Jewish Passover. In fact, the Greek word for Easter, Πάσχα, *Páscha*, which was accepted as the Latin word for it, *Pascha*, means Passover. It is a slight modification of the Hebrew word for Passover, פֶּסַח, *Pesach*. All European languages except

German and English refer to the Christian Spring Festival as Passover: Italian *Pasqua*, Spanish *Pascua*, Portuguese *Páscoa*, French *Pâque*, Dutch *Pasen,* Russian and Polish *Pascha,* Swedish *påsk,* and Irish *Cáisc* (P replaced by C and pronounced as *k*). The English Easter and German *Ostern* are named after the Teutonic Goddess of Fertility and Spring: *Éastre*, *Ostern*. The English word "paschal" pertains to both the Jewish and Christian Passovers.

Henceforth, I usually use the term Christian Passover for the Christian festival, to make it clear that it is a modification of the Jewish Passover. The mental connection with Judaism remains strong. The Spring Festival of the Teutonic Goddess of Fertility, *Éastre*, is not a concern here.

Some Early Christians celebrated their Passover each year on the day that Jews sacrificed their Passover lamb, because St. Paul had said that Jesus was sacrificed as a Passover lamb. This happened on the "14th day of the Moon," Full Moon Day, in the barley-harvest month in Judaea. Barley harvest usually occurred during the month that contained the Spring Equalday, but sometimes weather conditions advanced or retarded the harvest.

Other Early Christians celebrated the Passover of Resurrection three days after Jewish Passover, because Jesus' Last Supper was a Jewish Passover meal, a Seder. Death passed over Jesus, as it had the Jewish children in Egypt 1300 years earlier. These Christians celebrated on whatever day of the week their Passover occurred. Still other Christians celebrated their Passover only on the Sunday after Jewish Passover, because the first day of the week, Sunday, had been selected as the Christian Holy Day, to separate it from the Jewish seventh day Sabbath, the day of rest and worship.

Christianity was spreading through different countries and cultures, so there was no uniformity in Christendom.

The Hebrews had a lunisolar calendar. They still do. Each month begins with the first visible crescent of the New Moon, the first day of the Moon. Each day is taken to begin at Sun set. The Moon is usually Full on the fourteenth day of the Moon. Two thousand years ago, the year was taken to begin with the month of barley harvest. The month was called אָבִיב, *Aviv*, which means "head of grain filled, but still soft." The barley would be ready to harvest later that month, and Passover began at the Full Moon on the fourteenth day.

While many Christians in the early years were converted Jews, most of the growth of Christianity during the early centuries occurred among non-Jews. The official calendar of the Roman Empire was solar. The timing of Christian Passover was tied to a lunisolar calendar. It still is. Fitting a lunisolar festival date into a solar calendar is not straightforward, so politics had an influence.

Beginning with the Gospel According to St. John, written about one hundred years after Jesus lived, texts were modified and expanded a little to separate Jesus from his Jewishness. There was a movement to separate Christian Passover from Jewish Passover. In A.D. 190, Christians everywhere were urged to celebrate their Passover only on the Sunday after Jewish Passover. In A.D. 325 at the Council of Nicaea (a city 100 kilometres southeast of Constantinople), the date of Christian Passover was formally separated from that of the Jewish festival. It was *legislated* that Christian Passover should be celebrated only on the Sunday following Jewish Passover. Some Christians continued to celebrate their Passover on the fourteenth day of the Moon, the Full Moon on whatever day of the week it occurred, and were denounced as *Quartodecimans*, Fourteenthers. Later Popes condemned them as heretics.

The main objective of the Nicaean Council in A.D. 325 was to settle a dispute about the perceived relationship between the members of the Holy Trinity: God the Father, Jesus, and the Holy Ghost. Were they all the same, or was each slightly different? The meeting was dominated by controversy and acrimony. No record of it has survived into present times, if one was ever made. Several centuries later, a biased summary of the Council's decisions was pieced together, mainly from writings of Eusebius, Bishop of Caesaria, between A.D. 325 and 340. Eusebius was a participant in the Council, not a neutral observer.

Acrimony in later centuries surrounded many things, including one letter in one word that was supposedly used at that Council. Surprisingly the letter is an *iota*, which is used in English to symbolize "a tiny little bit." (Ever heard the order "Don't change one iota of that!", or "Not one jot!"? Jot is Anglo-German for iota. Here's where they come from.) The language of the Council was Greek. In later writings about conclusions from the Council, someone either inserted an *iota* into one word or removed it from the word that described the relationship between the members of The Holy Trinity. Some authorities said that God the Father, Jesus, and The Holy Ghost are

ὁμοούσιαν, *homoousian*, of the *same* essence, same being.

Other authorities said that the members of The Holy Trinity are ὁμοιούσιαν, *homoiousian*, of a *similar* substance, similar being.

The records I found are all from the side that wanted no *i* between the two *o*'s. But the surviving vitriolic attacks on people who used the extra *i* indicated that the *homoiousian* faction had political clout at some time. The corrosive language indicates that the theology was dominated by politics. I recall a philosophy prof in my undergraduate days admonishing us, "Don't get theology mixed up with religion!" Religion is a deeper, more soulful thing than theology.

While reading different versions of the first two thousand years of Christian Church history, the missing and erased Watergate tapes after the 1972 presidential election of Richard Nixon often came to mind. Historic records are continually revised. A recent example is America's fraudulent "Weapons of Mass Destruction" and "War on Terrorism" justifications for invading Iraq on the festival of Purim in 2003, to try to take control of the oil underground.

It amazes me that wars fought for the material gain of leaders are paid for by the blood and taxes of citizenries. Mental control of the taxpayers and soldiers is gained by a nonhomogeneous psychological process. Leaders offer a phantom of personal gain to the citizens, use the truncheon of patriotism, and generate fear by bestializing the people they want to rob, through campaigns of lies about "the enemy." It's a shell game rooted in the nearly universal characteristic of greed.

Dates of the Jewish and Christian Passovers

The two Passovers are Movable Feasts, because the Moon-phase dates in the solar calendar change from year to year in a 19-year cycle. Official dates of Passover were sent out each year from Headquarters in Jerusalem and Rome. As the beliefs of Christianity and Judaism spread around the world, it took too long for messages to reach regions far from Headquarters. The official dates were uncertain in remote regions. In Judaism, a second Seder was added to the celebration of Passover in countries far from Jerusalem, so that one of the ceremonial meals would probably be on the correct day. Christianity became embedded in many cultures, so the setting of a uniform date for Christian Passover was difficult. The Christian bureaucracy became more and more concerned that all Christians celebrate their Passover on the same date. Politics required that it be at least one day away from Jewish Passover.

Writings of Eusebius of Caesarea about the Council of Nicaea were later interpreted as meaning that Christian Passover should be celebrated everywhere on the Sunday after the Full Moon after Spring Equalday, Εἰαρινὴ Ἰσημερία in Greek, or Spring Equalnight, *Vernum Aequinoctium* in Latin.

However, people in different regions didn't agree on the Equalday/night date. The Syrians and Mesopotamians had one idea. The Alexandrians (Greeks in Egypt) had another. Romans had another. When Christianity reached Ireland, they had another. The struggle endured for centuries.

Alexandrians and Romans

Alexandrian astronomers, according to some of the reports that still survive, took the Spring Equalday as March 21 in A.D. 325. However, from all the cooking of the books that seems to have been done during the last 2000 years, I wonder whether the March 21 Equalday date applied to the year of the Council of Nicaea, A.D. 325, or whether it actually applied to the time of Julius Caesar and sexy Cleopatra, followed by the beginning of the Julian calendar in 45 B.C. Different reports suggest that Romans took the date of the Spring Equalnight in A.D. 325 to be March 18, 21, or 25.

The English word "equinox," with its physically impossible definition of day and night having equal length on the same date everywhere on Earth, did not exist at that time, so it is not relevant to the early dates.

By 45 B.C., Romans had learned the difference between the *Aequidiarium*, Equalday, of variable date and the *Aequinoctium*, Equalnight, of constant date. The date of the Equalday flip-flopped back and forth across the constant Equalnight date every two years during each leap year cycle. Julius Caesar and Tullius Cicero (died in 43 B.C.) both used the term *aequinoctium* in their writings. *Aequidiarium* and *aequidies* (another word for Equalday) were said to be ancient terms for *aequinoctium*. The switch was probably made to obtain a constant reference date for the calendar from year to year.

Romans probably chose the nights of March 21 to 22 and September 29 to 30 as the Equalnights when they adapted the Egyptian solar calendar to make their own in 45 B.C. (Dates for this period are the same in the Julian and the present Gregorian calendars). The purported March 25 "original date of the Vernal Equinox in the Julian

Calendar" seems to have been proposed more than 1600 years later; the three-day slippage of the Julian date between 45 B.C. and A.D. 325 was added to March 22, the original date of the end of the Equalnight. It is illuminating that March 25 is the date of the Christian festival of the Annunciation, commemorating an angel's announcement to the Virgin Mary that "The Holy Ghost shall come upon thee, and the power of the Highest shall overshadow thee: therefore also that holy thing which shall be born of thee shall be called the Son of God." (*St. Luke 1:35*, King James version, 1611.) And nine months later, December 25, is the Christian festival for the birth of the Son of God, Jesus.

The Greeks never switched from Equalday to Equalnight for their calendrical reference. The word ἰσονίκτιον, *isoniktion*, Equalnight, seems to occur only in a Latin-to-Greek dictionary, not in original Greek writings. The ancient terms ἰσημερία, *aequidiarium*, Equalday, were originally nearly equivalent to *aequinoctium*, Equalnight, differing by only twelve hours. The word "equinox" came into use less than a thousand years ago (the Old English word for Equalnight is *emnniht*), by which time the date of its parent *aequinoctium* had become uncertain and politically manipulable.

Council of Nicaea

By A.D. 325, the flip-flopping true dates of the Spring Equalday had most likely slipped to March 18 and 19 in the Julian calendar. The three hundred or so bishops who participated at Nicaea (estimated numbers range from about two hundred to one thousand) had greater things to argue about than the accuracy of the Julian calendar. They wanted a uniform statement on what Christians are to believe. Subsequent revisions of that statement produced the bureaucratic Nicene Creed with its group-committing "We believe - - -," which is still in competition with the crisp Apostles' Creed and its personally responsible "I believe - - -." The words indicate that the original Apostles' Creed was that of the ὁμοιούσιαν folk, whereas the later Nicene Creed is from the ὁμοούσιαν faction. The Nicaean revisionists removed the ι.

The violence of the *iota* quarrel caused the admonition, "Don't change one iota of that!" to remain in use for the next 1600 years.

The Councillors also wanted all Christians to celebrate their Passover on the same date, but they depended upon astronomers to determine the Equalday, so accuracy of the calendar was not a Nicaean problem. Unfortunately, astronomers in different places came up with different dates for the Equalday, because some of them were using theoretical estimates rather than direct observations of Sun rises and sets. The method of direct observation had been accurate and unambiguous for thousands of years. But theoretical estimates are based on models. Different models gave different values.

After many centuries of international councils and coercion, most branches of the Church adopted March 21 as the Equalday date. By A.D. 600, the true date of the exactly twelve-hour day had drifted to oscillating between March 16 and 17, but in the struggle to obtain a uniform date everywhere, a firm March 21 was more important than an accurate date of the Equalday. Besides, who would notice?

Perhaps the people of Ireland did.

Britain and Ireland

Christianity entered Britain under the Romans in the second century A.D., according to the historian Bede (an Old English or Saxon name possibly pronounced *Beedeh* or *Baydeh,* instead of the modern English *Beed*). Christianity declined with the Roman regime in the third and fourth centuries. Some of the Celts remained Christian. St. Patrick was a Celtic Briton missionary who took Christianity to Ireland in the fifth century.

The Celtic people who lived in Ireland were the original Scots. Patrick had Christianized many of them by A.D. 460. The Scots and earlier occupants of Ireland had known how to determine the Equalday for about 3000 years. But calendars were not uniform in Europe, and Ireland was a long way from Jewish Passover festivals, so the dating of Christian Passover was probably not a serious problem there.

Scots crossed from Ireland to invade the Picts in northern Britain about 1700 years ago. The Picts and Scots became Christianized a century or two later (Saints Ninian and Patrick). The Scots and Picts in A.D. 600 dated Christian Passover according to the Full Moon and Sunday formula, but might have used the correct date of the Equalday.

By A.D. 700, Christians in most of Europe had been coerced into using March 21 as the Equalday. But by then the true date of Equalday was March 15 to16. The Scots, Picts, and Britons were accused of celebrating Christian Passover too soon. The calendar in Stonehenge shows that the ancient Britons also knew how to determine the Equalday.

The only surviving record of goings-on in Britain during these early centuries is Bede's *Ecclesiastical History of the English People*. Bede lived from about A.D. 637 to 735, near the present Newcastle. He was a Priest when he wrote the *Ecclesiastical History*. He wrote a lot about the stubbornness of the Scots and Picts who refused to accept the Paschal dates issued from Rome. He did not say that the Scots had an earlier date for the Equalnight, but he recorded lengthy arguments about why they should obey the Pope, and not celebrate Passover early. He recorded an entire, long letter from Abbot Ceolfrid to King Naitan of the Picts in 710, which included the statement that the Egyptians exceed all other learned men in the calculation of the Equalnight, which usually happens on March 21, "as we also prove by inspection of a clock." The clock at that time must have been a sundial or a mechanical waterclock. Neither device would have been accurate to the minute over a twelve-hour period to determine the Equalday/night. So it was all smoke and mirrors to enforce uniformity.

By 716, the last of the Scots and Picts accepted the Alexandrian date for the Paschal Equalnight. At least the lunar-phase 19-year cycle that was used to calculate the date of the Paschal Full Moon was okay within a day or two. Thereafter they celebrated Christian Passover on the date dictated by Rome. It may have been then that the Scots pretended to Christianize their pagan celebration of the true Equalday by naming it after St. Patrick. The Spring Equalday, *earrachúil lá leathach*, actually Spring Equalnight Eve, is still commemorated as St. Patrick's Day.

At some later date, the Scots on the island of Ireland called themselves Irish, and the Scots who had taken over northern Britain called their land Scotland.

The English people never did accept the name Passover for the Christian Spring Festival. They continue to call it Easter after the Teutonic Spring Goddess of Fertility, *Éastre*. The Germans, who are the post-Roman ancestors of the Anglo-Saxons, also continue to name the Christian Spring Festival *Ostern*, after this Goddess. Her origins trace back to the Mesopotamian Goddess *Ishtar* and to the Vedic Goddess of Dawn, *Ushas*. The mythologies of *Ushas* and *Ishtar* flow into the mythologies of *Éastre* and Jesus.

The words Easter and east are from the Greek word ἠώς, *eos*, which means "red sky in the morning," dawn, and ἠώς is from the

Sanskrit *ushās*, dawn. Dawn is the harbinger of the Sun. A new beginning in the offing.

The English also continue with the Nordic God and Goddess names for six days of the week: Sun, Moon (wife of Sun), Tiw, Woden, Thor, and Frigg (wife of Woden). The seventh day is named after Saturn, the Roman God of Fertility and Agriculture, perhaps because there wasn't an appropriate seventh Nordic diety. However, Sun, Moon, and Saturn are a Celestial Holy Trinity. Saturn is the bright planet with the longest orbital period, twenty-nine years. After conversion to Christianity, perhaps the Anglo-Saxons were willing to pray to southern Gods, the Christian Holy Trinity, but northern winters could be deadly. So the northern Gods and Goddesses were most likely retained for good luck. Why take chances? The most powerful pagan deities, Sun and Moon, are still presented in Christian churches around the world. Insurance.

Many years ago, a Haitian in Port-au-Prince told me that 90 percent of Haitians are Christian and 100 percent are Voodoo. In fact I did not understand our Christian rituals until I learned something of the ancient Voodoo religion.

Five centuries of politics and papal bulls finally settled the universal dating of Christian Passover in 716. The calendar problem then lay dormant for another 800 years. In the meantime, the true date of the Equalday/night receded farther and farther from the papal March 21. But who noticed? Even the Irish seemed to forget why they celebrated St. Patrick on the true Equalday.

Portuguese in the South Seas

In 1471, Portuguese sailors on the Atlantic Ocean crossed the Equator for the first time. It is probably not a coincidence that soon afterwards, in 1475, the Italian astronomer/mathematician Paolo Toscanelli measured the error in the Julian calendar date of the Summer Solstice by putting a small hole in the top of the enormous dome of Santa Maria del Fiore in Florence, producing a pinhole image of the noonday Sun on the floor of the north transept, 90 metres below. The sharp-edged image of the noonday Sun moved south along the floor a few millimetres per day near the Solstice, then came to a standstill and reversed direction. This allowed the exact day of the Summer Solstice to be determined. I have not been able to find the actual date he recorded for the Solstice, possibly because his original records have been lost or destroyed. Subsequent fiddling with the calendar confused the result, and maybe it was not transmitted by later authors. But in the Julian calendar of 1475 the Solstice occurred on June 9, not on the "official Solstice date June 21."

The transept was not long enough for a direct determination of the Equalnight and Winter Solstice dates.

During the late fifteenth and early sixteenth centuries, European explorer/navigators sailed into the Southern Hemisphere and around the world. They navigated by the Sun and stars. The constellations in the night sky gradually changed as the explorers sailed south. In the Southern Hemisphere there is no North Star. There is a South Star, which rotates about the Celestial South Pole. For the past 6000 years, it has been one or another of the stars of the constellation Hydrus. Navigators had to make new sky charts for the southern region. The constant reference was the Sun, but the path of the Sun through the sky changed. The direction of the Sun's zenith moved northerly as they sailed south; from March to September, the Sun rise and set points on the horizon moved closer together, and days got shorter; from September to March, the rise and set points moved farther apart, and days got longer.

The voyages lasted several years. The Equalnights are the key to an exact solar calendar, and they also determine the exact compass points east and west, so they were probably determined each March and September as part of the sky-charting process. Equalday/night is when the Sun rise and set over flat land are observed to occur in opposite directions along the same straight line (Appendix 6). The true Equalnights in Europe were twelve days ahead of the official dates in 1471. But the dates of the Equalnights changed with latitude (see Table on page 223).

Among those who would have noticed the latitude dependence of the patterns of lights in the sky was Bartholomew Diaz, who in 1488 sailed from Portugal to the south tip of Africa and back. In 1497, Vasco da Gama sailed from Portugal to south of Africa and to India. He stayed in the zone of the Indian Ocean until 1499 and might have noticed the change in dates of the Equalnights. In 1505, Ferdinand Magellan sailed from Portugal to India by the same route as da Gama. He stayed in the zone of the Indian Ocean until 1513, and then returned to Portugal. In 1519 he sailed from Spain, south and west across the Atlantic, to find a western route to the East Indies. He sailed around the south end of South America,

54° S, into the Pacific Ocean in 1520.

The navigators almost certainly noted the change of Equalnight dates with latitude. Magellan was killed in the Philippine Islands in 1521, but one of his five initial ships made it back to Spain in 1522, by the route south of Africa. The survivors' navigation sky-charts would have created great interest in Portugal, the nation of great navigators.

In the North Temperate Zone where our calendar was developed, the Sun passes through a southerly arc each day. As one faces the direction of the arc, the Sun rises on the left and sets on the right. In the South Temperate Zone, the Sun passes through a northerly arc. As one faces the direction of the arc, the Sun rises on the right and sets on the left. The solar clock seems to move backwards in the southern region! This news almost certainly spread from the navigators to observer-astronomers and to people concerned with the calendar in Europe.

At the southern tip of Africa, 35° S, the March Equalnight is six days later and the September Equalnight is six days earlier than in Europe. At 20° S, the differences are even greater: the March Equalnight is ten days later and the September Equalnight is nine days earlier than in Rome. The waxing-waning Moon cycle is little affected by latitude, so the date of the Sunday after the Full Moon after the March Equalnight could be a month later south of the Equator than in Europe. Which date should be selected for the celebration of Passover south of the Equator? If Christians everywhere were to celebrate Passover on the same date, the formula used to determine the date had to be changed. This news must have reached the Pope early in the 1500s. The Christian Passover date problem was back again. Progress always has a down side.

Popes had struggled for many centuries to get Christians in all countries to celebrate Passover on the same date. It had taken six hundred years to settle on a uniform date for the Equalnight. Now, eight hundred years later, not only did *sailors* know that the official date of the March Equalnight in Europe was twelve days in error, they knew that the true dates vary with latitude. Correction of the calendar would have been a relatively minor problem. But the formula for setting the date of Passover would give different dates at different latitudes. Jesus resurrected only once. There could be only one Christian Passover date.

One can imagine Bishops telling explorers, "Stick to sailing!

That's what you're trained for!" I have been told the like myself, in several different subjects.

It took about thirteen Popes and nearly a century to solve the Passover date problem, from about Alexander VI in 1500 (lustful father of licentious Cesare Borgia, lascivious Lucrecia Borgia, and ten other bastards) to Gregory XIII in 1582. To understand the magnitude of the problem, consider the politico–religious environment in Europe at that time. The fifteenth and sixteenth centuries were a period of great religious turmoil, even without the resurfaced Passover date problem. There was corruption and scandalous behaviour within the Vatican and the Church hierarchy. For example, Alexander VI made his bastard son Cesare a cardinal at age eighteen. Cesare, a Prince of the Church, was the prototype of Niccolo Machiavelli's *Il Principe*. The book was written in 1505, but not published until 1515, eight years after the disgraced Cesare's death in battle.

Muslims and Jews had finally been cleared out of Spain in 1492. The Inquisitors of Heretical Depravity were back in business dispatching stragglers and Christian deviants. Protestants in France, Germany, and Switzerland were causing trouble for the corrupted papal bureaucracy.

Nicolaus Copernicus in 1515 wrote about a universe centred on the Sun, an idea that had been proposed by Aristarchus 1765 years earlier, but had not flourished. The official Christian position was that the Earth was the centre of the universe. The Earth-centred universe theory based on what was known at the time was no crazier than the BigBang-originated universe theory based on what is known now. Both explain some observations but not others. Both theories became enshrined in a Theological Establishment, the BigBang one being a faction of Applied Mathematics that is inadequately disguised as Theoretical Physics.

In 1515, Copernicus took part in a Lateran Commission on calendar reform under Pope Leo X. The Lateran Basilica is the Cathedral Church of the Pope as the Bishop of Rome. No calendrical change was accepted, but the Commission did forbid Priests to have concubines.

In 1517, Martin Luther nailed his *95 Theses* to the front door of the Wittenberg Castle Church. In 1543, Copernicus' book *On the Revolutions of the Heavenly Spheres* was published, just before his death. The book had been finished in 1530, but the aggressive attitude of the stressed Church toward revision of its model of an

Earth-centred universe, or the revision of any other opinion in the ecclesiastical domain, caused Copernicus to not publish it. A colleague urged publication of the book and tended it when seventy-year-old Copernicus was in failing health. It was published with a cautionary prologue, stating that the Sun-centred universe was a hypothesis, with the Earth rotating on its axis once per day and revolving around the fixed Sun once per year, and the planets revolving around the Sun in periods of different lengths. During the next few decades, the Copernican model gained increasing support among astronomers. It continued to be opposed by the Church.

More and more explorers and merchant mariners were sailing to and from the South Seas, so knowledge of the calendar error, and consequently the Easter date problem and the stubborn Church bureaucracy, would have spread.

In 1534, the English Parliament created the Church of England, with King Henry VIII as its head. It renounced the Papacy, evidently not solely because Henry was having difficulty siring a male heir and wanted to try more wives. During the following decades, England became a naval power on the Ocean Sea (Atlantic Ocean). After the defeat of the Catholic Spanish Great Navy (*L'Armada Grande*) in 1588, Protestant England was the dominant power on the oceans.

The 1500s were filled with strife and Church Reformation. The Catholic Church tried to rectify many of its errors and practices. The Council of Trent (1545–1563) failed to solve the Passover date problem.

Now consider a solution to the Southern Hemisphere Equalnight date complication in this tense ecclesiastical atmosphere. The Latin word *Aequinoctium* actually means, and had meant for nearly two thousand years, that the lengths of an adjacent day and night are truly equal. The Romans had switched the calendrical reference point from *Aequidiarium* (Equalday), which in Europe moves back and forth between adjacent dates every two years, to *Aequinoctium* (Equalnight), which has a constant date for many decades. Expressed in terms of the Julian calendar in 45 B.C., the exactly twelve-hour day was March 21 in the first two years of each leap year cycle and March 22 in the second two years of each cycle, whereas the exactly twelve-hour night was always March 21 to 22. The Roman measurement of Equalday/night dates at that time had to be accurate to the day.

The dates of the Equalday/night (Appendix 6) and the Full Moon are determinable by simple observations. But the date of Christian

Passover was in practice based on March 21 in the Julian solar calendar and calculation of the following Full Moon date from the not-quite-exact lunar-phase 19-year cycle. For centuries, Tables of future dates of Passover had been published and distributed to all churches. The Tables sometimes extended more than a century into the future. By 1570, the date of the March Equalnight in the Tables was wrong by thirteen days, and the phase of the Moon was out by several days. As long as the errors were the same everywhere, the correction was not urgent. But the latitude problem, and knowledge of it outside the ecclesiastical community, made revision urgent. And who knows what the Protestants would do if they attacked the problem?

Thirteen Popes, with their Councils of Bishops and astronomer advisors, struggled for more than eighty years to reform the calendar. Reform must not disrupt the traditional dating of festivals and must have them celebrated on the same dates everywhere on Earth. All variable-date festivals are anchored to the Passover date. Council after Council could not agree on a solution to the latitude problem. The latitude problem is not mentioned in any of the documents, but it seems to be the only reason that would complicate an otherwise simple calendrical adjustment. A deception seemed politically advisable, but evidently there was strong objection to it from some of the participants.

Gregory XIII the Lawyer Pope: The Gregorian Deception and the Equinox that isn't

It seems that by 1582, Pope Gregory XIII decided to force a conclusion. On February 24, 1582, he published his Proclamation *Inter Gravissimas*, "Among the Weighty Pastoral Duties ..." I have translated relevant parts of the Latin text to display the problem and the chosen solution.

There are seventeen sections in the document. It refers to how long and hard people worked, even at night. The calendar problem had to be resolved by better predictive cycles of the Sun and Moon, so that Tables of future dates of festivals could continue to be issued from Rome. Below are excerpts from the sections indicated.

    II.   ... concerns the annual recurrence of Passover and other festivals, which depend upon measurement of motions of the sun and moon.

    IV.   ... indisputably requires that calendar restoration be

V. ... to restore the vernal equalnight to 21 March, remove from the month of October 1582 ten days, including the fifth to the fourteenth, ...

XIV. ... we want all ... Church leaders to introduce the new calendar, and ... begin to use it after these ten days have been removed from the month of October 1582. **As for those who live in remote regions, ... they are allowed to make the same change in the month of October in 1583 or, of course, whatever year our letter reaches them.** (*My emphasis added*)

XVI. ... to places in the whole Christian world (orb) ..., all people everywhere ...

How did the Gregorian adjustment solve the problem caused by the latitude dependence of the Equalnight? The latitude dependence of the date of Passover was solved by changing the anchor date from the Equalday/night to the Sun Zenith Midaltitude, SZM, the time when the Sun is directly above the Equator. SZM refers to a unique latitude, the Equator, so is independent of latitude.

In Europe, roughly the middle of the North Temperate Zone, the March Equalnight occurs three nights before the Sun reaches the Equator. In the South Temperate Zone, March is in the autumn, and near the mid-South Temperate Zone, Equalnight occurs 3 nights after the Sun has crossed the Equator. To pick the Sun above the Equator as the anchor point, all they had to do was shift the anchor date to 3 days later in March in Rome. The Julian calendar was 13 days late. They cut 10 days instead of 13 from the calendar.

Why not just say so back in 1515, when Copernicus took part in an attempt to revise the calendar? Evidently the tension between astronomers and Church bureaucrats made such a solution dangerous to astronomers in those troubled times. In 1582, the Council said that the calendar had slipped 10 days since the Council of Nicaea in A.D. 325, and that Equalnight occurred on March 21 in 325. There is no evidence that Churchmen in 325 were aware that the date of Equalnight had slipped 3 days since the calendar was begun in 45 B.C. They might have "checked it with a clock," as they did in A.D. 710, and got just as wrong a result. It appears that the date of the Spring Equalnight in the original Julian calendar was the night of March 21 to 22.

Gregory XIII's *Inter Gravissimas* continued to use the old name *vernum aequinoctium*, Spring Equalnight, for the new SZM anchor date of Passover. This hid the fact that the nature of the anchor date had changed, and protected the concept of papal infallibility. It also gave an incorrect definition to the term Equalnight. The date when the Sun is above the Equator is not an Equalnight anywhere, not even on the Equator (see Table on page 223).

San Petronio Basilica, Bologna

In ancient times, all specialized knowledge was considered to be sacred, including calendars. The calendrical device, the readable lunisolar calendar, was constructed in a sacred place. Stonehenge and *Ómahkiyáhkóhtóohp* are sacred places. Pollen and hawthorn berries are still left as offerings at Stonehenge, and longleaf sage, tobacco, and raptor feathers at *Ómahkiyáhkóhtóohp*.

Several centuries ago solar calendars were built into a few Christian basilicas and cathedrals. In A.D. 1575, the Dominican friar Egnazio Danti constructed a *Meridiana* sundial in San Petronio Basilica in Bologna, Italy. A 25-millimetre diameter hole in a 9-millimetre thick stone slab, sloped at 60° toward the north from vertical, was put in the top of the south wall, and a marble meridian strip was laid south to north into the stone floor in line with it. At solar noon each sunny day, the circular image of the Sun crossed the meridian strip. The device acted like a pinhole camera. At the Winter Solstice, when the noon Sun was lowest in the sky, the Sun image crossed the north end of the meridian line near the north entrance of the Basilica. At the Summer Solstice, the noon Sun was highest in the sky, and the Sun image crossed the south end of the meridian line near the centre of the Basilica. The months, Solstices, and "Equalnights" were marked along the meridian line. The word *Aequinoctium* on the present form of the device, redesigned by Gian Domenico Cassini in 1655 when construction of the Basilica was nearing completion, will have to be changed to the Latin equivalent of SZM.

The date of construction of the original *Meridiana* in 1575 is so close to the 1572 election date of Gregory XIII as Pope, and to the Gregorian subterfuge of 1582, that this sundial in San Petronio might have been constructed as a theatrical prop to support the ten-day adjustment of the calendar. The adjustment hid the three-day switch from Equalnight to SZM for the calculation of the date of Passover, by keeping the old name for the new anchor date. Why was it built in San Petronio in Bologna?

Gregory XIII had been born Ugo Buoncompagni in Bologna, in 1502. He studied at the University of Bologna and graduated as doctor of canon law and civil law. He later taught jurisprudence at the University. His brilliance was recognized, and he was called to Rome for papal appointments. He was a papal deputy in the Council of Trent, 1545–1563, so was well aware of the longstanding calendar problem. To increase his official impact, he was appointed Bishop in 1558, without being ordained a Priest. He was appointed Cardinal Priest in 1564, and elected Pope in 1572. Evidently he was good at his job during the troubles. Law was more important than saintly behaviour. His bastard son Giacomo was appointed to high office within the Church, in the manner of the times.

San Petronio Basilica was planned in the late fourteenth century to be the largest church in Italy. It was the time of the Great Split in the Church between Rome and Avignon, 1378 to 1417. Construction of the church began in 1390, but was very slow. It never got beyond the huge transept. Popes finally decided that the biggest church would be built in Rome. The nave of a church is supposed to be oriented east–west with the altar at the east end, so the San Petronio transept was oriented north–south. The transept was finished off as the basilica, with its altar in the south end. San Petronio was a large church with a long meridional axis. Perfect for the construction of a *Meridiana* inside it. Pope Gregory XIII knew about that. The University of Bologna had a strong reputation in both law and science. Copernicus had studied canon law there in 1496 to 1500 and was also assistant to the astronomer Domenico Novarra.

San Petronio in Bologna was an excellent place to set up a deceptive switch from Equalnight to SZM as the anchor date for Christian festivals.

I admired the marble bust of Copernicus in a foyer of the *Accademia delle Scienze* in Bologna when I lectured there many years ago. Phyl and I have watched the noonday image of the Sun cross the *Meridiana* in San Petronio. If we are still mobile when *Aequinoctium* has been replaced by *Sol Vertex Medaltitudo* in that *Meridiana*, we'll go to see it again.

How *Ómahkiyáahkóhtóohp* Got Us Here

We had a frustrating few years looking for Equinox Sunrise and set observation lines in *Ómahk*, finding none. Finally, the calendar in that Temple led to the discovery that "Equinox" has since 1582 been a word intended to deceive, when Latin *aequinoctium* and its European equivalents were given a physically impossible definition: *when the Sun is directly above the Equator, day and night are of equal length all over the Earth.*

When the Sun is directly above the Equator the length of the night is 11.9 hours at the Equator and 0.0 hours at the North and South Poles. The length of the adjacent daylight period is 12.1 hours at the Equator and six months at each Pole. There is never an Equalnight at the Equator or the Poles. Days are always 12 hours 7 minutes long at the Equator, and nights are always 11 hours 53 minutes long. At the North and South Poles, it is either daylight or night for six months at a time, with daylight about one hundred hours longer than the night (see Table on page 223).

More than 2000 years ago, observers had determined that the Earth is a sphere. Astronomer theoreticians assumed incorrectly that at an Equalday/night the Sun was directly above the Earth's middle circle of latitude, *Circulus Aequinoctium*, Equalnight Circle. That's why it was called the Equator, where day and night were supposedly equated. Calculations made with this approximate model and the Julian calendar provided dates of solar and lunar events in Europe that seemed adequate if they were not examined closely. Church Authorities in Rome insisted that their calculated Tables of dates of Equalday/nights and Paschal Full Moons be used everywhere instead of local observations of the Sun and Moon. As Christianity spread over the globe and centuries passed, the calculated dates drifted farther and farther from the true dates.

Officials of the Christian Church struggled with imperfect calendars for more than 1500 years. The calendar problem was used in the second century A.D. as part of the movement to separate the Christian Πάσχα (*Páscha*, Passover) from the Jewish פֶּסַח (*Pesach*, Passover). After another 1400 years, a solution to the problem was legislated by Pope Gregory XIII, but it is not accepted in Orthodox Christian countries. It also created a small problem of language, by shifting the "official dates" of *Aequinoctia* to those of SZMs while keeping the no-longer-appropriate name.

The solar calendar that we use was not invented by Europeans. It was adopted by Europeans, modified and slightly distorted. I find it wonderful that the distortion has been uncovered by a solar calendar that was devised and built 5000 years ago by non-Europeans, here on Turtle Island, one of the Indian names for North America and for the World.

The enormous *Ómahkiyáahkóhtóohp* Temple and the extended Stonehenge Temple have many similar characteristics. Each is at 51° N latitude (similar to Calgary and London), at which the wobble of the Moon's orbit increases the angle between the rise directions of the Solstitial Full Moon and Sun to the sacred right angle once each 18.6 years. The angle between the set directions varies similarly. The stone ring at the centre of each Temple is nearly 30 metres in diameter. The design of each stone structure involves the numbers 1, 2, 3, 4, 5, 7, and 28. Each ring has a river two or three kilometres to the east. (Abundant water one to three kilometres east is also a characteristic of eight of the ten ancient, engraved Sacred Rock sites on hills in Alberta.) Each structure contains a bovid symbol, "buffalo stones" in the Sun Cairn and the silhouette of a Bull's head in Stonehenge. Each Temple contains a solar time machine that has a leap year cycle slightly more accurate than that of the Gregorian calendar.

Ómahkiyáhkóhtóohp includes an image of the Morning Star. The Temple appears to be dedicated to the Sun, Moon, and Morning Star, a Holy Trinity. I suspect that Stonehenge Temple is as well.

Ómahkiyáhkóhtóohp Temple is still relatively complete. The solstitial Sun rise and set observation lines can be dated because their directions change slowly over millennia, due to a slow decrease of tilt of the Earth's spinning axis relative to the axis of rotation of the Earth around the Sun. The oldest lines were made 5000 years, perhaps 5200 years ago. Some of the lines were adjusted every few centuries by adding fresh rocks, and other lines were built, up to about 300 years ago. Greater understanding of Stonehenge and its neighbourhood might continue to be obtained from studies of *Ómahkiyáahkóhtóohp*.

The similar calendars in Alberta and England are separated by 7000 kilometres, including an ocean and a continent. How similar, intricate devices came to be built in two such widely separated places at the same latitude at similar times remains a mystery. It may be answered in the future by examining the right places.

Fixing the Language

Dictionaries of European languages were compiled mainly during recent centuries, well after 1582. As a result, the word for *aequinoctium,* for example equinox in English and *tagundnachtgleiche* in German, was incorrectly defined as "one of two times per year when the day and night are of equal length everywhere on Earth; March 20 or 21 and September 22 or 23." There is no time of year when the first statement is true, and no place on Earth where the day and night are of equal length on the stated dates.

In future editions of the dictionaries, and dictionaries of American and Chinese, a term equivalent to Sun Zenith Midaltitude (SZM, pronounced *zem*) needs to be added: the dates when the Sun is directly above the Equator, March 20 or 21 and September 22 or 23; replaces the archaic word "equinox," because the lengths of day and night on these dates are not equal anywhere on Earth.

In French and German, Sun Zenith Midaltitude retains the same abbreviation with a similar pronunciation: *le Soleil Zénith Mi-altitude, SZM,* pronounced *zem*; *die Sonne Zenit Mittelhöhe, SZM,* also pronounced *zem*. In Latin it might be *Sol Vertex Medaltitudo, SVM,* pronounced *svem*; in Greek Ἥλιος Ζενίθ Μεσυψος, HZM, pronounced *zeem* instead of *eezm*? Greeks like the sound *ee*.

The definition of Equalday/night is: a 24-hour period in which the times between the first and last flashes of the Sun that bracket daylight and night, measured on a flat plain, are each 12.0 hours, equal within 2 minutes. The dates vary with latitude. The following Table lists examples for different latitudes at 0° longitude. At large values of longitude east and west, the dates might shift by one day. Abbreviation: Equalnight or Equalday, as it is in Latin or Greek.

The definitions of the ancient terms *ἰσημερία, lá leathach,* and *aequinoctium* will return to their literal, original meanings of Equalday, Equalday, and Equalnight, as will *tagundnachtgleiche* and שִׁוְיוֹן יוֹם וָלַיְלָה (*shivion yom valailah*) return to meaning Equalday/night, and so on. The word "equinox" is so corrupted that it will probably remain archaic and drop from use.

In recent centuries, the date of the Jewish Passover all over the world has also been anchored to the March SZM, rather than to the month of barley harvest in Judaea.

DATES OF EQUALNIGHTS*

Latitude (°)	North		South	
0	none			
2	none			
3	about Feb 3–9	about Nov 4–10	about Apr 30–May 6	about Aug 9–12
5	Feb 25–26	Oct 17–18	Apr 14–15	Aug 28–29
10	Mar 7–8	Oct 5–6	Mar 31–Apr 1	Sept 10–11
20	Mar 13–14	Sept 29–30	Mar 26–27	Sept 16–17
30	15–16	26–27	23–24	18–19
40	16–17	25–26	23–24	19–20
50	17–18	25–26	22–23	19–20
60	17–18	24–25	22–23	19–20
80	17–18	24–25	22–23	20–21
90	Sun rises about Mar 18, sets about Sept 24		Sun rises about Sept 20, sets about Mar 22	

*Calculated for 0° longitude, A.D. 2000. SZM: March 20, Sept 22. Solstice: June 21, Dec 21

What is Needed Now

The terms Equalday, Equalnight, Equalday/night, and Sun Zenith Midaltitude (SZM, *zem*) need to be included in English dictionaries, with definitions equivalent to those given above. Equivalent words and definitions need to be introduced into all European languages and many others. The misleading word "equinox" and its equivalent in other languages are now obsolete, but will take several generations to fall from use.

The language deception served a useful political purpose at the time it was done. It is fortunate that accurate calendars created long before the present era still exist, and can be read, so the no-longer-useful deception can be corrected.

Ómahkiyáahkóhtóohp is a vast Temple of the Sun, Moon, and Morning Star, an extensive stone-lacework that contains astonishingly accurate Stone Age solar and lunar calendars. It is gravely undervalued by the people in the Alberta Government who are responsible for its protection. Stonehenge is getting protection and care.

I cannot stress strongly enough that *Ómahkiyáahkóhtóohp* is in danger of being badly damaged by commercial exploits, and it needs official protection from further digging damage. Seduction of Government Officials by private interest groups and commercial organizations seems to have occurred since the beginning of Governments with Officials. It's called corruption. It needs to be opposed. **Forbid digging!**

Epilogue

here is adventure in archaeology and archaeoastronomy that leads us to places unforeseen, physically and mentally. Adventure has a strange attraction to amateurs and professionals alike. Amateurs, *lovers*, do the thing simply for the love if it, and usually have more absorptive minds than do their formally trained colleagues. That's why I have written this book mainly for amateurs, but have included enough description and data to carry along present and future professionals in the subject.

Great advances in knowledge are made through the intense curiosity, ingenuity, and persistence of a few individuals. Later, other people use the knowledge for something practical and create a need for it. A driving curiosity is like a monkey on your back that won't let you rest. (What's the story of that expression?) It seems that human societies have always contained a number of people with that affliction.

Some advances in knowledge branch out as they progress, and branches sometimes reach surprising places. It's like a mental flash of forked lightning. Such was the discovery of how Stone Age people on these plains measured time 5000 years ago.

Time is the curious dimension that cannot be stopped to examine it. It can only be measured in its passing. And although time is a physical thing, the perception of it is usually affected by emotion. Does a pot of water over a fire really take longer to boil if you watch it? Does time really pass more quickly if you are enjoying yourself?

People throughout the North Temperate Zone have similar methods of marking physical time, somewhat different from those in the Tropics, for example the Maya. About 5000 years ago, two communities at 51° N latitude, separated by an ocean and a continent, developed similar, accurate calendars that we still use. Why at 51° N latitude? Apparently it was because 5000 years ago at 51° latitude the Sun and Full Moon near the Solstices rose and set at the perceived-sacred right angle from each other once during each 18.6-year Moon cycle. North latitude, because at 51° S latitude there is very little land, and hardly any people.

Discovery of the ancient accurate calendars at 51° N latitude also led to confirmation of a Stone Age solar calendar at 36° N latitude, which had been widely ridiculed when it was reported. In fact, the calendar is more accurate than the discoverers thought.

Stone Age Calendar in New Mexico

Anna Sofaer and Rolf Sinclair took remarkable photographs of a "Sun Dagger" traversing a double-spiral petroglyph on Fajada Butte in Chaco Canyon, New Mexico, in September and March of 1983 and 1984. The Sun Daggers on the petroglyph mark the Equaldays, not the Equinoxes as claimed.

Fajada Butte is located at 36°.1 N, 108°.1 W and rises as a three-stepped pyramid, 135 metres above the canyon floor. Three large, vertical slabs of rock lean against the south side of the top section of cliff face, making a rock shelter. Light from the midday Sun shining through spaces between the three slabs forms vertical rods of light, "daggers," on the cliff face in the shaded shelter. The altitude of the near-zenith Sun varies throughout the year, so light-rods make annual cycles up and down, back and forth across portions of the shelter walls. There are several petroglyphs on the walls, and the light-rods interact with them differently at different times of the year.

Sofaer and Sinclair took photographs during a Summer Solstice, showing that a single light-rod vertically bisects a ten-ring clockwise-inward spiral at that time. They also found that at the Winter Solstice two vertical light-rods tangentially touch the east and west sides of the spiral. They photographed the passage of a light-rod across a west–east double-spiral in September 1983, and in both March and September 1984. Each spiral in the connected pair is two-ring clockwise-inward, making a fancy, recumbent S.

The marking of the Solstices by the light-rods on the large spiral is unambiguous. At the Equinoxes, the light-rod is unsymmetrically too far east in the double spiral. At an Equalday, the light-rod would be in the centre of the double spiral. In *Astronomy and Ceremony in the Prehistoric Southwest*, Sofaer and Sinclair's Figure 4.8 shows that the tip of the light-rod takes six minutes to cross from the bottom to the top of the horizontal double spiral near noon on a given day. Their Figure 4.9 records the left-to-right position of the light-rod at the same vertical level on different dates. The light-rod takes eleven days to cross the double spiral from west to east. On any particular Equinox, the light-rod is three-quarters the distance from left to right across the double spiral. Symmetry in the design would require that the rod be only halfway across. The Equinox date is away from symmetry by (11/4 = 2.8) three days, since from noon to noon means that only whole days are counted. The photographs in Sofaer and Sinclair's Figures 4.8 and 4.9 show that the light-rod would have been at the centre of the double spiral on September 25, 1983, March 17, 1984, and September 25, 1984. These were Equaldays.

The bisected double-spiral symbol for Equaldays is equivalent to the Babylonian symmetrical symbols of the Ram horns and Equal-arm Balance for the Equaldays.

There are spiral petroglyphs on stone slabs in *Nuaghrian*, 5200 years old. There has been no physical dating of the spiral glyphs on Fajada Butte. The petroglyphs, and hence the calendar, were attributed by Sofaer and Sinclair to the Anasazi of about one thousand years ago. *Anasazi* is Navajo for "Ancient Ones," people of the unknown past. The petroglyphs might be much older than one thousand years and, just as with *Ómahkiyáahkóhtóohp*, could have been used more or less continuously for several thousands of years.

Sofaer and Sinclair's attention to detail was rare for the era in which they worked. The recording of calendrical alignments and exact measurements in ancient sites was fashionable fifty years ago, but in the normal generational cycle of fashion change, such alignments and exactness fell out of style thirty years ago. Each generation wants to separate itself from the previous one. Travelogues and ethnology came into fashion. Sofaer and Sinclair's photographs and interpretation appear in *Conference Proceedings* published by the Maxwell Museum of Anthropology at the University of New Mexico in 1987. The articles that precede and follow Sofaer and Sinclair's, including a negative critique "Moonshine on the Sun Dagger," well illustrate the politics that governed archaeoastronomy during the last quarter century. In the context of the conference, Moonshine meant "Bullshit."

The pendulum is now swinging back because we are aware that unless measurements are made as accurately as possible the data are not worthy of placement in any context. Furthermore, the tone of many articles during the last thirty years indicates that the authors have not spent a lot of time with Indians when the authors did not want something from the Indians.

I will pass along a comment from an Indian Elder: "Anthropologists went onto Reserves with tape recorders and paid Indians for stories. They got stories." North American Indians from the Atlantic to the Pacific have told me that much of the ethnology now in university libraries is not correct. Furthermore, ethnology refers to people who are alive now, and no ethnology is applicable to societies of 3000 years ago, let alone 5000 years ago.

We have to begin with as accurate physical data as we can determine, and go from there.

* * * *

Now let's glance back at the Temples that captured our imaginations, in their reverse order of discoveries.

On Preseli Mountain

I visited Preseli Mountain as an afterthought, because I didn't believe that the Stonehenge Bluestones had been merely "quarried" there. They probably had exceptional value by being in an extremely sacred structure, to warrant the enormous labour of transport to enhance the glory of the site on the Salisbury Plain. Conquerors have taking ways. Venetians at the time of the Fourth Crusade in 1204 took four ancient bronze horses and other plunder from Constantinople to Venice. Spaniards during the sixteenth century took tonnes of precious gold objects from Central and South America to Spain, and melted them to bulk gold. During 1801 to 1803, Lord Elgin vandalized the Parthenon in Athens to take ancient marble statues and friezes to England. It is an unfortunate characteristic that many humans like to break things and steal. We are born savage, and in civilized societies parents train their children to resist temptations to do uncivil things. But power corrupts.

Was the mythical Celtic War Leader Arthur native to southwestern Wales, or to the Salisbury Plain? The Arthurian legend of 1500 years ago has been reinterpreted as a Christianized and embellished Arthurian myth of 4400 years ago. Is the name Arthur derived from the Welsh *Arth*, which means Bear? Bear-man? Was he responsible for moving the Bluestone Temple from *Foelteml* to the Salisbury Plain? That feat was so great that it could only be explained in a later era as work of a magician, Merlin. I think it no accident that Arthur's grave, *Beddarthur*, is purportedly a stone ring 1.2 kilometres due west of the ancient East–West Sanctuary in *Carnmenyn* on *Foelteml*, the same distance and direction as the other purported graves of Arthur in rings of stone at Stonehenge and Glastonbury from the New King Bowl Barrows and the Tor. West is where the Sun dies each day, but what does the 1.2 kilometres represent?

Any hunter who has skinned a bear sees that the body is unsettlingly like a human's. The interpretation of *Arthur* as Bear-man is intriguing. In many mythologies a bear is graced with the characteristics of wisdom and strength. The northern, always-visible constellation Big Dipper is also called *Ursa Major*, Latin for Great Bear. In some American Indian legends the four stars of the bowl of the Big Dipper are seen as a Bear, and the three stars of the Dipper handle are seen as three hunters who perpetually follow the Bear. During the annual cycle of the Bear constellation through the sky the Bear stands on all four legs part of the time, and stands on its two hind legs the rest of the time, just as real bears do. A bear is considered to be a two-legged animal, like a human.

Anyone who is familiar with *Ómahkiyáahkóhtóohp* will be excited about the similarities in the east portion of Preseli Mountain. This mountain will be much studied during the twenty-first century. The land is densely occupied by sheep, so watch where you step.

After reading this manuscript, anthropologist Alice Kehoe told me about Littleton and Malcor's suggestion that the Arthur legends had roots in Scythia, the western part of the Steppes, north of the

Caspian and Black Seas, in 3000–2000 B.P. That is the west end of the area to which I assigned the origin of Indo-European cultures, around the Aral Sea (now Kazakhstan and Uzbekistan), but I favour a first-wave migration date of 6000–5000 B.P. Major studies of the prehistory of Kazakhstan seem imminent.

At Stonehenge

My experience exploring *Ómahkiyáahkóhtóohp* taught me how to look at Stonehenge and helped me to find things. For example, two of the six season-pivot Sun observation lines at Stonehenge are grandly impressive, but four are hidden. I was able to find the hidden ones only because of what I'd learned at *Ómahkiyáahkóhtóohp*. They are so well hidden in the Sarsen structure that there is no previous report of an attempt to record the Sun along a Summer Solstice set, Winter Solstice rise, or Equinox set or rise line. The four hidden lines were probably used by the scientists of the day, who were the astronomers, calendar keepers, and prophets.

There is not even a report of an attempt to accurately record the magnificent Winter Solstice Sun set at Stonehenge. The calendar controversy was casual and fun.

The major lines for the Summer Solstice rise and Winter Solstice set probably marked focal events in the religion. They symbolize the perpetual cycle of growth, strength, decay, weakness, and regeneration. The Solstitial Sun rise and set observation lines cross in the middle of the Altar. What does that signify?

In the future, much will be made of the fact that about 5000 years ago people in places we now call southern Alberta and southern England had identified the Equalday/nights, the key to an exact solar calendar. That feat probably required keeping records through many centuries. Records might have been kept in an oral tradition that has been lost by people who write. Myths and stone markers would have been mnemonics.

The 28 lintels on the Sarsen Circle are analogous to the 28 Rays in the Sun Cairn Ring in *Ómahkiyáahkóhtóohp*. They seem to relate to the 28 stellar Mansions of the Moon. There are two lunar calendars of different eras in Stonehenge, which suggests that the Moon was the head deity when the Sarsen Circle was built, and that the Sun became the head deity when the lunar calendar was moved to outside the Circle.

In each lunar calendar, a pair of observation lines for the 18.6-year cycle of Summer Moon rise and Winter Moon set clasp the Inner Sanctum of the Sun. The Moon is the Sun Catcher. I have also seen an allusion to the Moon as Sun Catcher in Amerindian art.

The 4000-year-old symbolism and artistry are as amazing as the exact knowledge of the sky. The knowledge, artistry, and symbolism should not have been surprising, considering the realism of the 30,000-year-old drawings and paintings of animals on smoothed surfaces deep within the cave near Chauvet Pont d'Arc in southern France. The motivation, the power of observation, and technical ability needed to create the paintings in the narrow, dark end-chamber 300 metres from the entrance of the cave, were similar to those needed 25,000 years later to create the calendars in *Ómahkiyáahkóhtóohp* and Stonehenge. The intelligence of people hadn't changed much, but Alberta and England were under a kilometre of ice 30,000 years ago.

Average intelligence might only change with the subspecies, for example from *homo sapiens* to *homo sapiens sapiens*. If *homo sapiens sapiens sapiens* eventually evolves, I wonder if that subspecies will spend still more of its ingenuity than do we *sapiens saps* in devising ways to kill each other at ever greater rates.

Phyl and I have seen Venus bright as Evening Star above Stonehenge. Some day someone might seek markings of its eight-year pentagonal cycle among the constellations there.

At *Ómahkiyáahkóhtóohp*

Complex work in an isolated place can't succeed without help from other people. Sometimes the biggest problem is just to get there.

Ómahkiyáahkóhtóohp is located eighteen kilometres off a gravel road, which takes an hour to drive in *good* weather; when the weather turns, it becomes a real challenge. On the afternoon of December 18, 1996, the snow on the prairie had a hard crust, with greasy sugar-snow beneath it. Junior and Nancy Bertschy live at the gravel road a kilometre beyond the turn-off. Junior left his farm chores to bulldoze a trail onto the prairie to help us on the way. He got us to a knoll crest two kilometres from the road, from where we thought we could go it alone.

Half an hour later we'd managed another kilometre, with fifteen to go, and it was getting dark. The 4-wheel-drive and heavy tires of *El Escarabajo Oro* couldn't handle the crust and lack of traction. We turned back, which probably saved our lives, because a whiteout blizzard blew in on the 20th. When we called in at Bertschys to let them know we had come out, Nancy was relieved. But I wanted to get in, so I phoned Grant Armstrong from Bertschys' kitchen.

In August 1996, high-accuracy Global Positioning System (GPS) technology had been released by the US military for private use. Geodetic surface coordinates obtained with it were supposed to be accurate within an amazing one-third of a metre, and altitudes above Mean Sea Level within one metre. On December 16, I rented a Trimble unit from Cansel Survey for a week, for $214. A few hours of simultaneous GPS Base Station data were purchased from Pleiades Corp. for $128. After learning how to use the equipment and do the computer analysis of the signals, I wanted to calibrate the system at the Geodetic Survey Marker on Sun Cairn Ring Hill, and take measurements at particular rocks in the hilltop pattern.

As a back-up in case of bad weather or undriveable ground conditions, I had phoned Grant, a rancher north of the Bow River, who told me that if our truck couldn't get to the site, he'd fly me in. He's a flying cowboy with a large ranch, and checking the herd from a plane reduces the need for ranch hands. His father Arnold had been one of the first of the breed.

Phyl and I drove the 90 kilometres from the Bertschys' home to Grant and Marilyn Armstrongs', and stayed the night with them to be ready for the next day. It's a long way between bridges across the Bow River, so the 18 kilometres as the crow flies meant a 90-kilometre drive on roads.

On the cold December 19th, Phyl was nervous about my flying to Sun Cairn Ring Hill. Grant joked with her, "I guess you want me to take good care of him." She didn't smile.

I took my equipment with Arnold in his 4-wheel-drive pickup truck to the cow camp, where he spread hay for the cows and chopped a hole in the ice to water them. Grant flew in at noon to pick me up (Figure E-1).

Half an hour later, he landed the ski-equipped Super Cub between the rocks near Sun Cairn Ring Hill to drop me off. It was a dangerous task; a few years earlier his brother had landed his plane in that area, hit a rock, and died.

Figure E-1 Grant Armstrong talking with his father, Arnold, who is on the tractor at the cattle camp. 12^{h}03^m December 19, 1996.

Before leaving me to continue his ranch work, Grant said, "You must really love this place."

I said, "Coming here is like a sacrament." The place has wonderment but is as comfortable as a friend.

I watched him take off between the rocks. Grant is a skilled pilot, and a Super Cub has a big engine, so it doesn't need much space to land and take off. I trudged up the hill carrying the equipment, occasionally breaking through snowdrift crusts.

The windswept hilltop was nearly clear of snow (Figure E-2). The Trimble GPS equipment didn't mind the cold weather, and I had it supported half-a-metre above the ground on an iron stand to keep it out of the snow.

When Grant returned two hours later, the last GPS data collection needed seven more minutes. He didn't risk shutting off the engine (Figure E-3), and we were soon on our way back home.

That evening, Phyl and I played games with the Armstrong daughters.

Figure E-2 The Sun Cairn Ring on the windswept hilltop, looking west by south. The Trimble GeoExplorer II is on the Geodetic Survey Marker. 12^h55^m December 19, 1996.

Figure E-3 Grant returned to pick me up from the high west bank of the Bow River. Afternoon, December 19, 1996.

Figure E-4 Horses wondered what we were doing out on the prairie in a storm. A bit later, blowing snow reduced visibility to near zero, a white-out. 10h55m December 20, 1996.

The next morning, in an approaching storm and accompanied by Phyl, I tried to drive *El Escarabajo Oro* from the Armstrongs' about thirty kilometres to a portion of *Ómahkiyáahkóhtóohp* on the east bank of the Bow River. For the first twenty kilometres or so we had gravel roads. Blowing snow grew into a blizzard. I missed the correct turnoff onto a prairie trail and wound up with a bunch of horses (Figure E-4). We each knew that the other was not part of the expected scenery. I was lost, and turned back to try to slowly retrace our path. Once back on the invisible road with a truck-tilting ditch on each side, I stayed on it by feel. Phyl grew up in sheltered Ottawa, and here she was experiencing a white-knuckling white-out on the prairie! What a magnificent woman. Finally we got onto a main road and the blizzard subsided (Figure E-5).

When we got onto the four-lane highway toward home, accidents had caused police to stop all traffic at the first village we came to. There was even a Greyhound bus in the ditch. So Grant and Marilyn put us up for another night.

On the 21st, we went home satisfied. It's an interesting life.

Computer analysis of the GPS data gave north and west coordinates for the Geodetic Survey Marker only one-third of a metre different from the official Survey values, and an altitude above Mean

Figure E-5 The Prairie Schooner after we'd escaped the white-out and got to a main road. Noon, December 20, 1996.

Sea Level only two-thirds of a metre different. The amazing accuracy of the Trimble device was as good as advertised! A rare event! This technique has made a major contribution to progress in observational Archaeoastronomy.

Why *do* such things as try to go to the isolated Temple in bad weather? To do them you have to know who to have confidence in, beginning with yourself and continuing with the people you depend on to get you out of trouble if you get into it. To help understand *Ómahkiyáahkóhtóohp*, you need to learn the lie of the land and the look of the rocks throughout its zone in different weathers. People worshipped there and lived nearby in all seasons for more than five thousand years.

* * * *

When I discover a season-pivot Sun observation line of great length, I walk the land between the back and front sights in snow-free season to see what else lies between.

One Summer Solstice Sun set line is from the Sun Cairn to a large red granite two kilometres northwest. On a fine day in June, Phyl and I walked the line and found a few small cairns, stone rings, and a large rubbingstone near it, but nothing of note directly in it. (Buffalo and cattle like to rub their necks on large rocks, and upper edges of some granite rubbingstones are polished to a sheen by thousands of years of rubbing buffalo.) On the way back from the granite foresight, we heard a bull bellow on the far side of a crest to our forward left. No doubt a bull with his harem of twelve or so, who sensed our presence. Phyl tensed with fright and clung tightly to my arm. I shifted to the bull side of her as we continued along. A White Bull, a Charolais, came onto the crest about 200 metres away, bellowing at us. I doubted that he would challenge me for my harem-of-one if we remained aloof.

Phyl was terrified. Head down and trembling, she said, "I'd like to run, but my legs are jelly."

I said, "If you run it might be your last time. Pretend you are ignoring him. Just hang on to me tightly and don't change your pace."

The truck was a kilometre away, and we had to pass in front of the bull within about 100 metres. We didn't alter our straight-line path and didn't turn our heads to look at him. As we approached the closest point, he pawed the ground and snorted a bit but didn't agitate much from side to side. When we were well past he became silent. After we reached the truck, Phyl's strength began to return.

She doesn't love the place quite as much as I do.

* * * *

The crescent Moon and Venus are drawn with rocks near the Sun Cairn Ring (Figure 3-6). I have deciphered rudiments of the lunar calendar's *moonthly*, annual, and 18.6-year cycles in the Temple, but several years of Moon rise and set observations remain to be made. The 28 Rays in the Sun Cairn Ring might be related to the 28, sometimes 27 days that the Moon takes to travel around the solar zodiac, the so-called sidereal month. The Moon in the ancient Vedic religion had 28 *nakshatras*, night places in the stars, equivalent to the Arabic 28 *al manazil al-Qamar*, resting places of the Moon, and the European 28 Mansions of the Moon.

The number of *nakshatras* was later reduced from the Vedic 28 to the Hindu 27 because in most months the Moon makes the circuit in 27 days, and $27 = 3^3$ is a mystical number. Other mystical numbers in ancient cultures around the world are $1^1 = 1$, $1^1 \times 2^2 = 4$, and $1^1 \times$

$2^2 \times 3^3 = 108$. This sequence might have been the origin of 108 being held sacred, less anciently than the sacred $4 \times 7 = 28$.

In *Ómahkiyáahkóhtóohp*, viewed from the Sun Cairn, the north and south extremes of the Full Moon rise positions in the lunar-standstill 18.6-year cycle occur at major bends in the Bow River (for example, Figure 3-4). One might expect that the eight-year pentagonal cycle of Venus among the constellations is also marked in some way. Someone in the next generation of students might find it.

Accurate determination of the cyclic paths of lights through the sky required meticulous record keeping over many centuries. Multi-generational oral records assisted by stone markers, now a lost technique, could have done the job. Skywatchers marked accurate lines toward average rise and set positions on the horizon. Accuracy could be attained by successive adjustments over many years. Myths transmitted orally through the generations would relate the passage of the Sun, Moon, and planets through the constellations.

No doubt many storytellers, historytellers, and sciencetellers, were killed by the migrating Europeans, and many myths and other knowledge perished with them.

"Then you'll have to arrange it through my father."

An hour after the two *Siksika* had come to find out what I was doing on Sun Cairn Ring Hill, I had to begin the seven-hour drive to Edmonton, to give a chemistry lecture the next morning to two hundred and fifty students. I had shown the two men some of my calendrical discoveries, which made them increasingly nervous.

The men—a younger man and his uncle—were a grandson and son of a Holy Man who had recently died. When the nephew suggested I talk about the site with his Grama, a Sun Woman, the uncle shouted, "No! Dad said never tell!"

His nephew countered: "BUT WE'RE GONNA DIE! SOMEONE HAS TO WRITE IT DOWN!"

I didn't have time to visit his Grama that evening, so it would have to be during a later trip. The young man said, "Then you'll have to arrange it through my father."

It was the following June before I could arrange to meet Grama. On our way to the Temple site, Phyl and I met with the young man's father and mother at their home in Siksika Nation. The father said that we could visit his mother at the end of our stay in *Ómahkiyáahkóhtóohp*.

I said that after four days on the site we'd smell of sweat, so we'd rather visit her when we are clean on the way to the site. He said it would be better at the end of a trip. I finally understood that our living at the Sacred Hill would be considered a spiritual purification before our meeting with the Sun Woman. We agreed to visit at 1 P.M., four days later.

We arrived at their home a little before 1 P.M. and found a note attached to the screen door: "When we made the appointment for today we had forgotten about this sale which we planned to attend. We are sorry for the inconvenience." I put the gifts of a braid of sweetgrass and package of tobacco on the ground in front of the door, and put a hand-size stone on them to hold them secure against a wind.

The young man had been brash with emotion upon seeing and hearing about a few of my discoveries. The Tribal Elders apparently agreed with his uncle: "No! Dad said never tell!"

Things that are most sacred to Indians are not talked about to Whites. A *Piikani* Elder said, "White people just go in and trash them." Indians of various tribes who know of my long work tolerate it, some even respect it and show me bits, but they don't want their traditional knowledge written down by a White.

A *Siksika* Elder told me: "A lot of you fellas paid Indians for stories. The Indians added a lot that wasn't true. Soon we won't be Indians! You'll be the Indians, because you have all that stuff!"

Unfortunately, I know some White professionals who are "Professional Whites," and already think that way.

What I have written, here and in the much more extensive report in the University of Alberta Archives, is permissible because it records what I discovered myself, and bits that I have been given permission to disclose for the sake of future generations of all races. The information crosses cultures and is important for each culture that it touches. Perhaps some of my discoveries had been lost by Indian cultures that have been so tragically suppressed during the last three centuries.

What I have presented about the vast Temple of the Sun, Moon, and Morning Star will no doubt be rephrased by Indians who take it up. I think that *Ómahkiyáahkóhtóohp* is merely a name released into the White environment, an environmental name, like Jews' environmental use of Albert instead of Abraham in Europe. A Blackfoot sacred name probably exists for the Temple.

Science and the Perception of Nature Around the World

It would also be interesting to seek ancient roots of calendars developed in the Tropics. Why is Year One of the Mayan Long-Count calendar 3114 B.C.? I do not believe that the 365-day-year calendar used by the Mayans began only two or three thousand years ago, as commonly suggested. It probably had a precursor in an earlier culture. Five thousand years ago seems to be an approximate starting date around the world for detailed records that still survive. Genius within populations did not vary much with longitude. The types of technology did, perhaps due to differences in philosophy.

For Christians and Jews, the English word "nature" commonly means everything except mankind, as in "dominate nature." *Genesis 1:27–28* bids mankind to be *Masters of nature* (nature is a thing, and came to include humans who are not like Europeans). The religions of North American Aboriginals contain the philosophy that we are *part of Nature* (we are children of Mother Earth). This difference is so great that, to learn to read the patterns of stones on the ground, someone of European heritage must abandon the "we are Masters of nature" concept and adopt the "we are part of Nature" way of seeing things.

Plains Indians did not construct large buildings or powerful weapons. They asked forgiveness of, and gave thanks to, the Spirits of animals they killed for food. The cycle of life produced by Mother Earth involves death and regeneration. The food of all animals is plant and animal *beings* that have recently been alive. The concept of "from being to becoming" long predates Nobel Laureate Ilya Prigogine's book of that title, but he is one of the first European scientists to understand it.

The aggressive philosophy of the Christian religion with its military engine led to its spread around the world. When it leapt from the North to the South Temperate Zone five hundred years ago, the lunisolar framework of its annual festivals was disrupted because the festival anchor-date, the Equalnight in March, has different calendar-dates in the two hemispheres. To solve the Christian Passover date problem after a century of political struggle, the lawyer Pope Gregory XIII legislated a deception in the calendar in 1582. The recently discovered 5000-year-old calendar in *Ómahkiyáahkóhtóohp* revealed the deception. *Ómahkiyáahkóhtóohp* contains the equivalent of the Rosetta Stone for Stone Age calendars.

Many modern calendars are sheets of letters and numbers that we tear off and discard as time slips by. Nothing on them tells how they work. We are aware of long, warm days in the middle period of the year, and short, cold days in the period that joins the ends of years into cycles, a spiral. We accept by faith the exactness of the chart. Most people who use the Gregorian calendar don't pay attention to the Moon, except romantically or mystically when it is near Full, because the Moon cycles, *moonths*, shift in successive calendar months. The ancient calendars that I have described are working machines, with the Sun and Moon as moving parts. One sees how the lunar and solar calendars work during each *moonth*, year, and increasing cycles of years.

Human Evolution

The oldest existing books are *RigVeda* (PraiseKnowledge), dating back about 3700 years, and *Torah* (Instruction), about 3400 years. They are still held sacred today by Hindus, Jews, Buddhists, Christians, Muslims, and many others. The books might have been transmitted orally for generations before being written. Their dates of first writing are controversial.

Nature has been venerated as a holy thing by North American Indians for more than 5000 years. An increasing number of Whites on the prairies are participating in certain Indian rituals for spiritual healing. The flying cowboy once said, "With all the bad stuff we've done to Indians, wouldn't it be ironic if we all converted to their religion?"

Knowledge about spirituality has apparently not advanced during the last 5000 years. Different religions focus on different details, which generate different rituals, but the basic spirituality seems to be the same.

An understanding of spirituality cannot be approached by methods of physical science. For more than forty years I have pioneered interdisciplinary studies of behaviour in complex systems. We measure rates of changes in many different kinds of system, and try to discover what causes the changes. The conventional subjects included in this unconventional work are biology, chemistry, cosmology, geology, physics, sociology—anything in Nature. The overall name for this new interdisciplinary subject is Kinetics of Nonhomogeneous

Processes, KNP for short. It has also been called The Sciences of Complexity, and recently, simply Interdisciplinary Studies. KNP contains unifying concepts that apply to all the different conventional subjects, and "pattern recognition" is the most insightful tool. Surprisingly, similar patterns in different realms are generated by related mechanisms, so pattern recognition simplifies understanding of behaviour in all areas.

In sociology, love or fear, or any emotion, cannot be understood in terms of physics and chemistry alone. An emotion involves mental extrapolation beyond one's self, and love is much more complex than fear. Neither can dreams be understood through physics, nor can greed and therefore war. Nor can the desire to understand the swing of skirts and the oscillations of *glutei*, or how the universe works. An understanding of biology requires understanding of physics, chemistry, and something of an entirely different nature. I wonder at what stage of complexity in living things spirituality enters.

I use the term "spirituality" to include all phenomena in the realm beyond chemistry and physics, including but not limited to religious phenomena.

Consider a current example of a complex stable/unstable/stable spiritual cycle in human behaviour that requires several generations to pass into and out of society. All advanced forms of life have two sexes, each with different specialized functions, although both sexes absorb nourishment, excrete waste, and have many other functions in common. Each species reproduces by male-female interactions. Cross interactions between species are sterile. Part of the human species is now trying to recede mentally to a single-sex species, by encouraging women to try to behave like men, and by replacing female honorifics such as actress, Directress, Governess, hostess, Mistress, Priestess, Rectress, sorority, and waitress with the male terms. Women's societies at the University of Alberta are now called brotherhoods. The movement is called "feminism," and men are the main driving force, for reasons of selfish material gain. One result is that cheating (deceit, lying, stealing), instead of being meaningfully discouraged in our homes, the only place where ethical behaviour can be taught effectively, has, through the epidemic neglect of children by their parents, permeated our society (white collar crime, divorce, I HURT lawyers).

However, the female honorific *mother* will survive, and will seed the return of others. It's always the woman who gets pregnant, no matter who's on top. Mother Nature is reacting as one might expect, but the movement will take another two generations to decay. Two generations to grow and two to shrink.

The contents of hundreds of the magazines read by millions of men every day, and of hundreds of others read by women, indicate a major genetic male-female difference that permits our species to propagate and survive: on average men like to fight and fuck, women like to shop (gather), cook, and cuddle. We are still hunter-gatherers.

The range of human intelligence was probably the same forty thousand years ago as now, including the rare genius. What have evolved are the tools and gadgets we make. We learn how to do a new thing, and forget how to do an old thing.

Time Machines in a Creation Myth

By the time the *Torah* was recorded in its present form, the lights in the sky were believed to form omens of future events, including future season-pivot dates. The 5000-year-old Temples in Alberta, Ireland, and England show that accurate knowledge of the sky preceded the *Torah* by at least 1000 years.

From about 3500 years ago, we read that Skywatchers made prophesies and calendars:

And God said, Let there be lights in the firmament of the heaven
to divide the day from the night; and let them be for signs,
and for seasons, and for days, and years:
And God made two great lights;
the greater light to rule the day, and the lesser to rule the night:
He made the stars also.

–Genesis 1:14,16, the Hebrew fourth day of Creation

And from about 3060 years ago, allusion in song to skywatching:

The heavens declare the glory of God
And the firmament showeth his handywork.
Day unto day (the Sun) uttereth speech,
And night unto night (the Moon and Stars) showeth knowledge.

–Psalm 19 of David

Now, for the first time, I know what each of the words in the above quotations means. To understand them one has first to understand how the solar and lunar calendars work. It still amazes me that this understanding came from my discovery of the solar and lunar calendars that were built by people who lived on the Canadian prairies 5000 years ago.

In the fun of telling this story there has been the fun of telling how big, new discoveries are made, now and thousands of years ago. The Skywatchers of old were driven by the same consuming curiosity as are the best scientists today.

Genius existed on the prairies at least 5000 years ago, and it continues in their progeny today.

ki ánimaie-ikskako'tsi
and now the boiling is ended

APPENDICES

xact measurements of Sun rise and set directions in ancient archaeological sites, as far as I have been able to determine, have been made only by dedicated *amateurs*: people who love the subject so much that they work in it at their own expense. They take the needed time and care to be thorough, and haven't had their minds closed by the profession's taboos.

In spite of three centuries of speculation about the ancient functions of Stonehenge, the only record I found of an accurate Sun measurement there is that by amateur Howard Payn, who tried to record the rise along a carefully selected line each morning of June 21 to 25, 1901, and succeeded on the last morning. The Sun rise line he recorded was reported by astronomer Norman Lockyer in 1906. The conclusions derived from Payn's observation and Lockyer's calculations have been repeatedly ridiculed by archaeologists and archaeoastronomers during the last thirty years.

Storytelling has been the vogue in archaeoastronomy the last quarter century. It has been entertaining but hasn't advanced our understanding of Stonehenge. The gross distortion of Lockyer's data by storytellers, through inadequacy or intent, reflects the quality of their work.

The era for exact measurements has returned, as we seek to increase understanding.

Rosamund Cleal and coauthors (1995) published an enormous compilation of Stonehenge data that contains a few errors. One of the people involved in the publication told me that the book was compiled and published in such a limited time frame that errors in the Tables and text were inevitable. But it is a vital resource. Beyond that, I think the most useful books about Stonehenge are those by William Stukeley (1724), Edgar Barclay (1895), and Norman Lockyer (1906). Richard Atkinson's data and conclusions (1979) were included in Cleal and coauthors' book.

I rediscovered the Equalday/nights in *Ómahkiyáahkóhtóohp* in 1988, and in Stonehenge in 2001. The Stone Age Time Machines in Alberta and England were discovered through extensive, accurate measurements of Sun rises and sets during June 1983 to December 2005. In New Mexico, Anna Sofaer and Rolf Sinclair's thorough recordings of passages of a small bar of sunlight across a petroglyph in a rock shelter unknowingly recorded the Equaldays in September 1983 and March and September 1984, but the actual dates were not recognized until 2004. Accurate, reproducible observations clear away masses of casual measurements and mistaken conclusions.

To assist amateurs and professionals alike, my methods of measurement and calculation are briefly described in the following Appendices. The astronomical equations are explained in Appendices of the books by Fred Hoyle and John North, or chapters 1 and 2 of *Spherical Astronomy* by W. M. Smart, listed in the Bibliography.

Ómahkiyáahkóhtóohp and its calendar are described in much greater detail in the large report *Temple of the Sun, Moon and Morningstar near Majorville, Alberta,* which will be in my files at the University of Alberta Archives after completion in a few years. The files also contain 12,000 annotated photographs taken at this Temple, with their negatives, and eight field notebooks. My Stonehenge files in the University Archives contain 1400 annotated photos with their negatives, six small notebooks, and manuscripts.

A.1. Angular Distance Between Points on the Horizon in Photographs

Azimuth from a place of observation (the camera) is the angle measured clockwise from north, with east at 90°. Azimuth angles between points along the horizon are measured from photographs.

The exposed area of each photo negative is 24.0 mm x 36.0 mm.

The tangent of the angular distance θ of a point from the centre of the horizon in the negative is proportional to the horizontal distance **d** from the horizon centre divided by the focal length *fl* of the lens:

$$\tan \theta = \mathbf{d} / fl \quad (1)$$

or

$$\theta = \tan^{-1}(\mathbf{d}/fl)$$

Prints were usually made by masking 2% from each edge of the negative and enlarging the image 4.40 x to get a 101 mm x 152 mm print. A distance *d* from the horizon centre in a print corresponds to an angular distance θ:

$$\theta = \tan^{-1}(d / 4.40\, fl)$$

Calculations are most easily done in radians, where radians = degrees/57.3. The measured angles were always small, less than 0.2 radian, so, $\tan^{-1}\theta = \theta$, within 1%. Therefore,

$$\theta\,(\text{rad}) = d / 4.40\, fl$$

This formula is also valid for vertical small angular distances near the horizon.

Most people visualize angles in degrees, and focal lengths are given in mm, so the distance *D* mm that corresponds to an angular width of 1° near the horizon in a print is:

$$D(\text{mm}/°) = (4.40/57.3)\, fl = 0.0768\, fl$$

Most of the angles were measured in prints from focal lengths 80 – 200 mm, with

$$D = 6.1 - 15.4 \text{ mm}/°$$

A.2. Depth of Field in a Photograph

A clearer picture of objects both close to and far away from the camera is obtained by using a greater depth of field, which means a smaller aperture in the lens, hence a larger **f** setting:

$$\mathbf{f} = fl\,/\,\text{aperture} \qquad (2)$$

A smaller aperture requires a longer exposure and a steady camera. Use a sturdy tripod and a cable release.

A.3. Refraction by the Atmosphere, of Light from a Sun Rise or Set

Light from the Sun near the horizon bends slightly toward the Earth as it enters from the almost-vacuum of outer space into the denser atmosphere and is slowed slightly. The result is that we see the first flash from the Sun a few minutes before the upper limb (top edge) of the Sun is physically in line with the horizon. For the same reason, the last flash is seen a few minutes after the Sun's upper limb has physically passed below the horizon. As the rising Sun's altitude increases, the amount of downward refraction decreases, so the apparent angle of the Sun's ascent increases slightly with increasing altitude (Table A-1, Figure A-1). In the same way, the apparent angle of descent of the setting Sun decreases as the Sun approaches the horizon. The curved ascent/descent lines in Figure 1 were constructed from tables of F. Hoyle and A. Thom.

If the Sun was hidden by a narrow band of cloud or trees at rise or set, the position of its top edge observed at altitude a degrees above the horizon had to be extrapolated to the treeless horizon, which had an altitude h degrees above horizontal. A transparency was made of Figure A-1 adjusted to the scale (mm/°) of the photograph. The portion of the appropriate Equalnight or Solstice curve between altitudes $a+h$ and h was laid over the photo to join the top of the Sun to the horizon, to find the location of the first or last flash. Care was taken to match horizontal lines in the photo and graph.

Table A-1

Line of the upper limb of the rising or setting Sun or Full Moon, seen through refracting standard air.

Measured altitude (°):	-0.50	0.00	1.00	2.00	3.00	5.00
Refraction (°):[a]	-0.71	-0.59	-0.41	-0.31	-0.24	-0.18
True Altitude (TA,°):	-1.21	-0.59	+0.59	1.69	2.76	4.82
Horizontal axis (°):[b] Solstice	-1.94	-0.95	+0.95	2.72	4.43	7.74
Equalnight	-1.50	-0.73	+0.73	2.10	3.43	5.99

[a]Hoyle 1977, p. 141; Thom 1971, p. 26, adjusted slightly to match Hoyle in the overlap region. Air at 10° C and 100 kPa. Angle values are listed to two decimal places to minimize round-off errors in the calculations.

[b]TA / tan θ. The true angle of ascent or descent θ near the horizon, neglecting refraction, from eqn (16) of North 1996, p. 563: θ = $\cos^{-1}[\sin\lambda / \cos\sigma]$; where λ = latitude = 51°.178 N at Stonehenge; σ = declination = ± 23°.44 at Solstices (A.D. 1955–2030), and ± 1°.2 (= ± 23°.44 sin 3°) at Equalnights. Therefore, θ = 31°.9 at Solstices, and 38°.8 at Equalnights.

Figure A-1

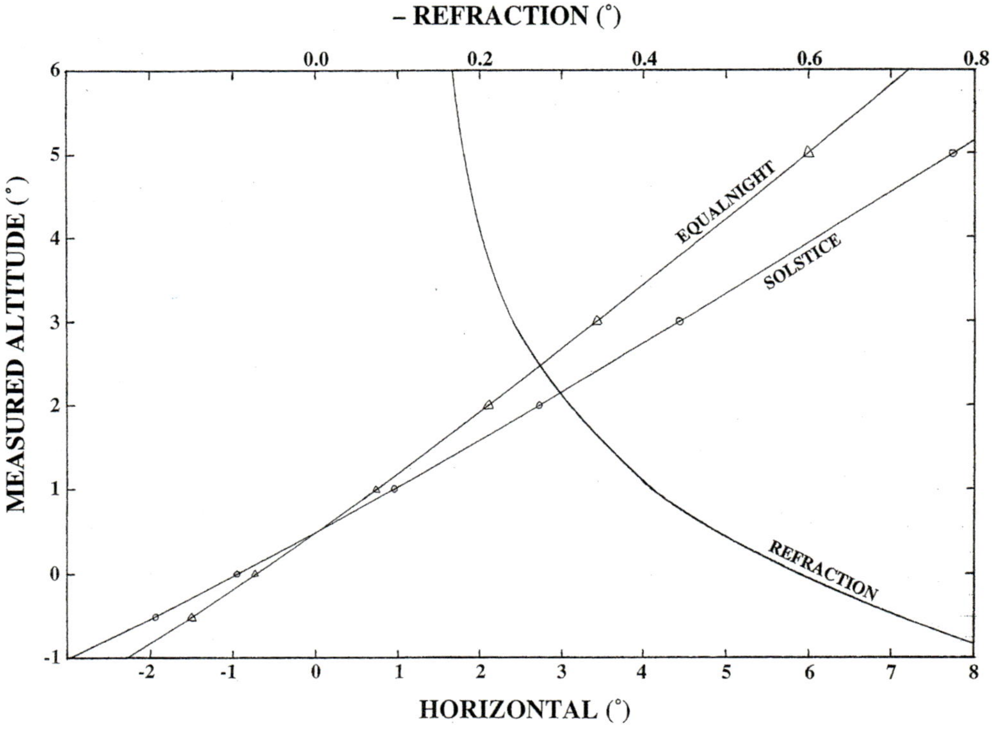

Figure A-1 Extent of refraction of light from the rising or setting Sun or Moon, by an average atmosphere (10° C, 100 kPa), at different observing altitudes above horizontal. Also, curves that are followed by the upper limb of the rising or setting Sun near a Solstice or Equalnight at different altitudes above horizontal. The same curves apply to the upper limb of the Full Moon. Data are from Table A-1.

A.4. Time Dependence of the Obliquity of the Ecliptic

The Earth's orbit around the Sun is called the Ecliptic, because an eclipse of the Sun or Moon can only happen when the Earth-orbiting Moon crosses the plane of the Earth's orbit.

The spinning axis of the Earth is the N–S Polar Axis. The Earth's Equator is perpendicular to the Axis. The Celestial Equator is the great circle in the sky directly above the Earth's Equator, centred at the Earth's centre.

The Ecliptic is at an angle ε to the Celestial Equator, and angle $(90° - \varepsilon)$ to the Earth's Polar Axis; ε is called the obliquity of the Ecliptic.

During the current epoch, the tilt of the Earth's Polar (spinning) Axis is slowly drifting toward the axis of the Earth's orbit around the Sun, so ε has been slowly decreasing during the last 10,000 years. The value of ε oscillates between about $22°.0$ and $24°.5$ with a period of about 40,000 years.

The decreasing tilt of the Earth's spinning axis causes the directions of the Solstice Sun rises and sets to drift slowly toward east and west. It does not affect the Sun directions at the Equalday/nights, because at those times the Earth's tilt is nearly broadside to the Sun and does not influence the rise due east and set due west.

The value of ε is presently $23°.44$. An equation for the value of ε and its variation with time is

$$\varepsilon(°) = 23.439 - 0.130T + 0.00050\ T^3 \quad (3)$$

or

$$\varepsilon(\text{rad}) = 0.40909 - 0.00227T + 8.7 \times 10^{-6}\ T^3$$

where T is the number of thousands of years (kiloanni, ka) measured algebraically from A.D. 2000; 1 radian = $57°.296$.

In A.D. 2000, the value of ε was $23°.439 = 0.40909$ rad, while in 4 ka B.P. it was $23°.93 = 0.4176$ rad, and in 5 ka B.P. $24°.03 = 0.4193$ rad.

A.5. Azimuths of Sun Rise and Set

The azimuths of Sun rise and set change throughout the year as the Earth travels along the Ecliptic. The Earth's orbit is taken to begin where the Ecliptic crosses the Celestial Equator in March, and the Sun is at SZM; this is the March Node. The angular distance of the Earth along the Ecliptic on a particular date, measured from the March (SZM) Node, is S_O.

The value of the azimuth θ_S^R of the first flash of the rising Sun depends upon the values of S_O, ε, the latitude λ of the observer's position on Earth, and the true altitude h_S^R of the centre of the Sun at the moment of the first flash. The governing equation is

$$\sin S_O \sin \varepsilon = \cos h_S^R \cos \lambda \cos \theta_S^R + \sin h_S^R \sin \lambda \quad (4)$$

The true altitude of the Sun's centre at the moment of the first flash is lower than the horizon, due to the angular radius of the Sun, which is 4.65 mrad = 0°.266, and to refraction of the light by the Earth's atmosphere, which is on average 9 mrad = 0°.52 at Stonehenge when the geographical altitude of the horizon in the rise direction is h^R = 8 mrad = 0°.46. The general equation for h_S of the Sun's true centre at the time of a first or last flash is

$$h_S = h - \text{Sun's radius} - \text{refraction} \quad (5)$$

For the preceding example of Sun rise,

$$h_S^R = 0.008 - 0.0047 - 0.009 = -0.0057 \text{ rad, or } -0°.32$$

Values of h_S at Stonehenge are all small, from −3 to −9 mrad, so $\cos h_S$ = 1.0000 and $\sin h_S = h_S$ (h_S must be in **radians**). Then equation (4) becomes

$$\sin S_O \sin \varepsilon = \cos \lambda \cos \theta_S^R + h_S^R \sin \lambda \quad (4')$$

and

$$\theta_S^R = \cos^{-1}[(\sin S_O \sin \varepsilon - h_S^R \sin \lambda) / \cos \lambda]$$

At the Summer Solstice, $S_O = \pi/2$ radians, so $\sin S_O = 1$, and

$$\theta_S^R = \cos^{-1}[(\sin \varepsilon - h_S^R \sin \lambda) / \cos \lambda]$$

At the Winter Solstice, $S_O = 3\pi/2$ radians, $\sin S_O = -1$, and

$$\theta_S^R = \cos^{-1}[(-\sin \varepsilon - h_S^R \sin \lambda) / \cos \lambda]$$

The Earth is at a node of the Ecliptic when the Sun's Zenith is at Midaltitude (SZM, zem). The March Equalday/night is on average 2.8 days before the March SZM, so S_O = 357°.2 = 6.234 rad; the September Equalday/night is on average 2.8 days past the September SZM, so S_O = 182°.8 = 3.190 rad. In both cases, $\sin S_O$ = -0.049, and

$$\theta_S^R = \cos^{-1}[(-0.049 \sin \varepsilon - h_S^R \sin \lambda / \cos \lambda]$$

The azimuth θ_S^S (rad) of the last flash of the setting Sun is (2π -

θ_S^R) rad if $h_S^R = h_S^S$. In general the two geographic horizon altitudes are different, so for the set directions,

$$\theta_S^S (\text{rad}) = 2\pi - \cos^{-1}[(\sin S_O \sin \varepsilon - h_S^S \sin \lambda) / \cos \lambda] \quad (6)$$

Values of θ_S, ε, S_O and λ in equations (4') and (6) may be expressed in degrees, but h_S must always be in radians to use the simplification $\sin h_S = h_S$. If one wishes to express h_S in degrees one simply replaces h_S by $\sin h_S$ in the equations, as in equation (4).

Altitudes of lines from the camera to the horizon free of trees at Stonehenge were estimated from the contour map Ordnance Survey Explorer 130, contour interval 5 metres, taking care to add the height of the camera above the ground to the map elevation of the observation point.

Data for the Seasonal Sun lines observed at Stonehenge are listed in Table A-2.

TABLE A-2

Geographical altitudes *h* of sight lines, and true altitudes *h*$_S$ of the Sun's centre, for Solstice and Equalday/night Sun rises and sets seen from Stonehenge Circle; Sun rise and set directions θ$_S$ in A.D. 2008 and 4.0 ka B.P.

	h [a]		Air refraction [b]		h_S [c]		θ_S [d]			
							A.D. 2008		4.0 ka B.P.	
	mrad	deg	mrad	deg	mrad	deg	mrad	deg	rad	deg
SSR [e]	8.5	0.49	8.57	0.491	-4.7	-0.27	0.875	50.2	0.859	49.2
ER [f]	7.5	0.43	8.74	0.501	-5.9	-0.34	1.595	91.4	1.595	91.4
WSR [g]	4.6	0.26	9.39	0.538	-9.4	-0.54	2.243	128.5	2.259	129.4
WSS [g]	8.4	0.48	8.60	0.493	-4.9	-0.28	4.032	231.1	4.016	230.1
ES [f]	10.1	0.58	8.32	0.477	-2.9-	0.16	4.684	268.4	4.684	268.4
	(2.9	0.17)	(9.76	0.559)	(-11.5	-0.65)	(4.696	269.0)	(4.696	269.0)
SSS [e]	6.3	0.36	9.04	0.518	-7.4	-0.42	5.412	310.1	5.428	311.0
Cursus Barrows 43 to 55										
ER [h]	7.4	0.42	8.78	0.503	-6.0	-0.35			1.595	91.4
ES [h]	5.0	0.29	9.25	0.530	-8.9	-0.51			4.691	268.8
	(4.8	0.27)	(9.30	0.533)	(-9.2	-0.53)			(4.692	268.8)

[a]Measured from 1.5 m above the ground at the place noted, except 0.7 m for SSR, to the distant horizon, along lines at 49°, 91°, 129°, 230°, 268°, and 311° on the contour map *Ordnance Survey Explorer 130* (1998). Recorded to two or three figures to minimize round-off errors in calculations.

[b]From Figure A-1, read to three figures to minimize round-off errors when added to the radius of the Sun, which is 4.65 mrad = 0°.266.

[c]$h_s = h$ - Sun's radius - refraction.

[d]Azimuth of the first or last flash, calculated from equation (4') or (6). $\lambda = 0.8932$ rad = 51°.178. In A.D. 2008, $\varepsilon = 0.4091$ rad = 23°.44; in 4.0 ka B.P., $\varepsilon = 0.4176$ rad = 23°.93.

[e]Summer Solstice rise or set; from near the centre of Oval Twin Disk Barrow **10** at 104 m MSL (above Mean Sea Level) to the SE side of Lark Hill at 130 m MSL, 3050 m away, or from SE of Circle Sarsen 8 at 104 m MSL to Lower Cursus ridge at 117 m MSL, 2070 m away.

[f]Equalday/night rise or set; from west of West Trilithon Sarsen 58 at 104 m MSL to the north base of New King Bowl Barrow **28** at 113 m MSL, 1200 m away, or from east of Circle Sarsen 3 at 104 m MSL to the top of a knoll at 121 m MSL, 1680 m away. Equalday/night is approximately 2.8 days before the Vernal SZM, and 2.8 days after the Autumnal SZM. (ES quantities in parentheses are from the top of New King Bowl Barrow **29** at 116 m MSL to a highland at 161 m MSL 11.7 km west; the effective altitude was reduced 11 m due to curvature of the Earth over 11.7 km.)

[g]Winter Solstice rise or set; from west of West Trilithon Sarsen 58 at 104 m MSL to SW of the summit of Coneybury Hill at 111 m MSL, 1520 m away, or from the SW face of the Heel Stone at 102 m MSL to the NW shoulder of a hill at 138 m MSL, 4270 m away. The altitude of the line from the Heel Stone at 102 m MSL to the SE groin of Bell Barrow **15** at 108 m MSL, 1020 m away, is 5.9 mrad = 0°.34. This is sufficiently close to the estimated altitude of the distant horizon that the exact altitudes should be determined with phase-analyzed GPS measurements. Eventually, a strip of trees will be cut out of Normanton Gorse to allow Bell Barrow **15** to be seen on the horizon.

*b*Equalday/night rise or set, viewed from a local slight crest at 111 m MSL, 100 m W of Cursus Bell Barrow **55**, to a saddle point at 180 m MSL, 8.5 km E, or to a hilltop at 178 m MSL, 11.3 km W. Corrections were made for the curvature of the Earth, which decreases the apparent elevation of the horizon by $\Delta h(m) = [\text{km to horizon} / 3.56 \text{ km}]^2$; $\Delta h = 6$ m in the E, and 10 m in the W. (The ES quantities in parentheses were calculated for observation from the base of Barrow **43**, 12.4 km from the horizon, with an Earth's curvature correction of 12 m.)

A.6. Extrapolation of Rise and Set Points to Their Positions N Days Away

Sometimes Sun rise and set cannot be observed on the desired date, for reasons of weather or access to the site. Rise and set points can be extrapolated accurately over several days from observed points to the positions on the Solstice or Equalday/night.

The period from the Summer Solstice to the Equalnight on either side is 96 days, and the average swing of the rise and set points to and from the Solstice points at Stonehenge now is $41°.4$. Each day near the Summer Solstice, the Earth moves along the Ecliptic approximately $90°/96 = 0°.94$. The change in rise or set azimuth during n days to or from the Summer Solstice is

$$\Delta\theta_S = 41°.4 \, (1 - \cos 0°.94 \, n) \quad (7)$$

This corresponds to $0°.006$ for $n = 1$, and to $0°.09$ for $n = 4$.

The period from the Winter Solstice to the Equalnight on either side is 86.6 days, and the average swing of the rise and set points at Stonehenge now is $37°.2$. Each day near the Winter Solstice, the Earth moves along the Ecliptic approximately $1°.04$. The change in rise or set azimuth during n days to or from the Winter Solstice is

$$\Delta\theta_S = 37°.2 \, (1 - \cos 1.04 \, n) \quad (8)$$

This corresponds to $0°.006$ for $n = 1$, and to $0°.10$ for $n = 4$.

The average period from an Equalday/night to the Solstice on either side is 91.3 days, and the average swing of the rise and set points is $39°.3$. The change in rise or set azimuth during n days to or from an Equalday/night is

$$\Delta\theta_S = 39°.3 \sin 0.99 \, n \quad (9)$$

This corresponds to $0°.68$ for each day during 10 days on either side of the Equalday/night, and an average $0°.67$ per day extends to 20 days on either side.

A.7. DETERMINATION OF THE CARDINAL DIRECTIONS AND THE EQUALDAY/NIGHT

Cardinal means "on which something hinges." The word derives from the Latin *cardo*, which means hinge, swing, pivot; it also means a mortise and tenon, a socket and knob joint, such as those between the Sarsen Stone uprights and lintels, for which Stonehenge is famous. Latin *cardo* in Old English is *henge*.

"Stonehenge," from *Stanhenge,* which is Old English for "Stonehinge," marks the cardinal directions and the swing of the direction of the Sun through the seasons. The calendar in *Ómahkiyáahkóhtóohp* also contains several Stonehinges, which I had been calling Pivot Rocks.

The cardinal directions are true north, south, east, and west. They are easily determined by carefully recording motions of the North Star and the Sun during a year. The Earth's Polar (spinning) Axis precesses slowly, so the identity of the northmost star changes in a 26,000-year cycle. During recent millennia, the northmost star is what we call Polaris, but 15,000 years ago it was what we call Vega (Wega, Stooping Eagle, Vulture), and the people at that time probably called it "North Star," or "Star That Doesn't Move Much."

North – south

The exact directions north and south can be determined by marking the direction of the northmost Star with a line on the ground, for example with a front stake and a back rock separated by 100 large paces (Figure A-2). The Star makes a complete circle around the North Celestial Pole (NCP) position in the sky every 24 hours. At latitudes between the Arctic Circle and the Equator, only part of the Star's circle is visible during any particular night. As the Star rotates, one adjusts the back rock to keep the line pointing accurately toward the Star, until it reaches a left or right extreme. The extreme line is left on the ground.

Several months later, when the northmost Star is visible on the other side of its circle, one uses a second rock and the same front stake to mark an accurate line to the other extreme of the North Star circle. One then stretches a cord between the two rocks to measure the distance, folds that length of cord in half, and marks the halfway point.

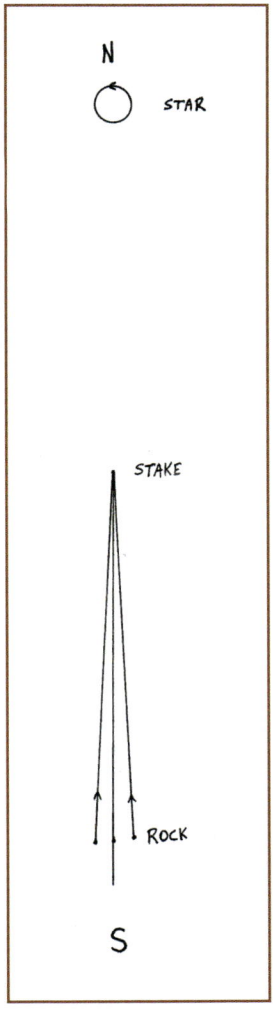

Figure A-2 Determination of true north–south by marking lines pointed at the left and right extremes of the northmost star in its circle about the Celestial North Pole. The midline is true S–N.

The halfway point joined to the front stake is an exact S–N line.

N–S is marked with an accuracy of 0°.1 in *Ómahkiyáahkóhtóohp*, by several lines from 700 metres to 1500 metres long. A pair of N–S lines apparently made by the above method is dated to either 2730 or 2910 B.C., with a precision of ±9 years: they are a 1500-metre, 0°.44-E line from the East House to a cairn on a hilltop, and a 1138-metre, 0°.54-W line from the V Rocks (West House) to the centre of a V of small cairns on a knoll top. In 2820 B.C., the NCP was exactly at α-Draconis (also called *Ath-Thu'ban*, The Snake), and it was moving counterclockwise at the rate of 0°.57 per century. The pair of lines from the East and West Houses is symmetrically ±0°.49 about True North within ±0°.05, and corresponds to pointing toward the E and W extremes of α-Draconis about the NCP in either 2910 B.C. before the NCP reached α-Draconis, or in 2730 B.C. after the NCP passed it.

East – west

East and west are determined by marking lines to the positions of Sun rise and set on a flat plain as the season passes through an Equalday/night. During the summer, both the rise and set lines have a northerly direction, so they do not join to make a straight line (Figure A-3). In winter both lines have a southerly direction, so they do not join to make a straight line. For one day in mid March, and another in late September, the rise and set lines join to make a straight line. That line is true E–W. An easy way to find it is as follows.

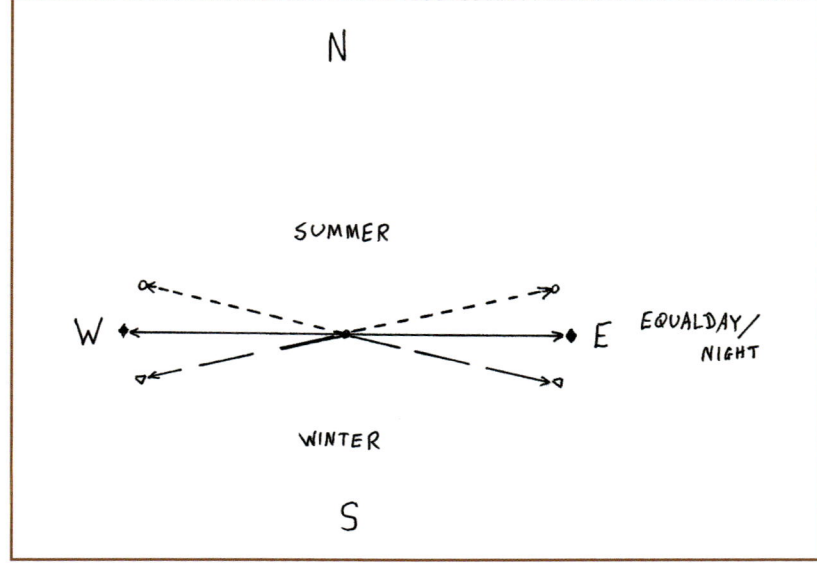

Figure A-3 Seasonal Sun rise and set directions. On the Equalday/night, the rise and set directions join to form a straight line, for one day each March and one day each September.

256　CANADA'S STONEHENGE

During the last half of September, the Sun rise and set points on a flat horizon move southerly by 0°.68 per day. When the rise and set lines are approaching a single straight line, place two rocks 100 large paces apart, approximately E–W. Rocks of 20 or 30 centimetres width and height can be seen each from the other. At Sun set, move the easterly rock to mark an exact line with the westerly rock to the last-flash position on the horizon (Figure A-4). Next morning, move the westerly rock southerly to make an exact line with the easterly rock to the first flash of the Sun. Each evening reset the easterly rock, and each morning reset the westerly rock, until the direction of re-setting reverses. The line between the most southerly positions, 3-3 in Figure A-4, is within 0°.3 of true E–W.

The Equalday/night is bracketed by the rises and sets closest to the bottom of a Figure such as A-4. In this case the Equalnight is between set E3 to W2 and rise W3 to E3; the Equalday is between rise W3 to E3 and set E4 to W3.

In March the Sun moves northerly, so the rocks would be shifted in the opposite directions.

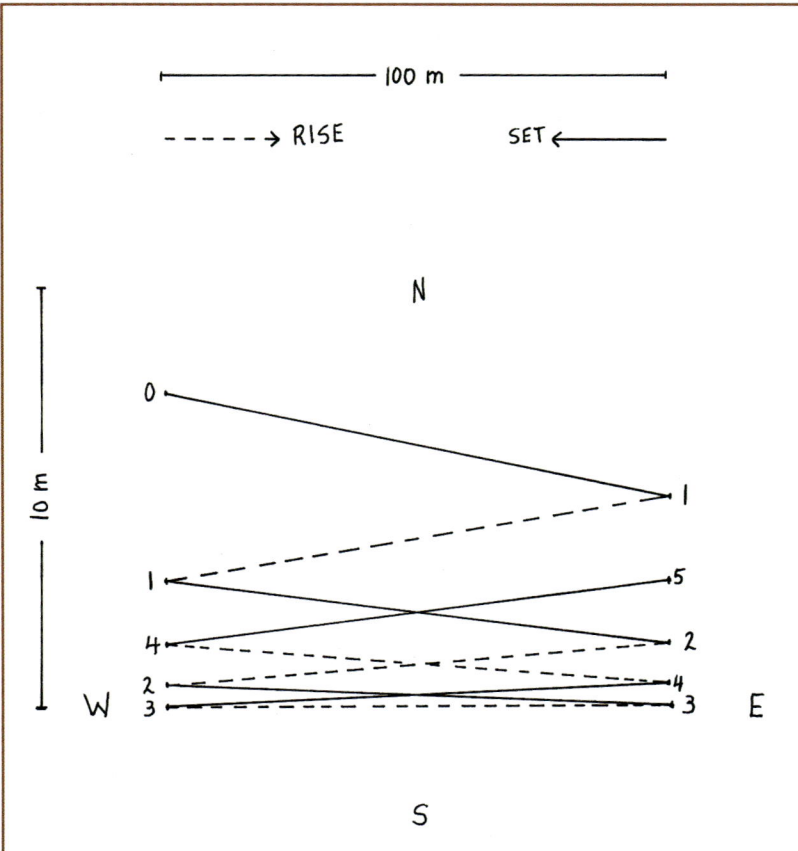

Figure A-4 Determination of true east–west by successively marking lines toward the last flash of the setting Sun and first flash of the rising Sun during September. The Equalnight is between set E3 to W2 and rise W3 to E3; the Equalday is between rise W3 to E3 and set E4 to W3. The line E3 to W3 is within 0°.3 of true east–west. The N–S scale in this Figure is expanded 8-fold to make the changes of direction clear. The displacement of the E rock from position 3 to 4 is 0.5 m.

The Equalnights at Stonehenge, and in Europe, are always September 25 to 26 and March 17 to 18. The Equaldays are September 25 and March 17 in the first two years of a leap year cycle, and September 26 and March 18 in the last two years of the cycle.

In *Ómahkiyáahkóhtóohp*, and in Canada, the Equaldays are always September 25 and March 17; the Equalnights spend two years on each side of the Equaldays during the leap year cycle.

By repeating the direction measurements in both March and September over several years and averaging the results, true east–west can be obtained within 0°.1. In *Ómahkiyáahkóhtóohp*, there is a remarkable string of calendrical cairns and oriented elongated rocks over a distance of 4 kilometres, crossing a low rise and the Bow River, which marks true E–W within 0°.1.

Once the dates of the Equalday/nights have been determined on flat land, the dates can be marked by Sun rise and set sight lines in any other place, whether the landscape is flat or not.

A.8. To Distinguish the First or Last Flash of the Sun from its Mirage

A mirage is caused by a high density-gradient in the atmosphere near the ground. Low-angle light from a Sun rise or set is bent toward the higher density layer of air. If the density gradient is large enough, light in the dense layer is reflected from the surface of the low-density layer, back into the high-density layer. That's why you see sky on the surface of a hot road, and stuff from beyond the normal horizon when air in a layer near the ground is much colder than the air above it.

Peculiar meteorological conditions sometimes produce several layers of alternating density near the Earth's surface, so a mirage sometimes appears as several thin horizontal layers on the horizon. Nonhomogeneous processes galore! Once you acquire the mindset of KNP, everything is interesting.

In horizon astronomy, the most common mirage effect is to produce a short, thin line of orange light on the horizon before the actual first flash. If one is not aware of mirages and how to take them into account, the error in a rise or set azimuth might be a degree or two.

A thin layer of high-density air near the ground might be caused by a warm air mass moving into a zone where the ground is much colder. When the Sun is still below the eastern horizon, light enters the band of dense air beyond the horizon and is bent around the curvature of the Earth to reach an observer who is in the dense band. The thickness of the dense layer at the distance of the horizon typically corresponds to an angular thickness of about $0°.05$, one-tenth of the Sun's diameter. This would be a layer 10 metres thick at a horizon 10 kilometres away.

The mirage is a horizontal line of orange light about $0°.05$ thick, which grows in length along the horizon to the maximum $0°.5$ width of the Sun's disk. This line sits on or slightly above the actual horizon, and moves southerly at the rate of the Sun's horizontal motion beyond the horizon. The line of orange light remains the same thickness because it equals the thickness of the layer of dense air at the horizon.

When the top of the rising Sun reaches the top of the dense layer at the horizon, the orange line begins to bulge in the middle and becomes yellow. To obtain the position of the first flash, one extrapolates the position of the top of the yellow bulge back to the normal horizon, using a normal angle of rising (Figure A-1).

First-flash positions can be obtained to an accuracy of $0°.1$ under conditions of mirage or haze. I have used both photographs and naked-eye sketches to record the formation and movement of the orange line, its bulging and change of colour, and extrapolated the location of the yellow upper limb to the first-flash position on the horizon. Examples are shown in my report *Temple of the Sun, Moon and Morningstar*, which, after completion in a few years, will be in the University of Alberta Archives.

■ ■ ■

Selected Bibliography

This is a partial list of works I have read that are relevant to this book, including those I think would be useful to anyone who pursues the subject.

Anati, Emmanuel. *Har Karkom in the light of new discoveries*. Capo di Ponte (BS), Italy: Edizioni del Centro, CCSP, 1993.
Reports extensive archaeological remains on the mountain that Anati believes is the Mount Sinai of the Biblical book of *Exodus*. Anati's overall work, centred on ancient rock art, displays an admirable breadth of scope.

Antrobus, Florence C.M. *A Sentimental and Practical Guide to Amesbury and Stonehenge*. 2nd ed. Amesbury, Wilts: Estate Office, 1902.
This elegant little book led me to Barclay, her source.

Astronomical Almanac. Vols. 1982 to 2003. Washington, DC: US Naval Observatory, US Government Printing Office. Published annually. *Explanatory Supplement*, 1992.

Atkinson, Richard J.C. *Stonehenge*. 2nd ed. Harmondsworth: Penguin, 1979.
Excellent source, rich with data. A minor point is that it gets the Altar Stone's original position, and some of the relative dating of features, wrong.

Aubrey, John (1626–1697). *Monumenta Britannica*. Edited by John Fowles. Sherborne: Dorset Pub. Co., 1980.

Aveni, Anthony F. *Empires of Time*. Rev. Ed. Boulder: University Press of Colorado, 2002.
Excellent book about Mexico and Central America, where Aveni did original work; poor about Stonehenge and "medicine wheels," where, apparently, he did not.

Aveni, Anthony F. *Skywatchers of Ancient Mexico*. 1st and 2nd eds. Austin: University of Texas Press, 1980 and 2001.

Aveni, Anthony F. *Stairways to the Stars*. New York: Wiley, 1997.

Baedae, Venerabilis (A.D. 673–735). *Historiam Ecclesiasticum Gentis Anglorum, Historiam Abbatum, Epistolam Ad Ecgberctum, Historia Abbatum Auctore Anonymo*. Edited by Charles Plummer, with commentary. Oxford: Clarendon Press, 1896.
Note the Latin pronunciation of the name, *Bayday*, compared with the Old Saxon pronunciation *Baydeh*.

Barclay, Edgar. *Stonehenge and Its Earth-Works*. London: D. Nutt, 1895.
Very insightful work.

Barnes, William. *Se Gefylsta: an Anglo-Saxon delectus*. London: John Russell Smith, 1849.

Beaubrun, Mimerose, lead singer of *Boukman Eksperyans*, a Haitian music group (Elipsis Arts, Roslyn, NY, 1997). "*Vodou* means spirit. . . . Everything is *Vodou* for us. . . . Water is a symbol of the feminine principle, of sweetness, of women. . . . The sun (is) the symbol of fire – the primary masculine symbol – you need the masculine and feminine. They are sacred. . . . In the morning, the first thing is to pour a little water, or throw it in the air, because water opens passages. You present the water to the sun. . . . When the sun goes down you light a candle. The candle is fire, the symbol of the sun."

Bede's Ecclesiastical History of England, also the Anglo-Saxon Chronicle. Edited by J.A. Giles, with notes. London: George Bell, 1907.

Bede's Ecclesiastical History of the English People. Edited by Bertram Colgrave and R.A.B. Mynors. Oxford: Clarendon Press, 1969.

Black Elk (1863–1950), told to John G. Neihardt. *Black Elk Speaks: being the life story of a Holy Man of the Oglala Sioux*. New York: William Morrow, 1932.
A valuable source of information about *Lakota* people.

Bullchild, Percy. *The Sun Came Down*. San Fransisco: Harper & Row, 1985.
Percy Bullchild is a Blackfeet in Montana, part of the large Piegan Tribe now divided between Montana and Alberta. The people in Alberta are called Blackfoot and Peigan. The spellings of Tribe names are not standardized. Related tribes in Alberta are the *Piikuni* (or *Piikani*, Peigan), *Kainai* (Blood), and *Siksika* (Blackfoot). This book is oral knowledge put into print, so you have to hear it as if it were being told to you. Language used in talking is looser than language used in writing. Print also lacks intonation and body language, but readers with appropriate experience can mentally supply some of it. The information will not be understood by Whites who have little or prejudiced knowledge of American Indian cultures. The more you know about the reality of Plains Indian cultures, the more you will see in the book. Interested uninitiated readers might enjoy looking for the numbers 1, 2, 3, 4, 5, 7, 14, 28, and 56 in significant contexts.

Burl, Aubrey. *The Stone Circles of the British Isles*. New Haven: Yale University Press, 1976.

Calder, James M. *The Majorville Cairn and Medicine Wheel Site, Alberta*. Ottawa: National Museum of Man Mercury Series, Archaeological Survey of Canada Paper No. 62, 297 pages, 1977. Detailed report of the Cairn excavation done in 1971.

Chippindale, Christopher. *Stonehenge Complete*, 3rd ed. London: Thames & Hudson, 2004.

Popular, humorous, but biased, sometimes distorted.

The Church in Crisis: A.D. 325–1870. Web site: **www.christusrex.org/www1/CHDN/coun2.html**.

Cleal, Rosamund, K.E. Walker and R. Montague. *Stonehenge in its landscape*. London: English Heritage, 1995.

Vital compilation of twentieth-century data, with inevitable errors increased by a limited publication schedule.

Coe, Michael D. *The Maya*. 7th ed. London: Thames & Hudson, 2005.

Cole, Peter. *Coyote & Raven Go Canoeing: coming home to the village*. Montreal: McGill-Queens University Press, 2006.

Peter Cole is so good at putting oral storytelling into print that, if you have experienced a good storyteller, your mind will provide body language to Peter's storytelling. This is remarkable, often understandably bitter, poetic prose, and sometimes you can hear the singing. Peter gives a lot of information that I'm not allowed to. His mind operates in the nonhomogeneous processes mode. He's a rare KNPer. Read page 69, leading to the visualizing "verbal pluming."

Cornell, James. *The First Stargazers*. New York: Scribner's, 1981.

Darvill, Timothy. *Ever Increasing Circles: The Sacred Geographies of Stonehenge and its Landscape*. Proceedings of the British Academy. Vol. 92, pages 167–202, 1997.

Darvill, Timothy and Geoffrey Wainwright. *Exploring Preseli*. British Archaeology. Vol. 83, July–August, page 29, 2005.

Dating Easter: Calendar Reform. Web site: **ancienthistory.about.com/library/weekly/aa040200c.htm**.

David, A. and A. Payne. *Geophysical Surveys within the Stonehenge Landscape*. Proceedings of the British Academy. Vol. 92, pages 73-113, 1997.

de Bhaldraithe, T. *Gearrfhoclóir Gaeilge-Béarla*. Baile Átha Cliath: Richview Browne & Nolan, 1981.

Irish, *Gaeilge*, to English dictionary.

Devereux, Paul. *Mysterious Ancient America*. London: Vega, 2002.

Easter Controversy, A.D. 190 to 716. Web sites:
www.newadvent.org/cathen/05228a.htm and
www.newadvent.org/cathen/11044a.htm.

Eddy, John A. *Astronomical Alignment of the Big Horn Medicine Wheel*. Science. Vol. 184. pages 1035–1043, 1974.

Eddy, John A. *Medicine Wheels and Plains Indian Astronomy*. Native American Astronomy. Edited by Anthony F. Aveni. Austin: University of Texas Press, pages 147–169, 1977.

In this article Eddy cautiously speculated a bit broadly. This might have seeded the attacks on "medicine wheel astronomy" that were fashionable during the next two decades.

Eddy, John A. and Thomas E. Hooper. *Probing the Mystery of Medicine Wheels*. National Geographic. Vol. 151, no. 1, pages 140–146, 1977.

Eddy's work is the most important precursor of my own.

Franz, Donald G. and Norma J. Russell. *Blackfoot Dictionary of stems, roots, and affixes*. Toronto: University of Toronto Press, 1989.

Freeman, Gordon R. *Kinetics of Nonhomogeneous Processes in Human Society: Unethical Behavior and Societal Chaos*. Canadian Journal of Physics. Vol. 68, pages 794–798, 1990.

Two years after this article appeared, it created a furor in the feminist-dominated public media (press, radio, and TV), and in pseudoscholarly publications such as the journal *Scholarly Publishing*. The furor was dubbed "The Freeman Affair" in humorous but penetrating comparison with "The Galileo Affair," and continued for several years.

Freeman, Gordon R. *Sacred Rocks of Alberta: Description of eleven glyphed boulders, a meteorite, and their sites*. Edmonton: University of Alberta Archives, Accession No. 2000-44, 126 pages of manuscript including index; 531 annotated photographs; 3 sketches; 14 site maps; the file also contains about 1368 photo negatives and their annotated prints; 2000.

Freeman, G.R. *Kekip Sacred Rock in Alberta: Moon, Morningstar and blood sacrifice*. XXII International Symposium of Valcamonica: Rock Art and the World Heritage, 2007. Edited by Emmanuel Anati. Proceedings in press.

Freeman, G.R. *Stonehenge Data and Files*. Edmonton: University of Alberta Archives, 1300 annotated photographs with their negatives, field notes, and manuscripts. In preparation, available about 2010.

Freeman, Gordon R. *Temple of the Sun, Moon and Morningstar near Majorville, Alberta*. Edmonton: University of Alberta Archives, about 500 pages of text, 2000 annotated photographs. In preparation, available about 2010.

The boxes of Sun Temple material contain about 12,000 annotated photographs with their negatives and eight books of field notes. The field notebooks also contain records of the *Sacred Rocks* field trips and photographs.

Freeman, Gordon R. and Phyllis J. Freeman. *Majorville Medicine Wheel Site: I. Distant outliers and accurate Solstice alignments*. 23rd Chacmool Conference, Calgary, Canada, November, 1990.

Freeman, Gordon R. and Phyllis J. Freeman. *Majorville Medicine Wheel Site: II. Marking the 12.0 hour day, not the Solar Equinox*. 23rd Chacmool Conference, Calgary, Canada, November, 1990.

Freeman, Gordon R. and Phyllis J. Freeman. *Stonehenge: Winter Solstice Sun Rise and Set Lines Accurate to $0°.2$ in 4000 B.P.* La Société Européene pour L'Astronomie dans la Culture, Conference, Dublin, Ireland, 2 September 1998.

Freeman, Gordon R. and Phyllis J. Freeman. *Variation in Estimated Positions of Sun Rise and Set Due to Atmospheric Conditions*. La Société Européene pour L'Astronomie dans la Culture, Conference, Dublin, Ireland, 2 September 1998.

Freeman, Gordon R. and Phyllis J. Freeman. *Observational Archaeoastronomy at Stonehenge: Summer Solstice Sun Rise and Set Lines Accurate to $0°.2$ in 4000 B.P.* 19 pages, 2000. Web site: **www.ualberta.ca/~gfreeman/stone/summer.htm**

Freeman, Gordon R. and Phyllis J. Freeman. *Observational Archaeoastronomy at Stonehenge: Winter Solstice Sun Rise and Set Alignments Accurate to $0°.2$ in 4000 B.P.* 33rd Annual Meeting, Canadian Archaeological Assoc., Ottawa 2000 Proceedings. Edited by J.-L. Pilon, M. Kirby, C. Thériault, pages 200-219, 2001. Web site: **http://epe.lac-bac.gc.ca/100/200/300/ont_archaeol_soc/annual_meeting_caa/33rd/freeman1.pdf**

Freeman, Gordon R. and Phyllis J. Freeman. *Observational Archaeoastronomy at the Majorville Medicine Wheel Complex: Winter and Summer Solstice Sun Rise and Set Alignments Accurate to $0°.2$.* 33rd Annual Meeting, Canadian Archaeological Assoc., Ottawa 2000 Proceedings, Edited by J.-L. Pilon, M. Kirby, C. Thériault, pages 220-229, 2001. Web site:

http://epe.lac-bac.gc.ca/100/200/300/ont_archaeol_soc/annual_meeting_caa/33rd/freeman2.pdf

Geoffrey of Monmouth. *Historia Regum Britannie*. About A.D. 1138. Many copies survive from the twelfth century, with variations between them. See the four volumes edited by Neil Wright 1985–1988. The first variant version is in Vol. 2, and a later version is in Vol. 1.

Geoffrey of Monmouth. *Histories of the Kings of Britain*. About A.D. 1138. Translated by Sebastian Evans, 1903. London: Dent, published 1912.

Goodman, Ronald. *Lakota Star Knowledge.* Rosebud, South Dakota: *Siŋte Gleska* University, 1992.

Gregorian Calendar Reform. Web sites:
ourworld.compuserve.com/homepages/khagen/GreyConv.html
and
ourworld.compuserve.com/homepages /khagen/Easter.html.

Gregorius Episcopus, *Inter Gravissimas*. Web site:
www.fourmilab.ch/documents/calendar/IG_Latin.html.

Hadingham, Evan. *Circles and Standing Stones*. New York: Walker, 1975.
Excellent summary of the history of proposals for Stonehenge's calendrics up to 1975. An apparent conflict between proposed construction dates of the Sarsen Circle and the Avenue was resolved by the new dating reported by Cleal and coworkers in 1995.

Hadingham, Evan. *Early Man and the Cosmos*. Norman: University of Oklahoma Press, 1984.

Hallendy, Norman. *Inuksuit: Silent Messengers of the Arctic*. Vancouver: Douglas & McIntyre, 2000.
The photographs are exceptionally beautiful; the text achieves a vital non-Caucasian mindset.

Hancock, Graham. *Fingerprints of the Gods*. New York: Crown, 1995.
Excellent book, but there are difficulties with numbers and hyperbole. For example: the original height of the Great Pyramid of Giza is quoted to the nearest one-thousandth of an inch, even though the top thirty-one feet are missing; monolith weights are sometimes quoted as eight times larger than those corresponding to the quoted length, height, and width, since rock densities are known.

Hancock, Graham and Santha Faiia. *Heaven's Mirror*. Toronto: Doubleday, 1998.

Hawkins, Gerald S. *Stonehenge Decoded*. Garden City, N.Y.: Doubleday, 1965.

Hoyle, Fred. *On Stonehenge*. San Francisco: Freeman, 1977.

Johnson, Anthony. *Solving Stonehenge: the new key to an ancient enigma*. New York: Thames & Hudson, 2008.

    Johnson made the exciting discovery that the area enclosed by the Y Holes ring (it is roughly a circle/spiral with 5 straight sections) is 2x that enclosed by the Z Holes (circling the squared circle). I found that the Y Holes ring area is 3x that of the Sarsen Circle, and that the area of the terrain within the Bank is 9x that of the Sarsen Circle. Much more will follow from these ratios. But Johnson used the wrong (distorted) map of Wood to conclude that Sarsen 56 is now not in its original location. The location of Sarsen 56 in Wood's good map, and Petrie's, was displaced 1.1 metres NE of the original, by Sarsen 56's 30° tilt NE and 2.3-metre subterranean depth. Sarsen 56 is now very close to its original position.

Jones, Inigo. *The Most Notable Antiquity of Great Britain Vulgarly called Stonehenge on Salisbury Plain*. London: James Flesher, printer, 1655.

Kehoe, Alice B. and Thomas F. Kehoe. *Solstice-Aligned Boulder Configurations in Saskatchewan*. Ottawa: National Museum of Man Mercury Series, Canadian Ethnology Service Paper No. 48, 1979.

    The Kehoes showed geoglyphs in Saskatchewan to John Eddy.

Kehoe, Alice B. *Shamans and Religion*. Prospect Heights, IL: Waveland Press, 2000.

Kehoe, Alice B. *America before the European invasion*. London: Longman, 2002.

King, Ross. *Brunelleschi's Dome*. London: Chatto & Windus, 2000.

    Filippo Brunelleschi designed and engineered the largest masonry dome ever constructed, on La Basilica di Santa Maria del Fiore, Florence, A.D. 1420–1446.

Krupp, Edwin C. *Echoes of the Ancient Skies: the astronomy of lost civilizations*. New York: Harper & Row, 1983. Rev. ed., New York: Oxford University Press, 1993.

    Contains the most beautiful dedication I've seen.

Lewis, C.T. and C. Short. *Latin Dictionary*. Oxford: Clarendon Press, 1879.

L'Heureux, Jean. *The Kekip-Sesoators, or Ancient Sacrificial Stone, of the North-West Tribes of Canada*. Journal of the Anthropological Institute of Great Britain and Ireland, pages 160–165 and Plate VII, 1886.

Liddell, H.G. and R. Scott. *Greek-English Lexicon*. Oxford: Clarendon Press, 1889.

Littleton, C. Scott and Linda A. Malcor. *From Scythia to Camelot: a radical reassessment of the legends of King Arthur, the Knights of the Round Table, and the Holy Grail*. New York: Garland Publishing, 1994.

Lockyer, Norman and F.C. Penrose. *An Attempt to ascertain the Date of the Original Construction of Stonehenge from its Orientation*. Proceedings of the Royal Society of London. Vol. 69, pages 137–147, 1901–1902.

Lockyer, J. Norman. *Stonehenge and other British monuments astronomically considered*. London: Macmillan, 1906.

> A photocopy of the Stonehenge portion, chapters 5 to 9, was kindly sent to me by Andrew Bourmistroff from Moscow, Russia, in January 2004. The full book was obtained from New York: Readex Microprint, 1970.

Malmström, Vincent H. *Cycles of the Sun, Mysteries of the Moon: the calendar in Mesoamerican civilization*. Austin: University of Texas Press, 1997.

> Fortunately, this book was shepherdessed between Scylla and Charybdis by Shannon Davies at UTP.

Marshack, Alexander. *The roots of civilization; the cognitive beginnings of man's first art, symbol and notation*. New York: McGraw-Hill, 1972.

> Moon cycle notation during the Ice Age more than ten thousand years ago.

McQuarrie, John. *Cowboyin': a legend lives on*. Toronto: Macmillan, 1995.

> Includes photos of Grant Armstrong and family at work and play, and landscapes north of the Sun Temple near Majorville.

Miller, Dorcas S. *Stars of the First People: Native American Star Myths and Constellations*. Boulder, CO: Pruett, 1997.

Newham, C.A. *The Astronomical Significance of Stonehenge*. Leeds: John Blackburn, 1972.

North, John D. *Stonehenge: Neolithic Man and the Cosmos*. London: Harper Collins, 1996.

Old Ordnance Survey Map, 1909. *North Pembrokeshire, sheet 210*, scale 1:63,360. Consett DH8 7PW, England: Alan Godfrey Maps, reprinted 2001.

Ordnance Survey Map. *Explorer 130: Salisbury & Stonehenge*, scale 1:25,000, contour line interval 5 m. Southampton, England: 1998.

Ordnance Survey Map. *Explorer OL35, North Pembrokeshire*, scale 1:25,000, contour line interval 5 m. Southampton, England: 2006.

Oxford English Dictionay, OED Online. 2007. Web site: **http://dictionary.oed.com/**

Pitts, Mike. *Hengeworld*. London: Arrow Books, 2001.

Quimby, George I. *Cultural and Natural Areas before Kroeber*. American Antiquity. Vol. 19, pages 317–331, 1954.

Richards, J. *Stonehenge Environs Project*. London: Historic Buildings & Monuments Commission for England, 1990.

Royal Commission on Historical Monuments (England). *Stonehenge and Its Environs: Monuments and Land Use*. Lord Adeane, Chairman. Edinburgh: University Press, 1979.

Three detailed maps in the pocket inside the back cover.

Sampson, R.D. *Atmospheric Refraction and its Effects on Sunrise and Sunset*. M.Sc. Thesis, Department of Geography, University of Alberta, Edmonton, Canada, 1994.

He did not recognize occasional mirages, so made no correction for them, and he obtained a correspondingly large mean deviation in his data.

Smart, W.M. *Spherical Astronomy*. 5th ed., chapters 1 and 2. Cambridge: University Press, 1965.

Soave, Pietro. *Historia del Concilio Tridentino, Seconda Editione, riveduta e corretta dall'Autore*. 844 pages plus 12 pages of index. Published posthumously (died 1623), no location or publisher named, probably Rome, inscribed date 1629.

Sofaer, Anna, P. and Rolf M. Sinclair. *Astronomical markings at three sites on Fajada Butte*. In Astronomy and Ceremony in the Prehistoric Southwest. Edited by J. B. Carlson and W. J. Judge. Papers of the Maxwell Museum of Anthropology, No. 2. University of New Mexico, pages 43–70, 1987.

This excellent work was ridiculed when it was presented because accurate measurements had temporarily fallen out of fashion. I have updated the interpretation of the data, and they agree with those from *Ómahk*.

Stover, L.E. and B. Craig. *Stonehenge: The Indo-European Heritage*. Chicago: Nelson-Hall, 1978.

Stukeley, William. *Stukeley's 'Stonehenge' An Unpublished Manuscript 1721–1724*. Edited by Aubrey Burl and Neil Mortimer. New Haven: Yale University Press, 2005.
   Publication of Stukeley's manuscript might be Burl's greatest contribution to future Stonehenge scholars. Put aside the Druids, and use Stukeley's observational acuity.

Thom, Alexander. *Megalithic Sites in Britain*. Corrected reprint of 1967 ed. Oxford: Clarendon Press, 1974.

Thom, Alexander, Archibald Stevenson Thom and Alexander Strang Thom. *Stonehenge*. Journal for the History of Astronomy, Vol. 5, pages 71–90, 1974.

Thomas, H.H. *The source of the stones of Stonehenge*. Antiquaries Journal. Vol. III, pages 239–260, 1923.

Thompson, J. Eric S. *The Mayans*. New York: Kraus, 1968.
   Reprint of 1927–1932 Anthropological Series XVII, Nos. 1–4, of the Field Museum of Natural History, Chicago.

Thompson, J. Eric S. *The Civilization of the Mayas*. 7th ed. Chicago: Field Museum Press, 1973.

Tilley, Christopher. *A Phenomenology of Landscape*. Oxford: Berg Publishers, 1994.

Tilley, Christopher. *The Materiality of Stone: explorations in landscape phenomenology*. Oxford: Berg Publishers, 2004.
   Tilley is struggling back toward the surface from deep immersion in the mumbo-jumbo of recent anthropology. His fieldwork and interpretations are analogous to that of my *Sacred Rocks of Alberta* (2000). On page 27, he states that most academics don't understand landscape as part of the artifact because "Landscape is not bodily experienced; it … [is] derived from maps, paintings, archives and texts. … Bodies remain at the desk rather than in the field (with the exception of the occasional afternoon site visit)." Archaeoastronomy suffers from the same attitude in many of its practitioners, which is why I stress *observational* archaeoastronomy. Someone of Tilley's mindset is needed to carry on the *Sacred Rocks* and *Stone Age Temples* work in Canada, England, and Wales. Decades of work remain.

Towards a Common Date for Easter, A.D. 100–1997. Web site: **www.elca.org/ea/Orthodox/aleppo.html**.

Uhlenbeck, C.C. and R.H. Van Gulik. *A Blackfoot – English Vocabulary based on material from the southern Peigans*. Amsterdam: Uitgave van de N.V. Noord-Hollandsche Uitgevers-Maatschappij, 1934.

Victoria History of the Counties of England. *A History of Wiltshire*, Parts 1 and 2. London: Oxford University Press, 1957 and 1972.

Wace, Maistre, A.D. 1155. *Le Roman de Brut*, 2 volumes, with commentary by Le Roux de Lincy. Rouen: Édouard Frère, 1836.
From the manuscripts of the Paris Libraries.

Walpole, Horace, 1762–1780. *Anecdotes of Painting in England*, in 4 volumes. Reprinted in New York: Arno Press, 1969.
In Volume 2, page 55, writing about the architect Inigo Jones (1572–1653), Walpole said of Jones' conclusion that Stonehenge is a Roman Temple, "It is remarkable, that whoever has treated of that monument, has bestowed it on whatever class of antiquity he was peculiarly fond of." Walpole put aside the Romans, Phoenicians, and the Irish Druidess Gealcopa, and said the origin of Stonehenge, "that mass of barbarous clumsiness," is inexplicable.

Websters Third New International Dictionary of the English Language Unabridged. Springfield, MA: Merriam-Webster Inc., 1993.
When, in about 1995, I sent Merriam-Webster (M-W) and Oxford English Dictionary (OED) correct definitions of the terms equinox, equalday, equalnight, and equalday/night, OED replied with thanks, and M-W replied with an attempt at sarcasm. But M-W will also change.

Williams-Thorpe, Olwen, M.C. Jones, P.J. Potts and P.C. Webb. *Preseli dolerite bluestones*. Oxford Journal of Archaeology. Vol. 25, pages 29–46, 2006.

Wright, James V. *A History of the Native People of Canada*. Vol. 1. Hull, QC: Canadian Museum of Civilization, 1995.

List of Figures

Photo identification and subject, locations of the negatives and prints in my files at the University of Alberta Archives: example, 20 Mar 1992, 1 3 36 means photo taken on 20 March 1992 with camera 1, film roll 3, negative 36.

M = Majorville, S = Stonehenge, P = Preseli Mountain.

Cover: M 30 Jan 2003, 1 1 7, part of aerial G0206022-105; Figure 3-29; Figure 4-47

About the Author: Gord, 16 Oct 2007, Canon A560, card Phyl, frame 479.

Frontispiece: M **top**, 18 Mar 1988, 2 2 28. ER sight line from V Rocks. **bottom**, 18 Mar 1991, 2 3 31. VR, 1st flash ER.

Prologue
P-1: M 20 June 1988, 2 2 35. Two patterns of rocks that archaeologists said are "just as the melting glacier left them 10,000 years ago."

Chapter 1
1-1: M 30 Jan 2003, 1 1 6, aerial photo G0206022-105 enlarged x 20, Moon-MrnStr-Sun pattern marked.
1-2: S 12 June 1999, 1 1. OTDB **10** to Great Trilithon, mist.
1-3: S 11 Apr 1989, 5 1. Heel Stone from Sarsen 55.

Chapter 3
3-1: M 17 June 1984, 3 0. Blue Shrine.
3-2: M 20 June 1992, 1 2 3. *El Escarabajo Oro*.
3-3: M **(a)** photo from Lee Francis 19 May 1999, Majorville about 1945. **(b)** 19 May 1999, 1 4 27. Lee Francis at Majorville.
3-4: M 18 Dec 1993, 1 1 32. looking SE to Sun Cairn and Bow River bend.
3-5: M 20 Mar 1992, 1 3 36. looking north at Sun Cairn Ring.
3-6: M 12 June 1983, 3 8A. looking NE to Moon, Morningstar, and Sun effigies.

3-7: M SSR line SE slope (a) 20 June 1989, 2 3 26. SSR line, 1st flash positions 1-5 ka B.P. (b) 19 June 1988, 2 1 14. 05^{h}15^m, rising Sun 43 sec after 1st flash, SSR marked. (c) 18 June 1994, 2 1 32. SSR line showing SW rock.

3-8: M 18 Dec 1993, 1 1 28. looking SW to Sun Cairn, 2^y SC Hill and SW Cairn Hill.

3-9: M SSR line from SW Cairn Hill
(a) 21 June 1987, 2 2 20A. 05^{h}15^m, 1st flash after slight mirage. SSR 1-5 ka B.P. (b) 20 June 1990, 2 2 4. Phyl standing behind middle foresight rock of (d). (c) 24 Sept 1987, 1 2 27. Phyl standing behind foresight rock of (b) and one to left. (d) 13 June 1996, 2 1 18. SSR line, SSR 1-5 ka BP. (e) 14 June 1997, 1 2 35, SSR foresights across GPS 23. (f) 14 June 1997, 1 2 33, SSR foresights across GPS 23.

3-10: M SSS line from NH 21 June 1990 (a) 1 6 24, 21^h 45^{m}30^s, last flash. (b) 2 3 25, 11^{h}35^m, Phyl standing behind foresight cairn, zoom of (c). (c) 2 3 26, SSS line from NH to Phyl behind foresight cairn. (d) 1 4 23, reverse of SSS line (c).

3-11: M Dec 1988 (a) 19th, 1 3 35, Norm Lee's truck and camper after a blow. (b) 20th, 1 5 22, looking NE at the rayed Sun Cairn.

3-12: M WSR from WH V Rocks 20 Dec 1988 (a) 1 5 10, 08^{h}48^m.
(b) 1 5 11, 08^{h}55^m.

3-13: M Bertschys 17 Dec 1992, 1 1 24.

3-14: M SCR Hill Dec 1993 (a) 17th, 1 1 7, hoar frost.
(b) 18th, 1 1 31, Priestess on WSR seat.

3-15: M WSS from EH to horizon marker (a) 16 Dec 1992, 1 1 10, hazy.
19 Dec 1993 (b) 1 3 14, 16^{h}04^m. (c) 1 3 17, 16^{h}06^{m}00^s. (d) 1 3 18, 16^{h}06^{m}10^s. (e) 1 3 19, 16^{h}06^{m}30^s. (f) 1 3 22, 16^{h}32^m.

3-16: M WSS line from EH to horizon marker 5 ka B.P., 4 Oct 2004, 3 19.

3-17: M 17 Mar 1991, 2 2 30. cowboys looking for horses.

3-18: M 21 June 1990, 1 5 36. horses came to visit me.

3-19: M 17 Mar 1991, 2 3 4. Sun Cairn to ES observation line.

3-20: M 18 Mar 1991, 2 4 27. zoom of 3-19.

3-21: M 16 Mar 1991, 2 1 5. Sun Cairn to setting Sun.

3-22: M 16 Mar 1991, 2 1 13. Sun Cairn to last flash.

3-23: M 17 Mar 1991, 2 3 12. Sun Cairn to last flash, ES.

3-24: M 18 Mar 1991, 2 4 35. Sun Cairn to last flash, set positions 16th to 20th.

3-25: M 18 Mar 1988, 2 **2** 28. V Rocks to ER observation line.

3-26: M 18 Mar 1988, 2 **2** 25. zoom of Fig 3-25.

3-27: M 17 Mar 1991, 2 **2** 7. V Rocks to first flash.

3-28: M 17 Mar 1991, 2 **2** 8. zoom of 3-27 fifty seconds later.

3-29: M 18 Mar 1991, 2 **3** 32. V Rocks to 10 seconds after first flash, ER.

3-30: M 19 Mar 1991, 2 **5** 29. V Rocks to first flash.

3-31: M 20 Mar 1991, 2 **6** 32. V Rocks to first flash.

3-32: M map, Sun observation lines for the Summer Solstice rise (SSR) and set (SSS), and Equalday/night set (ESS). Base map NTS 82 I/9 SW (1997).

3-33: M 6 May 2007 aerial photo G0206022-106 enlarged x10, neg. 13, Sun Cairn Ring hilltop portion showing Sun observation lines for the Summer Solstice Sun rise (SSR), Equalday/night rise (ESR), Winter Solstice rise (WSR), and Winter Solstice set (WSS).

3-34: M 30 Jan 2003, 1 **1** 5, aerial photo G0206022-105 enlarged x 20, Sun Cairn Ring: (**a**) Rays ticked; (**b**) Rays marked.

3-35: M 27 Sept 1996, 1 **5** 25A. East Bank looking west to Phyl and I, and SCR Hill.

Chapter 4

4-1: S 11 Apr 1989, **5** 0. South Trilithon seen from North Trilithon.

4-2: S 25 Sept 2002, **3** 3. Sarsen Circle completed by drawing.

4-3: S 11 Dec 1995, **3** 0. Bluestone 31 to Bell Barrow **15**.

4-4: S 5 Dec 1997, **1** 23. Heel Stone to Sarsen Circle in fog.

4-5: S 11 Dec 1995, **3** 15. setting Sun, Bluestone 31 to Bell Barrow **15**.

4-6: S 11 Dec 1995, **3** 22. setting Sun, as Fig 4-5.

4-7: S 20 May 1996, Dominey 11. WSS positions, Bluestone 31 to Bell Barrow **15**.

4-8: S 26 Sept 2002, **4** 0. Heel Stone to Circle, WSS line 4.0 ka B.P. Great Trilithon completed.

4-9: S 1 Apr 1997, 21A. SW of Ditch to Dominey at Heel Stone, reverse of WSS line.

4-10: S 1 Apr 1997, 16A. across SE groin Bell Barrow **15** to Heel Stone, reverse of WSS line.

4-11: S 1 Apr 1997, 12A. SE groin of Bell Barrow **15** to Heel Stone.

4-12: S 11 Apr 1989, **5** 2. Heel Stone from SW.

4-13: S 12 Dec 1997, **3** 7. first flash, Altar Stone toward SE.

4-14: S 13 Dec 1997, **4** 10. NW Bank to Sun in West Trilithon gap,

WSR line of 4 ka B.P.

4-15: S 12 Dec 1997, **3** 23. NW Bank to West Trilithon gap, WSR line.

4-16: S 12 Dec 1997, **3** 30. SE of Sarsen 53 to West Trilithon gap, reverse of WSR line.

4-17: S map out to Ditch, WSS and WSR lines. Base map composite of English Heritage maps in Cleal & co. (1995) and Hawkins (1965).

4-18: S 17 June 1999, **5** 6. OTDB **10** to rising Sun.

4-19: S 17 June 1999, **5** 11. as 4-18, 3 Suns.

4-20: S 17 June 1999. **5** 6. Sun rises extrapolated to first flash 4000 B.P., SSR lines.

4-21: S 25 Sept 2002, **3** 19. OTDB **10** N tump to Great Trilithon, SSR line, complete GrTri.

4-22: S 13 Dec 1997, **5** 17. SW of Ditch to Aubrey Hole 28 to 56 line, complete Sarsen bldg.

4-23: S 13 Dec 1997, **4** 30. Aubrey Hole 28 to 56 (Phyl) line.

4-24: S 13 Dec 1997, **4** 33. Sarsens 30-1 gap to Phyl in OTDB **10** SSR line.

4-25: S 24 Sept 2001, **3** 11. Peter's mound.

4-26: S 24 Sept 2001, **3** 25. north edge of Cursus to Great Trilithon, reverse of SSR line.

4-27: S 12 June 1999, **1** 29. Altar Stone to setting Sun.

4-28: S 12 June 1999, **1** 33. as 4-27, setting Sun and last flash positions. SSS lines.

4-29: S 12 June 1999, **1** 13. SE Bank to West Trilithon gap, SSS line.

4-30: S 15 June 1999, **3** 35. reverse of SSS line from trees.

4-31: S map out to Ditch, SSR and SSS lines. Base map composite of English Heritage maps in Cleal & co. (1995) and Hawkins (1965).

4-32: S 20 Sept 2001, **1** 27. Avenue to Trilithon lintels.

4-33: S 20 Sept 2001, **1** 29. Avenue to Sarsen Circle.

4-34: S 20 Sept 2001, **1** 32. Avenue to top Heel Stone.

4-35: S 20 Sept 2001, **1** 36. Avenue to Heel Stone.

4-36: S 5 Dec 1997, **1** 27. notch in Sarsen 58 to Altar Stone line for WSR.

4-37: S 24 Sept 2001, **3** 8. notch in Sarsen 58 east to Sarsens 2-3 gap.

4-38: S 24 Sept 2001, **2** 34. Sarsens 2-3 gap west to notch in Sarsen 58.

4-39: S 27 Sept 2001, **5** 36. Sarsens 2-3 gap east to New King Barrows.

4-40: S 25 Sept 2002, **3** 30. NKBB **29** to setting Sun.

4-41: S 26 Sept 2002, **4** 30. NKBB **29** to last flash, positions 22nd to 27th. Leap year cycle.

4-42: S 26 Sept 2002, **4** 22. NKBB **29** to ES. Leap year cycle positions above Sarsen Circle.

4-43: S 24 Sept 2002, **2** 20. notch in Sarsen 58 to last flash, positions 22nd to 27th.

4-44: S 24 Sept 2001, **3** 5. notch in Sarsen 58 to leap year cycle ES positions.

4-45: S 24 Sept 2002, **2** 14. Sarsen 3 to notch in Sarsen 58 ES line.

4-46: S 27 Sept 2001, **6** 1. Sarsen Circle east to Sarsen 3.

4-47: S 24 Sept 2002, **2** 11. East Bank to ES line west to Sarsen 3 and notch in 58.

4-48: S 25 Sept 2002, **2** 30. Sarsens 2-3 gap east to rising Sun, leap year cycle ER positions.

4-49: S 24 Sept 2002, **1** 35. west of Ditch to ER line gap between Sarsen 2 and 58.

4-50: S map of Sarsens, season-pivot-date Sun rise and set observation lines. Base map modified Figure 14 of Cleal & co.

4-51: S map out to Ditch, season-pivot-date Sun rise and set observation lines. Base map modified Figure 13 of Cleal & co.

4-52: S map of Stonehenge landscape, season-pivot-date Sun rise and set lines. Base map Royal Commission 1979, pocket map 2.

4-53: S map out to Ditch, Cardinal Directions. Base map composite of several English Heritage maps.

4-54: S 28 Sept 2001, **7** 0. North Bank south to N–S axis of Sarsen Circle.

4-55: S 28 Sept 2001, **6** 36. South Bank north to S–N axis of Sarsen Circle.

4-56: S 25 Sept 2002, **3** 3. East Bank west to E–W axis of Sarsen Circle.

4-57: S 26 Sept 2002, **3** 34. west of Ditch east to W–E axis of Sarsen Circle.

4-58: P 2 Oct 2006, **5** 34. WSW 300m to *Carngyfrwy*.

4-59: P 2 Oct 2006, **5** 36. from *Carngyfrwy* E 60m to 20m diameter ring of stones.

4-60: P 4 Oct 2006, **6** 28. centre *Carngyfrwy* SW to *Carnganol* gap and *Carnmenyn* V sight.

4-61: P 4 Oct 2006, (a) **6** 28. below *Carnmenyn* V sight, looking NE to NW ends of *Carnganol* and *Carngyfrwy* and to *Foeldrygarn*.

(b) **6** 35. on *Carnmenyn* V sight, looking NE to the NW ends of *Carnganol* and *Carngyfrwy* and to *Foeldrygarn*.

4-62: P 4 Oct 2006, (a) **6** 25. NE side *Carnmenyn*, N–S Sanctuary, S rock panel. (b) **6** 26. NE side *Carnmenyn*, N–S Sanctuary, N rock panel.

4-63: P 4 Oct 2006, (a) **6** 31. SW side *Carnmenyn*, E–W Sanctuary, E rock panel. (b) **6** 32. SW side *Carnmenyn*, E–W Sanctuary, W rock panel and *Carnbica*.

Chapter 5

5-1: S 27 Sept 2002, **5** 16. SE of Ditch to White Bull's head in West Trilithon gap.

5-2: S 25 Sept 2002, **3** 5. south of Ditch north to South Causeway and Sarsen 11.

5-3: S map of Sarsen Circle with light-rod lines from South Trilithon, and shadow from Sarsen 11. Base map modified Figure 14 of Cleal & co.

5-4: S map of landscape, 5 m contour interval, season-pivot lines, Cursus, Woodhenge. Base map Ordnance Survey Pathfinder 1221 (1988).

5-5: S map of renumbered Circle Sarsens, lunar-standstill 18.6-year cycle observation lines.

5-6: S 27 Sept 2002, **5** 5. NW Bank SE along SMR_{max} observation line.

5-7: S 25 Sept 2006, **3** 31. SEbyS Bank NW along WMS_{max} observation line.

5-8: S map out to Ditch, renumbered Y and Z Holes, Station-Stone Moon observation lines. Base map composite of several English Heritage maps.

Chapter 6

6-1: Newgrange drawings, (a) and (b) adapted from material of Tom P. Ray in *Nature, 1989, volume 337, pages 343–345*.
(a) horizontal cross section of passage and chamber,
(b) vertical cross section of passage and chamber,
(c) roof-box window seen from floor of end chamber in 5 ka B.P.

6-2: sky map, Full Moon positions in September to March. Sky maps containing the Full Moon were obtained from **http://www.fourmilab.to/yoursky**. Dates and times of the Full Moon at Stonehenge were obtained from **http://aa.usno.navy.mil/data/docs/MoonPhase.php**.

6-3: sky map, Full Moon positions in March to September. Sky maps containing the Full Moon were obtained from **http://www.fourmilab.to/yoursky**. Dates and times of the Full Moon at Stonehenge were obtained from the web site **http://aa.usno.navy.mil/data/docs/MoonPhase.php**.

6-4: sky map, Ecliptic and Celestial Equator background for 6-2. Sky map obtained from **http://www.fourmilab.to/yoursky**.

6-5: sky map, Ecliptic and Celestial Equator background for 6-3. Sky map obtained from **http://www.fourmilab.to/yoursky**.

Epilogue

E-1: M 19 Dec 1996, 1 **1** 26. Armstrongs' cow camp, Grant, Arnold, and plane.

E-2: M 19 Dec 1996, 1 **1** 29. Sun Cairn and GPS.

E-3: M 19 Dec 1996, 1 **1** 36. Grant's plane.

E-4: M 20 Dec 1996, 1 **2** 9. horses in snow storm.

E-5: M 20 Dec 1996, 1 **2** 18. *El Escarabajo Oro* after white-out.

Appendices

A-1: Light refraction against altitude, and Sun/Moon rise and set curves.

A-2: Determination of true S–N line.

A-3: Sun rise and set directions in summer and winter, and Equalday/night.

A-4: Determination of true W–E line and Equalday/night date.

Endpapers

Front cover inside map: Stonehenge and terrain out to the Bank and Ditch. Black spots are stones that remain, some no longer upright. Stones 1 to 30, joined by red dashes, are the Sarsen Circle; open spots represent missing Sarsen Stones. Uprights of the five Trilithons are Sarsen Stones 51 to 60, joined by green dashes, which form a "Horseshoe." The ring of 56 Holes inside the Bank is the Aubrey Circle. The various ditches are coloured brown. [The base map is a modified composite of several in R. M. J. Cleal & coworkers (1995) and G. S. Hawkins (1965), all produced by English Heritage, Ancient Monuments Branch. © English Heritage.] Aubrey Holes 28 and 56 make a straight line with Stone Hole 97; the ratio of the distances 28 to 56 and 56 to 97 is 7:3, two sacred numbers that total 10. This ratio indicates something about the builders' sense of proportion, and their counting system appears to have been based on 10, like ours, the number of fingers on two hands.

Front right-side map: Stonehenge Circle and Trilithons, with the traditional Stone-numbers.

Back left-side map: Stonehenge and terrain out to the Bank and Ditch, with the new (lunar calendar) numbers of the Circle Sarsens and of the Y and Z Holes in green. Base map © English Heritage. The various ditches are coloured brown.

Back cover inside map: Stonehenge Circle and Trilithons, with the new (lunar calendar) numbers of the Circle Sarsens in green.

Glossary

Words in the text are capitalized when they refer to specific items, such as Aubrey Holes, Bowl Barrow, 28 Rays in the Sun Cairn Ring, Sarsen Stones, Sun Temple. Words are not capitalized when used generically, such as a hole, rays of the Sun, a stone, a temple, and so on. If a single word has been capitalized it is an abbreviation for a previous name: for example, Cairn refers to the Sun Cairn in Ómahk, Carn refers to a recently-named Carn on Preseli Mountain, Hole refers to an Aubrey Hole, and Stone refers to a Sarsen Stone.

A.D. Dates *Anno Domini* in the Christian calendar, now sometimes designated C.E. (Christian Era), with year 1 placed at approximately the year when Jesus of Nazareth was born.

Alignment. Two sighting gaps or stones, like the back and front sights on a rifle, that point to the event or structure that is marked by it. Some alignments contain several rocks or pairs of rocks along their lengths.

Aubrey Holes. A circle of 56 Holes just inside the Bank around Stonehenge; named after the 17th century antiquarian and member of the Royal Society John Aubrey, who first reported on them.

Avenue. A 2.8-kilometre path that goes 0.6 km straight northeasterly from Stonehenge, then about 1 km easterly, then southerly to the Avon. It was probably used processionally in the opposite direction.

Barrow. Earth mound or tump surrounded by a ring-ditch in the Stonehenge zone.

B.C. Dates Before Christ in the Christian calendar, now sometimes designated B.C.E. (Before the Christian Era). B.C. is usually used to specify a particular year, because B.P. dates increase as time passes.

Bluestones. Stones in Stonehenge that were taken from Preseli Mountain in Pembrokeshire, southwest Wales. Most of them are bluish, hard, coarse-grained basalt (dolorites and rhyolite). About 4400 years ago, 80 blocks of them weighing several tonnes each were transported about 300 kilometres to the site now called Stonehenge, in southwest England.

B.P. Dates Before the Present date, used to designate approximately how long ago an event happened; for example the Jewish First Temple in Jerusalem was begun in 832 B.C., or about 2840 B.P., and the Sun Temple near Majorville is datable to about 5000 B.P., also written as 5 ka B.P.

Brave. A North American Indian warrior.

Cairn. A cluster or pile of stones, containing three or more, sometimes many thousands.

Cursus. A straight 2.8-kilometre "runway" that runs nearly east–west, one kilometre north of Stonehenge.

Daylight. The period between the first and last flashes of the Sun on the horizon, officially measured on a flat plain. This definition was used 5000 years ago by Sunwatchers in *Ómahkiyáahkóhtóohp*, and 4300 years ago by Skywatchers in Stonehenge, and is still used for Sun rise and set listings in Astronomical Almanacs today.

Equalday/night. A 24-hour period in which the times between the first and last flashes of the Sun that bracket daylight and night, measured on a flat plain, are each 12.0 hours, equal within two minutes. The dates vary with latitude. In much of the North Temperate Zone, during successive leap year cycles they now oscillate between 17 and 18 March, and 25 and 26 September; in much of the South Temperate Zone they oscillate between 23 and 24 March, and 19 and 20 September.

Equalday. A day for which the time between the first and last flashes of the Sun, measured on a flat plain, is 12.0 hours. The dates vary with latitude. In much of the North Temperate Zone they are now 17 or 18 March, and 25 or 26 September, dependent on the longitude and the year within the leap year cycle; in much of the South Temperate Zone they are 23 or 24 March, and 19 or 20 September.

Equalnight. A night for which the time between the last and first flashes of the Sun, measured on a flat plain, is 12.0 hours. The dates vary with latitude. In much of the North Temperate Zone they are now 16–17 or 17–18 March, and 24–25 or 25–26 September, dependent on the longitude and the year within the leap year cycle; in much of the South Temperate Zone they are 22–23 or 23–24 March, and 18–19 or 19–20 September.

Equinox (*now an obsolete term*). A translation of the Latin word *aequinoctium*, which literally means equalnight, but in A.D. 1582 its definition within the Gregorian calendar got changed to "one of the two dates in the year when the lengths of day and night are equal everywhere on Earth," which is physically impossible, and the dates selected were when the Sun crossed the Equator, 21 March and 23 September. The Sun/Equator dates have now drifted to 20 or 21 March and 22 or 23 September, dependent on the longitude and the year within the leap year cycle. A correct name for the time when the Sun crosses the Equator is Sun Zenith Midaltitude (abbreviation SZM, pronounced *zem*), see below.

Geoglyph. A manmade pattern of stones on the ground.

Glyph. A grooved pattern carved in something; in a rock, a petroglyph.

KNP, Kinetics of Nonhomogeneous Processes. Concerns all types of changes that occur in Nature; involves measuring the changes and their rates, and seeking to understand their causes.

Lintel. A capstone that bridges two upright stones.

Majorville Medicine Wheel. *An obsolete term*, see Sun Cairn Ring.

Medicine wheel. *An obsolete term in archaeology*: a pattern of cobble stones or rocks on the ground, comprised of a cairn, a ring, and radiating lines, or any two of these features.

In mental health, used by Indians: a circle with a red and black cross in it, used as a symbol of "The Balanced Way."

Moon wobble. Variation of the orbit of the Moon due to precession of the Moon's axis of revolution about the Earth, which has a period of 18.61 years.

Night duration. The period between the last and first flashes of the Sun on the horizon, officially measured on a flat plain. This definition was used 5000 years ago by Skywatchers in *Ómahkiyáahkóhtóohp*, and 4300 years ago by Skywatchers in Stonehenge, and is still used for Sun rise and set listings in Astronomical Almanacs today.

OldBigArrangement. See *Ómahkiyáahkóhtóohp*.

Ómahk. A Blackfoot prefix that means Old, Big; used as an abbreviation of *Ómahkiyáahkóhtóohp*.

Ómahkiyáahkóhtóohp (*the h's are aspirated, and the accented vowels are emphasized*). A Blackfoot word meaning Old, Big Arrangement, which I join together in the Blackfoot manner to OldBigArrangement. It is a widespread set of patterns of stones, distributed over about 30 square kilometres of hilly prairie (diameter about 6 kilometres), and includes accurate solar and lunar calendars. I call this large region a Temple to the Sun, Moon, and Morning Star, or briefly, a Sun Temple. Perhaps Sky Temple would be more appropriate.

Sarsen. A very hard sandstone, used to construct the most prominent parts of Stonehenge. Blocks weighing up to about 70 tonnes were transported southerly about 30 kilometres, from near Marlborough to the Stonehenge site.

Solstice (Sun-standstill). A period when the positions of the Sun rise and set on the horizon appear to remain constant at the northern or southern extreme for several days, centred on 21 June and 21 or 22 December, depending on longitude and the year within the leap year cycle. In the Polar Zones the Sun remains above or below the horizon for an extended period in these seasons.

Sun Cairn. A stone pile that is a Sun effigy; the main one in *Ómahk* is in the Sun Cairn Ring, it is about 9 metres in diameter, 1.5 metres high, and contains about 50 tonnes of rocks.

Sun Cairn Ring. The so-called "Majorville Medicine Wheel"; it includes a 28-metre-diameter Ring of stones, the central Sun Cairn, and 28 radiating lines of stones that join the Cairn to the Ring.

Sun Cairn Ring Hill. The Sacred Hill that has the Sun Cairn Ring on its summit; it has a diameter of about 400 metres. It is the northeast hill of a set of three of equal height.

Sunrise. The general event of the morning sun emerging from the horizon.

Sun rise position. The dot of the first flash of the rising Sun on the horizon.

Sunset. The general event of the evening sun passing below the horizon.

Sun set position. The dot of the last flash of the setting Sun on the horizon.

Sun Temple. See *Ómahkiyáahkóhtóohp*.

Sun Zenith Midaltitude (abbreviation **SZM**, pronounced *zem*). The dates when the Sun crosses the Equator, and the noonday Sun is half way between its maximum and minimum altitudes of the Summer and Winter Solstices; now 20 or 21 March and 22 or 23 September, depending on longitude and the year within the leap year cycle.

Trilithon (three-stone-thing). In Stonehenge, two upright Sarsens capped by a third Sarsen, weighing a total of about 120 tonnes. Five Trilithons are arranged in a "Horseshoe."

Tump. A small hump of dirt enclosed by a ring-ditch.

Warino. Irregular war waged by small bodies acting more or less independently. Like neutrinos, participants in a warino are difficult to detect, and individual impact events are irregularly spaced. Participants may be called revolutionaries or terrorists, depending on whose side the speaker is on. Warino is the English equivalent of the Spanish word *guerrilla*.

zem. Pronunciation of SZM, *see* Sun Zenith Midaltitude.

Zenith. Highest point above the horizon of an object crossing the sky.

INDEX

[Figures in ***bold italics*** are on, *or shortly after*, the preceding page number, which begins that particular entry]

51° N latitude:
  Kazakhstan, 186, 192
  Majorville, *Ómahk*, 5***F1-1***, 64, 175
  Stonehenge, 6***F1-2***, 175, 178
  Sun & Moon rise at right angle, set
    at right angle 175, 179, 186, 226

Alberta:
  depressions in cairns, 150
  Majorville, xvi, 4
  medicine wheels, ribstones, 4, 14, 24
  Rocky Buttes, 43
  Sacred Rocks, 190, 221, 263

alignments to Sun and Moon rise and set:
  do not exist?, 4, 19
  exist, 3, 6, 153
  time machines, 20

angular distances in photographs, 247

anthropologist/archaeologist, 18, 31, 228, 229, 245

Archaeoastronomy, observational, 19, 246, 264
  observational acuity, eyes, cameras, xii
  accurate, reproducible, 245

Arthur, War Leader, myth, 148, 150, 229
  Bear-man, 229
  grave of, 148***F4-63***
  King, legend, 142, 148-150

As in Heaven, so on Earth, 17, 71

Astrology, 187, 200

astronomer, 200, 207, 219

Astronomy, 20, 200, 227

Atkinson, Richard J.C., 246

aura, 15, 42, 186

Avon, *Afon*, 92, 168

azimuths of Sun rise and set, theoretical, 251

Balanced Way, The, 74

Barclay, Edgar, 246

Big Horn Mountains Sacred Ring, 3, 14
  vision quest site, 15

Blackfoot (*Siksika*), Blackfeet, xiii, xvi, 53
  Bullchild, 21
  death lodge, 73
  First Nation, 43
  Kekip Sousouators, 30
  Napi, 72
  Ómahkiyáahkóhtóohp, 39, 239, 240

Bluestones (*see* Stonehenge)

bovid symbol, 221

Buffalo, 13, 31
  Bulls, veneration of, 160
  effigies in stone, 221
  stones, 24
  White, 160

Bull:
  Buffalo, 160
  Equalday/night constellation, *Taurus*, 160, 181
  skull Altar, 160
  White, 159***F5-1***, 160, 237

burial mound, 84, 88, 98, 152

Caesar and Cleopatra, 201, 207

cairn, Majorville, xv, xvi, 27-29, 43
  see Ómahkiyáahkóhtóohp,
    Sun Cairn

calendar:
  accurate, xiii, 153
  accurate, 5000 B.P., 65, 68
  controversy:
    Julian, 216
    medicine wheel, 3, 18
    Stonehenge, xvi, 8
  counting device, 1, 185
  framework for religious festivals, 185, 202
  Gregorian,
    deception in its origin, 218
    deception uncovered by calendar in
      Ómahkiyáahkóhtóohp, 221
    Easter date, 202
    leap year, 68
    month, 17
  Hebrew, 204
  Hijri, 157
  history of Christian, 184-223
  Julian,
    Christian festival cycle frame, 202
    Church struggle with, 216
    correction of, 216-218
    inaccuracy, 203, 208, 211
    origin, 202, 207
    Spring Equalnight date, 207
  leap year cycle:
    and Equalday dates, 65, 68
    Roman, 207, 215
    seen at Stonehenge, 121-124, 182
  lunar:
    Islamic, 157
    Ómahkiyáahkóhtóohp, 68, 238
    Stonehenge, 170**F5-5** to 181, 230
    zodiac, 193
  lunisolar, 6, 169, 204
  Mayan, 2
  religious festival cycle, 1, 185
  season-pivot dates, 53, 83, 156
  solar:
    Fajada Butte, Chaco Canyon, 226
    "medicine wheel", 2
    Ómahkiyáahkóhtóohp, 68
    Stonehenge, 132**F4-51**, 158
  solar, key to exactness, 68, 212
  Stone Age, 1, 6**F1-2**, 156, 202, 223, 226, 240
  year-one date, 201

Cardinal axes, 137**F4-53**

Cardinal directions:
  east to water, from sacred place, 31
  east–west,
    Equalday/night, determination of,
      212, 257**FA-4**
    channel across Stonehenge,
      117**F4-37**, 126**F4-45**
    diameter of Stonehenge, 136**F4-53**
    "Houses" in Ómahkiyáahkóhtóohp, 39
  name origins, 21
  north to habitations, from Sun Temples,
    73, 140
  north–south, determination of, 255**FA-2**
    diameter of Stonehenge, 136**F4-53**
    New Kings Barrows Ridge, 120**F4-39**
  south to constellation effigies, from Sun
    Cairn in Ómahkiyáahkóhtóohp, 71
  west, prayer offering to, 53

Chaco Canyon, NM, accurate solar calendar, 226

Cleal, Rosamund, and coauthors, 246

Colt Hoare, Richard, 91, 100, 133

complex systems, 100, 242

constellations:
  effigies in rocks, constructions, 71, 72
  images and myths, 17
  navigation by, latitude dependence, 212
  Sun and Moon paths through, 151, 160
  zodiac, 193-200

culture classifications, European bias, 21

curiosity:
  a driving force, 152, 244
  and major advances in knowledge, 18, 225
  creativity from, 68

cycle:
  east to west, 16
  leap year, 2, 19, 121**F4-41** to 129
  life, death, rebirth, 14, 116
  Moon, Sun, Venus, 1, 17, 68, 182
  Moon, 18.6-year, 8, 70, 170**F5-5**
  religious ritual, 185
  Sun, 122**F4-51**

day and night, exact lengths, 7

day:
  longest and shortest, 20
  when does it begin?, 193

death and rebirth cycle, symbol, 98

INDEX   285

Eagle, Golden, 76, 77 **F3-35**

Easter:
  Christian Passover, 203-216, 240
  date problem, 202, 203, 216

east–west, exact determination in flat landscape, 212, 257 **FA-4**

Eclipses of Sun or Moon, 71, 198
  cycles, 201
  Stonehenge, prediction, 8

Ecliptic, 199 **F6-4**, **6-5**
  obliquity of, time dependence, data, 250

Eddy, John, 3, 4, 16

Egg-shaped, *see* Sacred Ring, *and* year

Equal-arm Balance, *Libra*, Equalday/night constellation, 160, 196, 200, 227

Equalday:
  at Fajada Butte, Chaco Canyon, 226
  at Stonehenge, 163 **F5-3**
  St. Patrick's Day, 66

Equalday/night:
  and exact length of the year, 67, 151
  at *Ómahkiyáahkóhtóohp*, 66, 75, 160
  at Stonehenge, 116, 130 **F4-50**, 160, 167
  dates, 223
  dates determined exactly, 65, 123
  definition, 222
  determination in flat landscape, 257 **FA-4**
  flat landscape, 135
  latitude dependence, 212, 223
  ritual, 157
  Sun rise, 60 **F3-29**, 128
  Sun rise and set lines, 63 **F3-32**, 64 **F3-33**, 130 **F4-50**
  Sun set, 58 **F3-24**, 121 **F4-41**, 124
  zodiac, in the, 193, 196

Equalnight:
  dates at different latitudes, 223
  Spring fertility ceremonies, 157, 210
  Stonehenge abandonment, 181

Equinox, 53, 64, 116
  definition is wrong in European dictionaries, 66, 222
  physically impossible definition, 207, 220, 222
  what happened to it?, 64-68, 217

European:
  cultural bias, 12, 21, 240
  Equinox, wrong definition, 66
  Equalday/night, correction, 222
  migration from Kazakhstan?, 192

Fajada Butte, Chaco Canyon, NM, marks Equaldays and Solstices, 226

Female nature, and symbol, 92, 98

genius on the prairie 5000 years ago, 5, 18, 202, 240, 244

Geoffrey of Monmouth, 79, 81

Glastonbury
  Abbey, 148, 149
  Arthur's grave, 148, 229
  Tor, 149

Global Positioning System (GPS), 37 **F3-9e**, 136, 232, 235

Gregory XIII, Pope Gregory's deception, 216-219, 240

henge, hinge, 81

hinges:
  due east and west for Sun rise and set directions, 20
  Stonehinges for Sun rise and set directions, 81, 144, 161
  for Moon cycle, 170 **F5-5**, 174, 181
  see also Rock Pivot

history:
  European, 202
  in New and Old Testaments, 23
  of the Christian calendar, 184-219
  pushing back the boundaries of, xvii, 5
  writing of, a plastic art, 203

iota, Don't change one iota of that!, 208

Ireland:
  Christian Passover date, 209, 210
  Merlin and The Round Dance of Giants, 79, 80**F4-2**, 149

Kazakhstan:
  51° N latitude, 186
  a source of Indo-European culture, 192, 230

Kekip Hill, 30, 43

Kinetics of Nonhomogeneous Processes (KNP):
  pattern recognition, insightful tool, 242
  unifying concepts in, 242
  visualize behaviour in complex systems, 100, 258

King Arthur legend, *see* Arthur, War Leader

landscape:
  at *Ómahk*, 33, 65
  at Stonehenge, 83, 103, 131-140, 155, 165
  flat for Equalday/night date, 65, 135, 258
  part of the artifact, 4, 142, 269
  to be viewed from ground level, 29

languages:
  Equalday/night, definition, 222, 280
  Equinox, wrong definition, 66, 280
  Indo-European roots, 192
  midsummer, midwinter, roots, 165
  translation, a plastic art, 203

leap year cycle, 2, 19, 65-68, 140, 165, 195, 202, 221, 258
  and the design of Stonehenge, 121**F4-41** to 129, 182

light refraction by atmosphere, data, 249**FA-1**

Lockyer, Norman, 6-8, 83

lunar-standstill 18.6-year cycle, 70, 174-182

Male symbol, 159

Mathematics, complex, 201

measurements of cardinal directions, Sun
    rise and set directions and times,
    accurate methods in Appendices,
    245+

medicine wheel (*inappropriate term*), 73
  Big Horn, 3, 14

Majorville, xv, xvi, 4, 5**F1-1**, 14, 19, 24, 29**F3-5**
  see also Ómahkiyáahkóhtóohp, Sun Cairn Ring
  modern, 73
  Moose Mountains, 3, 4, 14-16

Meridiana, 218, 219

mirage, distinguish from Sun rise or set, 258

Moon
  calendars, 156, 169-181, 193
  cupping Morning Star, 29
  Full,
    Christian Passover date, 204-207, 216
    in *Taurus*, 5000 B.P., 160
    positions among constellations, 195**F6-2**, **F6-3**
    right angle to Sun at 51° latitude, 175, 226
    rise and set directions, 8, 70, 150
  lunar-phase 19-year cycle, 171, 197, 206, 209, 216
  lunar-standstill 18.6-year cycle, 8, 70, 171-181, 226, 238
  lunar-standstill nineteen-year cycle, 70
  number **28**, 68, 70, 230, 237
  shape change cycle, *moonth*, 17, 20, 68, 151, 241
  Sun Catcher, 178, 231
  waning crescent, 30, 70, 157
  zodiac, 193, 195**F6-2**, **F6-3**

moonth, 17, 20, 68, 151, 241

Moose Mountains
  Sacred Ring, 3, 15, 16
  Sun-egg, 16, 165
  Sun-egg Hill, 16
  Winter Solstice Sun set, 16

Mynydd Preseli (Preseli Mountain), 143-150

Nature, perception of, 240

New Mexico, accurate solar calendar, 226

Newgrange, *Nuaghrian*, 187-193
  see also Nuaghrian

night and daylight, exact lengths, 7

North American Plains Indians:
  accurate calendar, 5000 B.P., 65, 156
  genius of 5, 202
  mobility and skill, 10,000 B.P., 24
  philosophy, 14, 21

North Pole Star, 18, 20

North Temperate Zone:
  accurate solar calendars, 226
  crude solar calendars, 2
  daily southerly arc of Sun, 213
  religions and the Sun cycle, 157

north–south
  axis, 13
  exact determination, 255**FA-2**

Nuaghrian, Newgrange, 188**F6-1**
  contemporary with *Ómahkiyáahkóhtóohp*, 192
  means Newsun, 191
  people, art style, 192
  roof box window, 189
  Winter Solstice Sun rise, 190

observation line, Solstice Sun rise or set: exact, 246
  Moose Mountains Sacred Ring, 16
  Ómahkiyáahkóhtóohp, 63**F3-32**, 64**F3-33**, 223
  Stonehenge, 7, 130**F4-50**, 166**F5-4**

Old World, New World cultures (*inappropriate terms*), 21

OldBigArrangement (*Ómahkiyáahkóhtóohp*), 23, 39

Ómahk (*see also Ómahkiyáahkóhtóohp*), 1, 39, 187

Ómahkiyáahkóhtóohp (OldBigArrangement), 23, 39-43,
    occurs throughout the book
  28 Rays in Sun Cairn Ring, xiii, xv, 69**F3-34**, 138, 171, 174, 230, 237
  aerial photograph, 29, 62, 64
  back sight V, 58
  Bow River, deep valley, xvi, 33, 234**FE-3**
    big bends, lunar 18.6-year cycle, 175, 238
    people lived north of, 73
    The Rocky Buttes, 43
  calendar, accurate, 5000 B.P., 35**F3-9**, 65-67, 223, 240
  cardinal directions, 31
  constellation effigies, 71
  contour map, 63**F3-32**
  East House, 39, 50**F3-15** to 52**F3-16**, 62
  Equalday/night Sun rise, 60**F3-29**
  Equalday/night Sun set, 58**F3-24**
  Forbid digging!, 223
  foresight V, 58
  habitations were north of it, 73, 140
  lunar calendar, 68, 238
  lunar-standstill 18.6-year cycle, 70
  map of calendrical Sun sight lines, 63**F3-32**
  Moon Crescent, 29**F3-6**
  North House, 39**F3-10**, 62
  Oxbow people, 28
  Preseli Mountain, key to, 142-150, 183

preservation, 223
Rock Pivot, 58, 81
Rosetta Stone for Stone Age calendars, 6**F1-2**, 240
Sacred Ring, 28 Rays, xv, 69**F3-34**, 137, 171
Sacred Rock north of the Temple, 29, 43
solar and lunar calendars, 68, 171, 175, 223, 244, 281
Solstice observation lines 5000 B.P., 36**F3-9**, 40**F3-10**, 52**F3-16**, 223
Stone Age calendar, 6**F1-2**, 156, 202, 223, 225
Stonehenge calendar, key to, 82, 115, 116, 122, 136, 140, 221, 230
stonehinge/pivot, 58
Summer Solstice Sun rise, 32**F3-7**, 36**F3-9**
Summer Sun rise, 5000 B.P., 36**F3-9**
Summer Solstice Sun rise and set lines, 63**F3-32**, **F3-33**
Summer Solstice Sun set, 41**F3-10**
Sun Cairn, 29**F3-5**, 30, 59**F3-25**, 234**FE-2**
  age and structure, 28
Sun Cairn Ring: 29
  4 quadrants, 69**F3-34**, 138, 174
  28 lines of stones, xiii, 69**F3-34**, 137, 237
  and an Equalday/night Sun rise line, 59**F3-25**
  diameter 3x Sun Cairn diameter, xiii, 97**F4-17**
  Hill, 35**F3-8**, 64**F3-33**, 77**F3-35**, 160, 232-234**FE-2**
  "Majorville Medicine Wheel", 29
  Sun, Moon, and Morningstar, xiii, xvi, 30**F3-6**
  Temple, 223, 246
  Temple core on three hills of equal height, 35**F3-8**, 142
  V Rocks, West House and Stonehenge West Trilithon, 132, 133
  Equalnight Sun rise, 59**F3-25**, 128
  Rock Pivot, 58, 64**F3-33**, 81, 161
  Winter Solstice Sun rise, 46**F3-12**, 64**F3-33**
  Winter Solstice Sun rise, 46**F3-12**, 62**F3-33**
  Winter Solstice Sun set, 48**F3-15**, 62**F3-33**
    in 5000 B.P., 52**F3-16**

Orion, 72

Oxbow People, 28, 71

Passover
  Christian, date, 204, 206, 217
  Jewish, 203, 220
  Jewish, date, 204, 206, 222

pattern recognition, insightful tool, 242

philosophy:
  Judeo-Christian, xvii, 240
  North American Plains Indian, 14, 21, 164, 240
  Winter Solstice Sun set and Summer Solstice Sun rise contrast, 116, 172

pivot, north-south, 20

planets:
  around the Sun, 215

cycles and myths, 185, 196, 238
omens, 186
paths through the stars, 17, 151, 200

politics, 201-206

Pope Gregory XIII, 216-219

precession of Earth's spinning axis, 196

Preseli Mountain, 79, 81, 142, 228
  Beddarthur, Arthur's grave, 148**F4-63**, 150, 182, 229
  Carn Meini, 142, 143
  Carnbica, 146**F4-63**, 150, 182
  Carnganol, 144-146**F4-61**
  Carngyfrwy, 144**F4-58** to 150, 175
  Carnmenyn, 143**F4-60** to 150, 175, 229
  Foeldrygarn, 144**F4-61**, 150, 182
  Foelteml, 144**F4-60** to 150, 175, 182, 229
  Mynydd Preseli, 143
  solar and lunar calendars, 150, 175, 182

Priest:
  and Skywatcher, 7, 98, 140, 151, 152, 181
  and Priestess, 98, 152, 157, 175

Priestess, title now temporarily out of fashion, 242

projectile points, dates, 23, 28

Prophet, 186, 201, 230

Quartz, white, 187, 190

Ram, *Aries*, Equalday/night constellation:
  symmetrical symbol, 160, 197, 200
  abandonment of Stonehenge, 181

refraction of light by the atmosphere, data, 248, 249**FA-1**

Religion:
  as in Heaven, so on Earth, 17, 71
  celebrate Spring Equalday, 66
  Christian Easter date problem, 202-220
  inappropriate classifications, 21
  philosophy and behaviour, xvii, 241-243
  ritual and symbolism, 152, 157, 178-181, 185-187, 231
  sacrifices, 30, 92
  Sun and Moon worship universal, xvi
  Vedic, 192
  Voodoo, 74, 161

Resurrection, 136, 204
  death and rebirth cycle, 98

right angle:
  cardinal directions, 135, 136, 172
  sacred, 74
  Stonehenge Altar, not, 108, 161
  Sun-Moon at 51° latitude, 175, 221, 226

RigVeda, 241

ritualization of time, 185

rock
  cairn, 27**F3-4**, **F3-5**
  crescent, 5**F1-1**, 30**F3-6**, 171
  pattern, xiii, xv**FP-1**, 29, 34, 39

Rock Pivot, Stonehinge, 81, 161

Rosetta Stone for Stone Age calendars, in *Ómahk*, 6**F1-2**, 240

Sacred place, xvi, xvii
  calendrical device in, 185
  Foelteml, Glastonbury, *Ómahkiyáahkóhtóohp*, Stonehenge, 149
  where observations for omens are made, 200

Sacred Ring of stones, 13-16, 73
  Egg-shaped, 14, 16

Sacred Rocks of Alberta:
  engraved boulders, 24, 30
  ribstones, 24

science, 18, 21, 22, 179, 241

scientist:
  Astrologer, Astronomer, Prophet, 200, 230
  Skywatcher/Sunwatcher, 27, 151, 244

season intervals, 165

season-pivot:
  date festivals, 200, 202, 240
  dates marked by Sun alignments in *Ómahkiyáahkóhtóohp*, 53, 63**F3-32**, **F3-33**
  in Stonehenge, 132**F4-51**, 158-166, 179-182
  Sun observation lines, 130**F4-50**, 163**F5-3**, 236

Siksika, see Blackfoot

Sky on the ground, 68

Skywatcher/Sunwatcher (scientist): 19, 64, 151, 230, 244
  accurate lines to rise and set positions, 83, 98, 238
  how does the sky work?, 17, 151, 201

leap year cycle, 140
Moon cycles, 171, 181
prophesies by, 201, 243
Sun rises and sets, 7, 34, 98, 151

Solstice:
   rise and set directions shift with time, 34, 252**Table A-2**
   Summer Sun rise and set, 3, 6, 18-20
   Winter Sun rise and set, 16, 20
   Winter, death and rebirth, 98, 157

South Pole Star, 212

South Temperate Zone, 213, 217, 240

spirituality:
   and mental health, 74
   and peace, 141, 203
   circles and cycles, 14
   instability cycle, 242
   purification, 239
   symbol, 131, 190
   understanding of, 241

St. Patrick's Day, Spring Equalday, 66, 210

stone:
   cairn, xiii, xv
   circle, xv, 5, 11
   crescent, xvi
   geometric pattern, xvi
   line, xiii, xvi, 24
   ring, xiii, 14
   ring, grave marker, 13

Stonehenge:
   28 lintels on Circle, 105**F4-22**, 138, 156, 162**F5-2**, 171, 230
   abandoned after 1500 BC, 181
   age, 5, 156
   Altar Stone, 93-96**F4-16**
      in the *sanctum sanctorum*, 98, 180
      in Winter Solstice Sun rise and Summer set directions, 112**F4-31**, 116, 130**F4-50**, 131
      is in original orientation, 96, 112, 161
      season-pivot, Stonehinge, 161, 163, 230
   Arthur's grave, myth, 148**F4-63b**, 149, 229
   Aubrey Circle, 8, 111, 124, 136**F4-53**
   Aubrey Hole **13**, 136
   Aubrey Hole **40**, 94**F4-14**, 95**F4-15**
   Aubrey Holes **28** and **56**, 105**F4-22**, **F4-23**, 106**F4-24**
   Avenue
      ditches, 105**F4-24**, 107**F4-26**
      photos of, 113**F4-32** to 115**4-35**
      Summer Solstice Sun rise line, 6, 105**F4-24**, 133**F4-52**

Winter Solstice Sun set line?, 113, 115, 165
Bank
   age, 82, 104, 160
   encloses a terrain, 82, 124
   Sun observation place, 93**F4-14**, 109, 115, 132**F4-51**
Barrows, 134**F4-52**
Barrow **10a**, 133
Bell Barrow **11**, 133
Bell Barrow **15**, 84-92, 107**F4-26**, 167
Bluestones:
   and King Arthur legend, 142-150, 229
   battle-axes, 149
   basalt, hard, 81, 149
   circle, age, 83, 86, 156
   rods of light, 162**F5-3** to 164
   source, 81, 143, 149
Bluestone **31**, 84**F4-3**, 86**F4-5**
Bluestone **69**, 94**F4-14**, 95**F4-15**
Bluestone **80**, Altar, 84**F4-3**, 96**F4-16**
Bowl Barrow **49**, 133, 134**F4-52**, 166**F5-4**
Bull, White, *Taurus* effigy, 159**F5-1**
calendars, 155
   accuracy, 4000 B.P., 153
   controversy, 8, 18, 82
calendrical Barrow symmetry, 166**F5-4**
cardinal directions, 136**F4-53** to 140**F4-57**
causeway entrances, 161, 162**F5-2**, 176**F5-8** to 179
Circle, Sarsen, 6**F1-2**, 80**F4-2**
   design, 111, 122-124, 134**F4-53** to 140**F4-57**
   lunar calendar, 169**F5-5**
Circle Sarsen **1**, 84**F4-3**, 86, 89**F4-8**
Circle Sarsens **2** and **3**, 120**F4-39**, 128**F4-48**
Circle Sarsens **8** and **9**, 93, 96, 115
Circle Sarsen **10**, Sarsen new **1** in lunar calendar, 170**F5-5** to 180
Circle Sarsens **10** and **25**, 133, 178
Circle small Sarsen **11**, 162**F5-2**, 163**F5-3**, 169**F5-5**
   Sarsen new **30** in lunar calendar, 170**F5-5** to 180
   shadow at Sun zenith, 163**F5-3**, 164
Circle Sarsens **15** and **16**, 90
Circle Sarsens **21** and **22**, 95**F4-15**
coded information, 178, 182
Cursus, 107**F4-26**, 133**F4-52**, 135, 168
   and Avenue contemporary, 167
   and Summer Solstice, 167
   Lesser, 110, 133
design of, 109, 111**F4-31**, 112, 122**F4-42**, 179
Ditch, 129**F4-49**
   age, 82, 160, 178
   causeways, 132**F4-51**, 161**F5-2**, 178, 179
East Trilithon, 141, 173
Equinox, 116
Equalday/night Sun rise, 128**F4-48**, **F4-49**
Equalday/night Sun set, 120**F4-41**, **F4-42** to 124**F4-44**, **F4-47**

E-W axis, 136**F4-53** to 140**F4-57**
female Moon Temple clasped male Sun Temple, 181
Great Trilithon
   and lunar 18.6-year cycle, 170**F5-5** to 173**F5-7**
   and Summer Solstice Sun rise line, 6, 8, 100**F4-20** to 103**F4-21**, 131
   and Winter Solstice Sun set line, 88**F4-8** to 91**F4-11**, 96, 131 **F4-51**, 179
   window, 102**F4-20** to **F4-22**, 152
Heel (Sun) Stone, 5, 7**F1-3**
   Winter Solstice Sun set observation place, 84, 89**F4-8**, 97**F4-17**, 131**F4-51**, 133
   Turtle head?, 92**F4-12**
landscape and the calendar, 83, 124, 131, 165
   proposed restoration, 135
Lesser Cursus Oval Enclosure, 110, 133**F4-52**, 166**F5-4**
lintel, 80**F4-1**, **F4-2**
   28 of them on Circle, 104**F4-22**, 156, 162, 171, 230
   none between Sarsens **10** and **12**, 104**F4-22**, 138, 162**F5-2**
   South Trilithon, rod of light, 162**F5-3** to 164
   Summer Solstice Sun rise above, 101**F4-20**, 103**F4-21**
   views from the Avenue, 113**F4-32** to **F4-35**
   West Trilithon, Bull's head below, 159**F5-1**
lunar calendar, 169-178
   Circle Sarsens renumbered, 170**F5-5**, 171, back endpapers
   Y & Z Holes renumbered, 176**F5-8**, 177, back endpaper
lunar-phase 19-year cycle, 171
lunar-standstill 18.6-year cycle, 170**F5-5**, 171
   cycle hinges, 170**F5-5**, 174
map,
   new numbers of Sarsens and Holes,
     back endpapers, 170**F5-5**, 176**F5-8**
   old numbers of Sarsens and Holes, front endpapers, 5, 97**F4-17**, 112**F4-31**
   solar calendar observation lines, 130**F4-50**, 134**F4-52**, 166**F5-4**
meaning of the name, 81
Merlin, 79
Moon 18.6-year cycle hinges (pivots), 170**F5-5**, 176**F5-8**
Moon and Sun intimately entwined, 174, 176**F5-8**, 181, 182, 231
narrow gaps in Sun rise and set alignments, 18, 89**F4-8**, 94**F4-14** to **F4-16**, 102**F4-20**, 110**F4-29**, 126**F4-45**, 127**F4-47**, 129**F4-49**, 130**F4-50**
   Moon 18.6-year cycle, 170**F5-5** to **F5-7**, 174
   still accurate, 153
New King Barrows, 120**F4-39**
New King Bowl Barrows, 135, 182
New King Bowl Barrow **28**, 120**F4-39**, 128**F4-48**, 129, 133-135, 148
New King Bowl Barrow **29**, 120-124, **F4-39** to **F4-42**, 182
North and South "Barrows", 133
North Trilithon, 129, 162-164**F5-3**
   and Equalday/night Sun set leap year cycle, 123**F4-42**
northeast causeway, 161, 162, 178, 179
N-S axis, 138**F4-53** to 140
observation line altitudes, 252**Table A-2**
Ómahkiyáahkóhtóohp teachings, 230, 231

Oval Twin Disk Barrow **10** (OTDB **10**), 100-104, 107, 111-115, 132, 133
rods of light and shadow, zenith Sun, 162-164**F5-3**, 179
sanctum sanctorum (Holy of Holies), 96, 138**F4-55**, 164, 173, 178-181, 231
sarsen, hard sandstone, 5
   source, 82
Sarsen Circle Moon counter, 169
   Moon Rectangle, 170**F5-5**, 173
   Sarsens renumbered, 170**F5-5**, 171, back endpapers
season intervals, 165
season-pivot Sun observation lines, 130**F4-50**, 132**F4-51**, 163**F5-3**, 166**F5-4**
site selection, 178
Slaughter Stone, 89**F4-8**, 92
solar calendar, 131**F4-51**, 134**F4-52**, 230
solar and lunar calendars, 155, 173, 174, 178
south causeway, 161**F5-2**
South Trilithon, 80**F4-1**, 96**F4-16**, 112**F4-31**, 173**F5-7**
   and Equalday/night Sun set leap year cycle, 123**F4-42**
   blocks N-S view, 138**F4-54**, 139**F4-55**
   rod of light, 162-164**F5-3**, 179
Station Stones, "Barrows," in Y-Z lunar calendar, 176**F5-8** to 178
Stone seat holes, 152
Stonehinges/pivots, calendrical, 81, 158 to 164, 170**F5-5**, 174, 176**F5-8**, 178
Stones straightened or re-erected, 152
Summer Solstice Sun rise, 5, 6, 101**F4-18**, **F4-20**, 112**F4-31**, 130**F4-50**, **F4-51**, 166, 181
Summer Solstice Sun set, 108**F4-27** to **F4-29**, 112**F4-31**, 130**F4-50**, **F4-51**, 161, 167
Sun (Heel) Stone, 7**F1-3**, 106**F4-24**, 115**F4-35**
   Winter Solstice Sun set observation place, 89**F4-8**, **F4-9**, 92
Sun rise and set horizons, from Sarsen Circle, 166
Temple to the Sun and Moon, 152, 181
Trilithon (Three-stone-thing), 80**F4-1**
   see East, North, South, and West Trilithon
   Horseshoe, 5, 98, 104**F4-22**, 141, 162
   design, 111, 123**F4-42**, 124, 171**F5-5**, 182
Turtle?, female and water symbol, 92**F4-12**
West Trilithon, 140**F4-57**
   Bull's head, 159**F5-1**
   Sarsen **58** notch, 93**F4-14** to **F4-16**, 110**F4-29**, 117**F4-36** to **F4-38**, 124**F4-44**, **F4-45**, **F4-47**
Winter Solstice Sun rise, 93**F4-13** to **F4-17**, 131**F4-50**, **F4-51**, 166**F5-4**
Winter Solstice Sun set, 86**F4-5** to **F4-8**, 89-93, 97**F4-17**, 130**F4-50**, **F4-51**, 163, 166**F5-4**, 180
Y and Z Holes lunar calendar, 175-181
   renumbered, 176**F5-8**, 181, back endpapers
Y, Z, Stations contemporary, 181

stonehinge, 58, 81, 158-164, 255

Stukeley, William, 6, 246

Sun
  cycle, 1, 17, 68, 158
  first and last flashes, 7, 19
    distinguish from mirage, 258
  rise and set
    alignments still accurate, 38, 153
    azimuths, data, 251-254
    definitions, 7, 282
    distinguish from mirage, 258
    exact shift over days, 254
    sight lines, 62**F3-32**, **F3-33**,
      132**F4-51**, 135
  zenith
    altitude, difficult to measure without instrument 158, 188**F6-1** to 190,
      211, 226
    altitude extremes and midaltitude (SZM), 67
    direction south, 73
    rod of light from South Trilithon gap, 139**F4-55**, 163**F5-3**
    south causeway, 162**F5-2**, 179

Sun-egg, 16, 165

Sun, Moon, and Morning Star, xiii, xvi, 223, 246

Sun Zenith Midaltitude (SZM, *zem*), 67
  definition, 222, 282
  Gregorian "equalnight", equinox, 200, 217, 222

sunrise and sunset, definitions, 7, 282
  upper limb altitude against time, 249**FA-1**

Sunwatcher/Skywatcher, xii, 7, 34, 46

Teampall Nuaghrian, Newsun's Temple, 191

Temple:
  evolution of, xvi, 187, 200
  Ómahk, near Majorville, 23, 39-43, 53, 60
  of the Sun, Moon and Morningstar, 223
  people lived north of it, 73
  Preseli Mountain, 145
  Stonehenge, 96, 152, 221

Time Machines, Stone Age: 18, 66, 81
  constructed in Temples, 183, 221
  in a creation myth, 243
  lines of stones on the ground, 20
  to Sun rises and sets, 151, 246

tipi ring, 13, 15, 73

Torah, 241, 243

Trilithon (Three-stone-thing), 80**F4-1**
  see Stonehenge

Tropics/tropical, 1-3, 226, 240

Turtle Island, 221

Venus, eight-year pentagonal cycle, 231, 238

visualize,
  powerful analytical tool, 17, 23, 100

Volga River, 193

Voodoo, 74, 160, 211, 261

Wace, Maistre, 79, 81

Wales, Preseli Mountain, 81, 142-150
  Arthur, War Leader, myth, 148, 229
  Temple to the Sun and Moon?, 186

warino, irregular small war, 197, 283

water, east of Sacred Place, 31

Western, Eastern cultures (*inappropriate terms*), 21

Woodhenge and the Cursus, 168

year:
  365.2422 days, 2, 122, 151
  Egg-shaped, 165
  Gregorian, 68
  Julian, 203
  when does it begin?, 193, 196

zem, SZM, *see* Sun Zenith Midaltitude

zenith, definition, 67, 283

zodiac, 6, 195
  Equal-arm-balance, 196
  Equalday/night, 196
  Full Moon positions among constellations, 195**F6-2**, **F6-3**
  seasons regress through it, 196
  Sun positions among constellations, 198, 199**F6-4**, **F6-5**

About the Author

Gordon Freeman was born in 1930 in Hoffer, Saskatchewan, and was introduced to Stone Age artifacts at the age of six. His father collected projectile points and stone tools from the Saskatchewan prairie after dry winds had blown away tilled soil.

He obtained an M.A. from the University of Saskatchewan, a Ph.D. from McGill, and a D.Phil. from Oxford. He is a Chemical Physicist, was for ten years Chairman of Physical and Theoretical Chemistry at the University of Alberta, and for thirty years Director of the Radiation Research Centre there. He is now a Professor Emeritus. For forty years he has pioneered interdisciplinary studies in chemistry, physics, and human societies. Interdisciplinarity is now the standard approach to understanding in the sciences and humanities. He has authored more than 450 publications in chemistry, physics, and other subjects.

As a hobby he visited many archaeological sites in Canada, the United States, Britain, Ireland, Europe, and Asia. In 1980 he discovered a 5000-year-old Sun Temple in southern Alberta, and has studied it ever since. In 1989 he took observation techniques he had developed in Alberta to England, to resolve the controversy that whirled about a possible calendar in Stonehenge. The astonishingly beautiful, ancient calendars in southern Alberta and Stonehenge are displayed for the first time in recent centuries, with far ranging implications for international prehistory and history.

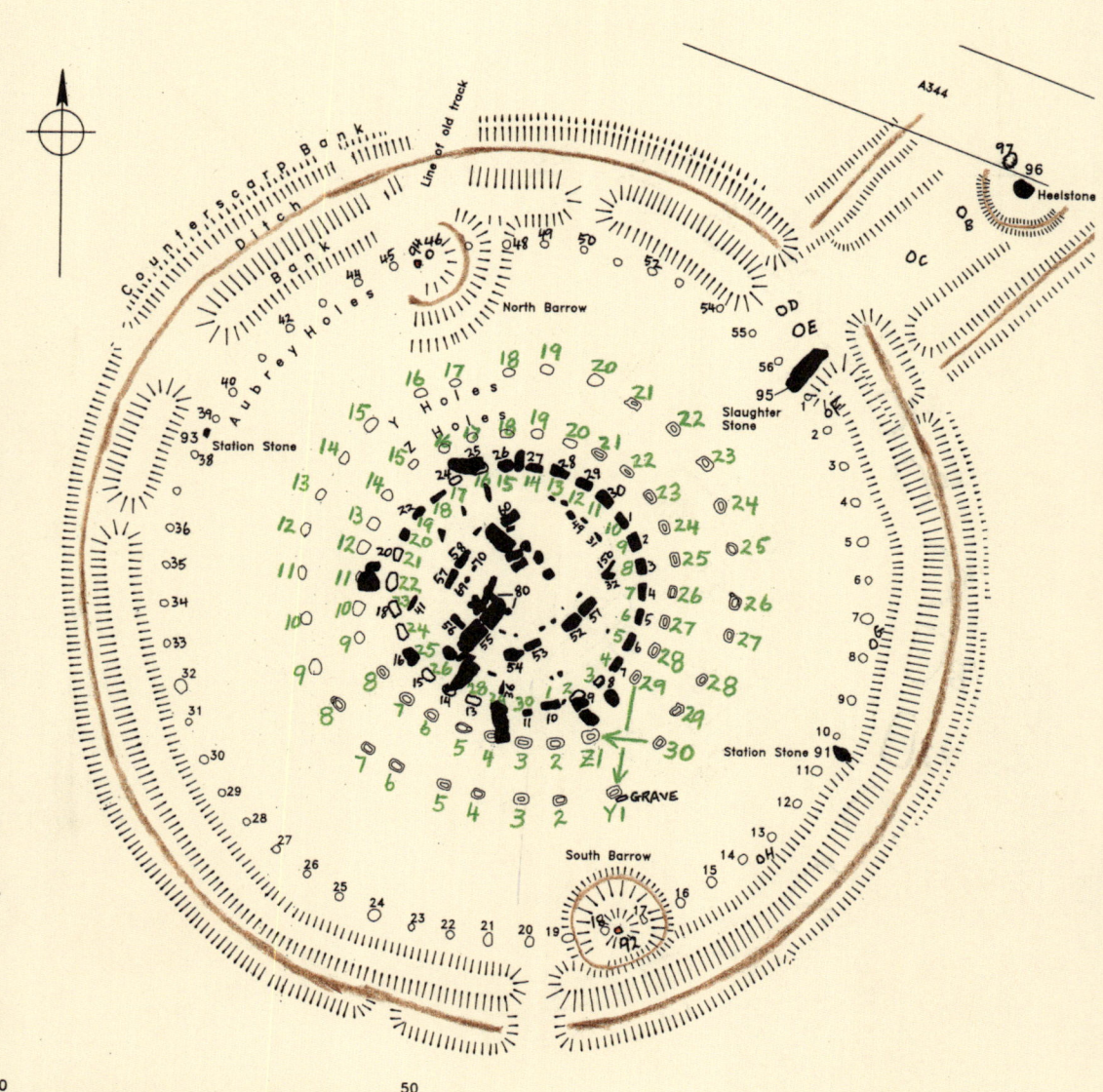